Capilar W9-CRJ-022

A PLACE FOR STRANGERS

A PLACE
FOR STRANGERS

*Towards a History of
Australian Aboriginal Being*

TONY SWAIN

School of Studies in Religion, University of Sydney

CAMBRIDGE
UNIVERSITY PRESS

Published by the Press Syndicate of the University of Cambridge
The Pitt Building, Trumpington Street, Cambridge CB2 1RP, UK
40 West 20th Street, New York, NY 10011–4211, USA
10 Stamford Road, Oakleigh, Melbourne 3166, Australia

Printed in Hong Kong by Colorcraft

National Library of Australia cataloguing in publication data
Swain, Tony, 1955–
A place for strangers: towards a history of Australian
Aboriginal being.
Includes index.
ISBN 0 521 43005 4 (hbk).
ISBN 0 521 44691 0 (pbk).
[1.] Aborigines, Australian – History. [2.] Aborigines,
Australian – Religion. [3.] Ontology. [4.] Aborigines, Australian
– Ethnic identity. I. Title.
306.0899915

Library of Congress cataloguing in publication data
Swain, Tony.
A place for strangers: towards a history of Australian Aboriginal
being/Tony Swain.
Includes bibliographic references (p.   ) and index.
ISBN 0-521-43005-4 (HB). – ISBN 0-521-44691-0 (PB)
1. Australian aborigines. 2. Philosophy, Australian aboriginal.
3. Australian aborigines – Foreign influences. 4. Australian
aborigines – Religion. I. Title.
GN666.S93   1993
305.89'915 – dc20   92-30379
                                                                CIP

A catalogue record for this book is available from the British Library

ISBN 0 521 43005 4 hardback
ISBN 0 521 44691 0 paperback

Contents

To take a strange land
as one's home,
Is folly beyond compare.
Cao Xueqin, *Hong Lou Meng*

for Dev and Max

Preface and Acknowledgements

Two pieces of paper were pinned above my desk as I wrote this book. The first was a newspaper clipping reporting that American astrophysicists had made a discovery that overturned the accepted view of the cosmos. It was a pulsar, formed by an exploding star, flashing at the unheard-of rate of 2,000 times per second. Re-evaluations were necessary, dozens of papers were written, until at last the novel phenomenon was fully embraced by theory.

Am I suggesting this work is a comparable attempt to reinterpret cosmologies so as to account for aberrant data? My answer, most certainly, is yes. But first I should finish the story of the scientists.

Those ingenious theorists were only slightly taken aback when someone amongst them observed that if the TV camera attached to their telescope was turned off, then the 'pulsar' too was gone. The event was hailed as 'an almighty cockup', but the scientists knew better. Said one of his paper: 'It's tremendously convincing. The only thing that's wrong with it is that it's wrong'. And another, even less perturbed: 'It's not a dead loss. I had a great time thinking about it'.[1]

Contained in this book is without doubt a radical reinterpretation of Australian Aboriginal existence, and search as I assuredly have, to date no trace of any interfering 'bug' has been found attached to my argument (although, quite frankly, I shall not be unduly dismayed if someone else gleefully spies it out for me). I appreciate that it is currently proper for academics to seek immortality through their work, but I am content to have had some fun trying to tame wayward data.

The other piece of paper on my desk bore the words of a writer who knew all this and much more. In what must stand as the most delightful preface ever written, he said:

> My friends are all broad-minded, and well educated, but we do not keep a record of our conversations. The reason for this is (1) we are too lazy, and do not aspire to fame; (2) to talk gives us pleasure, but to write would

give trouble; (3) none of us would be able to read it again after our deaths, so why worry; (4) if we wrote something this year we should probably find it all wrong the next year.[2]

And so, not wanting to write about those things he took even half seriously, he chose instead to produce 'a trifle', 'a hotchpotch', designed to give him pleasure whilst awaiting his friends' return.

Am I this time suggesting scholarship is to be treated as an interim plaything? My answer, once again, is most certainly yes. But before those holding tight to the earnestness of academic pursuits proclaim I have therefore succeeded, in terms of my credibility, in shooting off my own foot, let me now conclude the story of the writer of that preface.

His book was the *Shui-hu Chuan*, which came to be recognised as one of the four great classics of the most populous nation on earth, and which not only inspired millions upon millions of individual lives, but which also helped fire many anti-oppression and anti-imperialist movements, not least of them the Boxer uprising[3] and the revolutions of Mao Tse Tung.[4]

History threshes human endeavours, depending upon the whim of its passing. Some, like our astrophysicists, fall like chaff. Others change the world when that was not their ambition, and even had that been a goal to which the author of the *Shui-hu* did not object, he had the good statistical sense to predict it most unlikely he would be reborn in a form capable of appreciating its realisation. If scholarly pursuits have any value that transcends time, it must therefore be as play.

For reminding me of this fact, I have happily dedicated this work to two of my most loved companions, Devlin and Dominique, who are irrepressible, outrageous and, above all, filled with life's playfulness.

A final pleasant matter to be be dealt with in this preface is saying thanks to friends and colleagues who have offered their help. In return, as the author of the *Shui-hu* wrote, 'I shall be satisfied if a few of my friends will read it and be interested'. Eric Sharpe, Garry Trompf and Carole Cusack have, as always, been tireless in their support. For their critical comments on various chapters I am also grateful to John Clegg, Francesca Merlan, Peter Koepping, David Turner and Bruce Swain. Yvonne White's superb editorial skills were invaluable. All of these people should rightly share in any merit this book might have. The influence of Dany Flint goes deeper, however, and with her I will share the blame.

TONY SWAIN

NOTES

1. D. Anderson, 'Literary Theory Lightly Bends the Ear', *The Sydney Morning Herald* (April 21 1990), p. 72.
2. Shih Nai-an, *Water Margin*, translated by J.H. Jackson (Hong Kong: The Commercial Press, 1963), vol. 1, 'Introduction' (no pagination).
3. J.W. Esherick, *The Origins of the Boxer Uprising* (Berkeley: University of California Press, 1987), p. 294.
4. e.g. see S.R. Schram, *The Political Thought of Mao Tse Tung* (Harmondsworth: Penguin, 1969), p. 197.

Introduction

Sit with dignity and talk with composure!
No small talk! Elaborate on this:
What means more to you: The silly splinter that went in?
Or the spirit from heaven – which you really are –
To wait in the waterhole?[1]

Rarely are the verses of the first Australians so austere. Rarely are they more urgent. Just for a moment the full-bodied complexities of myth are cast aside and with a slap of reprimand and a Zen-like interrogation we find ourselves facing a choice of being. Are we determined by life's pains (and pleasures) or rather by some eternal abiding spirit?

We relax – too soon. For all its intensity, the question seemed rhetorical, but just as we attempt a nod at the expected answer, the real paradox emerges. Is the spirit from above? Does it wait in the waterhole? Or is it left dangling somewhere between Heaven and Earth?

Only the foolhardy attempt to resolve paradoxes. My task is merely to ask what it means to create one. Like Piruwarna, although with a less poetic air, I am going to pose questions of Aborginal ontology – about what they 'really are'. Like him, I am concerned with the relationship between the stuff of being and the cosmos as a whole. And, like him, I will stress antinomy.

Put in its briefest possible form, this book is about the historical coexistence of two spiritual principles in Australian Aboriginal Law. On the one hand there is the 'waterhole': a site-based life potential co-joined with specific human beings. This is immanent and radically pluralistic. On the other hand there is a continuum which can lead to 'Heaven': non-locative powers which, in their most extreme form, are relegated to a distant and unknown place. Here is a tendency towards social and spatial transcendence,

1

potentially pan-Aboriginal, and at times flirting dangerously with monistic ideals.

My thesis, quite simply, is that the latter principle has emerged, in varying degrees, as Aboriginal people sought to accommodate outsiders and make a place for strangers.

Already I have identified two of my main players. *Ontos* and *Chronos*, Being in Time. Both are enigmatic, both invite obscuritanist reflections, yet I cannot but echo Heidegger's insistence upon 'Time as the horizon of the understanding of Being.'[2]. Which leaves me running headlong into a dilemma.

Central to my whole argument is the position that Aborigines themselves do not, or at least once did not, understand their being in terms of time, but of place and space. Surely, therefore, it might be said that to insist upon the vantage of time and history undermines, or at best ignores, the Aboriginal notion of being-in-the-world. We could, of course, seek to give priority to one stance, but which one? If we evoke Bergson's rhapsodic phrase: 'time is but the ghost of space haunting the reflective consciousness',[3] we must then deal with Heidegger's dismissal and inversion of this stance: 'the "atemporal" . . . are also "temporal" with respect to Being'.[4]

Whilst it would satisfy neither of my philosophers, I see no need to adjudicate on the 'true' nature of existence. I am not concerned with what might most infelicitously be called ontological ontology (the very being of being) but with hermeneutic ontology (the interpretation of being). Indeed, it seems that this is as far as we can ever aspire if we accept Gadamer's important observation that 'language is not just one of man's possessions in the world, but on it depends the fact that man has a world at all'.[5]

When I say, therefore, that time is the horizon of the understanding of being, I am alluding to the central place of temporality in the Western mind. If nothing else, it is an indispensable component of our horizon of understanding. What, then, is to happen to this horizon when it encounters one that almost exclusively proclaims place?

For most of the history of the study of Aboriginal traditions, the scholarly solution has been 'objectivity'. Since Aborigines themselves had not nurtured the possibility of locating their being in time, they were deemed a 'timeless' people. For researchers to assert otherwise would have been for them to have allowed their own ontological heritage to contaminate those they studied. The condemnation reserved for those who did so was 'subjectivity', which has so aptly been called 'the prejudice against prejudice itself'.[6]

The price of object-ivity – of the intended absolute separation of the 'I and Thou' – has only recently become apparent. The divide between history and its self-imposed positivistic offspring, anthropology, can be viewed in this context. What initially distinguished the two fields of investigation was that the content of history alone was within our own ontological horizon. Bruce Trigger came close to this point whilst at the same time highlighting its political face: 'The original differentiation between history and anthropology was the product of colonialism and ethnocentrism. Anthropology was initiated as the study of peoples who were alleged to lack history.'[7] We can call this 'racism', 'ethnocentrism', or whatever, but beneath all this is the less laden realisation that while we have shared the world with Aboriginal people we have mostly failed to share our understanding of our being in the world. We have been unable to spare our time.

Until the 1960s, Aborigines were almost totally non-existent in history. Strictly speaking, there is no need to qualify this with 'European history' for, as Urry quite rightly maintains, history itself is a construction of the past which was alien to Aboriginal thought.[8] Historians simply kept aloof from Aboriginal people, content 'to leave the study of the Aborigines to anthropologists, and then to ignore the anthropologists'[9] – and rightly so, as the anthropologists, in turn, had themselves ignored history. In his famous Boyer lectures, W.E.H. Stanner dubbed this almost perfectly formed shun 'the great Australian silence'. This, he said, was the story of things we have unconsciously 'resolved not to discuss with [Aborigines] or treat with them about; the story in short, of the unacknowledged relation between two racial groups within a single field of life'.[10]

Much has changed since the 1960s. That decade opened with the publication of a collection significantly entitled *Aborigines Now*,[11] and the processes of change and the dynamics of history in Aboriginal society have ever-increasingly become the focus of scholarly attention. We now even require a journal of *Aboriginal History*. Yet, despite this thriving new industry, little has been uncovered about the fundamental changes to Aboriginal people's ontology. This is more than a neglected topic; it is a neglected world.

We have managed to be true to our own ontologic field of view, rooted as it is in time and history, but we have yet to turn this into an encounter with the Aboriginal understanding of being. We have, in short, largely failed to begin to achieve what Gadamer so evocatively described as a genuine 'fusion of horizons'.[12] Historical understanding demands not only that we be faithful to our own temporality but also that we recognise the fundamental otherness of those others who transform our history and hence our very being. As Peter Winch once said, 'seriously to study another way of life is necessarily to seek to extend our own – not simply to bring the other way within the already existing boundaries of our own'.[13] That Aboriginal and European world-horizons differ is therefore not a quandary but a promise that understanding itself is possible. There is indeed a tension between our being and theirs, but 'the hermeneutic task consists not in covering up this tension by attempting naïve assimilation but rather in developing it consciously'.[14]

A dominant theme of this book is that Australian Aborigines have themselves been engaged in a hermeneutic process in their encounter with outsiders. That this interpretative tradition has been cast in spatial rather than temporal terms would be disconcerting to most European hermeneuts. Husserl himself had his thinking shaken by his brief encounter with Aboriginal thought, and Merleau-Ponty added the question: is it actually 'possible for us, who live in certain historical traditions, to conceive of the historical possibility of . . . societies . . . in which our concept of history is simply absent?'[15] Husserl at least had no doubt that it was indeed of the 'highest importance' to 'feel our way into' this historical possibility. For such people 'this is the basis of the world which is no mere representation but rather the world that actually is *for it*'. Husserl also amplified that this was not merely a lack of historicity but positively 'a humanity whose life is enclosed in a vital . . . tradition'.[16] I would but add that the essence of that tradition is place and that the Aboriginal interpretation of changes to their life-world has been cast in terms of space rather than history (see chapter 1).

This work reciprocates by offering a history of that interpretative process. It explores the 'historical possibility' of a hermeneutics of ubeity. One might call this a hermeneutics of hermeneutics, but less pretentiously it is an attempt to view the Aboriginal understanding of others from the vantage of our own historical horizon. I call this 'a History of Australian Aboriginal being'.

Some readers may feel that my subtitle is presumptuous. After all, current evidence indicates that people in northern Australia were recording their 'view of nature' in art at least 60,000 years ago, and hence Australia can perhaps boast the oldest directly dated hint of ontological reflection in the world.[17] The period of human occupation of Australia, furthermore, feasibly goes back twice as many years as this.[18] Surely, it might be argued, a proper 'history of being' must do justice to those remarkably remote origins. My reply is firmly negative. Firstly, I would respond once again with Urry that 'history' is not an Aboriginal concept and that 'a history of Aborigines can therefore only begin with the establishment of white settlement in Australia'.[19] This at first might seem a *post hoc* semantic rationalisation, but my second point reveals otherwise: the more important fact is that everything we know of Aboriginal ontology has been recorded in a historical setting, and that history has then been denied.

This is not of course to suggest that reflection upon the nature of existence was not occurring in the ancient Australian past. Of those reflections, however, we know and can know almost nothing. Prehistorians have provided solid evidence that such contemplation was *occurring*, but even art, the most communicative of all archaeological evidence, cannot self-disclose its *meaning*. It is thus that interpreters of the Aboriginal symbolic past have always weighed the evidence in terms of the ethnographic present (itself a dubious procedure, which would be totally unacceptable were it employed with the so-called 'higher' civilisations). Clegg, for example, has made a most ambitious attempt to disclose those changes in religious beliefs accompanying changes in iconography, but his starting assumption had to be that engravings, some of which were perhaps 5,000 years old, could be understood in terms of nineteenth and twentieth century Aboriginal traditions – 'I assume that Aboriginal religion at the time of the engraving . . . was within the generality of the [ethnographic] model. If that model is false, there is no way of knowing so'. Even if we concede this, the most that can be concluded is that earlier engravings had a different form and therefore quite possibly a different meaning. Clegg concluded, 'I cannot yet see a way to infer from the changes in pictures what changes there were to religion'.[20] If meaning is not synonymous with that of the cultures recorded in ethnography, it remains virtually impenetrable in terms of its ontological significance.

Thus, not only has our ethnography been recorded within a silent historic context, but even our prehistory shares the interpretative signature of an image of Aboriginal traditions created in a post-colonial context. My resolve is to admit this history in the ongoing creative tradition of Aboriginal being.

This is not the place to examine in detail what has been said about non-Aboriginal impacts on Aboriginal cultures. I will discuss the relevant literature within each of the following chapters. Something must be said here, however, about a continuing heritage of inferred and conjectural pseudo-history in Aboriginal Studies. This is a shadowy doctrine, constantly present since anthropology itself began, but always peripheral to the mainstream positivist thrust of the discipline. J.C. Prichard's *The Natural History of Man* (1843) is among the earliest instance of this kind, presenting a crypto-Biblical picture of the spread of humanity. His tireless debate with those advocating multiple origins for the human species was seemingly silenced by the Herculean arrival of evolutionary theory but, once the tumult subsided, a history-of-kinds persisted in the form of diffusionary theory. Even its most excessive exponents could make some very valid observations. Grafton Elliot Smith once remarked that what ultimately distinguished diffusionists from their opponents was the realisation that human 'conscious activities make the principle of continuity and the historical method which expounds it the chief instrument of achieving a full and true interpretation of the data of *human history*'.[21]

Such sentiments are laudable, and their programmes had much promise. In particular, the German *Kulturkreise* school made a bold attempt to account for regional variation in Australian traditions. Chronicling a diffusionary path, however, is in itself not history, and by unnecessarily setting their research within the framework of an unobservable (and hence at best only reconstructable) past, they succeeded primarily in ensuring that they insulated themselves from the possibility of sound interpretative historiography.

I have no interest in agendas of this kind. I am not concerned with drawing gossamer-like lines of passage across a twilight world but rather with a vigorous tussle with Aboriginal ontology across the very tangible boundary of our historical being.

If, however, we once admit the historical circumstances in which *all* our texts on Aboriginal belief and practice were obtained, we realise there is little need to appeal to the remote past. As I will illustrate in chapters 2 and 4, Melanesian and Indonesian impacts on Aboriginal societies belong to the realm of genuine history.

Indeed, in both cases they possibly have a past which does not much exceed the arrival of Europeans in Australia.

I am, of course, not saying that prior to the eighteenth century nothing changed in Aboriginal societies. What I am suggesting is that a range of interpretations of existence within Aboriginal Australia cannot be separated from the varieties of ways of existing within their world. An explanation which merely appeals to ancient times cannot account for the ongoing significance of beliefs and practices. Diffusionists presenting ethnographic data collected in the nineteenth and twentieth centuries as the solidified remains of a once larval flow of 'Old Australian' and 'Boomerang' cultures are engaged in nothing less than a gigantic theoretical fudge.[22] This mangling of the integrity of an era's boundaries is the very antithesis of the historical enterprise.

My approach in this work is simply to examine ethnographic texts (along with my own field material) in terms of the historical contexts in which they were collected. I maintain that the array of Aboriginal understandings of existence at any one time reflects an array of ways of being at *that same time.* Our history can therefore begin almost precisely two centuries ago, and as the curtain of history parts, so to speak, there are, beside the Aborigines, three other kinds of actors on the stage. There are Melanesian people at the tip of Australia; there are Indonesians in Arnhem Land; and, of course, there are the recorders of these events who have just arrived from the Western world. I devote a chapter to each of these domains (chapters 2 to 4), before pursuing the continuing historical repercussions of White society on Aboriginal being (chapter 5).

Before attempting to reveal the historical impact of strangers upon Aboriginal ontology, it is essential to have some notion of what constituted the unintruded upon form of their traditions in the eighteenth, nineteenth and early- to mid-twentieth centuries. This is a difficult task, but not impossible. My approach to this had three phases. First, as all the outsiders were from agricultural traditions and came by sea to coastal areas, it follows that the desert interiors of Australia would be the last places to have their old order disturbed. (Thus studies from the Central and Western Deserts written in the second half of this century can sometimes be legitimately said to describe Aborigines having minimal contact with the non-Aboriginal world.) Second, I took this basically desert-derived model and

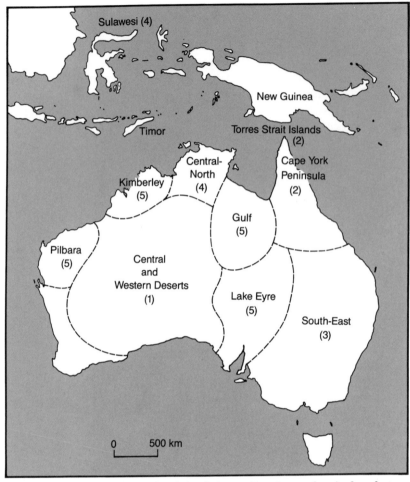

Sulawesi (4)

New Guinea

Timor

Torres Strait Islands (2)

Central-North (4)

Kimberley (5)

Cape York Peninsula (2)

Gulf (5)

Pilbara (5)

Central and Western Deserts (1)

Lake Eyre (5)

South-East (3)

0   500 km

Cultural blocs within Aboriginal Australia. A number in brackets indicates the chapter in which a region is discussed in full.

compared it with the evidence for other regions, such as the Kimberley, Arnhem Land, Cape York and the south-east. These data are presented in the relevant chapters of this book, and for the moment I will only note that in each of these regions the same pattern as is found in the desert can be observed, although accompanied by other, sometimes conflicting and logically posterior traditions. In most cases it is possible to roughly date these variations on an Aboriginal theme. Third, while it should hold no real authority, it

has comforted me (and will no doubt comfort others) to discover
that other scholars have argued for very much the same 'architectonic
idea' (to borrow Stanner's words)[23] underlying Aboriginal societies
continent-wide. This will be detailed in chapter 1.

The four subsequent chapters do not constitute any more than
my subtitle professes – a movement *towards* a recognition of history
in the construction of Aboriginal being. A comprehensive history
of the past two centuries, even were it based exclusively on documentary evidence, would be several times larger than the work in
hand. It would necessarily cover many topics that I have considered
at an intoductory level elsewhere.[24] Amongst them is the immense
impact of Christian missionary enterprises, and the responses of
Aboriginal people within individual, highly variable, mission
regimes; the spiritual life of Aboriginal people who have moved
toward rural and urban lifestyles; the impact of Black and liberation
theologies on post-mission Aboriginal Christianity; the vision of the
world captured by contemporary Aboriginal poetry, drama, novels,
art and song; and, most importantly, the radical transformations of
Aboriginal life and thought which have developed in the wake of
the land rights movement.

The four intensive case-study chapters forming the bulk of this
book can thus only claim to be the first stage of a far-reaching history.
What they cover is essentially the reformation of ontology within
entirely Aboriginal forms of expression. This, of course, reflects the
fact that I dealt with people who, no matter how disrupted their
lifestyle may have been, had managed to retain some autonomy over
their own domain, which thus allowed their ceremonial life to
continue. This is a genuine line of demarcation separating this study
from one examining Aboriginal reinterpretations of introduced
forms of worldview communication, be it the church service (even
though it incorporates 'traditional' ritual elements), the written
word, or the stage.[25]

Chapters 2 to 5 consider four different types of intrusions upon
Aboriginal worlds. The Melanesian contacts with Aborigines at the
tip of Cape York Peninsula were ones in which the respective peoples
recognised one another's land entitlements and forged links through
trade and occasional marriages. This is contrasted in the extreme
by the invasive arrival of Whites in south-east Australia. Chapter 4
then swings back to the central-north of Australia at much the same
time as the European invasion, where a morally regulated and yet

potentially land-threatening association with Indonesians was in progress. Finally, my last chapter pursues the presence of Australians of European descent as they spread across pastoral frontiers, forging relationships with Aborigines regulated by rations, wages and labour.

While I consider these four chapters as 'case-studies', both they and my first chapter embrace virtually the entire spectrum of writings on 'traditional' Aboriginal ceremonial life and belief. I have chosen here to take them as my focus because they have been most neglected in terms of historical analysis; because the data they contain seem to me to be desperately in need of reinterpretation; and, frankly, because they are the most difficult to translate in terms of the new approach to understanding Aboriginal ontology which I am proposing. With this groundwork in place, more recent developments in which Aboriginal people have employed (originally) non-Aboriginal forms of expresssion will be readily grasped.

There is one final introductory matter to be disposed of: method. Anyone familiar with the hermeneuts whose views I have cited might easily predict my response. Gadamer has produced his brilliant but Gaddish (a 'Gad' being the unit of measure of superfluous complexity) critique of the fetishisation of methodology.[26] Somewhat less brilliantly, I have already published reservations about methodology in the study of Aboriginal religious traditions.[27] I will repeat here neither my own nor others' arguments on this matter. Rather, I will conclude this introduction with an anecdote and a quotation.

Methodology is these days increasingly on the defensive. Instead of a slavish devotion to one methodological position, it has become fashionable to be poly-methodological and to have an impressive 'toolbox' of methods. I can boast nothing of this kind, but instead take refuge in the memory of my late neighbour in the country. Tom was an oldtimer who still worked a bullock team and disdained electricity. He had a few tools that experience had taught him worked, but in the bush he travelled lightly. We would fix boundary fences together, and I would inevitably bring with me a comprehensive collection of modern tools. Tom would always take an interest in these (just once or twice he reluctantly conceded their merit), but as I would fumble with technology to solve a problem that a twist of wire or an improvised bush-pole would mend (and mend very well), he would feign impatience: 'Forget your gadgets and fix the bloody thing.'

Wendy O'Flaherty once said, wisely: 'I do not want to talk of method right now; I want to get on with the job.'[28]

NOTES

1. Piruwarna in C.G. von Brandenstein & A.P. Thomas, *Taruru: Aboriginal Song Poetry from the Pilbara* (Adelaide: Rigby, 1974), p. 29 and pp. 73-4.
2. M. Heidegger, *Basic Writings: From Being and Time (1927) to The Task of Thinking (1964)*, edited by D.F. Krell (London: Routledge & Kegan Paul, 1978), p. 61.
3. H. Bergson, *Time and Free Will* (New York: Allen & Unwin, 1910), p. 99.
4. Heidegger, op. cit., pp. 62-3.
5. H.-G. Gadamer, *Truth and Method* (London: Sheed & Ward, 1975), p. 401.
6. ibid., p. 240.
7. B. Trigger, 'The Past as Power: Anthropology and the North American Indian', in *Who Owns the Past?*, edited by I. McBryde (Melbourne: Oxford University Press, 1985), p. 34.
8. J. Urry, 'Beyond the Frontier: European Influence, Aborigines and the Concept of Traditional Culture', *Journal of Australian Studies*, no. 5 (1979), pp. 2-3; see also the critique by B. Barker, 'Strange Tales from the Raj', and Urry's rejoinder, 'Aborigines, History and Semantics', *Journal of Australian Studies*, no. 6 (1980), pp. 63-7 and 68-72.
9. In R.H.W. Reece, 'The Aborigines in Australian Historiography', in *Historical Disciplines and Culture in Australia: An Assessment*, edited by J.A. Moses (St Lucia: University of Queensland Press, 1979), p. 265.
10. W.E.H. Stanner, *After the Dreaming* (Sydney: Australian Broadcasting Company, 1969), p. 25.
11. *Aborigines Now: New Perspectives on the Study of Aboriginal Communities*, edited by M. Reay (Sydney: Angus & Robertson, 1964).
12. Gadamer, op. cit., p. 273.
13. P. Winch, 'Understanding a Primitive Society', in *Rationality*, edited by B. Wilson (Oxford: Basil Blackwell, 1964), p. 99.
14. Gadamer, op. cit., p. 273.
15. M. Merleau-Ponty, 'Phenomenology and the Sciences of Man', in *Phenomenology and the Social Sciences*, edited by M. Natanson, vol. 1 (Evanston: Northwestern University Press, 1973), p. 103.
16. cit. ibid., p. 102.
17. Rhys Jones, cit. G. O'Neill, 'Java Man Art in Kakadu Cave, Says Scientist', *The Sydney Morning Herald* (May 14 1990), p. 2.
18. G.W. Trompf, *In Search of Origins* (London: Oriental University Press, 1990), pp. 116 & 141; see chapter 5 below for further references.

19. J. Urry, op. cit., p. 2. See also G.W. Trompf, 'Macrohistory and Acculturation: Between Myth and History in Modern Melanesian Adjustments and Ancient Gnosticism', *Comparative Studies in Society and History*, 31 (1989), pp. 621–48.

20. J. Clegg, *Prehistoric Pictures as Evidence About Religion* (Sydney: author's printed and distributed copies, 1985), pp. 9 & 47.

21. G. Elliot Smith, *Human History* (London: Jonathan Cape, 1930), p. 14

22. F. Gräbner, 'Kulturkreise und Kulturschichten in Ozeanien', *Zeitschrift für Ethnologie*, 37 (1905), pp. 15–24; P.W. Schmidt, 'Die soziolgische und religiös-ethische Gruppierung der australischen Stämme', *Zeitschrift für Ethnologie*, 51 (1909), pp. 328–77; L. Erlich, *Origin of Australian Beliefs* (Vienna: Francis Chamra, 1922), part 2.

23. W.E.H. Stanner, 'Some Aspects of Aboriginal Religion', *Colloquium*, no. 9 (1976), p. 19.

24. T. Swain & G.W. Trompf, *The Religions of Oceania* (London: Routledge, forthcoming).

25. See D. Thomson, *'Bora is Like Church': Aboriginal Initiation Ceremonies and the Christian Church at Lockhart River, Queensland* (Sydney: Australian Board of Missions, 1985). Perhaps the best example of a cultural revival through drama is Jimmy Chi's *Bran Nue Dae*, which has been described, without too much journalistic exaggeration, as a 'story rich in hope, even with hints of a second coming', D. Graham, 'The Chant of Jimmy Chi', *Good Weekend* December 1 1990), p. 37.

26. H.-G. Gadamer, *Philosophie und Lehrjahre: Eine Rückschau* (Frankfurt: Klostermann, 1977), p. 46.

27. T. Swain, *On 'Understanding' Australian Aboriginal Religion*, the Young Australian Lecture Series no. 6 (Adelaide: Charles Strong Memorial Trust, 1985).

28. W.D. O'Flaherty, *Women, Androgynes, and Other Mythical Beasts* (Chicago: University of Chicago Press, 1980), p. 3.

CHAPTER 1

Worlds to Endure

The country,
the little ones will be taking it,
in due time, this country here.
Holding this place,
looking after this country . . .
We, the old ones,
The old men
will all pass away . . .

In that other time,
'what's-it-called,'
the Ancestors set the world down as it is.
Therefore we will each pass away,
in the fullness of time.
We here,
The old men and women,
The old ones, will each pass away.
The old men too,
will each pass away,
in due time.

Then the young men will be taking the country,
in due time.
The world,
long ago,
the Ancestors set it in place as it is.[1]

Through the rhythm of Jack Bruno's 'Elegy', time defeats time itself.
Unedited, the effect is even more complete. In a short piece of oratory,
phrases asserting that people will 'pass away' in the 'fullness of time'
recur on more than a dozen occasions. The repetitive pulse seems
endless. Lives, no matter how beloved, do not matter as lives. They
are denied temporal extension; there is no room for them to be
protracted in memory and so to stretch into history.

Yet for all this we are not witnessing mere 'ahistoricity' or 'time-lessness'. Terms such as these linger unduly in the shadows of an often unremarked reality. Time and history are not left to decay passively but rather are stripped of their being by the uncompromising forms of space set down by the Ancestors. Only they endure, and the human lot is, ultimately and alone, 'holding this place'.

In this prologue of a chapter, I develop elements implicit in Bruno's words in order to provide the foundation for those chapters that follow. I establish the positive form of what I believe was once a transcontinental ontology of place. Like all philosophies, it was one which nurtured its basic premises so that they might flourish; and in doing so other possible interpretations of being remained of necessity embryonic, developing only later when the pressures of contacts with outsiders changed the structure of the Aboriginal cosmos. The two sections of this chapter take their titles from phenomena conspicuous by their absence in early Aboriginal thought – phenomena so taken for granted in Western understanding that this absence has led most scholars to focus unduly upon them as things which Aborigines at best have denied, and at worst of which they are downright ignorant. These I have labelled 'time' and 'the body'. My purpose is to show, from an Aboriginal perspective, that the two are one and that their 'suppression' is best understood simply as an inevitable cost of the affirmation of place.

TIME

DREAMTIME, DREAMPLACE

Few topics have more allure than the Aboriginal conception of time; few have been discussed with less care. For those seeking primal wisdom, New Age enlightenment or cosmic awareness, the subject has of course been irresistible. On the fringes of scholarship we encounter interpretations ranging from astounding superficiality to almost comical inventiveness. Aborigines, for example, have integrated nine kinds of time, each with its own 'distinctive energy potential', 'chthonic forces', 'fourth dimensions'[2] and so on. Before we smile, however, it is appropriate to recall that academics, whilst mostly more sober in their theories, have also largely failed to proceed far beyond chronic vagueness or even, sometimes, blatant contradiction.

It was A.P. Elkin who first made a serious attempt to understand the problem of time in Aboriginal philosophy. His words falter: 'But what is time? To us it is a series of then and now, the now almost immediately becoming then. To the Aborigines, however, time is now. Then is a past . . . that past, however, is present, here and now.'[3] Similarly, W.E.H. Stanner condensed groping words into the most often quoted phrase from his famous article on 'the Dreaming'. Considering the relationship between Dreaming and time, he concluded 'one cannot "fix" the Dreaming *in* time: it was, and is, everywhen'.[4] In a recent but less inspired attempt to define Dreaming, R.M. Berndt begins by locating it as 'the far distant past, the creative era, or the beginning' and then instantly retreating: 'In addition, however, they imply a condition of timelessness.'[5]

Faced with the apparent problem of expressing Aboriginal understandings of time in general, and their view of time as embodied in Dreaming in particular, it is not surprising to find scholars either avoiding definitions completely or attempting to dress obscurity in poetic guise. It is easy enough to find examples of the latter kind and, in fairness, I select a few examples from scholars whose work I admire. Diane Bell speaks of Dreaming as 'an era shrouded in the mists of time, from which people claim to be descended without actually tracing the links'. John von Sturmer says time, for Aborigines, is 'still and moving all at once – like days and seasons, in a regular sequence, a sequence (or a change) of sameness', while Deborah Rose chooses an aquatic image of Dreaming: 'a great sea of endurance on the edges of which are the sands of ordinary time . . . Dreaming can be conceptualised as a great wave . . . obliterating the debris of our existence'.[6]

Each of these quotations conjures something of the reality, but given the acknowledged cardinal importance of the issue it seems vital that we either abandon poetics or, better still, give our images the precision the art-form deserves. Indeed, the looseness of academic language must in part admit responsibility for both the romantic stereotypes of the 'timeless' Aborigines and the hackneyed criticism that Aborigines are never punctually 'on time'. Faced with this situation, other researchers have opted to devote themselves to minimalising any claims for a uniquely Aboriginal view of time,[7] but in so doing they unfortunately assume that Western historical consciousness is the 'natural' yardstick against which to measure other cultures. Thus, says Partington, a sense of historical time is not totally absent from traditional Aboriginal thought and . . . in so far as it is weak, this is a condition to be challenged and transformed rather than to be accepted as an immutable necessity.[8]

What Partington fails to appreciate in this backhanded compliment is that there might be some cost to the existing Aboriginal worldview were this embryonic temporality allowed to become a leviathan. In this, however, he has merely continued the tradition in Aboriginal Studies of presenting Aboriginal ontology in its negative form (i.e. time*less*).

Thus, between the overly hasty disclaimers and the amorphous assertions, falls the very basis of Aboriginal being. Those recognising this conundrum and wishing to say something (anything!) positive have assured us that Aborigines have a cyclical view of time. In a recent and relatively detailed analysis of the topic, Nancy Williams said time, for the Yolngu, is 'both cyclical and circular'. Again, 'Although no Yolngu person has explained it in precisely this way it seems to me that Yolngu perceive time as circular, so that from any particular time, what is past may be future, or what is future may be past.'[9]

The assumption that Aborigines have a cyclical time perspective is widespread and often to be found in the very same works advocating atemporality. The roots of the thesis lie in the Durkheimian notion that the human discovery of temporality was triggered by the sense of social rhythm. Stanner could thus assert that generation moieties 'arranged into named and recurring cycles' gave rise to *social* time which is itself ' "bent" into cycles or circles'.[10] Others have reaffirmed Stanner's position, although sometimes citing the natural rhythms of seasons or celestial bodies along with those of society.

This last refuge for those who would say something concrete about Aboriginal time has, alas, one vital flaw. It assumes Aboriginal people perceive natural or social rhythms as cycles, because that is how the scholars producing the ethnography interpret them. This may be partially true of lunar rhythms and subsections, to which I return below, but these exceptions aside it is vital we recall Williams' candid confession that no Yolngu person ever spoke to her of cycles *per se*, and underscore the point that social and natural 'cycles' are *not* facts but *interpretations* of observed phenomena. Aborigines, of course, observe these phenomena, but in the main I do not believe they share the 'cycle' interpretation.

At this point, it becomes necessary to explore some academic preconceptions about time. There still remains a prominent and largely unchallenged assumption that there is only a binary option in temporal constructions: that is, if time is not linear then, almost by default, it is cyclical. This, I am convinced, is what has led scholars to suppose that the Aboriginal understanding of time takes the form of cycles. I must therefore raise some comparative issues, not in order to fit the first Australians into some typology, but rather to refine the fideist task of understanding what is definingly unique to their subject matter.[11]

Cyclical time certainly exists in both Eastern and Western[12] thought. For convenience, I have selected a well known example from the Hindu *Manu-smrti*. In that Law book, time (*kala*) is marked by a series of articulated and quantified cycles. Four *yugas* of decreasing length (4,000, 3,000, 2,000 and 1,000 divine years) mark out human history and collectively form a *mahayuga*, itself but one thousandth of a *kalpa*, which is in turn only a day (or night) of *Brahma*, the creator.[13] Although the *mahayuga* contains a series of ever-decaying cycles, the larger cosmic process is one of unceasing changeless repetition.

If this is a cyclical vision of time, in what sense can we align it with Aboriginal thought? The only grounds that I can see for their equation is a totally unfounded ethnocentric and evolutionary model which assumes there is a linear history for the West and varying degrees of cycles for the rest. Such a view, of course, is nonsense. Indeed, the following quotation indicates that true cyclicity already *presupposes* the illusion of linearity. Says *Manu*, 'Those only, who know that the holy day of Brahman, indeed, ends after the completion of one thousand ages of the gods and that his night lasts as long, are really men acquainted with the length of days and nights.'[14] The reality of cycles appears only to those who have grasped this esoteric knowledge. It is thus entirely correct of Paul Ricoeur to say in one of the few papers to question our rigid categorisations of time:

> Cyclical time appears paradoxically as a particular case of, and not an alternative term for, linear time. We cannot help thinking of something cyclical except as 'a line returning into itself as to form a closed circle' (*Oxford English Dictionary*).

Ricoeur's conclusion is nowhere more needed than in Aboriginal Studies: a people's view of time must not be forced to cast its vote in a two-candidate typology but should rather be left to be 'understood in their own terms'.[15]

Insofar as Aborigines speak neither of lines nor of cycles of time, we are left to search for a more serviceable terminology. Edmund Leach, on the subject of 'Time and False Noses', once argued for a 'pendulum' type in which 'time is a succession of alternations and full stops',[16] but this again imposes too much on the Aboriginal world. Ricoeur's reference to a distinct 'rhythmic time', on the other hand, is important. Rhythmic time recognises recurrent and distinct patterns, but without suggesting that the patterns loop back upon themselves to form circles. If we remove our presuppositions re-garding Aboriginal statements about seasons, celestial activity, kinship and so on, we are left with the more faithful claim that these are presented as predictably patterned rhythms.

At this point, however, I must depart from Ricoeur's suggestion that this is a rhythmic form of *time*. Having disposed of cycles, I want to dispose of time itself. This is not as difficult as it might at first appear. Ricoeur argues, correctly, that numbered intervals are necessary to open-ended linearity, but I would go further to say they are indispensable to time itself. Certainly Plato saw them as essential to cyclical time:

> For simultaneously with the construction of the Heaven He contrived the production of days and nights and months and years, which existed not before Heaven came into being. And these are all portions of Time . . . which imitates Eternity and *circles round according to number*.[17]

If linearity, as Ricoeur suggests, requires 'the application of numbers', then circularity, that line returning upon itself, would likewise be a time which 'circles round according to number'.

Significantly, the rhythms of Aboriginal life are totally unnum-bered, as Aborigines traditionally used no counting at all. No doubt someone will wish to remind me that Aborigines could always count to three, or perhaps five, while John Harris felt he had made a breakthrough by discovering references (in a post-colonial trade context) to the use of units of twenty.[18] Aborigines can, of course, learn to quantify things, but we miss the point by labelling units of three or even five 'numbers'. As Elkin noted long ago, 'this is not counting; it is . . . a concrete method of indicating persons or places'.[19] At a glance, anyone can see a duality or a trio, and most Aboriginal languages constantly differentiate the singular, dual and plural without anyone ever counting. Even five (often literally 'hand') can be seen as a 'fivesome' (although this is my personal limit without occasional error). Thus, while Aborigines had words for what we call numbers, there is nothing to suggest these are counted. They are simply qualities of existence.

Rather than prejudicing the issue with the word 'time', I suggest it is best to state that Aborigines operate from an understanding of *rhythmed events*. The semantic clarity is important in order to avoid giving time an unfounded ontological autonomy in Aboriginal life. Time, as Plato reveals, is, for those who give it freedom, the arena in which events occur. It is prior to events and not determined by them. In the popular Western view, time still, so to speak, ticks on even if nothing occurs; its emancipation from events is ensured by its own subjugation of an ongoing numbered measure. But in Aboriginal thought there is nothing beyond events themselves. This is entirely apparent in their cosmologies, which lack any reference to ultimate pre-event origins. For Aborigines, there is nothing more fundamental than the statement: events occur.

Aboriginal appreciation of events is indeed impressive: subtle as well as aesthetically and philosophically well developed. The most sophisticated instance recorded of the understanding of natural patterns is an Aranda reading of what T.G.H. Strehlow refers to as the 'time-points of night and day'.[20] His father, Carl Strehlow, had recorded thirty clearly demarcated conditions of the world during both night (*ingua*) and day (*alta*). T.G.H. Strehlow adds some obviously clock-based guides for the Western reader ('the very early hours', 'the time after midnight', etc.), which are not intrinsic to the classification itself. Some of the Aranda states of the world might be rendered thus:

The Milky Way is stretched out across the centre of the sky.
The bandicoots back into their burrows.
Light glimmers.
The outline of trees and objects are clearly defined.
The sun is burning down.
The sun is low in the sky.
The shadows are variegated.
The sun is sinking.
The sky is aflame with red and yellow.

There is, as Strehlow says, a poetic gift here, but where is time? Where are cycles? These are concrete events, patterns of the condition of the world. They are acutely observed, rhythmic and predictable, but there is no suggestion the 'end' co-joins the beginning. 'Cycle' is one *interpretation* of patterns that repeat, but there is no evidence the Aranda employ that interpretation.

The inevitable example of a social event which has led to scholars 'discovering' the germ of time is the subsection. After all, from a Western perspective these not only return but are also numbered. The 'numbering', however, must be immediately qualified, for although there are always 'eight' subsections, they are not thus perceived by Aborigines. The 'number' is a byproduct of an organisation which von Brandenstein has shown to be a socio-philosophic division of a paired duality,[21] and in practice this is how Aboriginal people actually employ 'skin' names. As for the cycle, however, I am happy to concede that one can discern time beginning to break free through subsections, and I will explain why this is so in chapter 5. For the moment I merely note that the subsection is a post-colonial development.[22]

Thus far I have argued that Aboriginal people, prior to the intensive disruption of outsiders, had not allowed 'time' to develop as a determinative quality of being. Temporal constructs are, I believe, not a 'natural' human attribute but rather they are specific forms of intellectual organisation. Why Aborigines avoided this philosophical option is the more important issue to which I will soon turn, but for the moment it is enough to recognise that there was no fashioning of time, linear or cyclical, but rather a sophisticated patterning of events in accordance with their rhythms. In a musical context, Catherine Ellis has suggested the Pitjatjantjara have 'perfect rhythm', designed to transcend time itself.[23] Be this as it may, we can at least say theirs was a highly developed interpretation of rhythm which does not require extension into the arena of time.

This conclusion immediately raises the question: what type of time is then left for 'Dreamtime'? My answer is, of course, that it is not a time at all. It is here that the foregoing conclusions start to bear fruit, but to begin I will briefly trace the history of this bastardised word.

The English term 'Dreamtime' was initially derived from the Aranda *Altjiringa*. Carl Strehlow believed this was the name of a High God,[24] but this was certainly not its initial meaning nor one that endured. Apparently, the early Hermannsburg missionaries felt this word was the closest Aranda approximation to 'God', and perhaps some Aranda people partially accepted this redefinition.

The first published reference to the word, by the Rev. L. Schultz, hints at its true meaning. The Aranda, he said, ' "pretend" *tjurunga* were *altjira* – that is, were not made'.[25] More specifically, when asked by Spencer and Gillen if the word meant 'God', he replied, 'I beg to tell you that, so far as I know the language, it is not "God" . . . but it has a meaning of old, very old, something that has no origin, mysterious, something that has always been so, also, always.'[26]

'Dreamtime' or 'Dreaming', as T.G.H. Strehlow has noted, emerged with a mistranslation of the *altjira* root, which has the meaning of 'eternal, uncreated, springing out of itself'. *Altjira rama*, literally 'to see the eternal', is the evocative description for human sleep-dreams, but the so-called 'Dreaming' is derived from *Altjiringa ngambakala*: 'that which derives from *altjira*'. Strehlow grasps at 'having originated out of its own eternity' as the closest possible English equivalent.[27]

It is true that in several Desert languages there is a linguistic connection between the 'self-derived eternal' and dreams, but this is not a universal occurrence. The word 'Dreaming' or 'Dream Time' has, nonetheless, returned from academic coinage through popular culture to spread throughout virtually all Aboriginal English speech: a self-fulfilling academic prophecy which began with a concept of which the Aboriginal linguist Eve Fesl says: ' "Dreamtime" is a compound word "dreamed up" by an English speaker who couldn't understand the Aboriginal languages'.[28]

As for the scholarly differentiation between 'Dreaming' and 'Dream Time', it appears to be little more than semantic. Radcliffe-Brown once spoke of it as a 'world-dawn'[29] and that has remained at least one of its meanings. Early professional anthropologists such as Elkin popularised use of the phrase 'Dream Time', and while Stanner warned against (although continued) this practice, it is still used uncritically in contemporary literature. Even those who employ Stanner's preferred term, 'Dreaming', still seem to hold the echo of the 'time' suffix. Thus, for example, Rose makes the distinction between 'Dreaming Time' and 'ordinary time'.[30]

Yet for all this there is a general, quite contradictory, agreement that the Dreamtime or Dreaming (-Time) is not confined by time. Solving the dilemma from within the bounds of temporal presuppositions has spawned some wonderful feats of intellectual gymnastics. The old school, carried on today by, for example, Morphy, would translate the Yolngu *Wangarr* as 'Ancestral past', a remote 'period of time'.[31] Frustrated with this kind of thinking, Françoise Dussart and Eric Michaels have rendered the Warlpiri *Jukurrpa* as 'Ancestral present'.[32] And, dissatisfied with both forms, I took this process to its absurd logical conclusion by coining the 'Ancestral Now', alluding both to William James' famous reflection on the saddle-like thickness of the experience of the now and to St Augustine's dictum that eternity is the now of God.

These contortions are only necessary, however, if we allege there is some form of normal time against which the Dreaming stands in distinction. If we accept, on the other hand, that Aborigines constructed their world in terms of *rhythmed events* then we can instead inquire into the nature of the so-called 'Dreaming' as a class of events. Following Strehlow's rendering of the original Aranda meaning, 'eternal events' approaches the reality but perhaps still harbours too many unjustified time referents. The words that I find most applicable in English are *Abiding Events*. Collectively, I suggest these form an *Abiding Law* (which I will often hereafter abbreviate to Law).

'Abiding' has the advantage of not only adjectivally conjuring something of the transtemporal quality of 'eternal' or 'enduring' but also, and as we will see more positively and importantly, having the verbal significance of 'residing in a place'. 'Law', too, probably derives from the Old Norse *lag*, a due or fitting place, and thus shares the connotation. And this brings me to the rationale of the preceding extensive critique of Aboriginal time, for I now wish to show that the tragedy of 'Dream Time' is not so much the inaccuracy *per se*, but rather the fact that it has blinded us to the realisation that the true significance of the concept behind the word is not temporal but spatial.

ABIDING EVENTS

I have thus far proposed that precontact Aboriginal worlds consisted of an interplay of two kinds of events: rhythmic events and Abiding Events. Neither requires reference to time. Certainly, Abiding Events appear more clearly separated from the normal rhythms (and chaos) of life, and this is what has been interpreted as the pastness of a Dreamtime. This 'pastness' is no more in the past, however, than, by analogy, the land is only in the distance for a person observing a panoramic view from above broken clouds. She or he might say 'in the foreground are clouds, in the distance is land', but does this suggest there is no land (perhaps even partially visible) closer to the viewer? Likewise, to say one or two generations ago there were certain kinsfolk but somewhere beyond that were Abiding Events does not suggest those events then stopped. It is only that they stand there *alone*, unobscured by rhythmic events. There is every difference between rhythmic events from long ago (e.g. Warlpiri *nuruwirri*) and Abiding Events (Warlpiri *Jukurrpa*), which do not change and for which history is irrelevant.[33]

There remains one final objection that must be dealt with. Does the sequence from Abiding Events to the present (even if the former endure) not suggest temporality? Morphy has recently argued that the 'disjunction between the Ancestral past and the time when humans occupied the earth' is in fact a form of direct linear time.[34] For reasons I give later, this may not be entirely untrue in the changing Yolngu context, but the logic of the argument is not as self-evident as it first appears. Let me be quite clear: I am not for one moment suggesting Aborigines experience a world devoid of past, present and future, but I am saying they avoided allowing these to be worked into an ontology which conceded the sovereignty of time. This is nowhere more apparent than in Morphy's own example. If Aboriginal 'Ancestors' were in strict fact lineal *ancestors* his case would be unimpeachable, but Aborigines do not trace an extended lineage to the Beings who perform Abiding Events. Indeed, as Bell demonstrates, they do not trace their genealogies far beyond living memory. Where, then, is the time linking the 'Ancestral past' and the 'present'? It does not exist. Rather, Ancestral Abiding Events and rhythmic life events are co-joined quite literally through place. Bell puts this most succinctly:

> The shallowness of genealogical memory is not a form of cultural amnesia but rather a way of focusing on the basis of all relationships – that is, the *Jukurrpa* and the land. By not naming deceased relatives, people are able to stress a relationship directly to the land. It is not necessary to trace back through many generations to a founding ancestor to make a claim.[35]

Abiding Events and rhythmic events are coterminous, linked not through time but place.

It becomes evident, therefore, that the entire discussion of time – linear, cyclical or Dream – has diverted our attention from the uncompromising position of place in Aboriginal worldviews.[36]

Margaret Bain is one academic investigator to highlight the error
of temporal references. Casting a careful linguistic eye over the
concept of *Jukurrpa,* she observed the word 'has no time reference'
whatsoever.[37] Rather, it is used in two contexts. Firstly, it refers to
a class of events which are manifest in the myth and rite of an
Ancestral Being, and secondly, the word is used in reference to places
associated with specific Ancestors. Dubinska and Traweek came to
a similar conclusion in an insightful long-range reinterpretation of
Nancy Munn's work. *Jukurrpa* is not, they wrote, 'primarily a "time"
but rather a symbol which gives shape to the Walbiri experience of
the Ancestral realm. This "realm" is both a location and a source
of energy'.[38] Were we to cling to the dream-root, this would be best
rendered as 'Dreaming-Event' (a qualitative rather than temporal
distinction) or 'Dream place'.[39] It is these qualities I have attempted
to merge in the phrase 'Abiding Events'.

It is probably wisest to refer to these Events in the plural – to
'Dreamings' rather than 'The Dreaming' – but the scholarly temp-
tation has always been to pull these pluralistic concepts into a
unified whole. Elkin comes dangerously close to misconstruing
Aboriginal thought when forcing it into a common mould: 'The
Dreaming is universal, being the ground of every particular'.[40]

The whole exists in Aboriginal thought as a conceptual principle rather than an ontological existant. That principle is referred
to in Aboriginal English most often as 'Law', less frequently as
'Dreaming', and, significantly, never in my experience as 'religion'
or any other such secularist invention.[41] The Abiding Law, as I term
it, is a way of describing the process of relationship between Abiding
Events and the patterns of the world. The Law is the life-plan derived
collectively from Dreaming Events.

Several prominent Aboriginal thinkers have tried to translate these
terms for White audiences. Commissioner Patrick Dodson, one-time
Director of the Central Lands Council, has said:

> The English word 'dreaming' can be misleading because the concepts
> which it translates are exceedingly complex and largely unrelated to the
> English meaning of the word. These concepts are often alternatively
> described as 'The Law'. They are a coherent and all-encapsulating body
> of truths which govern the whole of life.[42]

Mussolini Harvey, Yanyuwa elder and Chairman of the Aboriginal
Sacred Sites Protection Authority, places the emphasis on distin-
guishing the Dreaming/Law and Dreaming*s*.

White people ask us all the time, what is Dreaming? This is a hard question because Dreaming is a really big thing for Aboriginal people . . . The Dreamings made our Law . . . This Law is the way we live, our rules. This Law is our ceremonies, our songs, our stories . . . The Law was made by the Dreamings.[43]

In other words, the Law is being–design collectively inherent in Abiding Events, but it must again be stressed that the locus of this Law is 'Dreamings', which are located spatially rather than temporally. Thus, adds the well known Yolngu theologian, Djiniyini Gondarra: 'To say "this mountain is my dreaming" or "that land is my dreaming" he is really saying to us that this mountain or that land holds very sacred knowledge, wisdom and moral truth.'[44] If there is one principle permeating the Law it is *geosophy*: all knowledge and wisdom derives, through Abiding Events (Dreaming*s*), from place.

To summarise my argument thus far, I am suggesting that precontact Aboriginal ontology was dependent upon that class of events I call Abiding Events and which collectively constituted the Abiding Law of an Aboriginal community. At first glance, the latter concept might appear comparable, for example, with the Hindu term for their own tradition, the *Sanatana Dharma* or 'Eternal Law', but what I have emphasised is that more than 'Eternal', the Law which abides is landlocked, entirely immanent and geosophical. 'Law', furthermore, is a quality of Abiding Events rather than a single plan of cosmic order. No Aboriginal person could say what constituted the full contents of *the* Law or *the* Dreaming, but all would assert that Lawfulness was an attribute of Abiding Events. This ensures that the ontological status of the Aboriginal world is always pluralistic. Dreaming*s* do not derive from, but rather themselves collectively constitute, 'The Dreaming'. Each Event gives shape to Law, but none is derived from a determinative pre-established Law. If for John the cosmic plan originated in the temporal priority of *logos*, then for Aboriginal people it sprang from the spatial priority of land-acts: Faust came close to this position:

> It says: 'In the beginning was the *Word*'.
> Already I am stopped. It seems absurd . . .
> The spirit helps me. Now it is exact.
> I write: 'In the beginning was the *Act*'.[45]

Not in the beginning was the Word, but beneath the rhythms are Abiding Events.

I will discuss the 'shape' of these Events in a moment. Before proceeding, however, it is necessary to pause briefly to examine some possible explanations for the emphasis on place–Events in Aboriginal life. To date, those who have recognised and queried this world-orientation have suggested an interplay of environmental and neurological causes. Graham Davidson's study of card-playing amongst the people of Bamyili is relevant here. He discovered the players did not add card numbers but rather, as one informant said, proceeded by 'see[ing] which cards fit together'. Davidson postulates that the Aboriginal storage of information is synchronous and spatial rather than serial and temporal, and indicates his preference for explaining this in terms of a nomadic lifestyle placing high stress upon location[46] – a view having points in common with one Bergson proposed many decades earlier.[47] Warren TenHouten goes further towards neurology, arguing that even urban Aborigines rely more than Whites upon 'right-hemisphere' thought related to spatial rather than temporal organisation. He seeks, however, to avoid accusations of any derogatory higher/lower mentality by simply stating that right-hemisphere activity is more appropriate to hunter-gatherer lifestyles.[48]

The difficulty with these views is that the environmental and neurological explanations are to date no more than conjectures in the realm of pure speculation. Differences in the processing of information have been recorded, but I know of no attempts to locate evidence for the hypothesised causes.[49] Until such time as some reasonable evidence is forthcoming, it seems preferable to remain agnostic as to ultimate causes, but what we must not overlook is that, once instigated, the philosophical content of ubietous thought has been a fundamental reason for its endurance. And while no doubt inviting cries of 'idealism', it is, of course, at least possible that Aboriginal people originally opted for place-based ontology on intellectual grounds.

My concerns in this book are not with origins but with why Aboriginal people might nurture the thought of place. One scholar to pursue the promise of spatial order is the Sioux author, Vine Deloria. He makes the acute observation that traditions which give precedence to time as a way of being-in-the-world must defend themselves from history. He notes the problems of communication between ontologies of space and time, and highlights their respective parameters:

Time has an unusual limitation. It must begin and end at some real points, or it must be conceived as cyclical in nature . . . Space has limitations that are primary geographical, and any sense of time arising within the religious experience becomes secondary to present geographical existence – the danger that *appears* to be lurking in spatial conceptions of religion is the effect of missionary activity on religion. Can it leave the land of its nativity and embark on a program of world or continental conquest . . .?[50]

Coming as it does from someone all too aware of the imperial message of missionaries,[51] the irony of this passage should be self-evident.

The thesis I develop in the following pages is that the Aboriginal focus on Abiding (i.e. enduring–place) Events has precisely the effect of undermining the conquest or incorporation of another's place. Time, in contrast, is inherently capricious; its indolent openhandedness paving the way for imperialism. Were I asked to offer a tentative typology of spatio-temporal location, I would suggest linear time was a 'fall' from place. History, associated quintessentially with the Hebrews, was something which intervened when the Israelites had lost their place. The covenant, God's promise, was to reinstate place, but this was only feasible by the Godhead entering a world given over to time. From the moment God said to Abraham 'Leave your country', instead of their place, the Hebrews had history and a promise of a land – and *Zakhor*, remembrance. We will see this scenario being repeated in Aboriginal contexts in later chapters.

Cyclical time, I believe, is a retreat from time's autonomy. It is not, as Paul Tillich suggests, inherently spatial[52] so much as it attempts to recapture the possibility of enduringness. In China, which had also developed a predominantly linear history, Buddhist cosmology appealed in part because it offered a haven from the tyranny of time. Yet even world cycles did not resolve the problem. Shao Yung, the Buddhist-inspired Neo-Confucian, while charting giant oscillating cosmic cycles, paused to reflect upon the whimsy of *all* time. Speculating beyond his conceptual abilities, he wrote:

The so-called past and present originated in a subjective point of view. It is quite possible that before the past of thousands of years ago, or after the future of many thousands of years ahead, mankind did, or will, relinquish the subjective point of view.[53]

Yet, paradoxically, he can only conceive of something beyond time's subjectivity in terms of another time *in* history. He did not imagine place as the object for the fixed point of *object*ivity. For Aborigines, however, Abiding Events remained victorious through the integrity of place. Stanner puts this with his usual assurance. Aborigines, he said, set

> a metaphysical emphasis on abidingness. They placed a very special value on things remaining unchangingly themselves. One may say their Ideal and Real come very close together . . . they are not simply a people 'without a history': they are a people who have been able, in a sense, to 'defeat history'.[54]

I would but correct Stanner's final words: they are a people who had defeated that place-depriving scenario which has so often made history a desideratum.

What would happen, however, were Aboriginal people to have their lands threatened? Would time develop? Would there be not only histories but eschatologies and millenniums? That, of course, is precisely the subject of this book, but before unravelling that story there is yet more to be said of the precontact structure of the Aboriginal world.

THE SHAPE OF EVENTS

Abiding Events are characterised by the fact that they take shape and are maintained as world-forms. So far I have depicted this as the victory of a spatial ontology over that of time. If, however, it has been necessary to retract all temporal projections onto the precontact Aboriginal understanding of events, it is equally essential to at least define what is meant by 'space'. In traditions where time is given autonomy, space itself has in turn been temporalised and construed as subject to change. Its durability undermined, we reach quickly for a definition in which space is not cosmic form but rather the vast empty domain in which forms reside in a state of flux. Space thereafter mirrors the face of time, measured, as it is, in numbered units. From a mainstream historical perspective it is Heidegger rather than Bergson who grasps the reality. Time is not the ghost of space but, instead, even the atemporal are temporalised (*supra* Introduction).

If time is shunned, however, space can endure. It is thus that Aboriginal thought was not fettered by the Euclidean notion of homogeneous abstracted Space which, since the time of the Deists, is well represented even in Christian theology. Instead, there is the structured world, unmeasured and unnumbered. Aboriginal understandings do not recognise the cosmos as a unified arena in which events occur; one cannot speak of space of any kind in the singular. The basic and only unit of Aboriginal cosmic structure is the place.

In terms of observing changes to Aboriginal models of the world it must be stressed that 'traditionally' all that was not localised was discarded. There was, in Jonathan Z. Smith's use of the word, no possibility of a Utopia (Greek *ou*, not; *topos*, a place).[55] All cosmology focused on discrete, known, observed sites.

This raises the philosophical problem of the origin of the cosmos. Even a cursory survey of cosmogonies indicates not only that they mostly postulate a single primordial event but, correlatively, also a single, although often unformed, world-substance which the first event transforms. All such cosmogonies, whether they refer to the divine sport of Brahma, the shadow of non-Being, the will of God or the Big Bang, situate something ontologically prior to the discrete place-Event.

The Aboriginal 'solution' to this problem, if indeed the problem ever presented itself at all, was simple, but to the Western reader disconcerting. There is, in their traditions, no first cause, world origin or creation. As Stanner said, 'taken as a whole the myths deal with cosmology rather than cosmogony. That is, they deal less with origins as such than with the instituting of relevances'.[56] Tonkinson, in contrast, entirely misses the mark when he writes approvingly, 'The Dreamtime . . . is typically described as the period of creation'.[57] Misinterpretations such as this are both widespread and informative, for upon closer examination, they reveal that false representations of Aboriginal world-order are linked to the surreptitious but unwarranted introduction of time into our models of Aboriginal Law.

The most sophisticated offender in this regard was Mircea Eliade, whose prominent work I shall take as an example for more detailed investigation. His reading of Aboriginal traditions was essentially in accord with his comparativist thesis that cyclical history is a mechanism for overcoming the terror of time. Thus, amongst Aborigines, 'the ritual reactualization of the mythical history reactivates communication with the Dream Time, regenerates life, and assures its continuation. In short, the ritual "re-creates" the world'. The cosmogonic emphasis here reflects Eliade's insistence upon the ontologic priority of history. 'There exists no culture without history,' he says, 'but this "history" is not acknowledged as such by the primitives.'[58] Through recreating the world upon the archetype of the first time, history itself is defeated.

The theory surely has applicability in understanding some forms of cyclical history (where, significantly, Eliade's own research began) but imposing this upon Australian data makes seemingly subtle shifts which entirely skew the Aboriginal view of existence. For if 'real' history is being *denied*, then time exists, and if time why not also first causes, creation, and unified space? To all of these Eliade readily replied – why not indeed?

In a remarkably Eurocentric reading of the ethnographies, Eliade has implied that throughout Australia people recognised a great first cause which amounted to a Supreme Being. His evidence for this claim was in fact confined to two regions, the seat of invasion in the south-east (which I consider in detail in chapter 3), and the intensively missionised Hermannsburg area.[59] Given the fact that the Aranda 'High God' held himself particularly aloof from the world, Eliade saw his opportunity to 'prove' the original universality of a single God. 'From the perspective of the history of religions, the transformation of a Sky Being into a *deus otiosus* seems to have reached its furthest limits among the western Aranda. The next step could only be his falling into total oblivion'.[60] Hence, by implication, all Aborigines once maintained (but have since denied or abandoned) a single first cause, just as they have denied time. What we are witnessing, of course, is Eliade's own cultural projection, for as he revealed in his journals, the 'secret message' in his history of religions was that 'myths and religions, in all their variety, are the result of the vacuum left in the world by the retreat of God, his transformation into *deus otiosus*'.[61]

If Aborigines have denied the primordiality of the one creator, however, Eliade still believes their understanding of space reflects the unified cosmic plan of the Godhead. Eliade cannot escape the image of a co-ordinated world co-joined to a distant Heaven. The self-created High God established the cosmic centre, 'an *axis mundi* which unites heaven and earth'. This opens the way for spatial homogeneity: 'the "centre" imparts structure to the surrounding amorphous space'.[62] Eliade thus bequeaths Aborigines, in turn, a history that they have suppressed, an Ancestral monism (against pluralism) and a universal space which itself becomes the arena in which events can occur. He articulates with consummate expertise an entire range of scholarly prejudices in the study of Aboriginal understanding of existence. What is particularly significant is the manner in which his studies reveal that misinterpretations of spatial structure are directly tied to misinterpretations of time.

I will propose as I proceed a detailed alternative to the views of Eliade, who has been singled out as only one example of a wide-spread misrepresentation. For the moment, to clear the ground, I will but make reference to Jonathan Z. Smith's comprehensive critique of Eliade's views. Perceptively, Smith writes

> By emphasising a 'rupture' between the world above and the world below . . . Eliade has placed the Northern Aranda tradition within a celestial and transcendental context, within the framework of his universal symbol of the 'centre'. Within such a frame of reference, place is established by its connection with cosmogony and by its 'opening toward a world which is superhuman and remote . . . But . . . the horizon of the [Aranda] Tjilba myth is not celestial, it is relentlessly terrestrial and chthonic. The emphasis is not on the dramatic creation of the world out of chaos by transcendent figures or on the 'rupture' between these figures and men. Rather, the emphasis is on transformation and continuity.[63]

Other writers have been more subtle than Eliade in the projection of Western notions of time, space and events. T.G.H. Strehlow is a case in point. In a justly famous article rereleased as a slim book, he concedes the pre-existence of the world and lack of creation, and while he also avoids models of Ancestral hierarchy he nevertheless cannot resist giving Abiding Events a co-ordinated unity as a single macro-event. Evocatively, he writes of 'semi-embryonic masses of half-developed infants' lying beneath the earth. 'Time began when these supernatural beings awakened from their sleep. They broke through the surface of the earth . . . the earth was flooded with light for the first time.'[64] Strehlow's error is perhaps primarily a stylistic one, but the fact remains that on scanning the author's less general-ised accounts it becomes apparent that the Aranda themselves do not present Ancestral activities as a single orchestrated event. To accommodate the reader, Strehlow unites a multitude of independent Events into *an* Event, but he would have served his purpose better had he instead attempted to derive a *principle* of Law behind separate Events. In speaking of the moment all Events together began and of the origins of time, Strehlow simultaneously introduces history and cosmic unity into the Aranda world.

Deborah Rose, in contrast, nicely stresses points antithetical to those of Eliade and Strehlow. Having insisted that Aboriginal people of the Victoria River District 'do not, and do not wish to have a supreme deity' she makes the correlative point: 'One of the most important moral principles of the whole cosmos is that the parts are autonomous'.[65] Barbara Glowczewski has made a significant examination of the spatial and so-called temporal aspects of Ancestral Events, concluding that they lack organisation either in time or in a unified spatial order: 'It is impossible to chronologize the tracks or hierarchize the totems. They can only be ordered in each specific place'.[66]

In brief, with the exceptions that form the substance of this book, Aboriginal cosmologies avoid the problem of a primordial or subsequent homogeneous spatial order, and this is achieved by avoiding cosmogony and creation themselves. There is no first cause, original world-stuff, moment of origin or co-ordinated emergence. Any author attempting to retell Aboriginal Ancestral stories as a unified macro-myth will destroy the principles of the stories thus amalgamated; the whole imagined by Western interpreters falls a long way short of the Aboriginal non-summation of the parts.

Rather than a world creation, Aboriginal narratives affirm a multitude of independent place-shaping Events. By avoiding a genesis of world-matter from a first being (or non-being), Aboriginal traditions are at liberty to attest that places are intrinsically discrete. The transformation of localised areas, on the other hand, does not threaten this principle. The world is not made, but worlds take shape.

The basic tenet of Abiding Events, as Nancy Munn has perceptively shown, is that something came out of, moved across, and went into, the earth. Graphically, Desert societies render this by employing two basic iconic elements: the concentric circle representing sites and lines standing for tracks between sites. In the boldest of terms, Aboriginal ontology rests upon the maxim that a place-being emerged, moved, and established an abode. This, Munn correctly concludes, is the basis of Aboriginal 'world theory'.[67]

Why must place move? There seem to be two facets to the answer to this question. The first is intentionality. Place itself is stretched by conscious action. Munn refers to this as the ability of sites to become humans or other species – subjects who travel only to conclude their sojourns with self-objectification as 'the Transformation of Subjects into Objects'. This she suspects reveals a free will exclusively open during Ancestral times, but in thus arguing she ignores a fact she herself documented: the Ancestors themselves are constrained by a pre-vision of their objectified form.[68] The issue seems not to revolve around time vs. the atemporal, nor free will vs. determination, so much as it simply states that place, like all existants, is conscious. From an Aboriginal vantage this, of course, reverses the order of logic: all life is conscious because it is an extension of the consciousness of place.

Such a statement obviously negates a great deal of the writing on Aboriginal life which rested upon the Durkheimian model requiring a distinction between mind (albeit social) and matter. In one of his happier phrases, Radcliffe-Brown softened Western categories, saying we are witnessing a conception of a 'larger whole' which represented 'the universe as a moral and social order',[69] but he predictably insisted upon the ultimate priority of the social. It was once again Stanner who saw beyond these dualities,[70] arguing that the social and even the 'religious' are each dependent relatum which in turn run back to 'a metaphysical object'.[71] That object is place.

The second reason why place must move is to relate sites and so overcome the monadology which would result from unextended place. In this context it is important to qualify the image of autonomy I have employed, for although countries are discrete and are ontologically prior to any larger whole, they are also interconnected and interdependent. What Morphy says of Yolngu political structure would, from a Yolngu vantage, be an extension of the structure of their lands, the organisation of which 'involves the continual maintenance of a balance between autonomy and exchange'.[72]

It is essential to note that the Ancestors do not move *from* one place *to* another but rather that they link sites by a common intentionality of place. As T.G.H. Strehlow significantly noted, the Aranda person 'believes in the simultaneous presence of the Ancestor at each of the many scenes which once witnessed the fullness of his supernatural powers'.[73] The movement of the Ancestors should therefore not be seen as a shift from pre-form to form so much as it should be understood to reveal that place has inherent extension and hence that places are related through structural networks. For those conceiving of space in the singular it is logical to believe each place is connected to an infinite number of other locii (an ideology in fact becoming evident in some recent Aboriginal re-formations of their cosmos). For Aboriginal peoples, on the other hand, the connection between sites is predetermined by the pathways which are the stretching of the being of conscious-place. God's grandeur could not charge the world, as Hopkins so astutely said, by gathering to greatness like the ooze of oil.[74] Rather, all that is land-derived – people, knowledge, cultural objects – is related along lines of place. Thus, in a passage which should be starkly opposed to Eliade's views of an *axis mundi*, Munn writes that the iconic symbol of a site-centre

> does not refer to the centre of the world as a *whole*, but only to a single place. Walbiri country consists of many such life centres linked together by paths. There is no single locality that focalizes all the others. Walbiri do not really give conceptual shape to the world as a whole in the sense of a single, centralized structure, but conceive of it in terms of networks of places linked by paths.[75]

The subjectivity of space sustained through Ancestral movement thus provides for a double relatedness of land; the channels between places on the one hand, and the links between sites and *other* (place-derived) conscious beings on the other. I develop both of these elements in the remaining sections of this chapter, but before I proceed to them, I need to briefly dispose of the issue of so-called 'totemism'.

Whilst Lévi-Strauss has pronounced 'totemism' dead,[76] the concept seems to persist in scholarship, either consciously maintained or, more often than not, used through analytical laziness. Yet, since Tylor, the early Radcliffe-Brown and many others, it has been seen as the anachronistic piece of Victorian thought which it in fact is. As Stanner said, ' "totemism" is a mentality and not an entity', and hence as a concept it is 'useless analytically'.[77] For Lévi-Strauss it was even less than a 'mentality' – it was 'not even a mode of classification, but an aspect or moment of it'.[78]

According to Stanner, the mentality of which 'totemism' was a moment was one which expressed a connection between humans and other existents 'within an ontology of life that in Aboriginal understanding depends for order and continuity on maintaining identities and associations which exemplify the connection'. That association, Stanner had already established, was a sense of world-design: 'Pattern, shape, form, and structure, occurring in what we call "nature" '.[79] In other words, 'totemism' was an aspect of an ontology which was based on the Aboriginal understanding of world-form. Lévi-Strauss came close, but inverted the reality, when he said that at root it was a classification intended to allow places to be incorporated as history,[80] for in the final analysis 'totemism' seems no more than a part of a metaphysic which insists upon the ultimacy of place. 'Totemism' as Strehlow maintained, uses a geographic order.[81]

The basic totemic assertion is that all Lawful existence emerges from the being of place. 'No matter,' says Harvey, 'if they are fish, birds, men, women, animals, wind or rain . . . All things in our country have Law, they have ceremony and song, and they have people who are related to them.'[82] Furthermore, given this emphasis on spatial plurality, it should not be surprising to realise that only specific human and other life essences emerge from specific sites. In other monistic traditions, thinkers retreating from a single cosmic order succeeded mostly in portraying the localised as self-sufficient micro-cosmic replicas. This is true of many philosophies, from the Taoist theory of 'the macrocosmic and microcosmic system of correspondences'[83] to the Hua-yen Buddhist view that each world particle contains a Buddha-being.[84] In Christendom, William Blake said

> . . . every Space that a Man views around his dwelling place
> Standing on his own roof or in his garden on a mount
> Of twenty-five cubits in height, such space is his Universe.[85]

True plurality of place, on the other hand, requires that while a location is autonomous, it is also unique and hence not equivalent to a larger whole. What emerges, therefore, is that sites which give rise to existence cannot be self-sufficient, that a species or specific people may be ontologically an extension of a country, but no country can contain all existents. The alternative view instantly lapses into a model of a unified space. 'Totemism' is but an affirmation that certain humans share their place-being with other place-derived existents.

I will say more on the emergence of life from place and the interdependence of lands in a moment. Before proceeding, however, let me summarise my exposition thus far. I have argued that Aboriginal ontology does not allow time or history philosophical determination because this is incompatible with an uncompromising insistence on the immutability of place. Abiding Events establish the shape of lands, but there is no world creation, cosmic centre, or recognition of any single unifying world principle. Rather, Abiding Events stress, firstly, that place is conscious (and hence consciousness exists), and secondly, that spatial intentionality gives place extension, linking sites in direction-determined pathways. In brief, space, for Aborigines, is a network of places resting upon

Ancestral mind-matter. Phenomena such as 'totemism' can be understood simply as a logical extension, 'a moment in thought', of the view that places, while autonomous, are unique and hence cannot contain the store of all existence. A place contains specific existence potentials, human and other, which form the 'totemic' nucleus of a place.

That is the ontology. I now turn to ontogeny.

THE BODY

TIME AND THE BODY

There are three themes in Aboriginal Studies which have been stumbling blocks for Western thinkers. High Gods, or the lack thereof, and 'totemism', we have already met. The third theme is the astoundingly tenacious debate revolving around the question: are Aborigines ignorant of the relationship between copulation and procreation? Sadly, the question has almost always been cast in the negative.

The tone for the debate was set early this century when James Frazer, faithfully summarising the poor ethnography of his day, concluded that Aboriginal people simply did not understand the role of physiological paternity. This claim gave rise to his theory that 'totemism' was nothing but a consequence of confusion about conception, and was also his proof for the profound primitiveness of Aborigines.[86] No sooner was Sir James' thesis pronounced than there were others grasping for a positive truth behind such dismissive claims: 'Denial of procreation is not "proof of pristine ignorance" but a philosophical inference from philosophic premises',[87] they said.

The debate, while voluminous, has unfortunately not progressed much beyond the opinions of 1905. Some have searched for evidence of the allegedly absent knowledge with thinly disguised ulterior motives such as, for instance, Géza Róheim's attempt to ensure the Aranda could be located within the universal paradigm of the Oedipal complex.[88] By 1937, the theoretical waters were so entirely muddied that M.F. Ashley Montagu devoted a book to resolving the matter – a book which in its second edition ran to over 400 closely printed pages.[89] Perhaps the story might have then faded into the obscurity it deserved had not Melford Spiro made a passing reference to Aboriginal ignorance which was refuted by Edmund Leach,[90] and thereafter the controversy has had the life to support a host of articles and yet another book.

It will, alas, remain forever impossible to say of what Aborigines were *ignorant* prior to outside contact. Studies from northern Australia provide solid evidence that some Aborigines were well aware of the physiological significance of sexual intercourse[91] but, of course, we cannot rule out the possibility of this being due to Melanesian, Indonesian and European influences. With this limitation acknowledged, however, we can still ask a question that has been almost totally overlooked – what is it that Aboriginal people affirm? It is my suspicion (although it cannot be proved) that the strength of this affirmation itself is what has provided an illusion of 'ignorance'. Warner's embarrassing realisation is indeed informative. He recorded:

> An occasion arose in which I could inquire of certain old men just what the semen did when it entered the uterus of a woman. They all looked at me with much contempt for my ignorance and informed me that 'that was what made babies'. I had not been able to obtain this information earlier because the [Yolngu person] is far more interested in the child's spiritual conception . . . than he is in the physiological mechanism of conception.[92]

This passage adds a little more support to the 'not ignorant' position, but more significantly reminds us that, ignorant or not, here is a categorical statement to which we must attend lest it be ourselves who are accused of what is at least an ethnographic ignorance.

The tension between physiological denial and spiritual affirmation has recently been brought to a head by the partially insightful re-examination of the issue by Warren Shapiro. His thesis, in brief, is that the disavowal of the physiology of the body in life processes is nothing less than a denial of death and hence of temporality itself. Spiritual birth in Aboriginal doctrine 'gives temporal and ontological dominance to the spiritual over the bodily': again, more fully

> Temporality is re-defined as eternally repeating sequences or, more importantly, is denied altogether. Thus, ontogeny is rendered not as a path to ultimate demise but as a sense of unending deaths and rebirths. Larger spans of time are collapsed, usually to cycles of two generations. Individuals seemingly trapped in temporal contingency have various avenues of escape into a timeless archetypal domain . . . known across Australia as 'The Dreamtime'.[93]

My departure from Shapiro's views will be easily anticipated. I believe his skewed perspective derives from reading Aboriginal traditions from within an assumed, if allegedly denied, ontology of time. If, on the other hand, the Aboriginal spatial order has in fact left no room for the emergence of temporality as a principle of being, the 'denial of the body' cannot be an adjunct to the 'denial of time'. Rather, the 'denial of the body' must derive from the 'affirmation of place'. As Turner has said, if there is something Aborigines deny it is precisely Shapiro's attempt to elevate the body at the expense of 'pre-established institutional ties focused on land'.[94]

Given Shapiro's reference to Becker's thesis that the 'Oedipus Project' is an attempted *Denial of Death*,[95] it is regrettable (although given his attitude towards alliance theory, predictable) that he did not in this context consider Lévi-Strauss' interpretation of Oedipus. For whatever it might have meant to the Ancient Greeks,[96] it seems certain that the *Oedipus Australis* Project hinges precisely upon the paradox Lévi-Strauss identified: have we sprung from our mother's body, or have we emerged from the land?

Aborigines 'across Australia' do *not, contra* Shapiro, avow a 'Dream*Time*' but rather they insist upon the primacy of place. Thus, says Harvey, whose plural, Event-focused use of 'Dreamings' should be noted,

> As the Dreamings travelled they put spirit children over the country, we call these spirit children *ardirri*. It is because of these spirit children that we are born, the spirit children are on the country, and *we are born from the country.*[97]

As Peterson states, Aboriginal conception beliefs serve primarily 'to relate conception to place',[98] or again, in Merlan's words, spirit child beliefs are an embodiment of a 'territorial aspect of . . . the order constituted by the activities of ancestral' beings.[99] This conception principle, taken to its logical conclusion, constitutes the foundation of what scholars who favour the social more than the geographical have called 'kinship'. But as Turner has so nicely shown, and Fred Rose so readily concedes,[100] Aborigines denied both the body and kinship in order to express the fact that all rights and obligations were derived from people's existence as extensions of places. T.G.H. Strehlow did not overstate the case when he wrote 'the whole countryside is [the Aranda person's] living, age-old family tree'.[101] Here is Leibnitz's fancied universe in which the order of space was 'made up of genealogical lines . . . wherein every person would have his place.'[102] Again, as Turner more recently argues, Aboriginal people dismiss procreation as irrelevant insofar as 'kinship' *is* cosmology and that 'each term in the relationship systems refers to a particular conjunction of Lands'.[103]

Aboriginal conception beliefs are so consistent in their basic orientation that they reveal, as Montagu has argued, a common core of Aboriginal ontology.[104] There are nonetheless highly significant variations on that trans-Aboriginal theme which reflect the impact of outsiders and consequent changes to the Aboriginal vision of space. I explore these in detail in the following chapters, but it is necessary here to begin to introduce history into the study of Aboriginal traditions.

The basic, precontact conception plan, I maintain, was one which derived all life from the lands embodying Abiding Events. As Ancestral beings gave extension to place they imbued it with their own being, and it is this stuff of existence, this life potential of land, which is lodged within a woman who thence is pregnant. The mother does not contribute to the ontological substance of the child, but rather 'carries' a life whose essence belongs, and belongs alone, to a site. The child's core identity is determined by his or her place of derivation. The details vary; the location might be directly linked with feeling the child enter the womb or, alternatively, dreams or foodstuffs may provide clues as to the site from which the spirit derived. Furthermore, the spirit may have taken the form of a fish, or a mischievous child, or may have been transmitted by some intermediary agent. At a fundamental level, however, all accounts agree that the mother carries, but does not contribute to, a life-potential of place. The Warlpiri take this unity of country and peoples to its logical linguistic conclusion. The word *kuruwarri* refers not only to an individual's spirit essence, but also to sites bearing the imprint of Abiding Events.[105] Life is annexation of place.

While there is general Aboriginal accord in affirming that the spiritual aspect of all humans (and other existents) is land derived, there are nonetheless significant variations in the degree to which this principle is *exclusively* affirmed. In Desert regions, for example, amongst the Pintupi and Aranda,[106] the 'accident' of location is the major determinant of all socio-geographical life. While patrilineally defined social groups do have certain territorial and sacral rights, the dominant claim is made by the person who has a direct spiritual identification with a site and who thus has an intrinsic association with the objects, ceremonies, songs and places embraced by the word *tjurunga*.[107]

It has long been observed, however, that in other regions the ritual unit has shifted from pure place derivation toward patrilineality. This would in fact occur spontaneously were families to reside in the vicinity of the husband's spirit-abode, but the widespread incidence of elaborate practices for 'finding' a child's true spiritual identity indicates there is considerable ambiguity involved and hence the shift to patrilineality would of necessity have been a case of conscious interpretation to favour children belonging to their fathers' place.

In some regions, patrilineality in fact appears to take precedence over the site as an ontological principle. This would indicate a shift from a geocentric order toward a sociocentric order, where kinship is allowed to be determinative over land. There are shades of degree between social and territorial extremes. For the Yir-Yiront in Cape York, for example, a child is almost always 'found' in its father's spirit abode, but if it is certain the mother conceived elsewhere then the child joins the 'clan' other than the father's[108] and place prevails. Amongst the Yolngu of Arnhem Land, on the other hand, a child's spirit comes from a 'clan well' but in the infrequent cases where this is not its father's Abiding place, patrilineality is the main principle appealed to. Some conception privileges are inherited, but the main rights and responsibilities are socio-determined.[109]

While there has been a longstanding scholarly concern to explain the interplay between the principles of locality and kinship, all have agreed that place is more fundamental, and with this I must concur. Were this not the case, we would be at a loss to explain the practice of 'finding'. It seems even those societies favouring patri-descent wish to legitimise lineage through an appeal to land. Why, then, the intervention of kinlines? At this point, I must begin to consider the historical elements fully pursued in the remaining chapters.

To the best of my knowledge, A.P. Elkin was the first to propose that place-identity (the 'conception site') was the initial Aboriginal world-organising principle. He suggested this would tend toward patrilineality in a patrilocal society, but would only become rigidly so in cases where people were separated from their homelands – in particular, after colonisation.[110] The tantalising suggestion that lineages, like time, only develop with the disruption of space will be developed in a moment, but before it is, it should be noted that Elkin's thesis is not quite as self-evident as it may initially appear.

First, it should be observed that it is not entirely necessary to actually be in a place to employ its powers of fecundity. Spirits can travel, especially during dreams, so a knowledge of a place can, if need be, substitute for physical proximity.[111] This would mean that longer term disruption (second generation) would be required to force Aboriginal people to partially abandon place. Secondly, however, we should consider Shapiro's suggestion that, while Elkin is correct in advocating the priority of land principles, patrilines seem more ancient than colonisation.[112] We need, therefore, to examine the associations and distribution of the two principles in more careful detail.

To date, Annette Hamilton's study of conflicting axioms of Law within the Western Desert is the most insightful of its kind. She notes that the anthropological orthodoxy is that people's spiritual ties with land are patrilineal, but that beneath this is a refracted, sometimes conflicting, land principle. If 'conception' occurs in a father's land, the paradigms merge, but, among the Pitjantjatjara and their neighbours, location is more fundamental: 'rights do not accrue primarily by being born to a particular father, but by being born at a particular place'. The paradox, nonetheless, remains.

> It seems as if the principle of patrifiliation to a real father is in opposition to the principle of filiation to a symbolic ancestor; in the former case it is the 'place' of the real father which counts; in the latter, the 'place' of the hypothetical ancestor, the country in which he left his marks.

Like Elkin and Shapiro, Hamilton is convinced that location is an historically prior principle, and that Desert ontology was in the process of shifting from 'a place-based to a father-based system', a process that had gone even further in Arnhem Land, where patrilineality has been victorious.[113]

Robert Layton has plotted in more detail the long observed shift towards patrilineality as one moves northwards from the Deserts. Layton's investigations, while convenient, are however, somewhat simplistic. In stating both the Aranda and Yolngu are mostly conceived on patri-estates,[114] he misses the point, for the real issue is that when conceived elsewhere the Aranda allow place to regulate affiliations,[115] whilst the Yolngu make an appeal to kinlines.[116] Layton's conclusion, nevertheless, is sound enough. From central to northern Australia, two principles coexist, but whereas the Deserts are governed ultimately by a site-based ontology, the northerners have given kinship its autonomy.

Returning now to the question of when the shift to kin-determination occurred, it seems that in the Deserts the situation was actually 'in a state of transition'[117] and hence was seemingly a very recent development. The evidence is quite clear that Aboriginal social organisation can change and transmit changes very rapidly indeed. Contemporary flux therefore indicates developments which had begun quite recently. Further to the north, however, the remodelling seems to have been more complete, and so is probably not the post-European phenomenon Elkin proposed. Nonetheless, the evidence for two principles is still quite apparent and thus neither can the transformation be exceedingly ancient. My own guess is that it should be dated to the period of first contacts with pre-European outsiders in northern Australia – a thesis I will expand upon in later chapters.

More complex is the question of why contacts with non-Aboriginal people would encourage a shift from place-based to *patri*-lineage-based orders. Given the consistency of links through the father, the gender of the parental line is clearly relevant, but there are serious problems with facile appeals to an emergence of male ideological manipulation.[118] In particular, such theories leave unexplained the fact that women contribute to their own 'downfall' by 'finding' children in their husbands' estates,[119] and make an unwarranted assumption that being co-joined with one's 'father's' (and father's siblings', etc.) place necessarily gives more power to men than being co-joined with one's mother's (and mother's brothers', etc.) place.

My own interpretation suggests both men and women were involved in the bolstering of the ontological status of the patriline, but that the father became victorious only, as it were, by default. Motherhood has one supreme disadvantage – it is convincing. But before I expand upon this point, let me gather together the implications of my preceding discussion.

I have hinted at the thesis that extended kinlines, like history and time, emerge with the disruption (or at least, threat to) place. Indeed, kinship determination is but the social face of time. I do not mean, of course, that without historical thought there can be no kinship, but the latter only achieves an ontological tenacity when it becomes historicised. Hamilton actually skirts this position when she notes Desert traditions oppose 'lineage' by eradicating the social memory of the dead with extensive taboos against referring to their past existence. Generations are therefore not amassed and thus in turn cannot (no more than uncounted seasons or other natural rhythms) constitute the measured units of time. To the north, however, where memorials are made to celebrate the dead, we hear a whisper of time, and 'there are also the areas where patrilineal descent is firmly articulated and socially embedded'.[120] Morphy makes a related point when he says the Yolngu, unlike Desert Aborigines, have not only myths about Abiding Events, but also myths of 'inheritance'. The latter, furthermore, are the basis of his argument that the Yolngu do have a form of time reckoning, and that their structure is linked more with ongoing clanlines than place. Inheritance myths bolster 'potential threat to their territorial integrity' by shifting emphasis from place-rights to kinship. In contrast

> myths of inheritance or their equivalents do not seem to have been reported from parts of Australia . . . where totemic cult groups are the product of a negotiated amalgam of individual ties to place. In such cases there is no need to state the once and forever transfer of authority to a particular group of people since the group is continually emerging and transforming through the coalescence of individual ties to land . . . as a part of a process of 'reallocating people to place'.[121]

In brief, the weakening of the absolute authority of place leads not only to the transference of dominion (at least in part) to kinlines but correlatively to the need for legitimising processes which appeal to the continuity of generations and thus nourish the germ of time.

If these observations are correct, then the reason for *patri* lineality is not difficult to ascertain. Where necessity requires the introduction of kinlines, fatherhood is the least threatening to the pre-existent order of the world. At this juncture, Shapiro is in the main correct, although his emphasis is misplaced: it is not, as he believes, that Aborigines flee from the carnality of women's bodies in order to escape time so much as they do it so as to prevent its philosophical possibility and hence to remain embedded in place. Fatherhood as a principle of land–identity inheritance is threatening enough, but motherhood would indeed swing the emphasis away from location toward the body. What is so frequently overlooked is that not only do Aborigines deny physiological paternity but, with even more energy, they deny maternity. And yet, as Andrew Lang said long ago, 'not being idiots, they are well aware of the maternal ties of blood'.[122] It is indeed *that* obvious, and to assert that people share inheritance-of-being with their mother is dangerously close to asserting they are in fact born from their mothers. The father's link, on the other hand, can bolster continuity where needs be without directly threatening the ontological status of land.

As I have already married the theories of Lévi-Strauss with the neo-Freudian conceptions of Becker (and Shapiro) to introduce the *Oedipus Australis* project, perhaps I might once more borrow from the Parisian scholar's examples, if only to invert his conclusions. Lévi-Strauss once maintained, with astounding inaccuracy, that the sacrality of men and the alleged profanity of women was mediated in Aboriginal societies by boys: biological males who were sociologically female.[123] If my preceding analysis is correct, we can recast his terms without lapsing into such bland false dichotomies as male: female :: sacred: profane. For the true polarity is not between men and women but the ontogenetic role of the body as expressed quintessentially by women versus land.[124] And the mediators are not boys but men.

In Aboriginal societies men, on behalf of all their community, are often ritually women and take upon themselves the symbolism of birth in order to affirm that humans are *not* born of women's bodies but are born of a place.[125] In other words, men use the body in order to deny it. Even women's actual birth rituals replicate this principle, when the newborn child is immediately placed in a small earthy depression from which it is then 'born' – an act surely stating unambiguously that the child comes not from a mother but from a location.[126]

My argument thus far can now be summarised. I contend that prior to contact with outsiders, the nucleus of Aboriginal ontology was a plurality of places. Their fundamental and uncompromising priority, encapsulated in the stories of Abiding Events, developed and flourished (as do all constructs) at the expense of other intellectual possibilities – in particular, time, unified space, and the autonomy of the body. Each of these doctrines, when pursued, poses problems for the enduringness of localities. The evidence seems strong that the biological determination of the body is downplayed or denied, but this should not be simultaneously interpreted as a 'denial' of time. Having refused kinlines' extension, events remain unprotracted, and time proper was no more than a germinal possibility. It did begin to emerge to the north, along with more robust kinlines, but that is a story that must be developed in later chapters.

If life for Aboriginal people is a billowing of the consciousness of country, then that life should pursue its natural rhythm of growth until, past its full extension, it again deflates into its home. Death,

whilst resisted when interrupting an incomplete life,[127] is accepted
as a part of a pattern of existence. Throughout the continent, the
human life-essence, upon death, returns to its rightful abode. To this
rule, every exception is profoundly important, and the significance
of these exceptions is something I pursue at length in the following
chapters. For while there is evidence that throughout the continent
the life-spirit always should return to the place from which it
emanated, there are in areas of intensive contact simultaneous and
paradoxically juxtaposed beliefs that the spirit also journeys to some
more distant Utopian domain, be it an Island of the Dead or a
Heaven. The significant point for the moment is that these *otiose*
lands always *coexist* with locative traditions and, as I will later show,
quite evidently postdate the arrival of strangers.

Death, then, is a return of place-being to place. A life as lived
can do absolutely nothing to alter this fundamental principle. In
Aboriginal belief there is no room for judgements or retributions
which might alter a spirit's course. Life's actions, as either rhythmed
or spontaneous events, do not have value in comparison with the
Abiding Events on which the cosmos rests. The culmination of a
life reaps neither rewards nor punishments for a further life. It is
enough that the spirit is restored to its place.

In this regard, the frequently used but loose reference in Australia
to 'reincarnation' requires very special qualification so as to avoid
unwarranted equation with Hindu traditions. Firstly, there is no
individual self (or, for Buddhists, no individual no-self) which is
reborn, as the dead do not retain their psychic identity. Rather, their
identity is as a fragment of the life-potential of the place-imbued
Ancestral being. Secondly, and most importantly, even if we speak
of a rebirth of an Ancestral particle, we must recall that for
Aborigines *samsara* (rebirth) does not stand subservient to any
principle of eternal moral causality (*karma*).[128] As 'prior births' make
absolutely no difference to the spirit-stuff, I can ultimately see no
sense at all in employing the laden concept of 'reincarnation'. It is
enough simply to assert that life is an outgrowth of a location, and
that when a life ends its essence returns to its place.

Given that death is for Aboriginal people an affirmation of the
enduringness of places, it seems appropriate to ask to what extent
they can be said to 'deny death'. Shapiro, of course, has avowed this
thesis, but it is in fact one inherent in most scholarship resting upon
the assumption that Aborigines 'deny' time. Eliade's words betray

this link between interpretations of cosmogony and beliefs about death. He writes: 'Once again [at death], though for the last time, man does what was done in the beginning by a Supernatural Being. With every new death, the primordial scenario is re-enacted'.[129] As, for him, Aboriginal cosmogonies are a denial of time, mortuary rituals become a denial of death through repetition of the cosmogonic plan. Yet, as the Berndts say in partial contrast to Eliade's views, while death might appear to Western interpreters as an end to a personality, it is to Aboriginal people a statement of the spiritual continuation of the Ancestral place.[130]

Upon more careful examination it appears that there are not only various theoretical interpretations but also variable responses to death within Aboriginal Australia itself. For the Desert areas it seems nothing short of an interpretative trespass to suggest there is a 'denial' of death, but to the north and in the south-east there is indeed a nostalgia for a lost possibility that individual lives might be un-ending. Kenneth Maddock has already and most perceptively noted this distinction between death orientations within Australia,[131] and I will here merely offer some analytical and historical interpretations of the differences.

The wistful regard of Aborigines concerning the possibility of continued life is to be found precisely in those areas of Australia where alien contact has been most extensive and where there has been the transfer of some of the organisational role of place to the body and to time. South-eastern Australia provides some instances of this kind,[132] but as this was a region rapidly thrust toward eschatological and even millennial views of history, the insights it provides lack subtlety (see, however, chapter 3). In this regard, Cape York Peninsula, central-northern Australia and the Kimberley are far more revealing areas of investigation.

It was Stanner who first gave credible form to the view that Aboriginal ontology was world-affirming, governed by a mood of assent, and yet harbouring a soft sorrow at the realisation that life might have been otherwise. For the Murinbata, life's wrongful turning was expressed foremost in the myth of *Mutinga*, the All-Mother, who would not have died had she not swallowed several children. The children themselves were cut open from her womb (not her stomach), but because she herself died, life was flawed. This, as R. Berndt notes, is itself paradigmatic of a range of (northern) myths dealing with death coming to the human race. Thus, for example, the Yolngu *Wawalag* sisters, through their menstrual and birth blood, bring death to all that lives: 'birth and death of animals as well as man's is all the fault of those two sisters', writes Warner. 'Were it not for them there would have been no copulation . . . no children'. 'If they had not done wrong in their own country, this would not have happened. If they had not menstruated in . . . [the well] this would not have happened. Everyone . . . would have stayed single'.[133] As Nancy Munn intriguingly adds, 'The women's sexuality generates the mortal cycle of generation and decay: it creates the alternating cycle of the seasons, the temporal "systole" and "diastole" which grounds the spatial order in the temporal process.'[134] Here we have a glimpse of the pattern (certainly overstated by Munn) whereby the temporalising of place, or at least the very beginnings of an intrusion of time upon place, is ultimately associated with the valuation of the carnal body on the one hand, and the consequent retraction from death on the other. Women's physiology is a central focus of symbolism in such contexts, but even more apposite is the image of the moon.[135]

The moon in northern Australia is restless, discontented, and to save itself will threaten the very world-structure. As Rose states in passing, 'the moon certainly had it in mind to dominate'.[136] The Yolngu Moon lives with his Dugong sister (both *Yirritja* moiety) but he refuses to die:

'I'm not going to die like other people,' the Moon answers.
'Why then do you not want to do that?' asked the Dugong.
'I want to die and come back alive again,' he told her.
'All right, but when I die, I won't come back . . .'
'Well, I'm different,' the Moon said. 'When I die, I'm coming back.'[137]

And thus the waxing and waning moon, unlike other Ancestral beings, refuses to allow death's finality to overcome him. In the beautiful 'Moon-Bone song cycle' his defiance of death almost gives him transcendence over the world:

Hanging there in the sky, above those clans . . .
Hanging a long way off, above Milingimbi Creek . . .
Slowly the Moon Bone is growing, hanging there far away.
The bone is shining, the horns of the Moon bend down,
First the sickle Moon on the old Moon's shadow; slowly he grows,
And shining he hangs there at the place of Evening Star . . .
Then far away he goes sinking down, to lose his bone in the sea;
Diving towards the water, he sinks down out of sight.
The old Moon dies to grow new again, to rise up out of the sea.[138]

In Cape York the symbolism is similar, for the Koko-Yalunyu Moon, after an incestuous liaison, is pursued and 'killed' several times, only to spring up saying, 'I'm not dead'. Finally, he is taken to the ocean, but, as his ghost, he lives on: 'He dies and comes to life again and everyone says, "Hello, there's the moon."' What is a little clearer in this example, however, is the link between the moon, rebirth and the body. Moon actually changes a male, Eaglehawk, into his wife and impregnates her.[139] Thomson has highlighted the fact that moon myths of this kind make explicit reference to physiological paternity and the role of semen[140] (an element also evident in the *Wawalag* myth just cited). Moon myths are body myths, but even more specifically they relate to women's biological procreative abilities. McConnel thus is certain the Koko-Yalunyu moon myth reflects a 'correspondence between the periods of women and the moon's phases, giving rise to a belief in the moon's power to cause physiological processes in women, associated, like the menstrual flow, with child-bearing'.[141] As the Cape York focus on the body and time was due to Torres Strait Islander associations, it is worth noting here that the Islanders believe Moon deflowers girls and begins their menstruation.[142] For Arnhem Land, although dealing with related serpent myths (such as that associated with the *Wawalag*), Chris Knight stresses the importance of menstruation and the fact that 'human female menstrual cycles can become phase-locked to the . . . moon'.[143] There is thus a very real association between women's physiology, birth, and the moon, making it a perfect symbol of a valuation of the body. In the south-east, the link is even clearer. Parker recorded that the moon 'is a sort of patron of women',[144] and more recently, Harry Buchanan, a Gambayngirr man of south-east Australia said, 'It's the moon that works the women . . . So if there's no moon, they'll all be dead'.[145]

We can thus make the following conclusions about Aboriginal attitudes towards death. In those areas least affected by outsiders, where a philosophy of place predominates, and where people affirm without qualification that they are born of their land, death is not denied, no more than is time. Rather these remain even less than shadowy possibilities. Where strangers enter Aboriginal worlds, however, and for reasons that will become apparent in later chapters, place can at least in part lose its hold. When that occurs, time and the body can subvert some of the power of place. Human biology comes more to the fore, physiological procreation is partially conceded, and there is a concern for the maintenance of the body *per se* rather than the body's maintenance of the country which it is. The desire for ongoing life and for the continuation of the individual life biography or the lineage (Hamilton sees this symbolised in Tiwi burial posts, which she contrasts with the ideology behind desert traditions)[146] opens the way for temporal ontologies. The perfect marker for the transition to both the temporal and bodily facets of a tradition which has felt compelled to annex place is the moon. Like history, like our carnal selves, it not only blisters from the land, but can break free of the world, rising like that Yolngu Moon, 'to grow new again, to rise up out of the sea'. All this is even more explicit in the Kimberley data, which I will save for consideration in chapter 5.

Here, once again, but this time in its individual rather than cosmological guise, there is the seed of a general theory of the origin of time as a fall from place. This, however, is something I cannot here pursue. This is a book about the vicissitudes of space. I have noted the first Aboriginal steps towards historical thought, the preservation of kinlines, and individual lives, and the endurance of bodily powers, only to highlight the fact that there is a huge cost to what have for so long been Western signs of 'progress'. I believe the evidence indicates that for Aboriginal people these first steps were taken reluctantly and that they resisted their continuation. For the sake of completeness I have noted these variations on an Aboriginal lifeplan, but they remain undeveloped consequences to more significant changes to visions of the shape of the cosmos.

I have argued that alleged denials of time, death and the body can all be better understood as affirmations of place, and that their emergence, whatever the gain, reveals a weakening of the ties of ubiety. Any sound interpretative history of Aboriginal ontology must therefore relentlessly focus on constructions of space. In the final pages of this chapter, then, I turn to ask what it is that Aboriginal people value in their locative visions of cosmic order. The answer is, worlds to endure.

WORLDS TO ENDURE

Despite the many departures from a basic plan of existence, throughout most of Australia a core can still be discerned. Whether or not a patriline mediates between the site and a life; whether or not the body is a necessary adjunct to the fecundity of countries, whether we die with regret or without, the lands still prevail. As Whitman wrote, 'Earth does not argue'.

Again, while we might witness the rudiments of new ontologies which might eventually (and perhaps even now begin to) dominate traditional Aboriginal orientations, throughout the continent there is a recognition that the cardinal human endeavour is to maintain the shape of the world. The entire Aboriginal spiritual commission is – to again employ Jack Bruno's words which opened this chapter – 'Holding this place'. Bruno speaks as a man of Cape York Peninsula, but it is a simple matter to find identical statements from other regions. For example, Mussolini Harvey, a Yanyuwa elder from the 'Top End', says

> When we wear the Dreaming mark, we are carrying the country, we are keeping the Dreaming held up, we are keeping the country alive. That is the most important thing, we have to keep the country.[147]

Whilst, in the Central Desert, Teddy Jampijinpa explains the logic of patrimoieties in ceremonial life: 'We got to have *kurdungurlu* [ritual overseers] and *kirda* [ritual embodiers of Ancestral Events], and like some people too. We hold the country every time, never lose him together'.[148]

There are two facets to holding place. On the one hand there is the realisation of *identity*, which has already been alluded to in my discussion of life as an extension of territory, and of death as a homeostatic return of a locality's being essence. But beyond the identity of people with estates, there is the equally important matter of how identified lands/people relate to other lands/people. It is the issue of *relationship* in world maintenance to which I now turn.

Earlier in this chapter I noted that the 'totemic' principle was essentially an inference of the consciousness of places whereby the uniqueness of sites was assured. That is, Aboriginal people avoided a scenario in which each country became a self-sufficient microcosm which replicated, in miniature, some spatially unified macrocosm. Had they done so they might have reverted to a monadology of sovereign, isolated yet identical, atoms of place. This they did not do.

In this regard, Rose's useful discussion of 'autonomy' needs careful handling. Her image of socio-spatial boundaries being 'maintained by being pressed against [through] the meta-rule of response'[149] is serviceable enough, but her discussion of countless 'Dreamings' acting in response to one another yet without causality and with seemingly total freedom, is at best vague and at worst undermines the very tangible and structured connections Aborigines have erected between lands.

The first point to be made regarding relationships between estates requires a clarification of 'identity'. It is essential to realise that the ontologic identity between a human being and an Abiding place does *not* provide him or her with exclusive social, political and economic rights to the site and its surrounding areas. Certainly, ontology informs human life patterns, but with a compound design rather than a bland reflection of axiomatic elements.

Anthropologists are still grimacing over their discipline's initial failure to distinguish between spiritual identity with, and 'ownership' of, land. The presupposition that the socio-political world mirrored ontology in a one-to-one fashion resulted in legal embarrassments for Aborigines and academics alike, and even today legislation bears the mark of our misunderstandings.[150] But it is precisely the fact that a person does not have exclusive rights over the location with which he or she is linked-in-being which ensures that places are structurally related to one another through their life manifestations. The knowledgeable Warlpiri men who introduced me to the areas in and around the Tanami Desert entered many areas other than those from which they had sprung. Indeed, I soon realised there were few places to which a well informed man could not legitimately claim a right of access. If he did not share the same patri-couple with the site's human extension (*kirda*), he could claim rights as a member of the *opposite* patri-moiety (*kurdungurlu*), and so on.[151] Furthermore, a simple distinction between ownership of 'ritual estates' and 'economic ranges', while useful, does not help here as we are dealing with multiple forms of 'ritual' rights and responsibilities.[152] Morphy's careful analysis of multiple rights in the use of sacred land-based designs in Yolngu society clearly illustrates the diversity of ritual-land rights.[153] The foundation principle is: the humans who are of a land's-stuff do not, and cannot, exclusively control that site. The immediate result is relationship.

Underlining this point is the fact that an abode is often more dangerous to those who spring from it than to others who stand in a different relationship to the place. Hiatt recalls a Gidjingali instance where an Ancestral yam protecting its site was said to be about to attack, but the man who diffused the danger was not the estate's descendant but his 'maternal uncle'.[154] The danger emanating from one's own place, Maddock comments, ensures social inter-dependence, alliance and relationships.[155] If we visualise the scene from the land's point of view, the self-instigated danger ensures that its own emanations do not return without the association of other land emanations.

At the economic level a land again does not favour people partaking of its spiritual substance. It is a fallacy that the 'estate' and 'range' overlap, even at the level of a Weberian ideal type.[156] This is not to say Aboriginal people neglect the economical face of their traditions, but they avoid equating identity with total ownership. Thus, while those who share in the site's being are absolutely essential (but not exclusively so) in ensuring that life essences effer-vesce from the location, and so maintain the balance of resources, they do not have exclusive rights to the foodstuffs produced. In terms of subsistence patterns many scholars, not least of them Frederick Engels,[157] have thus identified Aborigines as living examples of communist, or very near communist, activities.

It should be stressed, however, that from an Aboriginal vantage, the 'means of production' is access to ritual positions, and so it is not quite the stratumless context imagined by early Marxists. On the other hand, however, it is difficult to cast Aborigines in a gender-as-class Marxist mould,[158] for again there is the absolute rift between the ritual control of the 'means of production' and access to the species 'produced'. Indeed, Aboriginal men and women can and do order ritual custodians to 'work' to make them food: 'You make'm father – I want to eat'.[159]

At every turn, therefore, ritual and economic, Aboriginal people denied the possibility of the self-sufficiency of being. There was an absolute, irreplaceable and fundamental identity between a land and a people who were spiritually of that land, but the autonomy was always counterbalanced by relationships. Economically, people could not claim the emanations of their land's life source as their own – indeed, in many (not all) areas of Australia, people were prohibited from eating their own 'totem'.[160] Ritually, while humans of a place are required to embody Abiding Events in ceremonies (to *be* the Ancestral being) they cannot perform by themselves but are strictly controlled by overseers who are most felicitously (and also with a twist of irony) termed in Aboriginal English 'policemen' – guardians of the Law.[161]

Given these rigorous checks on autonomy as self-sufficiency it becomes evident that 'holding the country' weaves lands and their people into an interdependent network, yet one which requires neither a masterplan nor an overriding blueprint of a 'whole'.

This structurally assured interdependence in an ontology of unique rather than complete places leads to a feature of Aboriginal societies which, although first appreciated by T.G.H. Strehlow in his booklet *The Sustaining Ideals of Australian Aboriginal Societies*, has recently been more fully developed by David Turner, whose theories are considered in later chapters. Strehlow wrote, with great insight,

> In Australia . . . local differences in ritual and belief were held to be natural and worthy of respect. The site from which each totemic ancestor was believed to have sprung was the religious centre of the totemic clan that celebrated his rites, and that clan took its totem as its kin-group classification from him. These rites could therefore not be spread easily in historical times by preaching and proselytizing . . . the *precise* form of religious worship hence depended on the area where it was practised. No form of religious ritual was more important than another. The various totemic clans did not merely tolerate each other; they regarded one another as equally important, each with its own home area. Even more important: the . . . religion provided strong links between the totemic clans.

And immediately following these observations on the mutual interdependence of places and their 'clans' he draws the corollary:

> The form of grouping or segmentation practiced . . . made possible not merely tribal but inter-tribal social co-operation . . . No tribe sought to dominate or terrorize its neighbours. There might be blood-feuds . . . [but] there have been, as far as we know, no instances of organized inter-tribal warfare in Australia.

Strehlow does not miss the opportunity to starkly contrast this fact with recent Western history, challenging his readers that the world needs 'a new mentality and a new attitude towards our fellow human beings everywhere on the globe, if we are not merely to survive physically, but to save for future generations the treasures of the spirit'.[162]

Strehlow and, more fully, Turner have, I believe, communicated to the modern Western reader precisely why Aborigines might nurture an ontology of place at the expense of other possibilities such as time and the embodied self. Place, in its radical form – unique and thus not self-sustaining but requiring relationship – makes wars of territorial conquest all but an impossibility. Theirs were worlds to endure.

Given the current enthusiasm for borrowed world-saving panaceas, it is important not to romanticise what Aboriginal cultures achieved. Even Strehlow misses the mark when he suggests that a distaste for violence lay behind the lack of 'inter-tribal' warfare. The reality, insofar as anyone has bothered to attempt to quantify the matter, is that the chance of being murdered in an Aboriginal society was comparable to the likelihood of a bloody end in Europe during a war-ridden time.[163] Aborigines did not, therefore, protect the integrity of lives but rather the integrity of place. There was carnage, even 'warfare', but as Strehlow correctly notes elsewhere in more sober terminology, there was no 'territorial conquest'.[164]

This territorial principle permeated all of Aboriginal society. It was more than an assertion that land could not be taken, for as people embodied land, it is equally impossible to consume another person's being. It is thus that despite fears of cannibal neighbours, all records of 'cannibalism' in Australia are of acts ritually controlled by the deceased's kin.[165] No one eats those they have murdered to take over their essence, as that essence is their land. Structured locative interdependence means to consume other people/lands is to destroy the world-pattern upon which one depends.

To the rule that Aborigines do not take over others' land-being there are two ethnographic departures. Turner notes the case of a Pitjantjatjara-Jankudjara life and death struggle over resources and a subsequent annexing of territory.[166] The situation was caused by drought, and exacerbated by the atypical pressures of introduced species. To this can be added the Warlpiri-Waringari war at Tanami, a rabbit-infested, gold-laden area where post-colonial pressures added to drought and where a territorial war led to about a dozen deaths on either side.[167] What is revealing in the latter case is that we have what amounts to, if not the myth of the war, then at least the myth of the logic of the war context. I will conclude this chapter with that important myth and some interpretative observations, but before I do I will summarise the salient points for this backdrop of a chapter.

The entire discussion in this chapter has led towards an appreciation of precontact Aboriginal ontology. I have spent a considerable part of my exposition in refuting some stereotypes of Aboriginal temporal orientations so as to return the emphasis to place, where it rightly belongs. This has been necessary not only in order to ensure accuracy of scholarly detail, but more importantly, because time and place are to some extent antagonists in world-constructions. While the evidence is strong that, prior to contact, Abiding Events required no time referent, disruption to a locative tradition has seen a slight shift in some areas of Australia (and a marked shift in other regions not yet mentioned) toward temporally recurring lineages, the valuation of the body and a hesitation over the finality of death. I have drawn attention to these matters in this first chapter not so much to explore the issues *per se* but rather to help clear away some postcontact developments in order to ensure a clear view of the fundamental plan of the Aboriginal understanding of existence. Having found our base, it is now possible to let the history reveal itself, and we can then pursue those matters rather hastily brushed to one side in the preceding pages. What I trust is now evident is the almost ruthless extent to which Aboriginal people had abandoned all that contested the immutability of a cosmos composed of inter-dependent places. With these summary words behind us, we can leave the Warlpiri to search for a conclusion.

The following myth was recorded by Meggitt,[168] retold to me by two senior Warlpiri men, and first interpreted by David Turner.[169] To all these I am indebted, but the following reading, of course, is my own.

  i. At a place near Tanami, Two Men emerged from the same site and so are 'real brothers'. There is a rift, and older brother sets off alone, but is caught and mutilated by younger brother, his body scattered in all directions. Younger brother is regretful of dis-membering his real brother, however, and so sings him back to life. Older brother, enraged, now repeats the butchering but, still hurting, feels no remorse. And so older brother travels, transforms sites, deposits life essences, and finds women to be his wives. While he catches plenty of rabbits for food, water is scarce and the family is on the brink of death. He instructs his wives to urinate, sings somewhat excessively over the urine, and thus causes a flood sweeping them into a rockhole. Older brother becomes the Rainbow Serpent.

  ii. From his place-essences his 'sons' emerge, and also suffer for water as they push into Walmadjeri country. They too want wives, but their magic fails, and so the 'real brothers' stay together. They then meet two classificatory 'brothers' (same subsection) who are friendly but are cannibals, and while they claim to repent of their flesh-eating ways, the brothers depart in fear. Exhausted, they camp when another classificatory brother of the Waringari warns that his people are about to attack them. The next night an identical warning is issued. By the following night, they are in Walmadjeri country and would have been eaten by *Djanba* but for a warning from the demons' human wives. Finally, the brothers are surprised by a Walmadjeri party who turn out to be friendly, but in dancing of their exploits, the brothers' legs swell and burst. The brothers head for their home and in the final subterritorial journey, are transformed into country.

Before offering some insights into this myth a few contextual comments are required. Firstly, old Warlpiri men knew that rabbits were an introduced species and were quite specific about their significance in the myth.[170] Secondly, they could remember the introduction of subsections in the recent past.[171] Thirdly, although not entirely clear in the Warlpiri case, *Djanba* are associated with post-colonial thought,[172] as indeed we will see when both this myth and the matter of *Djanba* are reintroduced in my final chapter. And finally, the myth-tellers recalled that the war with the Waringari was precisely in the area of the myth. With these points in mind, we can turn to the myth.

The story has two scenarios. In the first, the place emanations (the brothers) separate. There is regret, the first separation is reversed, but finally not only do the brothers disunite, but one brother is literally scattered. The spreading of the place-being is then followed by alliance with other place-beings – marriage. This is now the subsistence group, but while they have rabbits they have no water. This is in fact probably the environmental cause of the historic war with the Waringari. Scenario one ends, however, not with war but with acceptance, remaining in the area, and a magical, if excessive, 'salvation'.

Scenario two almost exactly inverts its predecessor. In this case, the place emanations cannot find other place-beings and so stay united as a rather monadish unit. In this case, the threat is not of perishing in the environment but of being taken over, killed, or literally consumed by cannibals. Extended subsection-mediated brotherhood manages to keep the heroes a step ahead of subsumption, but the story finds no rest until they are heading back toward their own land.

Between the two scenarios the possibilities of place are mooted. On the one hand, land spread through its human manifestations and allied with other land-people is enduring, although if one's range becomes depleted, there is little room to move and bodily death must be faced. On the other, if places remain isolated and unfederated, then interdependence vanishes and the possibility of being consumed is exposed.

Lévi-Strauss once suggested a focal paradox of myths was: to be or not to be.[173] In this myth the issue is compounded by a *how* to be. To be of land related but perhaps not to be as an individual life, or not to be of land related but to be of a sovereign land and as an embodied person: *that* is the question.

There is no answer, only a choice.

Some Warlpiri once chose the latter possibility. This is not surprising. What is remarkable is that they did not, or other Aborigines did not, make that choice more often. Yet the evidence seems overwhelming that Aboriginal people were willing to 'hold place' with the relationship of places even where the cost was human life. What they resisted, at all costs, was the possibility of a fall from Abidingness, the shift of their lands, or a cannibalism of place.

Yet, of course, all these principles are embedded in myth. It is a myth to which I will return at the end of this book to show how it was later conscripted to a new and world-threatening cause. But that is a story centuries away. Having laid the foundations, it is now time for our history to begin to unfold at a time when, far to the north of the Warlpiri, at the very tip of the continent, Aborigines were encountering strangers differing from themselves in many ways, not least in the fact that they ate their enemies.

NOTES

1. J. Bruno, 'Elegy', in *Aboriginal Australians and Christian Missions: Ethnographic and Historical Studies*, edited by T. Swain & D.B. Rose (Adelaide: Australian Association for the Study of Religions, 1988), pp. 11-13.
2. M.J.E. King-Boyes, *Patterns of Aboriginal Culture: Then and Now* (Sydney: McGraw-Hill, 1977), pp. 42-4.
3. A.P. Elkin, *The Australian Aborigines: How to Understand Them*, fourth edition (Sydney: Angus and Robertson, 1964), p. 234.
4. W.E.H. Stanner, 'The Dreaming', in *Traditional Aboriginal Society: A Reader*, edited by W.H. Edwards (Melbourne: Macmillan, 1987 [1956]), p. 225.
5. R.M. Berndt, 'The Dreaming', in *The Encyclopedia of Religion*, edited by M. Eliade, vol. 4 (New York: Macmillan, 1987), p. 479.

6. D. Bell, *Daughters of the Dreaming* (Melbourne/Sydney: McPhee Gribble/Allen & Unwin, 1983), p. 90; von Sturmer, cit. N. Williams, *The Yolngu and their Land: A System of Land Tenure and the Fight for Its Recognition* (Canberra: Australian Institute of Aboriginal Studies, 1986), p. 35, n. 16; D.B. Rose, *Ned Kelly Died For Our Sins*, the 1988 Charles Strong Memorial Lecture (Adelaide: Charles Strong, 1988), pp. 13–14.

7. e.g. P. Harris, *Teaching about Time in Tribal Aboriginal Communities* (Northern Territory: Department of Education, 1984); N. Holm & K. McConnochie, 'Time Perspective in Aboriginal Children', in *Aboriginal Cognition*, edited by G.E. Kearney & D.W. McElwain (Canberra: Australian Institute of Aboriginal Studies, 1976).

8. G. Partington, 'The Australian Aborigines and the Human Past', *Mankind*, 15 (1985), p. 38.

9. Williams, op. cit., p. 30.

10. Stanner, op. cit., p. 232.

11. On fideism, see my *On 'Understanding' Australian Aboriginal Religion* (Adelaide: Charles Strong, 1985), pp. 11–12.

12. For the West, see G.W. Trompf, *The Idea of Historical Recurrence in Western Thought: From Antiquity to the Reformation* (Berkeley: University of California Press, 1979).

13. G. (Hans) Bühler, *The Laws of Manu*, 'Sacred Books of the East', vol. 25, edited by F.M. Müller (Oxford: Clarendon Press, 1886), pp. 19–21 [*Manu Smriti* 1, pp. 61–74].

14. ibid., pp. 20–1 [*MS* 1, p. 73].

15. P. Ricoeur, 'The History of Religions and the Phenomenology of Time Consciousness', in *The History of Religions: Retrospect and Prospect*, edited by J.M. Kitagawa (New York: Macmillan, 1985), pp. 15 & 19.

16. E. Leach, 'Two Essays Concerning the Symbolic Representation of Time', in *Rethinking Anthropology* (New York: Humanities Press, 1961), p. 130.

17. Plato, 'Timaeus', in *Plato with an English Translation*, by R.G. Bury, vol. 7 (London: Heinemann, 1929), p. 77.

18. J. Harris, 'Australian Aboriginal and Islander Mathematics', *Australian Aboriginal Studies*, no. 2 (1987), pp. 29–37. I am happy to concede Harris' point that Aborigines could count 'when the need arose' (p. 30) but ask in return, why did they create a culture negating that need?

19. Elkin, op. cit., p. 237.

20. T.G.H. Strehlow, *Songs of Central Australia* (Sydney: Angus & Robertson, 1971), pp. 706–8.

21. C.G. von Brandenstein, 'The Meaning of Subsection and Section Names', *Oceania*, 41 (1970), pp. 39–46; and *Names and Substance of the Australian Subsection System* (Chicago: University of Chicago Press, 1974). Von Brandenstein's intriguing thesis is that moieties are

based on a conceptual duality which is itself bisected by another conceptual pair to form sections. A final conceptual bisection results in subsections. He believes the warm–cold and dry–moist (sometimes he chooses other terms) pairs lead to a fourfold classification of existence identical to Empedoclean philosophical constructions.

22. P. McConvell, 'The Origin of Subsections in Northern Australia', *Oceania*, 56 (1985), pp. 1–33.

23. C. Ellis, 'Time Consciousness of Aboriginal Performers', in *Problems and Solutions: Occasional Essays in Musicology Presented to Alice M. Moyle*, edited by J.C. Kassler and J. Stubington (Sydney: Hale and Iremonger, 1984), pp. 149–85.

24. C. Strehlow's letters did more to spread his views than his book. See M.F. von Leonhardi, 'Über einige religiöse und totemistische Vorstellungen der Aranda und Loritja in Zentralaustralien', *Globus*, 91 (1907), pp. 285–90.

25. L. Schultz, 'The Aborigines of the Upper and Middle Finke River: Their Habits and Customs, with Introductory Notes on the Physical and Natural-History Features of the Country', *Transactions of the Royal Society of South Australia*, 14 (1891), p. 242.

26. In W.B. Spencer & F.J. Gillen, *The Arunta: A Study of A Stone Age People* (London: Macmillan, 1927), p. 596.

27. T.G.H. Strehlow, op. cit., p. 614.

28. E. Fesl, untitled circulated leaflet, 1986.

29. A.R. Radcliffe-Brown, 'Religion and Society', *Journal of the Royal Anthropological Institute of Great Britain and Ireland*, 75 (1945), p. 39.

30. D.B. Rose, 'Consciousness and Responsibility in an Australian Aboriginal Religion', in Edwards, *Traditional Aboriginal Society*, p. 262.

31. H. Morphy, *Journey to the Crocodile's Nest: An Accompanying Monograph to the Film Madarrpa Funeral at Gurak'wuy* (Canberra: Australian Institute of Aboriginal Studies, 1984), p. 17.

32. E. Michaels, 'Constraints on Knowledge in an Economy of Oral Information', *Current Anthropology*, 26 (1985), p. 508.

33. This has posed a nice dilemma for Bible translators. Wanting to avoid casting Genesis in an Abiding Event mould, they opted to translate 'In the Beginning' as *nuruwirri* and in doing so disempowered Biblical events. As I have shown elsewhere, however, the Warlpiri themselves have reversed this linguistic decision.

34. H. Morphy, 'Myth, Totemism and the Creation of Clans', *Oceania*, 60 (1990), p. 314.

35. D. Bell, op. cit., p. 90.

36. My suspicions in this regard were rewarded when I queried Gladys Tybingoomba, a Cape York woman, on the gloss of *auwa* as 'Dreamtime'. She immediately conceded the translation was infelicitous,

herself preferring the lovely phrase 'settling place'. Pers. comm. 6/12/1990 at the *Two Laws: Queensland Aboriginal Law and Spirituality Conference* (St Lucia: University of Queensland, 5–8 December, 1990).

37. M. Bain, 'No Pitjantjatjara Transformation', *Anthropological Forum*, 4 (1978–9), p. 319.
38. F.A. Dubinska & S. Traweek, 'Closer to the Ground: A Reinterpretation of Warlpiri Iconography', *Man*, NS, 19 (1984), p. 28.
39. T.G.H. Strehlow, *Songs* (pp. 614–15), says, for the Aranda, a person's 'Dreaming' (always a specific) refers to his or her place of emanation.
40. A.P. Elkin, 'Elements of Australian Aboriginal Philosophy', *Oceania*, 40 (1969), pp. 88–9.
41. see T. Swain, 'Dreaming, Whites and the Australian Landscape: Some Popular Misconceptions', *The Journal of Religious History*, 15 (1989), pp. 345–50; & K. Maddock, 'Australian Religions: History of Study', in *The Encyclopedia of Religion*, edited by M. Eliade, vol. 1, p. 566.
42. P. Dodson, 'The Land My Mother, The Church My Mother', *Compass Theology Review*, 22 (1988), p. 1.
43. M. Harvey, 'The Dreaming', in *Yanyuwa Country: The Yanyuwa People of Borroloola tell the History of Their Land*, by J. Bradley, (Richmond: Greenhouse Publications, 1988), p. xi.
44. D. Gondarra, 'Father You Gave Us The Dreaming', *Compass Theology Review*, 22 (1988), p. 6.
45. J.W. von Goethe, *Faust*, translated by W. Kaufmann (New York: Anchor, 1962), p. 153, lines 1225–6 and 1236–7.
46. G.R. Davidson, 'An Ethnographic Psychology of Aboriginal Cognitive Ability', *Oceania*, 49 (1979), pp. 284 & 287–8.
47. H. Bergson, *Time and Free Will* (London: Allen & Unwin, 1910), pp. 95–7. Bergson refers in this context to non-human spatial reckoning as an alternative to temporality, but the comparison is nonetheless of interest.
48. W. TenHouten, 'Right Hemisphericity of Australian Aboriginal Children: Effects of Culture, Sex and Age on Performances of Closure and Similarities Tests', *International Journal of Neuroscience*, 28 (1985), pp. 125 & 143.
49. Some research is currently being conducted, which may be informative in this regard, such as J. Klekamp *et al.*, 'The Growth of the Visual Cortex in Australian Aborigines and Caucasians', *Neuroscience Letters*, supplement 30 (1988), p. 86.
50. V. Deloria, *God is Red* (New York: Dell, 1973), pp. 76, 82 & 83.
51. idem., *Custer Died for Your Sins: An Indian Manifesto* (New York: Avon Books, 1969), chapter 5.
52. P. Tillich, *The Protestant Era*, translated by J.L. Adams (Chicago: University of Chicago Press, 1948), p. 20; cf. pp. 26–7.
53. cit. C. Chan, *The Development of Neo-Confucian Thought* (New York: Bookman Associates, 1957), p. 165.

54. Stanner, op. cit., p. 234.
55. J.Z. Smith, *Map is Not Territory: Studies in the History of Religions* (Leiden: E.J. Brill, 1978), p. 101.
56. W.E.H. Stanner, *On Aboriginal Religion*, The Oceania Monographs, no. 11 (Sydney: University of Sydney, 1959-61), p. 46.
57. R. Tonkinson, *The Mardudjara Aborigines: Living the Dream in Australia's Desert* (New York: Holt, Rinehart and Winston, 1978), p. 15.
58. M. Eliade, *Australian Religions: An Introduction* (Ithaca: Cornell University Press, 1973), pp. 61 & 69.
59. As already noted, the missionary Schultz explicitly denied that *Altjira* was a God, but used the word as 'God' for proselytising purposes. By the time of Carl Strehlow, who worked mostly with three or four knowledgeable but heavily missionised informants, the High God interpretation had emerged. Later, Géza Róheim confirmed Strehlow's opinion ['Primitive High Gods', in *The Panic of the Gods and Other Essays* (New York: Harper, 1972), pp. 64 ff.], making correlations with south-eastern traditions.

    Significantly Róheim compares cognate beliefs among the neighbouring 'Ngatatara' and Pitjantjatjara with those of the Aranda. While there was clearly a general conceit in the region that there was a sky father, in most cases he was merely a localised Ancestor associated with a particular constellation. Among some of the Aranda, however, he focused all power in himself and reigned supreme above the earth as a High God. Róheim says of such beliefs, 'The Altjirra in question is not the Altjirra iliinka of old mythology, but Altjirra or God of the Aranda Bible' (ibid., p. 69, n. 168). This is true perhaps of the origin of such beliefs, but their ongoing significance must be contextualised in the life-world of the mission regime.

    Clearly, the Aranda High God has a history comparable with that of south-eastern Australia. There are other isolated examples of this kind, such as those emerging on the Benedictine Mission of New Norcia [R. Salvado, *The Salvado Memoirs: Mission of New Norcia and of the Habitats and Customs of the Australian Natives*, translated and edited by E.J. Stormon (Nedlands: University of Western Australia Press, 1977), p. 126]. As however, this book deals with broader cultural processes rather than smaller mission pockets, I leave these matters to one side, but see also my brief references to *Djamar* in chapter 5.
60. M. Eliade, op. cit., p. 33.
61. M. Eliade, *No Souvenirs: Journal 1957-1969* (London: Routledge & Kegan Paul, 1973), p. 74.
62. Eliade, *Australian Religions*, p. 52.
63. J.Z. Smith, *To Take Place: Toward Theory in Ritual* (Chicago: University of Chicago Press, 1987), p. 10.
64. T.G.H. Strehlow, *Central Australian Religion: Personal Monototemism in a Polytotemic Community* (Adelaide: Australian Association for the Study of Religions, 1978), pp. 14-15.

65. D. Rose, op. cit., p. 266.
66. B. Glowczewski, 'Australian Aborigines, Typology and Cross-Cultural Analysis', paper presented at the *Fifth International Conference on Hunting and Gathering Societies* (Darwin: August–September, 1988), p. 3.
67. N. Munn, 'The Spatial Presentation of Cosmic Order in Walbiri Iconography', in *Primitive Art and Society*, edited by A. Forge (London: Oxford University Press, 1973), p. 197.
68. N. Munn, 'The Transformation of Subjects into Objects in Walbiri and Pitjantjatjara Myth', in *Australian Aboriginal Anthropology: Modern Studies in the Social Anthropology of the Australian Aborigines*, edited by R.M. Berndt (Nedlands: University of Western Australia Press, 1970), p. 145.
69. A.R. Radcliffe-Brown, 'The Sociological Theory of Totemism', reprinted in *Structure and Function in Primitive Society* (London: Routledge & Kegan Paul, 1929), p. 131.
70. For another false duality corrected, see W.E.H. Stanner, 'Sacred and Profane Reconsidered', unpublished ms.; also 'Reflections on Durkheim and Aboriginal Religion', in *Social Organization: Essays Presented to Raymond Firth*, edited by M. Freedman (London: Cass, 1967), pp. 217–40.
71. W.E.H. Stanner, 'On the Study of Aboriginal Religion', unpublished ms., p. 7.
72. Morphy, op. cit., p. 325.
73. T.G.H. Strehlow, *Aranda Traditions* (Melbourne: Melbourne University Press, 1947), pp. 28–9.
74. G.M. Hopkins, 'God's Grandeur', in *Poems and Prose of Gerard Manley Hopkins* (Harmondsworth: Penguin, 1953), p. 27.
75. Munn, 'The Spatial Presentation', pp. 214–15.
76. C. Lévi-Strauss, *Totemism* (Harmondsworth: Penguin, 1969).
77. Stanner, 'Religion . . .', p. 223.
78. C. Lévi-Strauss, *The Savage Mind: The Nature of Human Society* (London: Weidenfeld & Nicolson, 1966), p. 218.
79. Stanner, 'Religion . . .', pp. 225 & 215.
80. Lévi-Strauss, op. cit., pp. 242–3.
81. T.G.H. Strehlow, 'Geography and the Totemic Landscape in Central Australia: A Functional Study', in *Australian Aboriginal Studies: Modern Studies in the Social Anthropology of the Australian Aborigines*, edited by R.M. Berndt (Nedlands, W.A.: University of Western Australia Press, 1970), p. 92.
82. Harvey, op. cit., p. xi.
83. R. Homann (translator), *Pai Wen P'ien Or the Hundred Questions: A Dialogue Between Two Taoists on the Macrocosmic and Microcosmic System of Correspondences* (Leiden: E.J. Brill, 1976).
84. As expressed in the *Avatamsaka Sutra*, translated by T. Cleary as *The Flower Ornament Sutra*, esp. vol. 3 (Berkeley, California: Shambhala, 1987).

85. W. Blake, 'Milton, A Poem in Two Books', Book the First, Plate 29, lines 5-7, in *The Complete Poetry and Prose of William Blake*, edited by D.V. Erdman (Berkeley: University of California Press, 1982), p. 127.

86. J.G. Frazer, 'The Beginnings of Religion and Totemism Among the Australian Aborigines', reprinted in *Totemism and Exogamy: A Treatise on Certain Early Forms of Superstition and Society* (London: Macmillan, 1910), p. 160; 'The Origin of Totemism', reprinted in ibid., pp. 93-4.

87. A. Lang, 'Australian Problems,' in *Anthropological Essays Presented to Edward Burnett Tylor in Honour of his 75th Birthday, Oct. 2, 1907*, by H. Balfour *et al.* (Oxford: Clarendon Press, 1907), p. 212.

88. G. Róheim, 'The Nescience of the Aranda', *British Journal of Medical Psychology* 17 (1938), pp. 343-60.

89. M.F.A. Montagu, *Coming Into Being Among the Australian Aborigines: A Study of the Procreative Beliefs of the Australian Aborigines*, second edition (London: Routledge & Kegan Paul, 1974).

90. M. Spiro, 'Religion: Problems of Definition and Explanation', in *Anthropological Approaches to the Study of Religion*, edited by M. Banton (London: Tavistock, 1966), pp. 110-12; E. Leach, 'Virgin Birth', *Proceedings of the Royal Anthropological Institute* (1966), pp. 39-49.

91. Esp. D.F. Thomson, 'Fatherhood in the Wik Monkan Tribe', *American Anthropologist*, 38 (1936), pp. 374-93; Papuan influence is advocated to explain Thomson's data in M.F.A. Montagu, 'Physiological Paternity in Australia', *American Anthropologist*, 39 (1937), pp. 175-83. Arnhem Land examples are given in the following note, to which should be added the explicit place of sexual intercourse as a prerequisite to Ancestral fecundity in the All-Mother cults (see chapter 4).

92. W.L. Warner, *A Black Civilization: A Social Study of An Australian Tribe*, second edition (New York: Harper, 1958), pp. 23-4; cf. J.C. Goodale, *Tiwi Wives: A Study of the Women of Melville Island, North Australia* (Seattle: University of Washington Press, 1971), p. 136.

93. W. Shapiro, 'Ritual Kinship, Ritual Incorporation and the Denial of Death', *Man*, NS 23 (1988), pp. 276 & 280.

94. D.H. Turner, 'Denial of Death: Affirmation of Life', *Man*, NS 24 (1989), p. 521.

95. E. Becker, *The Denial of Death* (New York: The Free Press, 1973).

96. C. Lévi-Strauss, 'The Structural Study of Myth', *Journal of American Folklore*, 67 (1955), pp. 428-44.

97. Harvey, op. cit., p. xi, my emphasis.

98. N. Peterson, 'Totemism Yesterday: Sentiment and Local Organisation Among the Australian Aborigines', *Man*, NS 7 (1972), p. 24.

99. F. Merlan, 'Australian Aboriginal Conception Revisited', *Man*, NS 21 (1986), p. 474.

100. D.H. Turner, *Tradition and Transformation: A Study of the Groote Eylandt Aborigines of Northern Australia* (Canberra: Australian

64 *A place for strangers*

Institute of Aboriginal Studies, 1974); F.G.G. Rose, 'Boundaries and Kinship Systems in Aboriginal Australia', in *Tribes and Boundaries in Australia*, edited by N. Peterson (Canberra: Australian Institute of Aboriginal Studies, 1976), pp. 199-200.
101. T.G.H. Strehlow, *Aranda Traditions* (Melbourne: Melbourne University Press, 1947), p. 30.
102. H.G. Alexander (ed), *The Leibnitz-Clarke Correspondence* (Manchester: Manchester University Press, 1970), p. 70.
103. D.H. Turner, 'Cosmology is "Kinship": The Aboriginal Transcendence of Material Determination', *Mankind*, 19 (1989), p. 219.
104. Montagu, op. cit., p. 229.
105. N. Munn, *Walbiri Iconography: Graphic Representation and Cultural Symbolism in a Central Desert Society* (Ithaca: Cornell University Press, 1973), pp. 27-31.
106. F. Myers, *Pintupi Country, Pintupi Self: Sentiment, Place and Politics Among Western Desert Aborigines* (Washington/Canberra: Smithsonian Institute Press/Australian Institute of Aboriginal Studies, 1986), pp. 130-1.
107. Strehlow, *Aranda Traditions*, pp. 85-6.
108. L. Sharp, 'Ritual Life and Economics of the Yir-Yoront of Cape York Peninsula', *Oceania*, 5 (1934), p. 24.
109. Peterson, 'Totemism Yesterday', p. 17.
110. A.P. Elkin, 'The Secret Life of the Australian Aborigines', *Oceania*, 3 (1932), pp. 129-30.
111. This mechanism is revealed, for instance, in R. Tonkinson, 'Aboriginal Dream-Spirit Beliefs in a Contact Situation: Jigalong, Western Australia', in *Australian Aboriginal Studies: Modern Studies in the Social Anthropology of the Australian Aborigines*, edited by R.M. Berndt (Nedlands: University of Western Australia Press, 1970), pp. 277-91.
112. W. Shapiro, *Social Organization in Aboriginal Australia* (Canberra: Australian National University Press, 1979), pp. 18-19.
113. A. Hamilton, 'Descended from Father, Belonging to Country: Rights to Land in the Australian Western Desert', in *Politics and History in Band Society*, edited by E. Leacock and R. Lee (Cambridge: Cambridge University Press, 1982), pp. 101, 102, 103 & 99.
114. R. Layton, 'Anthropology and the Australian Aboriginal Land Rights Act in Northern Australia', in *Social Anthropology and Development Policy*, edited by R. Grilla and A. Rew (London: Tavistock, 1985), pp. 152 & 153-4.
115. O. Pink, 'The Landowners in the Northern Division of the Aranda Tribes, Central Australia', *Oceania*, 6 (1936), pp. 275-305.
116. Peterson, 'Totemism Yesterday', p. 17.
117. Hamilton, op. cit., p. 103.
118. Hamilton, op. cit., p. 106.

119. Merlan, op. cit., p. 476; Pink, op. cit., p. 290.
120. Hamilton, op. cit., p. 101.
121. Morphy, op. cit., pp. 324-6.
122. A. Lang, *The Secret of the Totem* (London: Longman, Green & Co., 1895), p. 190.
123. Lévi-Strauss, *The Savage Mind*, p. 94.
124. A related point is made by S. Hargrave, 'Two Sister Myths: A Structural Analysis', *Oceania*, 53 (1983), where, on p. 356, she stresses that the *Wawalag* myth (Lévi-Strauss' example) is not 'focused on the relative status and value of men and women. They are concerned with ability and perpetuity of the social group which is dependent on socially controlled relations between men and women'. Equate 'land-group' with 'social group' and her point is well taken.
125. see L.R. Hiatt, 'Secret Pseudo-Procreation Rites Among the Australian Aborigines', in *Anthropology in Oceania: Essays Presented to Ian Hogbin*, edited by L.R. Hiatt & C. Jayawardena (Sydney: Angus and Robertson, 1971), pp. 77-88.
126. D.B. Rose, *Dingo Makes Us Human: Life and Land in an Australian Aboriginal Culture* (Cambridge: Cambridge University Press, 1992), pp. 61-3.
127. K. Maddock, *The Australian Aborigines: A Portrait of Their Society*, (Penguin: Harmondsworth, 1974), pp. 161-9, suggests that inquests over deaths indicate that Aborigines believe death is an aberration. In actuality they indicate quite the opposite, insofar as there are no inquests for people who have lived a full life. Aborigines do not resist death but unfulfilled life.
128. M. Crawley ['Aboriginal Beliefs and Reincarnation', *Religious Traditions*, 6 (1983), pp. 1-29] is tenacious enough to suggest '*karma* is applicable for the individual Aranda man. For him, life is determined according to the activities and choices he exercized in his previous existence as an ancestor' (p. 17). One wonders why anyone would make such contortions to save a word. For a Hindu, *karma* without time (which Crawley has depicted) would be simply silly.
129. Eliade, *Australian Religions*, p. 171.
130. R.M. & C.H. Berndt, *The World of the First Australians*, second edition (Sydney: Ure Smith, 1977), p. 488.
131. Maddock, op. cit., pp. 159-61. Cf. Berndt & Berndt, *The World . . .*, pp. 488-9.
132. Radcliffe-Brown ('Religion and Society', p. 41, n. 18) refers to the death and resurrection of *Daramulun* as being based in the three-day resurrection of the moon. Radcliffe-Brown disclaims any Christian influence, but cf. chapter 3 below.
133. Warner, *A Black Civilization*, pp. 385 & 297.
134. N. Munn, 'The Effectiveness of Symbolism in Murngin Rite and Myth', in *Forms of Symbolic Action: Proceedings of the 1969 Annual*

Spring Meeting of the American Ethnological Society, edited by R.F. Spencer (Seattle: University of Washington Press, 1969), p. 186.

135. Maddock, *The Australian Aborigines,* pp. 159–61; Berndt & Berndt, *The World . . .,* p. 487.
136. D. Rose, *Dingo,* p. 230.
137. R.M. Berndt, 'A "Wonguri"-Manjikai Song Cycle of the Moon-Bone', *Oceania,* 19 (1948), p. 20.
138. ibid., p. 46.
139. U.H. McConnel, 'A Moon Legend from the Bloomfield River, North Queensland', *Oceania,* 2 (1931), pp. 13, 14 & 6.
140. Thomson, 'Fatherhood . . .', pp. 386–9.
141. McConnel, op. cit., p. 13.
142. G. Seligmann, 'Women's Puberty Customs', in *Reports of the Cambridge Anthropological Expedition to Torres Straits: Volume V: Sociology, Magic and Religion of the Western Islands,* edited by A.C. Haddon (Cambridge: Cambridge University Press, 1904), pp. 206–7.
143. C. Knight, 'Lévi-Strauss and the Dragon: *Mythologiques* Reconsidered in the Light of an Australian Aboriginal Myth', *Man,* NS 18 (1983), p. 32.
144. K. Parker, *The Euahlayi Tribe: A Study of Aboriginal Life in Australia* (London: Archibald Constable, 1905).
145. H. Buchanan, transcript of interview at Nambucca Heads, original source unknown.
146. Hamilton, op. cit., p. 101.
147. Harvey, op. cit., p. xi.
148. cit. W.J. Kearney, *Mount Allan Land Claim,* Report no. 19, Aboriginal Land Rights (Northern Territory) Act 1976 (Canberra: Australian Government Publishing Service, 1985), p. 9.
149. Rose, *Dingo,* p. 223.
150. The definition of 'ownership' in the *Aboriginal Land Rights (Northern Territory) Act 1976* equates spiritual and economic elements in a simplistic and largely unworkable manner: the traditional 'owners' thus are a 'local descent group' who have 'primary spiritual responsibility for' and are 'entitled . . . to forage' in an area (Part I: Section 3).
151. See K. Palmer, ' "Owners" and "Managers": Ritual Cooperation and Mutual Dependence in the Maintenance of Rights to Land', *Mankind,* 13 (1983), pp. 517–30.
152. G. Barker, 'The Ritual Estate and Aboriginal Polity', *Mankind,* 10 (1976), pp. 255–89.
153. H. Morphy, 'Rights in Paintings and Rights in Women: A Consideration of Some of the Basic Problems Posed by the Asymmetry of the "Murngin System" ', *Mankind,* 11 (1978), pp. 208–19.
154. L.R. Hiatt, *Kinship and Conflict: A Study of an Aboriginal Community in Northern Arnhem Land* (Canberra: The Australian National University, 1965), p. 55.

155. K. Maddock, 'Dangerous Places and Their Analogues', *Mankind*, 9 (1974), pp. 206-17.
156. A position maintained by W.E.H. Stanner, 'Aboriginal Territorial Organisation: Estate, Range, Domain and Regime', *Oceania*, 36 (1965), pp. 1-26.
157. F. Engels, *The Origin of the Family Private Property and the State: In the Light of the Researchs of Lewis H. Morgan* (New York: International Publishers, 1942 [1844]), pp. 38-40.
158. e.g. J. Bern, 'Ideology and Domination: Toward a Reconstruction of Australian Aboriginal Social Formation', *Oceania*, 50 (1979), pp. 118-32. For an extensive critique by an Aboriginal Marxist, see M. Langton, 'Looking at Aboriginal Women and Power: Fundamental Misunderstandings in the Literature and New Insights', in *Aboriginal Perceptions of their Heritage: Papers Presented at the ANZAAS Festival of Science*, pp. 92-111 (Melbourne: Aboriginal Research Centre, 1985).
159. Munn, *Walbiri Iconography*, p. 186.
160. The Warlpiri with whom I worked, for instance, have, and do not recall having had any such restriction. On the logic of these taboos, where they exist, see my reference to D. Turner in the next chapter.
161. Also referred to, less commonly, as 'lawyers'. 'Managers' is perhaps the most frequently used gloss, as juxtaposed to the 'owners'. The latter, alas, was a less felicitous choice of terms insofar as it has confused Western reinterpreters of its meanings: 'owner' does not mean having authority and control over a land, but rather that one is ontologically identified with it.
162. T.G.H. Strehlow, *The Sustaining Ideals of Australian Aboriginal Societies* (Adelaide: Aborigines Advancement League, 1956), pp. 9, 10 & 12.
163. Warner, *A Black Civilization*, pp. 158-63. Warner's sample consisted of some seventy killings over a twenty-year period. Fifty were revenges for previous inflictions, ten were due to stealing or unlawful sexual relations, five were due to alleged sorcery and improper use of sacred objects. There was no reference to territorial dispute. Hiatt, *Kinship and Conflict*, p. 103, concurs, saying 'disputes over property were rare and usually trivial'. For comparisons with European death tolls during war, see G. Blainey, *Triumph of the Nomads: A History of Ancient Australia* (Melbourne: Sun Books, 1975), pp. 105-12.
164. Strehlow, 'Geography', p. 130.
165. See Berndt & Berndt, *The World of the First Australians*, pp. 467-70.
166. Turner, *Life Before Genesis: A Conclusion: An Understanding of Australian Aboriginal Culture* (New York: Peter Lang, 1987), p. 84; cf. N. Tindale, 'The Pitjandjara', in *Hunters and Gatherers Today*, edited by M. Bicchieri (New York: Holt, Rinehart and Winston, 1972), p. 219.
167. M.J. Meggitt, *Desert People: A Study of the Walbiri Aborigines of Central Australia* (London: Angus & Robertson, 1962), p. 42.

168. M.J. Meggitt, *Gadjari Amongst the Walbiri Aborigines of Central Australia*, The Oceania Monographs, no. 14 (Sydney: The University of Sydney, 1966), pp. 120–5.

169. Pers. comm., 9 June 1987; see also D.H. Turner, 'Australian Aboriginal Religion as "World Religion" ', *Studies in Religion*, 20 (1991), pp. 175–6.

170. Meggitt, *Gadjari*, p. 122, n. 248.

171. Meggitt, *Desert People*, pp. 165ff.

172. I consider the relevant data in chapter 5. Meggitt contested the post-colonial elements in his 'Djanba Among the Walbiri, Central Australia', *Anthropos*, 50 (1955), pp. 375–403.

173. C. Lévi-Strauss, *The Naked Man* (London: Jonathan Cape, 1983), p. 716.

CHAPTER 2

Songs of a Wayfarer

He might have been born there, or he must have
   a mother.
Or God put him there . . .
Then he stop there, stop there, stop there.
He must have been doing great things like got a nice
   house or big house.
And he do all that game there, all Bora things . . .

He go, he go, he go, he go.
Come out in the river mouth.
Him say, 'Well, I think I go now leave this place' . . .

He look back, 'Oh, country there I leave him long
   way', he say, 'right to south'.
He start make one sing there, make sing then.
He still go . . .
He never stop
Em keep sing.[1]

This is a fragment of a story which is itself a fragment from the
borders of a truth. The story, as we have received it, has a mirrored
pair (although perhaps once that rim was refracted in yet other ways),
and together they tell of wandering Heroes who leave Australia,
singing order into life as they search for new homes.

If anything, the symmetry of their symbolism is amplified when
translated into Western cartographic images. The Heroes leave from
adjacent points from the eastern and western coast of Cape York
Peninsula, heading northward for that narrow strait, a mere 150
kilometres wide, separating New Guinea from Australia. Draw a line
of latitude exactly midway between the extremities of the two land
masses, and then intersect it twice at the longitude of the eastern-
and western-most islands of Torres Strait. The two points of
intersection fall uncannily close to the tiny islands of Mer and

Mabuiag, the eternal homes of the Heroes. There they stand like
sentries guarding that median.

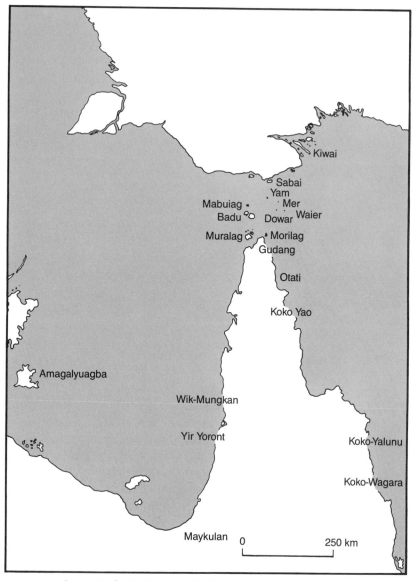

*Cape York Peninsula, Gulf of Carpentaria and the
Torres Strait Islands.*

The image, of course, is too neat; the geometry lifeless. Nevertheless, the question lingers: against what are the Heroes barring the way? My answer is this: not a people, as these passed freely. Nor a culture, as the boundary was at least partially permeable in that regard.

As intangible as it may seem, the songs of the wayfarers guarded against the passage of an idea.

THE SPLIT COSMOS

Scholars have rebuffed the possibility that Aboriginal worldviews might respond intelligibly to the changes caused by encounters with outsiders. The more radical and disruptive the contact, the stronger the academic dissent. There seems almost to exist an implicit evolutionary assumption whereby Aborigines can only meaningfully engage those close to their 'lowly level'. In the next chapter, I show that the effects of White invasion were met with nothing less than total denial. Indonesian impacts could safely be acknowledged, so long as they were belittled, as I show in chapter 4. The Melanesians of New Guinea, however, were so close in terms of geography and alleged cultural 'development' that the influence could not easily be overlooked. Given the fact that six or seven thousand years ago the two land masses were cojoined, and furthermore that there is a mammoth list of New Guinean influences on Aboriginal societies,[2] it would seem that we have no choice but to come to terms with the reality.

But even in this instance the 'repulsion' is evident, although the naïve observer might have imagined scholars had been left with little room to manoeuvre. Change and innovation can to some extent be neutralised if it is ancient enough or absurdly remote. Finding mummies in the Torres Strait came as a godsend. It is not the Melanesians at all we should look to for answers, but the Ancient Egyptians, and as the Egyptians influence *all* culture, then this amounts to no special impact at all. Grafton Elliot Smith first made this, as it now appears, absurd claim and Perry gave it currency.[3] What is truly amazing is the number of scholars who were convinced by such reasoning. Elkin, who confessed to me shortly before his death that he believed his old doctoral supervisor Elliot Smith to be a 'genius' (Perry was merely indefatigable), allowed this pan-Egyptianism to be apparent in his highly influential books. Eliade observes:

> Elkin is inclined to believe these Melanesian influences brought ideas and techniques that originally belonged to other, higher cultures. If he does not insist upon the final Egyptian origin of the ritual of mummification, he compares the parapsychological powers of the Australian medicine men with the feats of Indian and Tibetan yogis.[4]

While here (but not elsewhere – see chapter 3) baulking at Egypt, Eliade is at least content to accept the Asiatic explanations for certain features of Aboriginal culture.

There were many others seeking Egyptian roots for Australian traditions. W.H. Thorpe, writing on 'Some New Guinea Cultural Influences Found Amongst the Aborigines of Australia', could not resist opening by eulogising Perry's *Children of the Sun*.[5] R. Hamlyn-Harris, in a similar survey of Melanesian influences upon Aborigines, states: 'There is distinctive evidence of an influx of certain rituals appertaining to "heliolithic culture" of Egypt'.[6] Again, Warren Dawson, surveying 'Mummification in Australia and in America' was prone to abandon all moderation when pronouncing that certain Islander traditions 'exactly resemble[d] those of the Twenty-First Dynasty mummies of Egypt'.[7]

Not all historical thought has been this bizarre, although Margaret Lawrie's contention that Torres Strait Islanders came from China and are related to Eskimos offers some stiff competition.[8] The German *Kulturkreise* school was far more restrained, however, and Gräbner and Schmidt in particular did much sober spade work in an attempt to uncover the cultural levels of the south-west Pacific.[9] But once again there is a safe distance between them and 'real' history. Theirs was a global programme so encyclopedic that each detail, no matter how well observed, could only be fully understood in terms of the total scheme. Furthermore, as they placed cultural diffusionary processes in the distant past, they could happily ignore the active role of people as agents in historical processes. Theirs is a passive diffusion which at times seems to be no more than an intercultural incontinence.

Finally, when researchers have actually allowed themselves to focus on the continuities between Australia and New Guinea they have done so employing that most blandly innocent of all means of ethnographic restraint: the inventory. The oft-published

catalogues of cultural affinities are not unlike Foucault's description
of the timetable, but whereas the timetable enables one 'to lay hold
of and recreate the soul',[10] the inventory seems to be more an eternal
prison from which the soul of history is never to be freed.

In brief, the presentation of the cultural associations between
Aborigines and Melanesians has been theoretically constrained by
setting them in the remote past, by making them into instances of
a grander historical plan, or by binding the data to voiceless inven-
tories. Throughout, the attitude is of unbridgeable gulfs in time and
amorphous diffusionary processes. Having stated the undeniable,
they refuse to view the encounter as one with purpose or the history
of exchanges as having meaning. Thus, I do not know of a single
study which attempts to understand the logic of the dynamics in
the Aboriginal relationships with Melanesians. This chapter is a first
attempt to redress this situation.

Whilst our data are imperfect, my task is not as impossible as it
might first appear. Too much stress has been placed upon the
antiquity of the Torres Strait Islands as a bridge between Australia
and New Guinea. The common view, which Mulvaney rightly notes
is merely a 'facile explanation',[11] is that the islands became refuges
for people who had taken to higher ground as the land bridge was
submerged about 6,000 years ago. Others, such as Vanderwal, suggest
waves of migration to the islands between 5,000 and 2,000 BP,[12] but
again Mulvaney notes that except for one conflicting date from
Sabai, just off the coast of Papua, 'none of the five other dated sites
within Torres Strait may exceed one thousand years'.[13] The Islanders'
own understanding, says Laade, is that their ancestors arrived only
a little over two centuries ago, and Laade believes genealogical
evidence supports this view. Certainly, the islands were populated
in 1756, when Captain Gonzal of the *Rijder* saw huts on Muralag,
but prior to this we have no Western observations of any value at
all to help ascertain the time of arrival of the Torres Strait Islanders.[14]

Were Islander traditions correct in terms of Western historiography,
we would be provided with an intriguing case indeed, for Melanesian
contacts at Cape York would have been almost coterminous with
(at least the last wave of) Indonesian traders arriving at central-north
Australia (chapter 4), and invasion in the south-east (chapter 3). Even
if we must anticipate an earlier date, however – and this seems quite
likely – we are still probably dealing with associations from within
our millennium. Furthermore, as will be apparent throughout this

chapter, Aborigines and Islanders reveal through their traditions an ongoing concern with how they relate to one another, and the variety of socio-religious forms in northern Cape York indicate that people were still experimenting with new ways of accommodating outsiders. In short, we have every reason to treat these traditions as dynamic movements revealing to us something of the principles of Aboriginal responses to non-Aboriginal peoples.

My account is in four sections. I begin by continuing to broaden the usual investigative domain of 'religion' to include that which I have termed Abiding Law, showing that land, subsistence patterns, cosmology and ritual are all equally and mutually embraced by this latter concept. The differences between Melanesian and Australian Law are stressed, but so too is the evidence of a well-structured accommodation between these Laws. In the second section I turn to focus on cosmologies and the significance of the Hero stories in understanding Aboriginal relationships to Islanders. To highlight what is particularly Aboriginal in this understanding, I then contrast, in the third section, Islander Hero myths with those from Australia. Specifically, I examine the respective significance of warfare and song in the Heroes' symbolism. Finally, I return to broader socio-religious issues, cult structures and principles of spiritual descent in order to reveal that the traditions of northern Cape York are best defined as coherently organised ways of Lawfully engaging outsiders in such a manner as to transcend that perennial problem of transcendence itself.

LAND LAW

The Aborigines of northern Cape York had their moment and it slipped away. Until quite recently, this was the tone of the literature discussing Aboriginal associations with Melanesians. The Islanders[15] had brought to the shores of Australia an example of what was regarded as the first faltering step of agriculture's infancy, but even this offer of technological salvation was too much to grasp, for those allegedly so steeped in the sin of conservatism. The best that could come from such contact was an unintegrated replication. Hamlyn-Harris could but reflect that the Aborigine 'was never an inventive genius . . . but that he is a born mimic and imitative is very apparent'.[16] A borrower occasionally, but never one to creatively control broader cultural processes.

Later writers made their apologies for Aborigines. Thus, wrote McCarthy, subsistence

> conservatism is to be explained partly by the non-occurrence, or non-introduction, of the staple food plants . . . of the Pacific Islands; also, because a great portion of the continent is arid and entirely unsuitable for primitive cultivation . . . it might be concluded, therefore, that the culture, historical background and conservatism of the aborigines are not conducive to a change to a settled gardening life.[17]

A handsome apology indeed, but unfortunately one almost totally devoid of substance. Firstly, Aboriginal diets in Cape York consist of vegetables of the same genera as those cultivated in New Guinea, and the climate is quite suitable for agricultural purposes.[18] Furthermore, according to Barbara Thompson, a White survivor of a shipwreck who was rescued by and lived with the people of Muralag (1844–48) – the closest Islander neighbours to mainland Australia and trading partners 'of some antiquity' – the Kaurareg, as they were called, in some cases saved seed and cultivated yams and other crops in a climate virtually identical to that at the tip of Australia. Aborigines thus had the requisite environment as well as evident access to sources of seed and technological information. More significantly, however, the Kaurareg, themselves influenced by mainland traditions, had among them only five men who set aside land for agriculture, and we must assume the rest chose deliberately not to follow suit.[19]

We therefore are faced with Peter White's conclusion: 'In fact, northern Australia seems to be one of the very few areas of the world which *could have become agricultural and did not*'. I would go further and change the last words to read '*intentionally did not*'.[20] The evidence indicating that Aborigines consciously rejected aspects of Islander technology is quite unambiguous. The bow and arrow is a clear example. These were never given a place within the Aboriginal mode of subsistence, although they were thus used on the nearby island of Muralag.[21] Aborigines nonetheless knew everything that could be known of these weapons. They were incorporated into their cosmology, although the myths tell why these objects properly belong only to Islanders, and were actually made as toys for children.[22] Adults declined their use, however. Some time later Thomson likewise observed that the Koko Yao toyed with European goods, but discarded them readily as they were said to lack the sacred power that gave their own cultural items legitimacy.[23]

Again, the myths of Cape York tell of the removal of cultivated crops to the Islands: 'Shiveri he took all the food from the mainland to Torres Strait Islands: banana, taro, yam, kassava, sweet potatoes. And what he left behind: only wild yam and wild roots'.[24] Readers miss the point if they see this as a discourse on the different species to be found in the two regions. Rather the difference is between cultivation and 'wildness'. But the *knowledge* of cultivation is here if only to explain why it should not be practised. Stanner made a similar observation regarding myth in central northern Australia. The Murinbata, he said, took offence when they were said to be ignorant of agriculture. It was all there in their stories![25]

Recently it has become acceptable to acknowledge that Aborigines deliberately spurned some Melanesian traditions, but why this occurred is still a matter of diverse opinion. Most popular is Marshall Sahlins' contention that hunter-gatherers possess the 'original affluent society',[26] a view which has been grossly romanticised whilst being conscripted to the cause of a now fashionable neo-Noble Savagery. The problem with this view lies in the ambiguity of 'affluence'. It must not be equated with constant abundance, and only the most starry-eyed would ignore Aborigines' stories of hunger and shortage. Barbara Thompson records her experiences of bad seasons in Muralag, and Moore adds the comment that this may have been a factor in deciding upon some supplementary agricultural activities.[27] Given all their leisure of 'affluence', why did Aborigines also not at least develop some form of interim agriculture?

It is here that the concept of affluence reveals its Western, post-Industrial and secularist bias. For while scholars may consider Aboriginal subsistence strategies allow much leisure (for men, at least), Aborigines say with an insightful use of English, that much of their 'leisure' is in fact 'work'.[28] Ritual is 'work' and if we are to take this into account as an *essential* component of Aboriginal subsistence then the image of excessive affluence is reduced. It also removes an imposed division between sacred and profane life, and hence the simplistic assumption that new subsistence methods might simply be appended to the Aboriginal world. In other words, I am suggesting Aborigines had to devote too much time to maintaining an order, of which hunting and gathering was but one facet, to contemplate introducing new strategies merely for the sake of subsistence. Futhermore, the ecological–ritual complexes of Aborigines were incompatible with those of Melanesians for 'religious' reasons that secularists might mistakenly argue had nothing to do with subsistence technology.

Meggitt came close to this position when he argued that an Aboriginal religious philosophy which relied upon non-technical ritual action to maintain fertility was at odds with an agricultural tradition.[29] But this still only states the problem without actually specifying its form. What is it about Aboriginal philosophy, we must ask, which places it in conflict with the cultivation of land? In a book to which I alluded in the closing pages of the previous chapter, David Turner makes a far more penetrating observation regarding the reason Aborigines were disinclined to incorporate Islander culture. This is an instance of his broader classification of societies into two categories. The Australian structure allowed for stable accommodation.

> The cost, however, was a lack of dynamism in technological and economic affairs which conventional 'band' . . . societies enjoyed as a result of allowing socio-economic relations to flow from proximity in space, encouraging (collective) self-interest and permitting a greater degree of pragmatism in economic activities . . . In the Australian case, stable accommodation was achieved by federative mechanisms . . . at the institutional . . . levels, in the form of intermarriage, trade, totemic prohibitions and spacing processes.[30]

The key to our inquiry that emerges from this understanding is the focus on the relationship between peoples and places. What unites subsistence patterns, social order and cosmological belief and practice in the cultures we are considering is land. More specifically, the encounter between Melanesians and Aborigines is best approached as one between divergent ontologies of space.

At this point it is valuable to summarise briefly what I believe to be the core section of Turner's *Return to Eden*, for although dealing with Amagalyuagba (Bickerton Island), which is on the other side of the Gulf of Carpentaria from Cape York, the principles he elucidates hold across this region of Australia. Turner's inquiry addressed the maxims governing the divisions of lands, peoples and species. He had initially supposed that spatial boundaries were imposed around scarce economic resources. If this were so then people of a land would be the custodians of species upon which other lands and their peoples were dependent. No matter where a person might reside, they would retain their initial home and as these were eternal there emerged a network of mutually interdependent

lands/peoples, none of which was self-sufficient. This was a highly
structured and radical pluralism. As it turned out, however,
Amagalyuagba, like all good Edens, was often superabundant and
Turner could discover no absolute resource basis to the spatial
boundaries. The people of the island, it seems, simply had to make
do with too much, and, significantly, although they could have
fragmented *ecologically* into self-sufficient communities, *philosophically* it was a case of nurturing a very slight tendency towards natural
abundance in certain areas into a cosmology insisting upon the
principle of non-self-sustaining mutually interdependent lands.[31]
The result was a rich tapestry in an apparently seamless expanse
of space.

If this interpretation is correct (and it will become evident as I
proceed that it is well supported by Cape York data) then clearly
Aboriginal traditions quite explicitly opposed the premise that the
spiritual potentialities of a place are in any way influenced by
humans or other species who merely happen to occupy it. Whatever
might occur in the mundane world of events, a land is, and can be,
metaphysically linked only with a limited and specific range of
people and other species and it is those land–people–species unions
which provide the principle for continual cosmic order. This is a
conclusion also reached in my discussion of 'totemism' in chapter 1.

It is evident that an agriculturalist worldview poses fundamental
obstacles to such an ontology. To give a stark comparison – and one
which comes into its own in later chapters – when Captain Cook
claimed Australia on behalf of George III, he did so on the understanding that Aborigines did not own their lands.[32] By his time,
admittedly, European agricultural lands were being increasingly
allocated in terms of secularist, anti-feudalist principles, particularly as articulated by John Locke and the Swiss jurist de Vatell.
Locke's definition of ownership is nonetheless informative. As is
well known, he said the right to property was determined by humans
placing themselves in land. His words, so perfectly inverting the
Aboriginal understanding of the relationship between individuals
and place, are informative: 'Whatsoever then he removes out of the
State that Nature hath provided, and left in, he hath mixed his
Labour with, and joyned to it something that is his own, and thereby
makes it his *Property*'.[33] Behind this statement is the presumption,
here very clearly phrased, that a human can, through his or her own
bodily effort, unite with a place. Moreover, the species planted or

grazed are also thus co-joined. By this stage in European thought, it is fair to suggest we are also witnessing a manifestation of the notion that space is undifferentiated and homogeneous and hence, so to speak, that one has to dig one's spirit into the land by the ritual of labour.

Certainly this is an extreme contrast, but from an Aboriginal perspective I believe the differences between European and other forms of agriculture are only matters of degree. All cultivation to some extent removes the locus of power from land and locates it in persons; again, to some extent at least, it allows geocentric organisation to be compromised by sociocentric authority. This is evident in rituals for ensuring species' abundance. In Cape York, which reveals a typically Aboriginal form of 'increase' (actually 'homeostasis') ceremony,[34] the stress is wholly upon releasing the pre-existent fecundity from a site. The land alone has this life-potential spirit. In Melanesian traditions, however, including those of the Torres Strait Islands, agricultural rituals are directed towards ensuring the success of human activity. The use of symbolism replicating human sexual behaviour[35] (denied by Aborigines as being of more than incidental significance) reveals this shift from the fixed potency of places to the human body, and to the person or social group as a (spatially mobile) centre.

Presuming for the moment that this model of the Australian/ Melanesian distinction is correct, we would expect to be able to discern at least some wrestling between the two spatial ontologies within the Torres Strait Islands, as indeed we do. In the Eastern, and culturally most Melanesian islands,[36] such as the Murray Island group of Mer, Dowar and Waier, there is something akin to the Australian understanding of a person's rightful abode, a permanent land such that, as Beckett has it, 'no matter where they lived, the place where they *belonged* determined their social placement'. The principle of inheritance of land affiliation was approximately patri-lineal, but the ties of the locality were emphasised more than the derived attributes of kinship, which were themselves land deter-mined. Inland, where gardens are cultivated, however, individuals gain ascendency over land. Garden land belonged to those inheriting the right to work it, and they in turn could pass it on as they wished. These holdings were particularly disjointed in terms of kin-groups, with neighbours sometimes having little in the way of close family relationships.[37] This comes close to Harding's characterisation of

New Guinea garden land which 'is viewed much as Europeans view real estate'.[38] One consequence of this organisation, essential to the understanding of the Hero cults, was boundary disputes.

For reasons that are not as historically clear as some writers suppose,[39] the Western Torres Strait Islands are closer to the mainland Australian order. Agriculture was far less important and more authority resided with the patrilineally regulated land-based group. Although communities here were more mobile, site affiliations were stronger and most land was 'owned collectively' by 'clans'. Territory was relatively fixed and boundary disputes become increasingly, but not completely, unthinkable.[40] Yet even Muralag, just off the tip of Australia, retained some distinctively Melanesian features.

Muralag has confused several researchers and deserves closer examination. Lauriston Sharp baldly stated that the Kaurareg recognised that 'the totemic organisation . . . centres entirely around localized named totemic clans regulating land tenure'. This he sees as being the same system as found in Cape York, explained by the fact that the Kaurareg 'had a hunting and gathering economy little more advanced than that of the mainland Aborigines'.[41] Were this the case I would happily concede these 'Islanders' were 'Aboriginal', but Sharp's conclusion seems overly hasty. Wilkin had earlier noted some ambiguity and, quoting J. MacGillivray's journals of 1846–50, cited the view that while land is not cultivated it is divided amongst children in a manner leaving much latitude for individual whim.[42] The solution to this apparent contradiction lies once again in a distinction between agricultural and unworked land, for in fact, as I have already noted, a handful of Kaurareg men actually did cultivate gardens. Barbara Thompson recalled:

> The places in the scrub where they cultivate the *koti* [yams] are called *pods*. When a man and woman become old and infirm they will divide their *pod* amongst the children. The youngest child gets the most. When a father or mother dies, the grandchildren take the land. The place is cultivated by the [heirs?] and also the ground or place which belongs to them. Girls get as much land sometimes as boys. The parents will give most land to a favourite child! *There is no particular rule in that respect*.[43]

Moore adds correctly that land ownership in this Kaurareg sense 'is totally alien to the Aboriginal thinking'.[44]

It is evident that there was a range of views on the relationship between peoples and places in the Islands of Torres Strait. A continuum can be drawn from the most Melanesian islands of the east to those like Muralag, which the perfunctory observer may fail to distinguish from mainland cultures. The distinction, no matter how slight, nevertheless exists. As we have seen, there is a direct correlation between the extent of agriculture and the degree to which the ultimate and eternal authority of land is fractured. The custodianship of cultural land rests not on the metaphysical identity of the human spirit which has emerged from and which indeed is the land-spirit, but rather on the people who have worked themselves into their land. To use what has now become something of a cliché: whereas agriculturalists own their land, Aborigines are owned *by* their land.

As I will presently show, this was far more than merely a socio-economic dilemma. It was a dilemma of Law.

But agriculture has been an ever-present problem in Aboriginal associations with strangers. Melanesians, Indonesians, and Europeans shared this much at least, and I have dwelt on the issue here as it underlies the discussion of the following chapters. I will simply assume what I have said here in my examination of the effects of other classes of aliens on Aboriginal traditions, but beyond the common problem of worldview themes shared by all cultivators there also lies the issue of the specific relationships with diverse agricultural peoples. After all, there is every difference between encountering agriculturalists through invasion, transitory trade, and long-term non-intrusive residence of close proximity.

What I therefore maintain is reflected in the Hero cults is the association with a particular class of cultivator, and before proceeding to the stories of the Heroes themselves, I must establish several features of the Aboriginal relationship with the Islanders. In particular, it is crucial to note that Islanders and other Melanesians, no matter how different their Law, were never perceived as a Lawless people. Nor did their traditions pose an uncontainable threat to Aboriginal Law. Accommodation was certainly necessary, but it was achieved with comparatively little disruption. If, as we will see in the next chapter, Whites were initially seen as essentially un-Lawful beings, while Indonesians (chapter 4), although not Lawless, were nonetheless a people difficult to engage through ordered, place-bound and marriage-regulated associations, then Islanders emerged as an 'other' that could be virtually brought into the Australian world. It was an oddly matched but workable marriage of cosmologies, with both parties assuming the other had entered the contract on its terms.

Both Australian and Melanesian Laws place a premium upon reciprocity, and although there are fundamental differences in the two cultures between what is given and what gifts signify, exchanges were almost inevitably the medium for their Lawful associations. Trade was one such form of reciprocity. The full list of influences in terms of material culture is indeed impressive, but the main transactions were drums, bamboo pipes, tobacco, and double outrigger canoes (the last originating from the Trans-Fly region of New Guinea) for Australian spears, spearthrowers and ochres.[45]

These exchanges should not be romanticised, nor should we assume the principles of reciprocity did not require constant displays of force. It has been observed for both Australian and Melanesian societies[46] that violence is an important means of maintaining the Law, and that, as Garry Trompf has so cogently shown, negative 'payback' (revenge) is as legitimate a means of reciprocity as positive 'payback'.[47] The points where Australian and Islander traditions meet seem to reveal a higher than average degree of organised violence, yet far from fracturing relationships, it in fact seems to have strengthened them.

This brings us to an important distinction between Indonesian and Islander relationships with Aborigines. As I will later show, Indonesian seafarers were all men, and reciprocal marriages, so fundamental to the Australian order, were thus impossible. This was not so in the case of Islanders, and hostilities erupting from unfulfilled trade responsibilities and other infringements led, at times, to marriages. Brierly makes the following notes from Barbara Thompson's Muralag recollections:

> There are some people among them who they call *gassimigi* – caught people (from *gassimi* – to catch). They are women and men that they have saved in fights with the mainland blacks . . . They were caught when they were young and brought away when they were young women. Some of the older men are *gassimigi*. They are all married and for the most part have children grown up on the island.[48]

While the consequence may not have been a major motivation, it is clear that violence actually led to affinal relationships. Aborigines and Islanders were thus linked through trade, marriage and children. If we bear in mind the land-spirit connection which constitutes the Aboriginal understanding of what defines a person's essence, then we readily see why these contacts were far more enduring and stable than any that might be achieved with the Indonesian seafarers.

As I have said, however, this reciprocity, although well established, could not have had entirely the same significance for both parties. The differences relate to the place of exchange within the wider forms of the respective Laws and, in particular, to land. For, as Turner argues, the process of 'placing part of one in the other and vice versa',[49] which constitutes trade and marriage for Aborigines, is foremostly a means of federating lands. People and even material objects containing sacred powers (which can include apparently mundane trade objects)[50] are manifestations of a spiritual force which is ultimately derived from a known site. Reciprocity, for Aborigines, is the temporary gift of an embodiment of part of a land-spirit which will eventually return to its abode. Melanesian reciprocity, as will later become apparent, does not share this premise.

In this context, it is important to stress that, despite the many simplistic interpretations of the Hero stories, which see them as garbled memories of the history of respective invasions of Islander and Aboriginal territories, ethnographic evidence does not support this view at all. At the places where the two cultural horizons meet, furthermore, we have glimpses of some fascinating means of adjusting divergent understandings of reciprocity: something of an ontological currency exchange. Moore has noted the importance of the small island of Morilag (Mt. Adolphus Is.) in this regard. This was indisputably the land of the Gudang Aborigines,[51] but although a place of natural abundance, it was not permanently inhabited, but apparently set aside as a neutral place of reciprocal relations with Islanders. Brierly's account captures the main points. His rough pencilled notes on 'The Neutral Ground of Morelag' read

> Morelag: or Adolphus Island. A high island standing at the entrance to the Straits, close to Cape York. It appears to be a kind of neutral ground to which at certain seasons of the year people from different islands in the Straits meet and here exchange by way of presents to each other, such as drums, shields, and different articles, either of ornament or use. All these islanders have a feeling of dislike and distrust of the mainland Blacks in the neighbourhood of Cape York, excepting the small tribe on the extreme of the peninsula with whom they are friendly. On this account, although they land from their canoes, they never camp upon the mainland.[52]

It is noteworthy that while there is total reluctance to enter each other's territory proper, and hence boundaries are quite rigid, there is also an institutionalised means of permeability in the form of Morilag. As Moore comments, the 'whole basis of the Islander and Aboriginal ethic was reciprocity . . . every gift sooner or later called for a counter-gift, every deed, whether good or bad, demanded a counter deed'. Morilag provided a means by which the two traditions might communicate: 'The Torres Strait goods owned by Aborigines were given [to them] by Central and Eastern Islanders in exchange for landing rights'.[53] The greater variety and complexity of Melanesian material culture was compensated for, appropriately, by access to land, the very thing which we have seen had prohibited Aborigines from annexing the goods into their own domain.

In this section I have sketched the features essential for understanding the contexts of the Hero cults. I have rejected both the position that Aborigines could not develop agriculture and the supposition that Aborigines and Islanders were constantly attempting to invade the domains of others. Both views falsely stress an image of cultural chaos and creative ineptitude. In contrast, I have attempted to show that the northern tip of Australia was the limit of a particular ontology of space and that the associations with Islanders are best seen as a very carefully ordered means of bringing two cosmologies into a mutual association which did not threaten the integrity of either. It was a Lawful association, secured through trade, marriage, and even controlled access to land. These arrangements were so successful that Aborigines and Islanders could see themselves as having a shared cosmological tradition, to which I will now turn. But even so, we should never lose sight of the fundamental difference between Aboriginal and Islander worldviews. When I consider the myths and rituals of the Heroes, my concern will be to show how all I have so far said could be encapsulated by deeming Islanders to be cosmologically the 'same' as Aborigines, yet ontologically 'other'.

OF HOMES AND HEROES

Is there any question more fundamental than: where do I belong? What is my place in the world? Or, to ask it negatively, what place is not mine, and where must I remain homeless? Even those who would deny the primary quality of these questions must conjure them if only to reveal that theirs is the greatest of all illusions. Thus said one of the most finely honed minds in history: 'No thing is not "other", no thing is not "it". If you treat yourself too as "other" they do not appear, if you know of yourself you know them'.[54] From an Aboriginal perspective, this would be mere sophistry (or more accurately, Hui-Shih-istry).[55] In the traditions of the first Australians there exists a prevailing insistence that every self has its Abiding place.

One of the greatest dilemmas for such an understanding is the encounter with peoples whose place is unknown and perhaps unknowable. How Aboriginal cosmologies can expand to accommodate strangers with homes as ethereal as 'England' and even 'Macassar' will be discussed in detail in later chapters. Melanesians from the Torres Strait Islands and New Guinea, however, were not from such *otiose* realms, but before I explore the significance of this fact I must dispel a fallacy about Cape York cosmologies.

Displaying a flair for overly tidy explanations, Thomson once put forward the dogma that there was an 'absence of the talk of White men from mythology' in Cape York.[56] Whites, he said, belonged to the present; 'Dreaming' was reserved for the Heroes and their kind. Yet, as Laade observes, one of the Hero's songs is:

> White Man, white man
> comes this way, he been come, he here now
> deep blue sea.[57]

The Aboriginal translator could offer no answer to the rather Eurocentric question of why Whites were represented in Abiding Events. They were simply there, providing a glimpse of a Law which now embraced newcomers.

This is hardly an exceptional case. As early as 1908, Seligman recorded the following myth among the Otati, neighbours of the Koko Yao, amongst whom Thomson was to work two decades later, and who shared a common Hero cult.

> Long ago all men were white; they lived in houses and food was abundant and easily obtained. Their chief was wise and powerful, and told them what was good to eat, and what to avoid. One fruit, a berry growing in clusters and called *unmoi*, he particularly told them not to touch. One day, some men and women saw this fruit and said, 'why should the chief prevent our eating this; it looks good, let us try it; he will never know we have eaten it.' So they plucked some and ate it and found its taste good. But a man saw them and went to the chief saying, 'Look at these people; they have plucked and eaten *unmoi*.' Then the chief got very angry and calling the culprits said, 'you bad men, did

I not give you plenty of fruit to eat, was there not plenty of white fruit and green fruit growing on the trees? Now, because you have not obeyed me but have eaten black fruit (*unmoi* = black) you and your children shall have black skins; you shall have no more houses and no more clothes, you shall walk about naked and you shall have hard work to find your food, which, since you like dirty food, you shall find in the ground. But I and the people who have obeyed me will go to another place.'[58]

What is central to this story is not so much the use of Biblical mythemes but an account of a cosmic split in which Whites leave for an unknown place far to the west. There is no romanticism, no self-congratulation at being the 'original affluent society' insofar as they 'shall have hard work to find . . . food'. But the fall might yet be seen as what Turner would call a fall *into* Eden; the loss of houses, clothes and easy foods in itself being part of their salvation. However we read these details, there is no denying that this story cosmologically accounts for a split into two worlds and two divergent Laws.

This theme is repeated in other myths from the area. The story of the two brothers found in the western Cape region (Yir Yiront, etc.) is almost of the Hero kind. The men travel through the land, demarcating place through song, and in some versions they 'disappeared to the west, out to sea, leaving three islands behind them'.[59] Like the Heroes, the brothers instigate initiation ceremonies, but initially they are thwarted by non-co-operation. Determined on revenge, they later set fire to the humpy in which the dancers are sleeping after the ceremonies.

Those who escaped serious burning went from there to their homes in other places. Those who jumped out of the fire first were White people. They were not burnt at all. Those who were a little burnt were half-castes and Chinese. Others were charred fairly badly, and these became the ancestors of the Aborigines and Torres Strait Islanders. Some were badly burnt and jumped into the water of a nearby pool to ease the pain. There they sank down and their ashes became the conception spirits of the . . . clan members.[60]

At face value the myth tells how non-co-operation and lack of accord lead to the separation of peoples into 'homes in other places', a separation marked by phenotypical differences. The section I have recounted ends, however, with the antithesis of the notion of distant, unknown lands: the entering of the eternal spirit into an Aboriginal site. Highly illuminating here is the inclusion of Islanders with

Aborigines. They belong to a shared cosmos; they extend continuously along the lines which give structure and purpose to space.

It must at this point be stressed that Aborigines could and did attempt to Lawfully come to terms with those whose homes were *beyond* the horizons of their cosmology – this process is discussed fully in the following chapters. But the Melanesians of Torres Strait and New Guinea came from *within* the known world order, and this is the key to the distinctive qualities of the Hero cults, to which I now turn.

Who, then, are the Heroes? The four that concern us are those most conspicuous in the literature and most prominent in Aboriginal and Islander ritual life. Two of them, *Shiveri* and *Iwai*, belong to mainland traditions. These Heroes travel to flank the centre of the Torres Strait Islands, as I recounted in the opening paragraphs of this chapter, where they had found their new homes. The other two, *Kuiam* and to a lesser extent *Bomai*, belong to Melanesian narratives and for comparative purposes are discussed in the next section.

There can be no doubt that at the very least the Hero cults of Cape York were inspired in their inception by contact with the northerners. Thomson readily sensationalised the facts with titles such as 'The Masked Dancers of I'wai'i: A remarkable Hero Cult which has Invaded Cape York Peninsula',[61] but in resorting to such ham-fisted images as 'invasion', he largely negates the realities of the exchanges. McConnel is far more restrained, suggesting that, apart from the Hero's association with Island fashions, there was nothing to indicate his cult had originated anywhere but in Australia.[62] While he tends to jump from this to the unwarranted conclusion that there therefore has been little innovation of significance, we can at least concede his point that symbols associated with Islanders do not prove that the cultic-complex *per se* has been borrowed, let alone allowed to 'invade' Australia. My own position is that while there are undeniable points of congruence, there are differences so fundamental that only at a very shallow level could Aboriginal and Islander Hero traditions be said to be entirely the same.

Much, of course, hinges on the criteria for determining 'sameness'. In some contexts Aborigines state, quite unambiguously, that *Shiveri* is the same as *Kuiam*. In the words of Dick Luff of Mapoon: 'Shiveri . . . – that's our lingo; the [Torres Strait] Islanders call him Kuiam'.[63] Most scholars have assumed statements like this signify that the two Heroes are identical. Thomson simply fuses them in another of his revealing titles 'Sivirri and Adi Kwaiam: A Culture Hero from Western Cape York . . .'[64] In an observation somewhat at odds with her claim of minimal Islander impact on Aboriginal cults, McConnel says the Mabuiag dance of *Kuiam* was, like that of *Shiveri*, associated with the seagull and hence that 'Shiveri was one and the same as . . . Kwoiyam'.[65] And from Mabuiag northwards the path is clearly defined, as Landtman has recorded the myths of *Kuiam* among the Kiwai in the delta of the Fly river in Papua New Guinea.[66]

What we are therefore presented with is a continuous Ancestral passage from Australia to New Guinea. In this sense we are dealing with one being: 'the same'. The differences, however, are equally and complementarily important. I will discuss these in a moment, but before I do it is necessary to examine the connections from eastern Cape York to the eastern Torres Strait Islands. This is a greater cultural gulf, and the continuity is not as evident. *Bomai*, who travels from New Guinea to Mer,[67] comes to reside at the same place as *Iwai*, but, of course, the two Heroes have converged at a point from opposite directions.[68] Nor do we have any records of *Bomai* taking the form of a crocodile – *Iwai*'s main manifestation. Laade notes, nonetheless, that people of Mer have hypothesised that *Iwai* and *Bomai* are the same being. As Laade suggests, this is possibly a recent merging, but we should also note that *Sagai*, *Bomai*'s brother who travelled with him as far as Yam, is represented by a hammerhead shark and a crocodile,[69] which, to my eye, seem to be conflated into the form of the main mask of the cult of *Bomai* at Mer (the mask's significance was not explained to Haddon, but is apparently a hammerhead shark with crocodile-like eyes and snout, front legs and hide).[70] It is therefore not impossible that the travels of *Bomai* and *Iwai* meet at Mer, where the two become one. At the very least there is a connection between *Bomai* and Australia in the fact that Aborigines are said to have supplied him with oil and ochre.[71]

The permutations and possible conflations of Heroes are indeed dizzying. One could, for instance, explore lateral links, as *Bomai*, *Sagai* and their other brothers are sometimes said to be the maternal uncles of *Kuiam*.[72] This, however, goes beyond our concerns. For my purposes, it suffices to have confirmed mythic passages through the islands which link Australia and New Guinea. In the western *Shiveri–Kuiam* path, the narrative line is continuous, in the eastern *Iwai–Bomai* association, it is a mirror image. In either case, however, it is recognised that there is a cosmic continuity; an unbroken procession which holds places together like beads along a shared thread of myth. There is no need to resort to the explanation associated with Whites, where the cosmos splits and some 'go to another place' or make 'their homes in other places' (*supra*). The cosmos is continuous, and this is what is meant when it is said that Heroes of the mainland and the Islands are 'the same'. I call this a *cosmological* 'sameness', and this reflects, more broadly, the fact that, as I have already shown, Aborigines and Islanders had developed a form of Lawful association through which their divergences could indeed be embraced by a shared cosmos.

Bisecting this cosmological sameness, however, is an *ontological* otherness. From the perspective of the deeper structures of being-in-the-world, there is every difference between *Shiveri* and *Kuiam*; between *Iwai* and *Bomai*. I will spell these out later in this chapter, but before I do it is necessary to establish a correspondence largely neglected in the literature. For while they transverse different paths and are thus cosmologically separated, *Shiveri* and *Iwai*, the two Aboriginal Heroes, share an almost identical ontological form. From this more fundamental perspective, it is *Shiveri* and *Iwai* who are 'the same'.

There is no need for me to relate the stories separately yet again. *Shiveri*'s tale has been told by McConnel, Thomson and Laade,[73] while that of *Iwai* can also be found in the works of the last two of these researchers. My composite presentation highlights what I believe to be the most significant episodes of their myths.

1. *The origins of the Heroes are unknown.* Of *Iwai* it is said, 'God been made him . . . He born on more other country . . . I don't know where he born and where he really been come from.[74] As this statement was a response to direct questioning, we may simply say origins are not relevant. Homes, however, are. Iwai's first home was a site on the Upper Pascoe River. *Shiveri*'s was on the north of Janie Creek. *Shiveri*'s maternal uncle, *Nyunggu*, inhabited the southern side of the creek.

2. Both Heroes are, *par excellence*, the *innovators of song and dance*. Shiveri 'did nothing but dance morning, noon and night'.[75] *Iwai*, as my opening quotation suggests, was always 'singin', singin', singin', singin', singin' '.[76] Both develop the initiatory cults associated with them, introducing the 'houses' (shelters), dress, masks and 'play' (ritual).

3. While still on the mainland, the Heroes *establish objects* which European history deem to be of *Melanesian origin*. Both make drums, found only in this region of Australia, and certainly introduced via the Islands. *Shiveri* also makes the bow and arrow, the double outrigger canoe and, as we have already noted, takes with him all the cultivated foods of the Islands.[77]

4. In both cases it is *a sexual infringement which dislodges them from their home*. *Iwai* takes Echidna's wife, cutting fat from her thighs, forming her vagina, and then raping her. *Shiveri* takes *Nyunggu*'s daughters. Fearing revenge, they flee; *Shiveri* to escape *Nyunggu*'s sons, *Iwai*, the people of the area – 'one big heap'.[78]

5. The Heroes *depart along rivers by canoes which are destroyed* or lost. *Iwai*'s, stolen from a relative, goes astray on his sojourns up the east coast. *Shiveri*'s crashed on Red Island, where it turned to stone.

6. Both *leave womenfolk behind*. *Shiveri* places *Nyunggu*'s daughters on islands, one because she has a sore breast, the other for an unspecified reason. *Iwai* leaves two girls on Quoin island because he is shamed when they discover the bullroarer.

7. After losing their canoes they *travel in their animal form*. *Shiveri* the seagull hops, creating islands wherever he touches down. *Iwai* attempts to persuade a skate, a cod, and a stingray to be his boat, but when these fail he becomes the crocodile-canoe upon whom his neophytes travel.

8. Finally, they *reach their new homes* at points almost exactly halfway between Australia and New Guinea. *Shiveri* goes to Mabuiag, *Iwai* to Mer. The locations are chosen in different manners. *Iwai* had periodically dived below the ocean surface to discover if he could hear his relatives. Only at Mer was he far enough away. *Shiveri* was actually intending to reach New Guinea, but was repelled by the inhabitants and so settles at Mabuiag (one might say *Iwai* goes until he is just far enough away, while *Shiveri* returns until he is just close enough). *Shiveri* is, however, never fully accepted, even though he marries and has a child. His 'hair is different'. 'Well, he make friends with those Mabuiag people. But in their hearts they never been friends – different race: Don't want him to breed there – but too late: his son already there'.[79] (*Nyunggu* is forced by his sons to pursue *Shiveri* and in fact does make his home in New Guinea.)

9. The Heroes *find an eternal home* on the island. *Shiveri*, in Australian versions of the myth, is killed. *Iwai* simply remains at Mer, and his drum may still be heard from the mainland, underwater or during dreams.

To grasp the significance of this composite summary it is once again helpful to contrast it with other Aboriginal stories dealing with outsiders. One Amagalyuagba myth central to their outlook,[80] which Turner has had occasion to suggest reflects the intrusion of Indonesians,[81] is particularly illuminating as it is an almost exact inversion of the Cape York Hero myths. As Turner has recounted the story several times,[82] I will simply note a few salient points. The myth of *Nambirrirrma* is about a man who, like *Iwai*, falls from God. He does not know where he belongs and hence to whom he is related, and the narrative is about how he finds his place within a pattern of places. He then marries correctly, has a child, and dies. (His son adds some discord to this order by marrying a relative who is a little too close.) Turner correctly suggests that when taken at face value this is a myth which dwells on how the unlanded are located within the country. If *Nambirrirrma* is a Macassan, then the story concerns the possibility of bringing strangers into the Aboriginal world-order. The whole tale contracts, bringing that from without into alignment with land and people.

Nambirrirrma offers one solution to one class of strangers: Lawful incorporation (although, as we will see, this was in practice never realised with Macassans). The Hero cults are the antithesis of this solution. Their structure expands, their theme is Lawful separation. The Heroes begin knowing their place and how they relate to those of other lands. Whereas *Nambirrirrma* ends with right place and right marriage, the Heroes breach these rules at the outset and cause a fragmentation of place. It must be stressed that such episodes cannot be reduced to mere examples for those who would flaunt moral codes,[83] as the Heroes, although pursued, are neither caught nor punished, and their infringement adds to, rather than detracts from, their sacred status. The Heroes' significance is as the founders of a Law, not its flaunters, and their transgressions are a means to a new order. Thereafter they expand the boundaries of the cosmos, giving 'otherness' itself a place within the Law.

The continuity of the cosmology must be stressed. It is not at all like those stories which tell of Whites, Indonesians and others belonging to an unknown distant domain, as the Heroes travel outwards to the Islanders' homes. *Shiveri* actually brings these into existence as he hops towards the north. *Iwai* does not create the islands in this fashion, but as he travels he does give meaning to the world by naming, and the places he visits thus receive sanction and significance. Although Mer was as yet unknown, *Iwai*'s searching was guided by an intuitive awareness of its direction. Billy Daniels chose precisely the right image to convey this to the European mind: 'He must have got chart'.[84] Within *Iwai* was the paradigm of the form of the world.

I am not so foolhardy as to offer an opinion on *the* meaning of the Hero stories but I have at least uncovered something unique in Australia in their understanding of space: an ontologic separation within a single cosmological field. Space is continuous, the 'same' Hero extends his path from place to place, and yet there is a separation. This will be analysed further in the next section, but already we have glimpsed the pattern. *Shiveri* was disliked by those already at Mabuiag because he had an (Aboriginal) appearance and the Islanders didn't want him to marry and 'breed'. His son, of mixed descent, is indeed a problem child according to Islander traditions, but more on this in a moment. The point to be made here is that the extended cosmos contains socio-geographic boundaries. Aborigines and Islanders not only belong to different places, but belong to place in different ways which make marriage alliances a dangerous option. As I have said and will continue to illustrate, ultimately the divide is between ontologies of space.

This helps to make sense of something which so disturbed Laade. Like so many scholars who have written on Cape York myths, Laade was fettered to the idea that Hero stories were a form of history, and where Aboriginal views failed to square with Western understandings of the past he could but conclude that Aboriginal myths were rather poor chronicles. Indeed, he seemed almost offended: 'To claim, as Dick Luff does, that all garden plants were carried from Cape York to New Guinea sounds both absurd and arrogant'.[85] Laade would like to dismiss Luff's account as aberrant, but then he too must dispose of other versions where *Shiveri* introduces the bow and arrow to the Islands, and so on (*supra*). If, however, we view the Hero myths not as history but as expressions of the basic order of their world, then the Aboriginal invention of Melanesian culture is an apt way of reinforcing the necessity of perpetuating the border between the Aboriginal and Islander plan of life. It is not so open-ended as a case of a missing aetiology for Islander ways; the Heroes' narratives state that these things were taken away so as to belong rightfully to another. The northern world is one to which Aborigines are tied, but which they can never subsume.

Once again, therefore, there is connection without union, a cosmic continuity which itself establishes a disjunction of being. It is now time to specify precisely what that rift reveals.

A WILD THROAT AND A HALF-WILD HEART

The essence of the Aboriginal Hero is song, and the essence of song is place. This is true for all Australia, but a nice example from Cape York is provided by the myth of *Iwai*. When his sojourn had just begun he encountered Eagle, who had travelled into the Hero's land. Billy Daniels described the encounter thus:

> Anyhow, he bump him that old crocodile . . . bump him. Him say, 'Eh, where you come from, inside our ground?' Him say, 'I come from Pascoe.' 'Have you got any Bora dance up down here?' Then the Eagle tell him, 'No. We got little bit but not that really.' 'Well, will you start that thing for me? I give you something: some sing.' He start him off sing belong one island, from Lockhart River, on other side of river. He say, 'Keep them sing and take him.'[86]

The implications of the meeting are quite clear: people outside their territory must know their true home. Intrusion is thus met with song. The myth does not say one cannot enter another's land, but rather that in doing so it is essential to understand one's own sacred links to country, and this is embodied in cultic-song. It is therefore entirely appropriate that *Iwai* gives Eagle the *Bora* song that provides him with an eternal connection to land.[87]

As I said when discussing the Heroes' stories, they were the quintessential innovators of ritual-songs. *Shiveri* would dance 'morning, noon and night' while *Iwai* created songs at almost every significant juncture of his journey. As songs and sites overlay one another,[88] the distribution of songs provides a foundation for a pattern of lands and, hence, interpersonal relationships. The structure of that pattern has already been discussed earlier in this chapter as well as in its predecessor, and here I simply remind readers that, insofar as the Aboriginal mode of spatial organisation federated people associated with sites into enduring and mutually interdependent lands, territorial warfare was virtually rendered an institutional impossibility.

Aboriginal song-land forms are therefore structured in a fashion quite opposed to those principles of warfare designed to allow the victor to subsume the land or being of the victim.

Let me now return to the issue of the 'sameness' of Aboriginal and Melanesian Heroes. I have argued for a cosmological continuity, but will now detail an ontological breach. For in the case of the *Shiveri-Kuiam* identity, the former is a song-maker, the latter a master of war. That the difference between song and slaughter has so often been overlooked should warn us that studies of the symbolism of Hero myths is particularly undeveloped. Such a glaring discrepancy could not go entirely unnoticed, however, and several scholars have at least noted it in passing. Haddon, who initially brought us the Mabuiag saga of the Hero, although in essential agreement with Thomson's view that *Shiveri* was *Kuiam I* (for in some accounts, as we will soon see, there are two *Kuiams*), was not without some reservations: 'The message of each [Hero] was different. It is quite evident that the headhunting and fierce war-like traits of . . . Kwaiam were not due to residence in Australia, they are typically Papuan.'[89]

Laade alone has stressed the differences between *Shiveri* and *Kuiam*, arguing their sole identity 'is most unlikely'.[90] I believe his either/or approach to sameness/difference lacks subtlety, but he has at least taken the contrasts seriously. *Kuiam*, he correctly notes, is an outstanding warrior 'and no such character can be found in an Australian tale. Moreover, he is a headhunter, and head-hunting is unknown in Cape York. In his fights, Kuiam behaves exactly like an island warrior'. In contrast, 'ceremonial dancing such as Shiveri used to perform at Janie Creek is absent from what Haddon calls the "Kuiam cult" of Mabuiag'. Alas, since Laade, like many others, is bound to the preconception that *Shiveri* and *Kuiam* were historical persons,[91] he can but conclude that they began as two entirely divorced legendary figures. To reiterate in slightly different form what I have already argued, my own view is that we are witnessing one myth with two meanings.

The myth of *Kuiam* has been recorded several times, the most authentic version having been handwritten late last century into a 281-page book, *Net Warian Polazinga. Muruigao Tusi. Lag Nel Mabuiagi* [Ned Waria's Writing. Old Man's Book. Place Name Mabuiag].[92] Other Mabuiag versions are Haddon's account, based on information from Papi, Ailumai, Nomoa, and Waria, and Lawrie's as related by Maurie Eseli, who had the benefits of her late father's written account.[93] Laade also adds some important myth fragments.[94]

While the exact location is open to some question, the people of Mabuiag agreed that *Kuiam* came from Cape York. He heads north, in one version somewhat randomly, following the direction of falling blades of grass. The Hero walks across the water to Mabuiag, bringing with him his spear and spearthrower. Reluctantly, the people there befriend him, and later he excels in a spearthrowing test of skill. His prowess so impresses *Kuiam* that she falls in love with him. As husband and wife they go to a place set apart on the island, but even so there is friction; he wants to sleep outdoors as Aborigines do, while she wishes to follow Island ways. *Kuiam* thus returns to the mainland, but his wife remains and gives birth to a son, also named *Kuiam*.

Kuiam I is indeed rather similar to *Shiveri*, and the splitting of *Kuiam* into two beings is perhaps a tidy means of radically changing a Hero whilst maintaining the continuity of the narrative tradition. *Kuiam I* is explicitly an Aborigine, and it is for this reason that he is never fully at home at Mabuiag. It is not his place and this results in gentle conflicts which are simply resolved by his return to the mainland. A happy ending, perhaps, except for his legacy: *Kuiam II*, who is the real focus of the Mabuiag cult.

Kuiam the son mysteriously inherits his father's interest in the Aboriginal spearthrower and with the aid of some charmed emblems he becomes virtually invincible; he was said to be like a rock upon whom the islanders crashed as waves. One day he visits his now old and blind mother and, not recognising him at first, she curses him, but apologises as soon as she recognises her error. Her son cannot be appeased, however, and he runs her through the eyes and mouth with a three-pronged spear. This horrendous crime is something he spends the rest of his days attempting to 'pay back' with a frenzy of killings.

Accompanied by his mother's brother, *Kuiam* journeys northwards, massacring the inhabitants of two islands and showing mercy only to those who display extreme subservience. 'I am like poison vines and bushes,' he says, 'killing all whom I touch.' Finally, his uncle and then *Kuiam* himself are defeated, but unlike *Kuiam's* own victims, the Hero's head is not taken. 'Kuiam's head was a good head, a head which teemed with ideas, a clever head . . . unlike ours, which are bad, useless, stupid heads.'[95]

The praise of these last words may surprise some readers, but *Kuiam* was a great man precisely because he took so many heads. Much of our information on headhunting is very equivocal as this was amongst the first things prohibited by colonial rule, but Zegwaard provides some insights based on his observations of its practice in southern New Guinea. He notes that the ultimate compliments are *juus aptsjam ipitsj* (man with soul), *nao pimir ipitsj* (man of frequent killings) and *kusfé juro ipitsj* (man with fine bunch of heads). The first is equivalent to the latter two, as a man who has taken no heads is 'nothing' or 'has no soul'.[96] In stark contrast to *Shiveri*'s, *Kuiam II*'s sacred status is derived not from his ability to sing meaning into place but rather his capacity to accrue power through slaughter.

And yet, even from a Melanesian perspective, there is something excessive and even purposeless in *Kuiam*'s actions. Says Madu Paul of Muralag, 'Kuiam only big name for fight. He no make anything good: he [got] no property, nothing', of which Laade observes that this is about the worst that can be said of a person as the passage refers to a failure to cultivate *garden* land.[97] The ambiguity in *Kuiam II* is that he seems to incorporate power through warfare but does not put this power into any positive creative form, and, in particular, the control of land.

To appreciate the religious–economic significance of *Kuiam*'s symbolism it will be necessary to venture a little further into Melanesian thought. When discussing the 'ideology' of headhunting, Zegwaard stressed cosmological, economic and other factors, emphasising that 'the motives for headhunting are many, and they are undoubtedly interwoven'.[98] Trompf, in a most insightful forthcoming book, entitled *Payback*, makes this point more strongly. Including the taking of heads as a form of negative retribution, he shows

> that retributive actions – to pay back the enemy or punish some offender – constitute powerful expressions and integral parts of tribal religious life. It is simply not feasible to dissociate Melanesian war from Melanesian traditional religion; the two were interlocked – just as so-called 'economic' and 'political' forms have been 'religious'.[99]

The most common explicit reason given for warfare in Melanesia is disputes over garden land or theft of domestic animals,[100] but theorists miss their mark if they reduce this to mere economics. Nor, on the other hand, need we resort to theoretically bland and culturally insensitive dogmas, such as Hallpike's conclusion about a people he so patently disliked: 'they killed, and still do kill, for the pleasure of killing'.[101]

As is the case in Aboriginal Australia, we find in Melanesia an ontologic link between 'religion' and 'economics' in attitudes towards space and in images of how persons stand in relation to their world. Identity, in both its social and geographical dimensions, rests on an understanding that, as Trompf argues, 'what is essential to "salvation" is the strength to succeed in the fight against others: in pidjin *strong bilong winim arapela long pait*'; again, in a slightly different form, 'survive or be struck down'. Trompf locates such views within the Melanesian vision of socio-geographic space, of an 'otherness' and 'self' in which patterns of ill-blood sustain and strengthen identity: 'Blood vengeance [is] central in cultivating a logical basis for collective action'.[102]

More fundamentally, what is articulated by such a worldview is the notion that a person or group can add to itself by subtracting from others; what Turner describes as a 'locality-incorporative' model of existence.[103] The explicit economic causes of warfare over property disputes expresses the constant awareness that land can be appropriated, but more broadly this stems from the recognition that one's place in the cosmos is not eternally fixed and that one can incorporate another's land, spirit, substance and being.

Kuiam was a headhunter; he subsumed the essence of others. Zegwaard's detailed study reveals this as the key symbolic value of the practice. The Asmat seek heads on ritual occasions, especially during the initiation of their own clan members. The neophyte is identified with the victim, taking on his or her name. The person to be attacked is spoken to as a woman, and the head is later placed almost touching the youth's penis in a symbolic sexual union. Eating the beheaded is the ultimate culmination of these images. Quite simply, the enemy's very being is taken over. The motivation for a raid may at one level be said to be to appease the dead clan members, but as such spiritual lineages pass back to the Ancestor who selected a site it can simultaneously be argued that 'the main background of head-hunting seems to be safe-guarding the territory'.[104] Put positively, headhunting asserts that it is possible to take over the land/being of others in order to add to the power of one's own existence. In some Melanesian traditions the position that one's own group cannot continue without 'eating' the other is taken to its logical conclusion. Killing others becomes a prerequisite for procreation.[105]

This brings my discussion back full circle to the principles previously established in this book. The Aboriginal understanding was that people participated in spirit in the land of which they were but a manifestation. Fertility was also dependent upon the land-spirit, aided by the ritual of its human custodians. I have suggested why neolithic principles posed a dilemma for Aborigines, and the practice of headhunting is one of its clearest symbolic forms. It states unambiguously that land boundaries are fragile – easily threatened and in need of constant vigilance, and that even if it is not necessary to take over another people's land *per se*, it is at least unavoidable that one's own group's spiritual continuity depends upon drawing off the power of others, of their lineage, and ultimately, of their place.

Kuiam, the headhunter, however, is also very Aboriginal. More correctly, he is a Melanesian image of an Aboriginal Hero. He has Australian features and personality. Haddon was told that, although not the case in recent times, 'the mainlanders [used to] fight all the time just like Kwaiam'. They had a 'wild throat and a half-wild heart'. There is no doubt that Aborigines can respond violently when their territories are infringed upon, but *Kuiam*'s methods of warfare are always distinctly Melanesian. If by 'wildness' we read 'according to principles we do not recognise', then it seems the problem *Kuiam* introduces is that he plays the game of warfare without its rules. He begins poorly, killing his mother who, of course, is far too close to be a legitimate victim. All his subsequent killings are based on that error. 'I think Kwaiam will kill me to pay for his mother'; 'Now he has killed his mother he will kill us all soon.'[106] His is a wild killing and it is thus that he does not benefit from the process. He does not incorporate the powers or essence of those he slaughters; and ultimately he does not establish his place – to repeat the phrase already quoted: 'Kuiam only big name for fight: he [got] no property, nothing'.

The final message the myth of *Kuiam* gives is perhaps the limit of Melanesian ontology. It states from an Islander perspective the incompatibility of their world with that of the mainland. The Melanesian principles of warfare are fundamentally at odds with the Aboriginal assertion of the immutable ties between lands, powers, and peoples. An Australian participation in Islander warfare is nothing but wildness; violence without purpose, the taking of life without the capacity to use it creatively within one's own group. The conclusion of the myth of *Kuiam* hints at its overall significances, for when the Hero is himself at last defeated and the knife drawn to remove his head, the butchering is stopped: 'Don't, that's a proper head'.[107] *Kuiam's* essence is not taken, and his Australian weapons are thrown back to the mainland. As Mulvaney observes, 'Incidents after his death are suggestive of the Australian–Papuan dichotomy. His spear and spear-thrower were hurled south towards Australia, and a warrior who began to decapitate Kwoiam was ordered to leave his body intact'.[108]

I will not linger long on an analysis of other myths on Melanesian-Australian relationships as they do not reflect the critical associations revealed in the stories analysed thus far. The *Bomai–Iwai* path is primarily of significance in that they meet from opposite directions but fail to become mythologically continuous. When they are said to be the 'same', it is as an inverted image which in fact only serves to emphasise differences. There was less tension along the eastern story line and the respective domains seemed to maintain a discreet distance with far less effort. It was the western associations which were more intense and culturally ambiguous, and it is precisely because of this that the *Shiveri–Kuiam* traditions are the most revealing of all. Whilst stretching taut one common mythic path they also, and at the same time, erect a boundary. From the Australian perspective, *Shiveri*, like *Iwai*, ensures that there is a Lawful and enduring spatial separation, whereas *Kuiam* acknowledges that, although the Melanesian's southern neighbours are people to whom they may relate and even be related, Aborigines would always be, from the point of view of those who fought for their very being, a people who were without order and hence wild.

Having begun this chapter with the problem of agriculture, and having argued this was in fact a problem of being, I have now come to the point of specifying precisely how the divergence between Melanesian and Australian ontologies is embedded in myth. It is time, therefore, to leave the Islands and the frontier of two worlds and instead return to focus on some broader consequences of the arrival of the Hero tradition. In particular, with an Ancestral figure of such wideranging significance, how is it possible to stop him shaking himself free of the world and becoming a Transcendental Being?

TRANSCENDING TRANSCENDENCE

While the myths of the Heroes are important expressions of an underlying philosophy of a people's relationship to space, it is only when we examine these and other beliefs in the context of ritual practice that a balanced picture emerges. Specifically, it is essential to ascertain how people were located in the world after they had encountered Melanesians. How did their spirits relate to their lands? How was northern Cape York socio-religiously demarcated? And what were the territorial implications of having introduced the Heroes?

To answer such questions it is necessary to keep in mind that model of a widely distributed and, it seems, once trans-Aboriginal understanding of ubiety or being-in-place which was discussed in the preceding chapter. Before I proceed it will not be out of place to recall some of the salient features of that standard.

Stanner once put on record what he saw as the basic plan of Aboriginal ontology throughout the continent. He wrote:

> If Aboriginal culture had an architectonic idea I would say that it was a belief that all living people, clan by clan, or lineage by lineage, were linked patrilineally with ancestral beings by inherent and imperishable bonds through the territories and totems which were either the handiwork or parts or the continuing being of the ancestors themselves.[109]

The patrilineality was both widespread and significant, but not, strictly speaking, paradigmatic, for as I argued in chapter 1 it was consequent upon an adjustment to the truly trans-Aboriginal *'Oedipus Australis* project', which had denied birth from mother in order to affirm birth from land. Perhaps, as we have seen, it was at first the case that people were recruited to those lodges directly associated with the place where their mother first felt herself to be pregnant, but more often than not, as Stanner suggests, this was expressed in terms of patrilineality. A transitionary case may actually be observed in Cape York.

Sharp wrote, 'since the responsible ancestor sends "spirit children" only to the countries of his own clan in his own tribe, the resultant offspring is affiliated with the clan in whose country the natural agent was "found". With the aid of various obvious fictions, the "spirit child" is usually found in the clan country of the child's real father.'[110] Despite Sharp's loaded terminology, it is here at least clear that patrilineality did not place emphasis on the body and biology as identity-makers, as birth-from-womb links do. Rather it directed the focus towards sites. What was said to be important was not the patrilineality *per se*, but lands with which people so happened to share a patri-heritage. The fundamental element, therefore, is not the affiliation of people with other people but of *people* with their sites. Again, in Stanner's words,

> The conception I have formed can be put simply. There are two data to which Aboriginal life conformed: a cosmic datum and a social datum. Under the cosmology a soul, which could never die, entered a human being. Under the same cosmology soul and human host were linked insolubly until the host died. When death came, a man's undying soul and his bones or ashes completed the cycle by returning to his 'bone or soul country'. Under this religious system human society and cosmos were made and kept co-relative.[111]

Precisely this model of the spirit emerging from a place and thence returning to it, thereby affirming the authority of a fixed and permanent cosmic form which regulates life, is evidently present in Cape York. Clearly, this region once shared fully the basic ontologic pattern outlined in my opening chapter. While authors have quibbled over semantics regarding the existence of an ideology of 'reincarnation', it is plain that there is a self-sustaining balance between the spirits emanating from a site and those returning to it upon death. Thus, for example, McConnel argues that the Ancestral essences or *pulwaiya*[112] emerge from their home and that the spirits of the dead return to this place. She concludes that 'the dead eventually become the pulwaiya' and hence ensure the homeostasis of the sacred power of a place. Add to this the fact that cult groups are all patrilineal in Cape York,[113] and it seems we have arrived back at Stanner's 'architectonic idea'.

Life principles, like linguistic elements,[114] reveal that Cape traditions were once very close indeed to those observed in central Australia. There were, however, cardinal variations such that the 'normal' arrangements stand out like peaks in a rising tide of innovation. The first is that in the lower parts of the Peninsula and the Gulf region it was often stated that spirits did *not* return to their home upon death. Our data for this region are decidedly imperfect, but solid enough to confirm that here we witness the place-less destiny for spirits which I discuss at length in the next chapter. There is no need to detail this now, and I will simply offer enough evidence to show that this is no more than a very northerly instance of that innovation which emerged in the south-east as a consequence to invasion.

It was Lauriston Sharp who brought this 'aberration' to our attention,[115] and Sharp's main sources were Edward Palmer, Francis Richards and Walter Roth. Richards gives us little but the bare inessentials regarding the fate of the Koko-Wagara spirits, but he does provide an all-important context. At the time of his research, this was an area of anti-White and quasi-millennial sentiments, indicating a region responding to the severe effects of invasion (I discuss his data more fully in chapter 5).[116] Again, Palmer's Maykulan data seem to be a northerly manifestation of the All-Father scenario: 'They do not fix the [home of the dead] anywhere, only say it is far away somewhere, and they think it among the stars'.[117] There they travelled along roads and ladders. Palmer rightly plots a continuum from this view to those of New South Wales. As for Roth, he is explicit: the spirit of Aborigines in the Cape Bedford region 'travels in the direction of the east, and enters a white person'.[118]

I will discuss the significance of such views in the next chapter, where they properly belong. They are beliefs which spread increasingly throughout Australia, and even Sharp's own Yir Yiront data seem touched by them. His is a sad image. The dead must depart for an unknown land, but some wish instead to return so that they might be reborn in their own land. These are the spirits of babies stillborn or miscarried.

In contrast, in the north of Cape York there are other, subtler variations on the 'architectonic' theme, which relate directly to Islander influence and ultimately bring us back to the Heroes. As I have said, the *cultic* unit in this area, as in all the Cape, was patrilineal, but at the very tip of Australia and a little way down the east coast – the very areas with the most intense contrasts with Islanders – it is said that the spirit which enters a body and returns to its place upon death actually emanates from the person's mother's territory. While the lodges *per se* are patrilineal, the powers of such groups are weakened by the fact that a human's very being, the place they visit in dreams throughout life and to which their spirit returns upon death, is determined matrilineally.

This shift might easily be dismissed as a random local quirk. Thomson, enthusiastically but at times somewhat over-dramatically, thought otherwise: 'Evidence is not lacking for the belief that there has been extensive invasion, or invasions, of culture, and it seems probable that the motives of Cape York were originally matrilineal and were invaded by a patrilineal people'.[119] There is, of course, no evidence of 'invasion', but more to the point McConnel reminded Thomson that as the unusual matrilineal elements were a small apex of a region otherwise patrilineal, 'it would be the matrilineal rather than the patrilineal organisation that was "superimposed" '.[120]

In the last analysis, McConnel wonders if the issue is significant in terms of cultural contact at all, as matrilineal links are widely distributed in Australia. In this she was partially correct. No one could deny the importance of matrilineality, and even associations with a mother's land. But these are not the same as postulating an ontologic root in, and an identity of, being with one's Mother's land.

The problem, however, with Thomson's thesis of 'invasion', even after we have corrected the arrangement of his term, is that the Islanders themselves did not have such a matrilineal system. Perhaps, though, 'borrowing' is the wrong image to pursue, for as Hart and Pilling noted in another distinctive case amongst the Tiwi, it was the encounter of two patrilineal peoples that had disrupted old principles and caused a necessary readjustment and a shift to matrilineality.[121]

A clue to why this may have occurred in Cape York is to be found in Thomson's data. He illustrates the fact that patrilineal 'clan totems' still direct territorial organisation and 'increase' ceremonies,[122] but even though these were called *gola* (father's father) at the time of his research they did not regulate spiritual descent, which was determined through the *ngartjimo* (mother's father). Only the latter are hedged by taboos; they brim with spiritual power. All the patrilineal 'clan totems', on the other hand, were relatively free from this numinosity that required such careful handling. All of them, that is, save one – the Hero.

There were dangers in the Hero's powers, and had these been allowed to be contained patrilineally, they might well have escalated. This is perhaps even evident in Islander images of Aboriginal power. As Haddon notes, in the myth *Kuiam* the warrior is associated only with his mother and mother's brother,[123] and yet though he never even sees his father, who belongs to another land, it is his father's spiritual energy (associated with the spear and spearthrower) which is somehow passed on to the son, and which gives rise to his terrifying behaviour. *Kuiam* drew on an uncanny link with his father's spiritual power. How much more worrying were this to have been institutionalised.

Shifting the locus of ontologic vitality to matri-lands which crossed and diffused the territory defining cultic patri-units would certainly curtail the Hero's supremacy. And a Supreme Being he might have become, since his site was a sacred centre 'for the tribe as a whole'.[124] As it was, however, he added his own contribution to solving the 'Melanesian problem' whilst leaving unaltered a basic pattern of land-based plurality. All the evidence points to the fact that the patri-lodges could continue to perform a multitude of interdependent rituals for cosmic balance ('increase' rituals)[125] and that, with the same diffusion of lodge power, there was a minimum of disruption to the pre-existing order.

The genius of the arrangement was that although *Shiveri* and *Iwai* both had a pan-Aboriginal significance insofar as they demarcated the essence of the Aboriginal against the Melanesian world, they never became transcendental beings. Clearly, things could have gone otherwise. *Iwai* had begun to take on the qualities of a Melanesian 'big man'. Other Ancestors were merely his 'helpers'.[126] Harry Siyu put it thus: 'Alligator [*Iwai*] he just like boss of (all) Bora'[127] and Laade adds there is almost a cosmic hierarchy developing. *Shiveri* too had taken on this potentially dominating position.[128]

The relationship between the Heroes and other Ancestral beings is particularly important. Thomson wavers between models of superimposition and juxtaposition. In the latter case, he notes that Koko Yao initiation ceremonies are of two kinds. Those instigated by *Iwai* (*Okainta*) are naturally his cult, but the *Mon'ka* ceremonies are associated with others, notably the trans-Aboriginal serpent, and are believed by Thomson to represent the pre-Melanesian tradition. Given that the Hero's cults are associated with Islander drums, masks, clubhouse-like huts, and songs,[129] this seems to at least contain some truth.

Once again, however, I would stress that we must avoid images of either passive superimposition or unintegrated juxtaposition. Instead, there appears to have been a careful, creative working of old practices into new ceremonial forms. The issue is not just that of old and new or first and later, but rather the locative and place-bound in relation to that which could potentially transcend the geo-social order. McConnel shied from the latter possibility, thinking it simply too un-Aboriginal,[130] but in reality her own data do little to disincline us to accept Thomson's position that the cult of *Iwai* 'is non-totemic' and has been married to 'a totemic culture in which it belongs not to one clan or moiety, but to the tribe as a whole. The cult associated with it is practiced by all the clans of the tribe, and this forms a basis for tribal rather than clan solidarity'.[131] Instead of having gone too far, Thomson has not gone far enough, for Laade rightly reminds us that Iwai's cult was trans-'tribal', binding together various linguistic groups. Indeed, it was *Iwai* who made these linguistic divisions as he transversed the areas involved, and all participants in his cult look to him as their common ritual founder.[132]

In contrast to the significance of their stories, however, *Iwai* and *Shiveri* themselves are not ubiquitous. In this sense, they are a part of the locative religious order. *Iwai*'s story place was unusually powerful and sacred, but rites performed at his place were only ever performed by the patri-group of that area.[133] *Iwai* was therefore simultaneously both the wayfarer who expanded space and a being bound by place. Thomson seems to be grasping rather awkwardly to make just this point:

> The new cult of I'wai with its localized centre on the Upper Pascoe must therefore have tended to weaken the totemic cult for all but one clan . . . The cult of I'wai is non-totemic, but has acquired a totemic significance for one clan only.[134]

McConnel felt the assertion that the Heroes were both 'totemic' and 'non-totemic', 'clan'-based and [trans]-'tribal' to be downright contradictory; and she is no doubt correct, but the contradiction seems to result from an Aboriginal paradox rather than an ethnographic blunder. After all, is McConnel not making a statement akin to the one she criticises when she says 'though totemic in structure like those from southern tribes which follow, it affords a link between the latter and the Torres Strait Islands and Papua, where legends are predominantly heroic and the totemic element is lacking or surpassed'?[135] Surely that 'link' must be precisely the trans-territorial elements to which Thomson alluded.

McConnel is nevertheless correct in reining in Thomson's tendency to overstate the evidence. There was no evidence that the Hero had invasively subjugated 'totemic' traditions. The evidence reveals that the broader pluralistic site-based associations were entirely healthy, and it is precisely this factor which makes this region an important yardstick against which to measure the effects of true invasion upon Aboriginal spiritual life. To a remarkable degree the Heroes left the original Australian order in place, yet at the same time introduced a new element which, whilst never abandoning the known world, broadened the boundaries of the cosmos and introduced something of a pan-Aboriginal Law standing separated from, but not opposed to, the Melanesian world.

Had Cape York Aborigines needed a warning as to what might befall a Hero who had freed himself from the immanence of their eternal lands, they need only have looked northwards to the western islands where 'totemic' principles were under threat,[136] or to the eastern islands, where land had cast its immutability aside and *Bomai* had ascended to the status of the Supreme Being.[137]

And failing that, were they were bold enough, they might have looked to the south.

NOTES

1. W. Laade, 'Notes on the Boras at Lockhart River Mission, Cape York Peninsula, North-East Australia', *Archiv für Völkerkunde*, 24 (1970), pp. 277, 278 & 279. My arrangement of paragraphs.
2. e.g. F.D. McCarthy, 'The Oceanic and Indonesian Affiliations of Australian Aboriginal Culture', *The Journal of the Polynesian Society*, 62 (1953), pp. 243-61; and 'Aboriginal Australian Material Culture: Causative Factors in its Composition', *Oceania*, 2 (1940), pp. 241-69; 294-320 & 268 ff; R. Hamlyn-Harris, 'Some Evidence of Papuan Culture on Cape York Peninsula', *Memoirs of the Queensland Museum*, 3 (1915), pp. 10-13; & 'Some Anthropological Considerations of Queensland and the History of its Ethnography', *Proceedings of the Royal Society of Queensland*, 29 (1917), pp. 1-44; W.H. Thorpe, 'Some New Guinea Cultural Influences found Amongst the Aborigines of Australia', *Report of the Australian Association for the Advancement of Science*, 17 (1924), pp. 491-4.
3. G. Elliot Smith, 'On the Significance of the Geographical Distribution of the Practice of Mummification: A Study of the Migrations of Peoples and the Spread of Certain Customs and Beliefs', *Memoirs and Proceedings of the Manchester Literary and Philosophical Society*, 59 (1915), pp. 1-143; W.J. Perry, *The Children of the Sun: A Study in the Early History of Civilization* (London: Methuen, 1923).
4. M. Eliade, *Birth and Rebirth: The Religious Meaning of Initiation in Human Culture* (London: Harvill Press, 1958), pp. 99-100.
5. Thorpe, op. cit., p. 491.
6. Hamlyn-Harris, 'Some Anthropological Considerations of Queensland . . .', p. 29.
7. W.R. Dawson, 'Mummification in Australia and America', *Journal of the Royal Anthropological Institute of Great Britain and Ireland*, 58 (1928), pp. 114-38.

8. cit. W. Laade, 'The Torres Strait Islanders' Own Traditions About Their Origins', *Ethnos* 1-4 (1968), p. 141.
9. e.g. F. Gräbner, 'Melanesische Kultur in Nord-Ost-Australien', *Ethnologica*, 2 (1913), pp. 15-24.
10. M. Foucault, *Discipline and Punish: The Birth of the Prison* (Harmondsworth: Penguin, 1979), p. 11.
11. D.J. Mulvaney, *Encounters in Place: Outsiders and Aboriginal Australians 1606-1985* (St Lucia: University of Queensland Press, 1989), p. 61.
12. R.L. Vanderwal, 'The Torres Strait: Protohistory and Beyond', *Occasional Papers of the Anthropology Museum, University of Queensland*, 2 (1973), pp. 186-7.
13. Mulvaney, op. cit., p. 61.
14. Laade, op. cit., pp. 151-2.
15. Laade, ibid., *passim*, says the Islanders themselves suggest their origins are either New Guinea or, in some cases, Polynesia. For my purposes, it is not necessary to make a Melanesian/Polynesian distinction and, as to whether there is real substance to the distinction at all, see N. Thomas, 'The Force of Ethnography: Origins and Significance of the Melanesian/Polynesian Division', *Current Anthropology*, 30 (1989), pp. 27-41.
16. Hamlyn-Harris, op. cit., p. 10.
17. McCarthy, 'Aboriginal Australian Material Culture', pp. 241-2. Cf. P.M. Worsley, 'The Utilization of Food Resources by an Australian Aboriginal Tribe', *Acta Ethnographica*, 1-2 (1961), p. 178.
18. J.P. White, 'New Guinea and Australian Prehistory: The "Neolithic Problem"', in *Aboriginal Man and Environment in Australia*, edited by D.J. Mulvaney & J. Golson (Canberra: Australian National University Press, 1971), p. 184.
19. D.R. Moore, 'Cape York Aborigines and Islanders of Western Torres Strait', in *Bridge and Barrier*, edited by Walker, pp. 333 & (cit.) 341.
20. White, op. cit., p. 183.
21. J.M. Creed, 'Aborigines of the North Coast of Australia', *Journal of the Anthropological Institute of Great Britain and Ireland*, 7 (1878), p. 267.
22. U.H. McConnel, 'Totemic Hero-Cults in Cape York Peninsula, North Queensland', *Oceania*, I, no. 6 (1936), pp. 452-77; II, no. 7 (1936), pp. 69-105, 78; Hamlyn-Harris, op. cit., p. 10.
23. D. F. Thomson, 'The Hero Cult, Initiation and Totemism on Cape York', *Journal of the Royal Anthropological Institute of Great Britain and Ireland*, 63 (1933), p. 468.
24. W. Laade, 'Further Material on Kuiam, Legendary Hero of Mabuiag, Torres Strait Islands', *Ethnos* 1-4 (1967), p. 73.
25. W.E.H. Stanner, *On Aboriginal Religion*, The Oceania Monographs, no. 11 (Sydney: University of Sydney, 1959-61), p. 88, n. 9.
26. M. Sahlins, *Stone Age Economics* (London: Tavistock, 1974), chapter 1. Note that Sahlins' calculations for time spent by Aborigines on

108   *A place for strangers*

subsistence (pp. 14 ff.) do not include periods for ritual maintenance of the environment.

27. Moore, op. cit., p. 142.
28. Even at the Ancestral level this is true. The Hero *Iwai* invented cults but other beings were 'working for him'. Yet this work is 'play'. Clearly, Western terminology makes distinctions Aborigines do not employ. (Thomson, op. cit., pp. 461-2.)
29. M.J. Meggitt, 'Aboriginal Food Gatherers of Tropical Australia', in *The Ecology of Man in the Tropical Environment*, edited by H. Elliot (Morges: International Union for the Conservation of Nature, 1964), p. 35.
30. D.H. Turner, *Return to Eden: A Journey Through the Promised Landscape of Amagalyuagba* (New York: Peter Lang, 1989), pp. 280 & 285.
31. ibid., chapter 5 & pp. 147ff. See my review of Turner's book in *Method and Theory in the Study of Religion*, 1 (1989), pp. 231-5. Having found the boundaries did not have substance at the ecological level, Turner rightly shows they were manifest at a philosophical level. But he also suggests they exist at a metaphysical level (as 'forms'). I am agnostic on this latter point, and certainly it is necessary to neither my nor his main argument.
32. J.C. Beaglehole (ed.), *The Voyages of Captain James Cook* (Cambridge: Cambridge University Press: 1955), vol. 1, p. 396. The relevant words were: 'We never saw one inch of cultivated land in the whole country'.
33. J. Locke, *Two Treatises of Government* (Cambridge: Cambridge University Press, 1960 [1690]), chapter 5, 'Of Property', p. 306.
34. The inappropriateness of 'increase' is made apparent by Thomson, op. cit., pp. 501 & 503-4, where he notes some rituals inhibit overabundant species. The point, obviously, is to maintain a cosmic balance. See also McConnel, op. cit., p. 456.
35. A.C. Haddon, 'Magic and Religion', in *Reports of the Cambridge Anthropological Expedition to Torres Straits: Volume V: Sociology, Magic and Religion of the Western Islands*, edited by A.C. Haddon (Cambridge: University Press, 1904), pp. 345-8.
36. This is a general conceit. Haddon's expedition of 1898, and volume I of *Reports of the Cambridge Anthropological Expedition* provide a convenient overview of their findings and the division of the cultural areas of the Torres Strait which the expedition's reports first systematised. See also D.R. Moore, *The Torres Strait Collection of A.C. Haddon* (London: The Trustees of the British Museum, 1984).
37. J. Beckett, 'The Torres Strait Islanders', in *Bridge and Barrier*, edited by N. Walker, pp. 320 & 321-2.
38. T.G. Harding, 'Land Tenure', in *Anthropology of Papua New Guinea*, edited by I. Hogbin (Melbourne: Melbourne University Press, 1973), p. 111.
39. There is no unambiguous evidence as to whether there has been, in places, an Australisation of an originally Melanesian people, a

Melanesianisation of an Australian culture, or both. From the linguistic perspective, S.A. Wurm, 'Torres Strait – A Linguistic Barrier', in *Bridge and Barrier*, edited by N. Walker, pp. 345–66, succeeds primarily in conveying the futility of any simple answer. Nonetheless, quite apart from other considerations, Turner's view (*Return to Eden*, p. 281) that the world perhaps historically fell from the grace of Australia is certainly provocative.

40. Beckett, op. cit., p. 324.
41. R.L. Sharp, 'Tribes and Totemism in North-East Australia', *Oceania*, 9 (1939), pp. 255 & 258.
42. cit. A. Wilkin, 'Land Tenure and Inheritance at Mabuiag', in *Reports of the Cambridge Anthropological Expedition to Torres Straits: Volume V: Sociology, Magic and Religion of the Western Islands*, edited by A.C. Haddon (Cambridge: University Press, 1904), p. 285, n. 1.
43. In D.R. Moore, *Islanders and Aborigines at Cape York: An Ethnographic Reconstruction based on the 1848–1850 'Rattlesnake' Journals of O.W. Brierly and Information He Obtained from Barbara Thompson*. (Canberra: Australian Institute of Aboriginal Studies, 1979), pp. 171–2.
44. ibid., p. 262.
45. F.D. McCarthy, '"Trade" in Aboriginal Australia and "Trade" Relationships with Torres Strait, New Guinea and Malaya', *Oceania*, 9 (1939), pp. 405–38; 10 (1939); pp. 80–104 & 179–83.
46. The pioneering study for Australia was L.R. Hiatt, *Kinship and Conflict: A Study of an Aboriginal Community in Northern Arnhem Land*. (Canberra: Australian National University, 1965). His focus is on conflict to maintain socio-political law but it equally addresses, by implication, the use of conflict to maintain the Law. For Melanesia see G.W. Trompf, *Payback: The Logic of Retribution in Melanesian Religions* (forthcoming), *passim*.
47. Trompf, ibid., pp. 28 ff. of ms.
48. In Moore, *Islanders and Aborigines . . .*, p. 197.
49. Turner, *Return to Eden*, pp. 285–6.
50. e.g. Thomson, 'The Hero Cult . . .', p. 468, notes spears that he could not purchase no matter how high his offer, yet which were passed on to other Aborigines.
51. Moore, 'Cape York Aborigines: Fringe Participants in the Torres Strait Trading System', *Mankind*, 11 (1978) p. 321.
52. In Moore, *Islanders and Aborigines*, p. 233.
53. Moore, 'Cape York Aborigines: Fringe Participants . . .', p. 322.
54. Chuang-Tzu, in A.C. Graham, *Chuang-Tzu: The Inner Chapters* (London: Unwin, 1981), p. 52.
55. Hui Shih, the famous Chinese 'sophist', was Chuang-Tzu's friend and intellectual protagonist.
56. Thomson, 'The Hero Cult . . .', pp. 461–2.
57. Laade, 'Notes on the Boras . . .', p. 283.

58. C.G. Seligman, 'An Australian Bible Story', *Man*, 16 (1916), p. 44.
59. J.R. von Sturmer, 'The Wik Region: Economy, Territoriality and Totemism in Western Cape York Peninsula, North Queensland' (Ph.D. thesis: University of Queensland, 1978), pp. 366-8.
60. J. Taylor, 'Gods and Goods: A Follow-Up Study of "Steel Axes for Stone Age Australians"', in *Aboriginal Australians and Christian Missions: Ethnographic and Historical Studies*, edited by T. Swain and D. Rose (Adelaide: Australian Association for the Study of Religion, 1988), pp. 441-2.
61. D.F. Thomson, 'The Masked Dancers of I'wai'i: A Remarkable Hero Cult which has Invaded Cape York Peninsula', *Walkabout*, 23 (1956), pp. 15-19. Equally sensationalistic and inaccurate is his title 'The Secret Cult of I'wai, the Crocodile: An Australian Aboriginal "Mystery" of Papuan Origin', *The Illustrated London News* (23 July 1938), pp. 166-9.
62. McConnel, 'Totemic Hero-Cults . . .', p. 88.
63. In Laade, 'Further Material on Kuiam . . .', p. 71.
64. D.F. Thomson, 'Sivirri and Adi Kwoiam: A Culture Hero from Western Cape York Who Invaded Torres Strait and Died a Warrior Hero', *Walkabout*, 23 (1957), pp. 16-18.
65. McConnel, 'Totemic Hero-Cults . . .', p. 78.
66. G. Landtman, *The Folk-Tales of the Kiwai Papuans*. Aeta Societatis Scientiarum Fennicae, vol. 47 (Helsingfors: Finnish Society of Literature, 1917), pp. 152-9. For Islanders' versions, from just off the New Guinea coast, see W. Laade, *Oral Traditions and Written Documents on the History and Ethnography of the Northern Torres Strait Islands, Saibai-Dauan-Boigu: Vol. 1, Adi-Myths, Legends, Fairy Tales* (Wiesbaden: Franz Steiner, 1971), pp. 9-11.
67. See H. Kitaoji, 'The Myth of Bomai: Its Structure and Contemporary Significance for the Murray Islanders, Torres Strait', *Japanese Journal of Ethnography*, 42 (1977), pp. 209-24. It is significant that Kitaoji sees the myth as dealing with issues such as private vs. communal property, as well as Islander vs. New Guinean traditions.
68. Another New Guinean Hero, *Sida*, passes Mer and thence returns to the Trans-Fly region in the northern direction that *Iwai* was travelling (Haddon, *Reports of the Cambridge Anthropological Expedition*, vol. 1., pp. 374-80) but I know of no indigenous equation of these figures.
69. Haddon, 'Magic and Religion', p. 374.
70. A.C. Haddon and C.S. Myers, 'The Cult of Bomai and Malu', in *Reports of the Cambridge Anthropological Expedition to Torres Straits: Volume VI: Sociology, Magic and Religion of the Eastern Islands*, edited by A.C. Haddon (Cambridge: Cambridge University Press, 1908), p. 291.
71. M. Lawrie, *Myths and Legends of Torres Strait* (St Lucia: University of Queensland Press, 1970), p. 326.

72. A.C. Haddon, *Reports of the Cambridge Anthropological Expedition: Volume I: General Ethnography* (Cambridge: Cambridge University Press, 1935), p. 393.
73. McConnel, 'Totemic Hero-Cults . . .', pp. 72-7, retold in *Myths of the Mungkan* (Melbourne: Melbourne University Press, 1957), pp. 20-7; D.F. Thomson, 'Notes on a Hero Cult from the Gulf of Carpentaria, North Queensland', *Journal of the Royal Anthropological Insitute of Great Britain and Ireland*, 64 (1934), p. 226; Laade, 'Further Material on Kuiam . . .', *passim*.
74. Laade, 'Notes on the Boras . . .', p. 277.
75. Thomson, 'The Hero Cult . . .', pp. 463-7; Laade, 'Notes on the Boras . . .', pp. 274-91.
76. Laade, 'Notes on the Boras . . .', p. 276.
77. McConnel, 'Totemic Hero-Cults . . .', p. 73.
78. Laade, 'Notes on the Boras . . .', p. 277.
79. Laade, 'Further Material on Kuiam . . .', p. 72.
80. Turner, *Return to Eden*, p. 87.
81. D.H. Turner, *Dialectics in Tradition: Myth and Social Structure in Two Hunter-Gatherer Societies*, Occasional Paper no. 36 of the Royal Anthropological Institute of Great Britain and Ireland (London: The Royal Anthropological Institute, 1978).
82. These are noted in D.H.Turner, 'The Incarnation of Nambirrirrma', in *Aboriginal Australians and Christian Missions*, edited by Swain and Rose, pp. 470-1.
83. On this view of myth in Aboriginal Studies, see my *Interpreting Aboriginal Religion*, pp. 112-14.
84. Laade, 'Notes on the Boras . . .', p. 279.
85. Laade, 'Further Material on Kuiam . . .', p. 79.
86. Laade, 'Notes on the Boras . . .', pp. 276-7. This episode does not appear in Thomson's account.
87. On issues of the relationship between song ownership and power in Cape York, see J. von Sturmer, 'Aboriginal Singing and Notions of Power', in *Songs of Aboriginal Australia*, edited by M. Clunies Ross, T. Donaldson and S.A. Wild, Oceania Monograph No. 32 (Sydney: Oceania Monographs, 1987), pp. 63-76.
88. At least at the ideal level, but, of course, there is a great deal of flexibility and room for innovation and negotiation in transferring this theory to practice. An excellent examination of the issue is H. Payne, 'Rites for Sites or Sites for Rites?: The Dynamics of Women's Cultural Life in the Musgraves', in *Women, Rites and Sites: Aboriginal Women's Cultural Knowledge*, edited by P. Brock (Sydney: Allen & Unwin, 1989), pp. 41-59.
89. Haddon, *Reports . . . Volume I*, p. 384.
90. Laade, 'Further Material on Kuiam . . .', p. 90.
91. ibid., pp. 88, 83 & 87.

92. S.H. Ray, *Reports of the Cambridge Anthropological Expedition to Torres Straits: Volume III: Linguistics* (Cambridge: Cambridge University Press, 1907), pp. 194-219, transcribes with interlineal and free translations the section from Ned Waria's book on *Kuiam.*
93. Haddon, 'Folk-Tales', in *Reports . . . Volume V*, pp. 67-83; see also vol. 1, pp. 380-5. Lawrie, *Myths and Legends . . .*, pp. 88-101.
94. Laade, 'Further Material on Kuiam . . .', *passim.*
95. ibid., pp. 95 & 99.
96. G.A. Zegwaard, 'Headhunting Practices of the Asmat of Netherlands New Guinea', *American Anthropologist*, 61 (1956), pp. 1020-41.
97. Laade, 'Further Material on Kuiam . . .', p. 77.
98. Zegwaard, 'Headhunting Practices . . .', p. 1040.
99. Trompf, *Payback*, p. 32.
100. For a recent overview with a particularly full bibliography on this subject, see B.M. Knauft, 'Melanesian Warfare: A Theoretical History', *Oceania*, 60 (1990), pp. 250-311; for disputes over garden land etc., see pp. 35 & 41.
101. C.R. Hallpike, *Bloodshed and Vengeance in the Papuan Mountains: The Generation of Conflict in Tauade Society* (Oxford: Clarendon Press, 1977), pp. 33 & 7.
102. cit. Trompf, *Payback*, pp. 45 & 51, & Trompf, p. 57.
103. D.H. Turner, *Life Before Genesis: A Conclusion: An Understanding of the Significance of Australian Aboriginal Culture* (New York: Peter Lang, 1987), pp. 15-6.
104. Zegwaard, 'Headhunting Practices . . .', p. 1032.
105. Trompf, *Payback*, p. 57.
106. Haddon, 'Folk-Tales', pp. 81, 72 & 71.
107. Ray, *Linguistics*, p. 217.
108. Mulvaney, *Encounters in Place*, p. 63.
109. W.E.H. Stanner, 'Some Aspects of Aboriginal Religion', *Colloquium*, 9 (1976), p. 19.
110. L. Sharp, 'Ritual Life and Economics of the Yir-Yiront of Cape York Peninsula', *Oceania*, 5 (1964), p. 24.
111. Stanner, 'Some Aspects . . .', p. 30.
112. U.H. McConnel, 'Mourning Ritual Among the Tribes of Cape York Peninsula', *Oceania*, 7 (1937), p. 362. For expansion on this view, see von Sturmer, 'The Wik Region', p. 140.
113. Overviews can be found in Sharp, 'Tribes and Totemism . . .', or even more summarily in his 'Notes on Northeast Australian Totemism', in *Studies in the Anthropology of Oceania and Asia*, edited by C.S. Coon and J.M. Andrews, Papers of the Peabody Museum of American Anthropology and Ethnology, vol. 20, pp. 66-71 (Harvard University, 1943); J.G. Frazer's *Totemica: A Supplement to Totemism and Exogamy* (London: Macmillan, 1937), while theoretically flawed, contains a convenient summary of data up to its time.

114. On the affinities between Arandic and Cape York languages see, for instance, Wurm, 'Torres Strait'.
115. Sharp, 'Tribes and Totemism . . .', and 'Notes on North Australian Totemism'.
116. F. Richards, 'Customs and Languages of the Western Hodgkinson Aboriginals', *Memoirs of the Queensland Museum*, 8 (1926), pp. 249–65.
117. E. Palmer, 'Notes on some Australian Tribes', *The Journal of the Anthropological Institute of Great Britain and Ireland*, 13 (1884), p. 291. Palmer's most unexpected data are confirmed by D. Roughsey, *Moon and Rainbow: The Autobiography of an Aboriginal* (Adelaide: Rigby, 1977), a century later. In chapter 9, Roughsey discusses good and evil spirits and the manner in which the evil block the road to peoples' home in the Milky Way so that some fall into 'Hell'! 'The teachings of the missionaries were not much different from our own,' he says (p. 93). Indeed!
118. W.E. Roth, *Superstition, Magic and Medicine*, p. 17.
119. Thomson, 'The Hero Cult . . .', p. 509.
120. McConnel, 'Totemic Hero-Cults . . .', p. 456.
121. C.W. Hart & A.R. Pilling, *The Tiwi of North Australia* (New York: Holt, Rinehart and Winston, 1960), pp. 111–12.
122. Thomson, 'The Hero Cult . . .', pp. 499ff.
123. Haddon, 'Folk-Tales', p. 80.
124. Thomson, 'The Hero Cult . . .', p. 502.
125. Thomson notes the similarities with Central Desert traditions. 'Stripped of the elaborate ceremonial of the Arunta, the rite still has the essential features of the typical *intichiuma* . . .' (ibid., p. 503).
126. Thomson, 'The Hero Cult . . .', pp. 460–1.
127. Laade, 'Notes on the Boras . . .', p. 289.
128. McConnel, 'Totemic Hero-Cults . . .', pp. 80, 83.
129. Thomson, 'The Hero Cult...', pp. 472ff, 488ff, 468 & 516; Laade, 'Notes on the Boras . . .', p. 291; McConnel, 'Totemic Hero-Cults . . .', p. 75.
130. ibid., p. 82f.
131. Thomson, 'The Hero Cult . . .', p. 504.
132. Laade, 'Notes on the Boras . . .', pp. 275, 287–8 & 297.
133. Thomson 'The Hero Cult . . .', p. 471. 'I have been unable to find any evidence of the existence there, past or present, of tribal, as distinct from clan, ceremonies.'
134. ibid., p. 514.
135. McConnel, 'Totemic Hero-Cults', pp. 83–4; *Myths of the Mungkan*, p. 20.
136. see A.C. Haddon & W.H.R. Rivers, 'Totemism', in *Reports... Volume V*, edited by Haddon, pp. 153–93.
137. Kitaoji, 'The Myth of Bomai', p. 210.

CHAPTER 3

A New Sky Hero From a Conquered Land

These strangers, where are they going?
Where are they trying to steer?
They must be in that place Thoorvour, it is true.
See the smoke coming in from the sea.
These men must be burying themselves like the sand crabs
They disappeared like the smoke.[1]

According to Aboriginal traditions this song records the Badjala response to seeing HMS *Endeavour* passing Australia's coast. The date would have been Sunday May 20, 1770.

Such a claim would be disconcerting to those who maintain that Aborigines were initially incapable of cognitively grasping Western cultural phenomena. This, however, is not an exceptional case. The Badjala had another public ceremony concerning the sighting of Flinders' vessel in 1802, which closely parallels the well authenticated *Koorannup* ceremony based on encounters with Flinders and his crew in the previous year on Australia's opposite coast. Other ship ceremonies have also been recorded.

The symbolism of the *Endeavour* ceremonial song is rich. For a people who buried their dead in the sand the self-inhuming crew must have constituted a powerful image. Indeed the suggestion that the sighting may have been interpreted as a portent is intriguingly appropriate.[2]

Less than two decades later death had landed. The year after the arrival of the First Fleet the initial lethal epidemic erupted. Collins gave an eyewitness account of the horror of the event.

In the year 1789 they were visited by a disorder which raged among them with all the appearance and virulence of the small-pox. The number that it swept off, by their own accounts, was incredible. At that time a native was living with us and on our taking him down to the harbour to look for his former companions those who witnessed his expression of agony can never forget either. He looked anxiously around him in the different caves we visited: not a vestige on the sand was to be found of human foot; the excavations in the rocks were filled with the putrid bodies of those who had fallen victims to the disorder; not a living person was anywhere to be met with. It seemed as if, flying from the contagion, they had left the dead to bury the dead. He lifted up his hands and eyes in silent agony for some time: at last he exclaimed 'All dead! All dead!'[3]

DEATH AS AN ETHNOGRAPHIC CONTEXT

In this chapter I reinterpret early accounts of Aboriginal worldviews in south-east Australia in their ethnographic context. That context was death and dispossession. Everything we know of this region comes from records made after the titanic population declines which followed colonisation. Even in Collins' account, which is our only significant eighteenth century source, we read of one 'tribe', reduced to three people, 'compelled to unite with some other tribe, not only for their personal protection, but to prevent the extinction of their tribe'.[4]

By the 1830s, when missionaries and explorers began to compile their hasty and superficial reports of Aboriginal beliefs, only one-third of the quarter of a million people in New South Wales and Victoria survived. By 1850, 10,000 people – four per cent of the 1788 population – were alive.[5] And it was yet another generation before the first serious account of the region was provided by Smyth in his *The Aborigines of Victoria* (1876). Works of the standard of Howitt's *The Native Tribes of South-East Australia* and R.H. Mathews' numerous articles, themselves severely wanting by current ethnographic standards, were the best part of half a century away.

To massive population declines caused by disease we must add the fact that these early accounts appeared in the wake of dispossession of traditional lands either through pastoral pressures or the effects of blatant racial hatred. This was not an issue in the immediate vicinity of Sydney, and by the 1830s only about 500 Aborigines remained within a radius of 200 kilometres of the town. Thus, for example, the first mission to Aborigines, founded in 1826 at Lake Macquarie, was forced to close in 1837 because only three inmates had survived.[6] Such diminution, coupled with a rapidly growing White population, led to the assertion that this region had been 'pacified'.

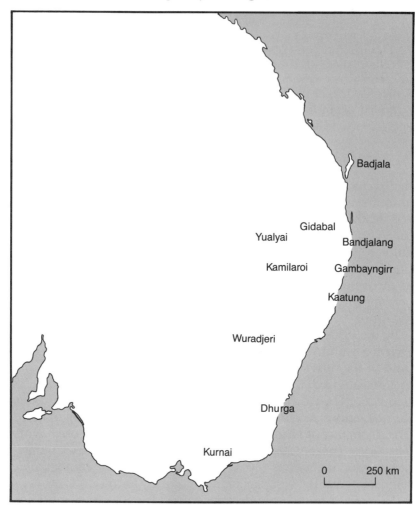

South-east Australia.

Farther afield, however, hostilities continued as intensive pastoral activity spread, using primarily convict labour. Under these conditions, Aborigines were compelled to leave their homelands and form new social aggregates on the outskirts of towns, on the few benign stations, or on mission settlements. Those refusing to comply were visited by punitive expeditions sent to 'teach the blacks a lesson', which at times was synonymous with murdering every Aborigine in a district.[7] The second Christian mission to Aborigines which, as I will argue, was a significant centre of Aboriginal ceremonial innovation, was thus established at Wellington Valley in 1831 with what Rowley has called 'a collection of beaten tribal remnants'.[8]

For a people whose Law simultaneously embraced 'religious', 'social' and 'geographic' realms, severe depopulation and dislocation would have conspired to deal a blow jarring its very foundations. The common but unexamined scholarly assumption has been that this was a trauma from which Aboriginal spiritual life simply could not recover. As early as 1825 Baron Field made the melancholy prediction that 'in a few years, perhaps, the corrobory will be no more'.[9] This became the catchcry of the nineteenth and early twentieth century studies of Aboriginal ceremonial life and the sworn duty of investigators was to salvage remnants of traditions which were seen as being no more than the shattered ruins of the glory that was pre-colonial life.

What has rarely been seriously entertained is the possibility that south-east Australian conceptions of existence could have been adapted so as to accommodate the devastating effects upon social and territorial organisation. My thesis is that not only were Aboriginal worldviews restructured but that Aboriginal people responded with remarkable speed to the seemingly insurmountable challenge before them. I contend that the major changes had already occurred by the 1830s, when the initial reports on Aboriginal societies were being prepared. Indeed, even at a *prima facie* level, it is virtually impossible to conceive how Aboriginal traditions in this region could have survived had it been otherwise.

Needless to say, this is a radical interpretation of the ontologies of south-east Australia. With the exception of one paragraph and one footnote,[10] I am unaware of any mention of the possibility of major cosmological reformation in this region. The nineteenth-century High God debate is, of course, relevant here, but those advocating mission influence on Aboriginal beliefs in that context were only concerned with postulating confused, unconscious and purposeless borrowings which had polluted a fine store of primitive ethnographic data. The dynamics of intellectual adjustment were entirely beyond their research programmes, and change was considered by them to be symptomatic of forgetfulness, loss, degradation and, ultimately, extinction.[11]

It is a simple matter to employ the wisdom of hindsight to criticise early scholars. As far as possible I wish to avoid this pointless exercise, but one ethnographer receives careful scrutiny in the following pages. Alfred Howitt's classic study of south-east Australia, after the best part of a century, retains its authoritative status. Significantly, Howitt is the only Australianist to be given a separate entry in the recent *Encyclopedia of Religion*. His seamless presentation belies a rather ruthless tendency to edit from his writing data contradictory to his general thesis. As John Mathew wrote to R.H. Mathews (the latter a fine researcher whose studies rivalled Howitt's and which were consequently totally ignored in his *magnum opus*): 'The trouble with Howitt is that European writers seem to take him as the sole and absolute authority on South East Australia whose *ipse dicit* [*sic*] is final. He is leading several of them astray on important points.'[12] As a passionate advocate of the unchanging nature of Aboriginal ideals in the south-east he has, I believe, led *all* of us astray. He was a man who easily ignored the missionaries' warning that their Kurnai inmates, who provided Howitt with his most complete data, could not be expected to reveal the pristine precontact information he sought. As Brian Attwood recently commented in this regard, Howitt would not accept that these Aborigines were 'better described as "transitionalists" than "traditionalists" '.[13]

My exposition is in two parts. The first part documents major changes to the relationship between people and places consequent to depopulation and dislocation. I show that, following the failure of initial overtures to locate White invaders within the pre-existent structures of space, Aboriginal people subsumed key elements of Western ontology. Specifically, they adopted the understanding, verified by their life experience, that the earth had been impoverished and that power now resided with the sky. This was linked to a notion of cosmic instability and the possibility that the re-establishment of moral equilibrium might only be attainable by purging the world of intrinsically bad (evil) elements. I argue, however, that Aboriginal people resisted allowing that possibility to become a means of salvation.

In the following pages, I develop themes alluded to in my first chapter. The section headed 'Utopia' is about a revolution in the Aboriginal understanding of space. The next section concerns time. I show that balance, instead of being a ritually maintained reality, became increasingly articulated as a radical and somewhat threatening future event. I discuss innovative ritual practices and, in particular, those which appear to have 'millennial' and 'cargoistic' elements. I suggest, however, that these terms prejudice our understanding of Aboriginal ontology in post-colonial south-east Australia. I call this section '*eschatogony*', which I define to encapsulate the essence of these peoples' temporal predicament – 'the origin of the end of this world'.

UTOPIA

LOCATING INVASION

We must accept the limitation that we will never be able to satisfactorily reconstruct pre-colonial views of the world in south-east Australia. To pretend otherwise is delusion. What we have to work with are frequently contradictory reports recorded following devastation, death and dispossession.

While ethnographic contradictions are the bane of scholarship and at times the hallmark of confused research, textual analysis suggests another source of these 'inconsistencies'. I consider many of them to be reasonably faithful records of Aboriginal peoples' presentations of a range of beliefs at variance with each other.

Let me unambiguously state that I am not advocating a version of Lévy-Bruhl's thesis of a pre-logical mentality. Certainly Aboriginal people maintain contradictory beliefs, but from my experience they are quite aware of the paradox this creates. Far from ignoring contradiction, they savour its expressive chromatic tension. Indeed, recent analysis indicates that Aboriginal societies expend considerable energy in actually forestalling the possibility of resolving opposition and paradox.[14]

My own field research in central Australia confirms this opinion. The Warlpiri with whom I worked have been in contact with White Australians for approximately the same period of time (although with less devastating results) as the Aboriginal peoples of south-east Australia had been when the first reports on their culture were being written. I encountered two opinions concerning the fate of Warlpiri spirits. In the more traditional version the spirit returned to the local site from which it had emanated. In the other version, inspired by both their social and intellectual encounter with Whites, the spirit ascended to an unspecified place in heaven. Individual people held both views simultaneously, perceived the contradiction and, for the time being at least, had no intention of resolving it. As I have argued elsewhere, such assertions articulated far more evocatively their experiences of the dilemmas of invasion than any form of syllogistic or synthetic logic.[15]

When discussing the two opposed orientations of Warlpiri thought, I began to employ Jonathan Z. Smith's distinction between locative and Utopian visions of the world (which I briefly introduced in chapter 1). It was the recent experience of applying these categories to a contemporary tradition in a state of transition which made the ethnographies of the south-east suddenly appear to me in a very different light.

My reading of these texts indicates the coexistence of locative and Utopian cosmologies in New South Wales and Victoria in the nineteenth century. Readers of Howitt's classic study will not detect this dual orientation as he has judiciously edited one scenario from the work. He concludes his survey of beliefs in the afterlife, for example, by asserting the 'universal' belief that the spirit 'finds its way to the sky-country, where it lives in a land like the earth, only more fertile, better watered, and plentifully supplied with game'.[16]

It is surely noteworthy that, with some other significant exceptions discussed in full elsewhere in this book, this understanding radically opposes Aboriginal opinion in the rest of the continent, but more intriguing is its variance with other reports from the south-east itself. Howitt's shunned rival Mathews, for instance, maintained that Kamilaroi spirits or *gundhaddyiba* followed the Barwon River up-stream to live beneath the mountains at its source. Other people on the southern Victorian coast are said to locate spirits on islands off the coast and to bury the dead with their heads toward their 'clan/phratrie' island.[17] The Dhurga of southern New South Wales, according to Mathews, direct spirits towards the country of the deceased's mother. Indeed, Howitt himself, with no indication as to its significance, produces an illustration of burial procedures in which the corpse's head is pointed toward the land of its 'clan and totem'.[18] This again suggests greater significance being attributed to the location of spirits than Howitt's conclusion would allow. In fact, if the fickle evidence of archaeology is employed, we might even suspect that the relationship between the dead and territory played a *more central* role in the south-east than elsewhere in Australia.[19]

The origin of human spirits is an equally divided issue. Montagu concludes his survey of the literature for this region by highlighting the anomalous lack of 'reincarnation' beliefs, yet Mathews wrote

of localised spirits waiting to be 'reincarnated'.[20] Although early
ethnographies are devoid of references to spirit essences residing in
the land, a late survey conducted by Radcliffe-Brown revealed that,
by formulating appropriate research orientations, one could uncover
information concerning 'increase' rites and ceremonies in northern
New South Wales, including several places for the 'increase' of
djadjam or human babies.[21] Such data, like the reference to the return
of the deceased's spirit to specific earthly sites, suggest the presence
of a locative tradition at odds with Howitt's Utopian model of a
vaguely defined, heaven-dominated cosmology.

Another textual contradiction concerns what Nancy Munn has
very aptly called 'the transformation of subjects into objects'.[22]
In some accounts from the south-east there is a preponderance
of transformations of subjects into other subjects (e.g. humans
into birds) which, in comparison with myths from other regions,
have a rather impoverished 'just-so' story quality, lacking land
connections. Even more atypical is the dominance of transformations
of Ancestral beings into non-located sky dwellers.[23] R.M. Berndt
claims, mistakenly I think, that 'in Wuradjeri belief, all "totemic"
beings went to a place named Wantanggangura "beyond the
clouds and sky"'.[24] In other accounts, however, and in particular
those associated with 'increase' sites, we do encounter abundant
references to Ancestral beings transforming into identifiable places
in the landscape.

My interpretation of these contradictions, some of which are
apparent in the works of eminent anthropologists, is that they
reflect a twofold cosmological orientation. The locative tradition,
which seems to approximate traditional beliefs found elsewhere in
Australia (as outlined in chapter 1), emphasises the association
between creative powers and sites, and the affiliation of human
spiritual essences with these places. It stresses ubiety and earth-based
powers. The Utopian tradition, on the other hand, removes both
human and Ancestral spirits to an *otiose* sky realm and, as I will
show, consequently defines the sacred realm as standing in a single,
ubiquitous relationship with all people.

The coexistence of dual cosmologies in post-colonial Aboriginal
Australia is a widely-spread and well documented phenomenon. It
is a major component of what Aboriginal people today consider to
be their 'two Laws'. What is peculiar to the early south-east is not
the plurality of cosmologies *per se* but the dominant position the

Utopian vision ultimately achieved. While locative elements, as I have shown, persisted into the twentieth century, they were no longer central to ceremonial activities. This, I will suggest, reflects the life experiences of people in this region. Unlike Aborigines in some parts of pastoral Australia (see chapter 5), invasion was for them a reality so devastating as to render impossible the maintenance of a locative cultic life. At the same time the Utopian understanding of the cosmos, for reasons that will become apparent, increasingly articulated their existential condition. I will discuss this matter presently, but proceed initially by briefly considering some of the tragically unsuccessful attempts by Aboriginal people to ally colonists with their place-based traditions.

In a penetrating analysis of Aboriginal appropriation of White Australian myth, Deborah Rose has identified a central intellectual concern to come to grips with a dilemma of colonisation: 'that of locating conquest in any sort of moral order'.[25] One attempted resolution of this dilemma was reported frequently from frontier situations, but does not appear to have persisted for long as a significant factor in structuring colonial ethnic relations. It is symptomatic of a general poverty of scholarship in this area that these conciliatory overtures have typically been misunderstood as no more than a quaint instance of Aboriginal failure to comprehend novel events. I refer, of course, to the frequently noted classification of Whites as deceased Aboriginal people.

It is a serious misrepresentation to suggest that Aborigines saw their invaders as 'ghosts' or 'spirits' – a view which Roth dismissed at the outset of this century for being 'as absurd as it is wide of the truth'.[26] Certainly there may have been initial perceptual errors on both sides of the frontier but, like the European ethnoclassification of Aborigines with subhuman species, the identification of Whites with deceased relatives was a *conceptual* equation. Unlike White Australian taxonomy, however, the social implications of the Aboriginal construct were generous to a fault.

In the Sydney region alone there was initially a wider range of interpretations of Whites. While at Port Stephens they were identified as previous 'countrymen', there was no such tradition at Port Jackson.[27] Mahroot, the last survivor from the Botany Bay district, on the other hand, said of Phillip's crew: 'They thought they was the devil when they landed first'.[28] Other models were also explored. It seems, however, that the 'deceased kin' classification was felt to be the most satisfying, and it subsequently dispersed from region to region, often in advance of the Whites themselves.[29]

The value of defining intruders as deceased kinsfolk was that it provided a mechanism for expanding the pre-existent cosmologically and morally established social order to accommodate alien people. While a 'malevolent spirit' category would have an inherent logical attraction it would place White Australians outside the domain of sanctioned human relationships. The generosity and genius of equating invaders with departed relatives was that it invited them to modify their behaviour and (re-)establish morally acceptable interactions with their former kin.

This explains the impassioned concerns, frequently reported in mocking tones, of Aborigines to identify their specific relationships with Whites. The 'recognition' of the escaped convict Buckley and the explorer Grey as kin are cases too well known to need retelling. A quotation from Eyre, emphasising both kinship and location, reveals the persistence of Aboriginal people in this regard and the frustrations they experienced.

> It is a general belief among almost all the Aborigines, that Europeans, or white people, are resuscitated natives, who have changed their colour, and who are supposed to return to the same localities they had inhabited as black people. The most puzzling point, however, with this theory, appears to be that they cannot make out how it is that the returned natives do not know their former friends and relatives. I have often been asked, with seriousness and earnestness, who, among the Europeans, were their fathers, their mothers, and their other relatives.[30]

Such offers to affiliate were, at a broader level, offers to accept small parties of Whites as co-habiters of land under the charter of the principle of an Aboriginal spatial ontology. To be socially related to members of a locative tradition, such as those I maintain to have existed in pre-colonial south-east Australia, was to be geographically placed on the one hand and spiritually linked to site-based Ancestral powers on the other. More accurately, social groups, places and mythic beings were but various interrelated manifestations of an all-embracing Law.

The reasons for the failure of attempts to locate invasion are as obvious as the results were tragic. There are records indicating Aborigines anticipated the impossibility of Lawful territorial coexistence with Whites and thus adopted ritual practices traditionally reserved for removing spirits living in the wrong place. Mitchell, for instance, reports an encounter with Aborigines who made ritual overtures 'to induce us to go back, whence we had come, and as I felt we were rather unceremonious invaders of their country, it was certainly my duty to conciliate them by every possible means'. To this end he took out his pistol and fired a shot.

> As if they had previously suspected we were evil demons [*sic*] and had at length a clear proof of it, they repeated their gesticulations and defiance with tenfold fury, and accompanied their action with demonic looks, hideous shouts and a war-song, crouching, jumping, springing with a spear, and throwing dust at us as they slowly retired.[31]

That this ritual practice was not merely the result of perceptual error is substantiated by the persistence of these practices well after close communications with Whites had been established. Ridley, for instance, having noted Whites were classified as deceased relatives, immediately proceeded to refer to elaborate all-night ceremonies 'to drive away the spirits of the dead'.[32]

But the spirits of the dead did not leave. Nor would they establish sanctioned relationships with Aboriginal people. Offers of alliance and kinship went unheard and few Whites could even perceive the structural reasons for the devastation their very presence caused. In 1845 Bishop Polding reported to the Parliamentary Committee on the conditions of the Aborigines that 'there is established in the mind of the black population a sentiment that the whites are *essentially unjust*... founded on the fact of the whites coming to take possession of their lands'. Dr. J.D. Lang disbelievingly questioned: 'Do you think they have such an idea of the value of land, as to lead them to the view its settlement is an act of aggression?' Polding replied: 'I am convinced of it, and I think that it is the root of the evil'.[33]

It was rapidly realised that, by the standards of an Aboriginal land-based Law, White Law was indeed 'unjust' *in essence*. The challenge could not, in the last analysis, be met by locating the invaders within the existing order. Rather it was necessary to establish a means of accommodating what were seen as fundamentally immoral people.

In the remainder of this chapter I will argue that the Aborigines of south-east Australia were left with no other genuine option than subsuming some of the ontological principles of the invader's own cosmology. I am not referring to syncretisms or mythic borrowings, although these did occur, but to a major reformulation of their understanding of the nature of existence. My argument is that in this area there occurred what Rose presents as, to date, a tentatively entertained possibility for Aboriginal people in northern Australia. She writes of the appeal of Pentecostal cosmology:

> It encapsulates conquest, providing a moral frame for brutality. And it mirrors social processes of invasion and conquest, offering a larger frame in which conquest, undertaken through immoral means, is granted moral values. It thus offers at least the illusion of resolution to the paradox of conquest through a radical reforming of cosmic principles.[34]

In the following pages I suggest that south-east Australian cosmology, as portrayed in the bulk of the records we have, reveals precisely the hallmark of restructured cosmological principles fashioned to mirror processes of invasion.

THE UTOPIAN VISION

It should be made quite clear that Aborigines in early colonial south-east Australia were not in any conventional sense becoming Christians. This did not occur. At best, by mission standards, 'success' was superficial and short-lived. More common were reports that Aborigines disdained the new teachings and institutions, and enjoyed the opportunity to gently, but very humorously, ridicule their proselytisers.[35]

It was, furthermore, not until the mid-twentieth century that ethnographers began to produce evidence that Aboriginal people in this area had equated the 'old Law' with Christian myth, although, as I will later explain, unpublished documents do suggest a link extending these syncretistic developments back to the time of Mathews' and Howitt's field research. The only explicit identification of Aboriginal and Christian beliefs in the nineteenth century was noted, much to his later chagrin,[36] in Howitt's own writing. His sensitivity as a student of dynamic worldviews is clearly revealed in the following passage.

> Being desirous of learning what Brewin, Bullumolut, and Baukan were supposed by the Kurnai to be, I questioned two of the most intelligent men. Both were Tatungolung – one, a member of the Church of England, the other an intelligent savage and a scamp. I said, 'What is Brewin?' They consulted, and after a few minutes one of them said, 'We think he is Jesus Christ'. I said 'Well, I think you had better consult again'.[37]

While Aborigines avoided aligning themselves with Christian institutions and mythic traditions, they nevertheless extrapolated from the latter essential ontological principles which benefited their conceptualisation of post-colonial life. Some investigators claimed that 'upon cross-examination' Aborigines confessed that 'they had learned [certain beliefs] from a missionary or some resident in the district',[38] but if this was so it merely underscores their reluctance to identify with the established forms of their conqueror's creed. On the other hand the restricted nature of these beliefs does not, as Eliade and others suggest,[39] indicate that they were autochthonous but only that Aboriginal innovation had subverted these elements into the secret realm – a process which has been unambiguously documented elsewhere in Australia. (See chapter 5.)

The principles which I believe Aboriginal people in south-east Australia adapted from White discourse and society postulated a radical and unbalanced dualism which was poised to achieve stability by resolving into a singularity. Unlike the pluralistic pre-mise of their locative cosmology, which rests upon the discrete yet affiliated site-based socio-religious units (sometimes federated into balanced reciprocal pairs), the eccentric dualistic orientation disempowers places and deprecates this world which stands in impoverished opposition to the Utopian skyworld. This opposition contained a momentum which sought its state of rest by allowing the greater to subsume the lesser, the heaven to destroy earth, and the good to vanquish the evil. The specifically Aboriginal contribution to this worldview, as I will later argue, was to deny it its fulfilment.

Utopian cosmology in the south-east of Australia begins with a single creator. This again suggests a mythic contradiction as there are well documented narratives for this region explaining how a multiplicity of Ancestral beings transformed the country.[40] As Kolig suggests

> All that was essentially required was to place this [monotheistic] figure outside and above the totemic and kinship order, thus elevating him to a status more exalted than the other beings of the theorimorphic pantheon who remained tied to the order to which the whole universe was thought to be subject.[41]

The consequences of this deceptively simple move were, however, monumental.

Residing with the All-Father were the total potentiality and responsibility for establishing moral, social and geographic order. Our earliest reference to the All-Father comes from the Wellington

Valley Mission. Rev James Günther says for the Wuradjeri: 'There is no doubt in my mind that the name Baia-mai . . . refers to the Supreme Being; and the ideas held concerning Him by some of the more thoughtful Aborigines are a remnant of original traditions prevalent among the ancients of the Deity.'[42] He proceeds to argue that *Baiami* has three of the attributes of the Biblical God – eternity, omnipotence and goodness. He had created the entire world but long ago decided to leave this earth. From his heavenly realm he rewards and punishes people and through his mediatory son *Daramulun* he knows all things.

A similar account, based on notes written in 1844–5, was provided by James Manning. Several critics have accused this author of embellishing his report with Christian details, although they were in accord with the underlying cosmic principles he proposes (they are, for instance, identical with those suggested by Howitt).[43] I find these ontologic principles every bit as alien as the specific details and hence see no *prima facie* reason to dismiss them. As Manning himself suspected some White influence, and subsequently checked his information to ensure its accuracy, this further inclines me to believe that he faithfully reported what he was told by Aboriginal people.

According to Manning's informants, *Baiami* dwells in heaven on a throne of transparent crystal surrounded by beautifully carved pillars from which emanate the colours of the rainbow. Out of his loneliness he creates his son *Grogorogally* who mediates between heaven and earth. 'The son's spirit they represent as being in every part of the habitable world, spreading – as was expressed to me – over the supposed distance of England to Sydney.'[44] Another intermediary, *Moodgeegally*, was the first human who now lives in an earthly paradise and periodically ascends by a path called *Dallambangel*, complete with ladders and steps, on a three-day journey to heaven.

Leaving the anachronistic details to one side for the time being, the theme of a single creator who leaves the earth is solidly supported by the ethnographies for this region. Instead of the more usual Aboriginal cosmogony, in which a host of transformative agencies come ultimately to reside at myriad earth-bound localities, there is only one source of spiritual vitality dwelling beyond the world. As R.M. Berndt says, 'All power, whether religious or magical, emanates from Baiami'.[45] Power, in brief, has been dis*placed* to become Utopian.

From the All-Father's oneness, however, emerges a duality caused by his departure from the world. Sky and earth stand opposed and the latter is impoverished. I have already quoted Howitt's opinion that there was a 'universal' belief that the spirits of the deceased ascended to a paradisical heaven. When a Wellington Valley woman was asked where she would go at death she replied 'to Heaven, I believe'[46] – although, significantly, other inmates at that mission suggested their spirit might travel to England, the distant home of God, where it would be made White.[47] In the Utopian scenario spirits do not return to the earth. Eyre's exceptional account only proves the rule:

> One old native informed me, that all blacks, when dead, go up to the clouds, where they have plenty to eat and drink; fish, birds, and game of all kinds, with weapons and implements to take there. He then told me, that occasionally individuals came back, but that such instances were very rare.[48]

That the fate of the human spirit denies the possibility of returning fertile essence to Ancestral localities is, by Aboriginal standards, anomalous enough, but even more disconcerting is the frequently reported claim, supported by Howitt, that the earth was depreciated by Aborigines in the south-east. This is already evident in previous passages in this chapter. To them I add Ridley's account: 'As for a future state, they generally have a lively expectation . . . Many of them die with a cheerful expectation of being soon in a "better country" '.[49]

Little imagination is required to understand why Aboriginal people in this region were predisposed to supplement and to some extent replace their locative traditions with another which transcended specific social affiliations with sites. As Maddock observes, the All-Father undermines site-kin based affiliation with Ancestral beings by asserting that all people stand in an identical relationship with the single cosmic power. This, he notes, sits comfortably with the Christian tradition asserting the brother/sisterhood of all people, but in Aboriginal societies produces a distortion between social and cosmological realms.[50] Why this tension was tolerated and, indeed, encouraged, is understandable if we see the All-Father *not* as an aberration in a locative site-kin tradition but as a dislocated Utopian innovation developed as a response to the destruction of the relationship between people and their countries. In a region where death devastated traditional social networks, and dispossession broke ties with the land, there could be little hope of maintaining the cosmos through a locative tradition. In a single move the All-Father created a new, potentially pan-Aboriginal, social base and removed the cosmological centre of gravity beyond known places to an unspecified realm in the sky.

This, however, is only the first level of analysis, for the spatial structure of the cosmos has a moral counterpart.

A central feature of traditional Aboriginal Law was the concern to maintain a stable balance of spiritual, social and environmental elements. 'The cosmos,' Rose suggests, 'can be seen as a closed, self-regulating system which seeks a steady state in which all life is maintained at optimum levels of productivity, knowledge, and so on.'[51] Homeostasis is achieved through a pluralistic network in which specific people take responsibility for regenerating the spiritual potencies residing at localities with which they are identified. In such an ecology of existants nothing is dispensable. An ideology of unchanging balance demands the constant regulation of the temporal world so that it conforms to the Law. What this cosmology cannot accommodate is non-regeneration nor, so to speak, system leaks.

The removal of spiritual essences from the earth which I have documented was, of course, one notable disruption to the equilibrium of this worldview. Essentially it postulated that the world could not maintain itself but rather was dependent upon another largely unknown and otiose domain. The moral counterpart to this view was the concept of evil.

The idea of evil is usually, and quite rightly, said to be absent from traditional Aboriginal thought. Unlike the notions of 'wrong' and 'bad', evil postulates an intrinsic corruption. To be evil is not to disobey the Law but to be incapable of being restored to a Lawful state. A cosmology which admits evil can no longer achieve balance through regeneration alone, and typically the understanding is that ultimately there is no option but to purge the world of its irredeemably immoral components.

From my earlier discussion of the failure of Aborigines to persuade Whites to enter into sanctioned relationships with them, we can deduce that Aboriginal people felt their invaders were beyond the Law and hence, from their perspective, evil. This encounter, I believe, was the experience which induced Aboriginal cosmology to admit the concept of evil. While in some contexts, as I will later document, Whites are specifically identified as the elements which must be abolished, it would be simplistic and, in a perverse way, somewhat vain to suggest that evil was a concept confined to the area of inter-ethnic relations. Although invasion provided the conditions under which evil became a necessary ontological postulant, Aboriginal people were concerned less with Whites *per se* than with the broader problem of re-establishing some kind of existentially relevant Law. Evil thus emerged as a fundamental feature of the cosmos attributable to Aboriginal people as well as the colonists.

The view that there are intrinsically immoral beings takes three forms. Firstly there are many references in the literature on south-east Australia to the All-Father having an adversary. In at least one account this is a subterranean creature with long horns and a tail – a striking image for a country with no indigenous horned animals.[52] In many versions it is the All-Father's relative who takes on the malevolent role. In an early report of this kind Strzelecki wrote: 'They do not dread the Deity; all their fears are reserved for the evil spirit, who contrasts the doing of the "Great Master"; and consequently it is to the evil spirit that religious worship is directed'.[53] In another version, *Baiami*'s brother, who lives in the far west, is prone to irrational and immoral behaviour, sending small-pox epidemics for no other reason than he was vexed that he didn't have a tomahawk.[54]

Because of the ease with which Western researchers can project the notion of evil onto Aboriginal beliefs, I am reluctant to rely too heavily on this first category, although in the wider context of reports from this area they do not seem anomalous and, in fact, there are records of specific instances of Christian notions of the Devil infiltrating Aboriginal doctrine so that, for example, spirits departing their bodies are consumed by Satan.[55]

The second category, while ambiguous, is more telling. The ambiguity is that it is uncertain whether evil resides with humans or the All-Father himself. It is frequently stated in the descriptions of the Sky Hero that his creative goodness and wrathful fury are somewhat at odds with each other. He is particularly associated with introduced epidemic diseases such as tuberculosis, pneumonia and smallpox. In one early reference to initiation ceremonies in the Hastings River district, the All-Father is asked to spare the neophytes from smallpox.[56] Is the omnipotent Sky-Father himself prone to unprovoked Lawless fury? Or is his action a just response to the evilness of humans? We are not unequivocally told. Manning describes *Baiami* as a 'benevolent though dreaded being. When any recover from sickness or other calamity, it is supposed their guilt has not been too great to pardon'.[57] In other accounts, however, the God's anger does not seem to have been reasonably provoked. Although I have found no evidence establishing a direct link, I am inclined to suspect Aborigines inherited this ambiguity from the God of their conquerors. Thus when Threlkeld reflected upon the closing of the first mission to Aborigines he said that although many had died while resisting invasion 'most died by the act of God'.[58] The same man, who was liberal for his time, attributed the Tasmanian population devastation to 'the will of God'.[59]

In the third category, which establishes the notion of evil, it is quite clear that evil is a human attribute. Although there are constant references to a paradisical afterlife this is not an inevitable fate. There was, apparently, a need to judge the dead in order to free heaven of earthly imperfections. Cameron, a reliable reporter,[60] took pains to verify the authenticity of what he suspected was Christian doctrine. While these are clearly notions alien to traditional Aboriginal thought, his informant flatly denied any foreign influence. Upon death the released spirit confronts two roads. The cleaner one, maintained by malevolent entities, leads to an unhappy fate. Other tests are presented, including a challenge of strength against the All-Father himself. Those who fail are thrown into a fiery destructive pit.[61] Assistant Protector Parker wrote of *Bunjil* subjecting the spirits to an ordeal of fires to determine whether they were good or bad. The good are liberated but the bad suffer for an indefinite time.[62]

Before proceeding to pull together the arguments of this first section I must comment on some of the mythic details in the data I have just presented. Clearly there are elements of Christian doctrine here, and I have deliberately chosen examples revealing these details. Since the nineteenth century scholars have been aware of their presence. E.S. Hartland, who lists more examples than I have space to include, suggested such details only crept in long after colonisation.[63] Andrew Lang, in turn, correctly pointed out that they were present in even the earliest records – a claim Hartland was forced to accept.[64] My citations are all very early and underscore Lang's point. What neither of these anthropologists noted, however, was that identifiable Christian mythemes actually progressively *decrease* until, by the turn of the century, they had all but vanished only to be rediscovered a generation later. The radical ontological dualism (sky vs. earth, good vs. evil), on the other hand, persisted. What I believe we see in the earlier more conspicuously Christian versions is therefore not primarily a case of mythic borrowings, but rather the appropriation of fundamental cosmological principles to which certain mythic elements initially and rather incidentally adhered. Once the structure of the post-colonial Law was established, Christian narrative segments were replaced by those which were more authentically Aboriginal.

What remained at the end of the century, and what all the ethnographers for this area maintained existed, was an unbalanced and unequal dualism. The most conspicuous features of this cosmology, which I have detailed, can now be summarised in four points.

(1) All existence and all power derives from a single source.
(2) From that singularity a duality emerged between earth and heaven. Ultimate significance and Law reside in the latter non-locative or Utopian domain.
(3) The earth is consequently depreciated in comparison with the sky realm, and its maintenance as a closed system is undermined by a dependency upon the potency of the heavens.
(4) Morally, the earth again loses its capacity for self-regulation, and the future of a homoeostatic process of regeneration becomes problematic as parts of the world are intrinsically Lawless or evil.

I suggested earlier that these innovations emerged to render colonial life meaningful by mirroring the process of invasion. I have argued that the idea of evil arose out of (although was not confined to) the Aboriginal understanding of Whites as an immoral and unLawful people. Conquest simultaneously fractured the living spiritual relationship of people with their lands, although I have shown that knowledge of locative beliefs persisted in a secondary capacity into the twentieth century. The impoverishment of the earth was indeed the experience of dispossessed Aboriginal people for whom identity shifted from place to Utopia. Finally, as Turner has so insightfully shown in *Life Before Genesis*, the notion of unequal duality is the fundamental premise for conquest which, rather than accepting a plurality of socio-religious units, proceeds by subsuming the other into the one, resulting ultimately, and often eschatologically, in a re-established monism.

Given this summary of the new Aboriginal cosmology we might suspect that their vision of the eschaton anticipated and welcomed an imminent millennium. It is precisely here, however, that Aboriginal thought diverges from our expectations. For while Aborigines were willing to accept an image of the world informed by an ontology of invasion, their soteriology largely denied monistic solutions. Such a stance, in a sense, rejected their new cosmology's right to fulfil itself. Why this should be so, and how it was ritually possible, is the subject of the next section of this chapter.

ESCHATONOGY

MILLENNIANISM AND ESCHATOLOGY

It has become something of an anthropological truism that Aborigines do not envisage the end of their world-order. Thus, for example, Berndt writes as follows about the lack of Aboriginal eschatological themes:

> They may become emotionally upset owing to physical circumstances, and see their culture toppling around them; but as far as we know they cannot really envisage complete destruction, the cessation of the 'eternal dream time' stream, and the life they know, even under the most intensive and disastrous form of contact.[65]

While Berndt has quite correctly highlighted the rarity of references to an eschaton, he has, I believe, misrepresented Aboriginal thought by suggesting this possibility 'cannot' be envisaged. Burridge correctly counters this stereotype by asserting that 'from the moment they perceived [Cook's] ship . . . millenarian activities among Australian aborigines became possible',[66] and the following data indicate that south-east Australian Aborigines clearly articulated the likelihood of an imminent end to their world.

Given their inability to continue the maintenance of the balance of the cosmos through the spatially discrete rituals of a locative tradition; and given the simultaneous emergence of the notion that some parts of the world possibly could not be made Lawful and hence might need to be withdrawn from the socio-religious ecology; it is not difficult to appreciate why Aboriginal thought was directed toward the future. As I suggested in chapter 1, an emphasis on temporal change and futurity emerges as a consequence to the disequilibrium of space.

Post-colonial south-east Australian cosmologies focused on liberation embodied in time and forthcoming events. One of the notable
features of the 'clever man' of this region was his ability to 'thrust
his mind forward into the future'.[67] The vision, however, was unclear.
On the one hand there appears the promise of the millennium in
which Whites are destroyed. On the other there is the looming threat
of an end to Aborigines themselves. I will examine these possibilities
in turn, examining particularly their respective capacity to resolve
the dilemma of unequal dualism.

Anti-White sentiment was central to a range of ritual activity
during the nineteenth century. At the more public (non-secret) end
of the spectrum was the description of an elaborate performance
staged near Surat and attended by over 500 Aborigines. The
ceremony begins with men dancing as a herd of cattle. A party of
hunters then stalk the 'cattle' and 'spear' two of them. This scene
perhaps deserves comparison with the nineteenth century photographic plate by Charles Kerry entitled 'Drafting the Sheep'.[68] In
the Surat sequence the successful hunt is followed by the arrival of
'Whites' on horseback, painted in detail, including representations
of their cabbage-tree hats. The 'Whites' drive off the hunters, but
the latter rally and a battle ensues. Gideon S. Lang reported:

> The native spectators groaned whenever a blackfellow fell, but cheered
> lustily when a white bit the dust; and at length, after the ground had
> been fought over and over again, the whites were ignominiously driven
> from the field, amidst the frantic delight of the natives.[69]

While this appears to have been an open ceremony or 'corroboree',
this does not negate the importance of the performance. The general
disposition toward Whites, furthermore, was identical to that found
in ritual intended to have very tangible consequences.

The earliest reference I have encountered that hints at millennial
expectations comes, appropriately enough, from the Sydney region.
Collins wrote in the late eighteenth century of an Aboriginal
woman, who lived in the clergyman's home, predicting Whites were
to soon encounter major misfortune. The portent was a shooting
star. He wrote: 'To the shooting of a star they attach a degree of
importance, and once, on an occasion of this kind I saw the girl
Boo-roong greatly agitated and prophesying much evil to befall all
the white men and their habitation'.[70] Collins does not mention the
suggested cause of the stellar activity, but it would be reasonable to

infer that, in keeping with information collected from a later period, it was understood to be due to the activities of the 'clever men'.

A similar case was witnessed by the explorer Eyre. He observed a comet on the 2nd March 1843, and an Aboriginal informant interpreted it as

> the harbinger of all kinds of calamities, and more especially to the white people. It was to overthrow Adelaide, destroy all Europeans and their houses, and then taking a course up the Murray, and past the Rufus, do irreparable damage to whatever or whoever came in its way. It was sent, he said, by the northern natives, who were powerful sorcerers.[71]

The major millennial movement of the nineteenth century was the 'clever-man'-controlled *Mulunga* cult, which I discuss in detail in chapter 5. I have not found direct evidence of it spreading into the region I am discussing, although it was documented as skirting its entire boundary from north to south-west. (See chapter 5 for references.) Howitt, who extends his survey of south-east Australia into the Lake Eyre basin, does include references to *Mulunga*, which he illustrates with three photographic plates.[72] Like Roth and Bates, however, he totally failed to comprehend its significance. According to the missionary Siebert, the cult's focus was a future war between Aborigines and Whites which climaxes with the appearance of the 'mother' who swallows all the colonial Australians.[73]

Returning eastwards into Victoria we do find details of at least one form of millenarian practice. In unpublished notes Howitt briefly describes a ritual in which one large and two small (serpentine?) figures are cut in bark and painted. Men, and often women also, danced in single file holding aloft small 'wands' of tufts of feathers, and then proceeded to reverently touch the carvings. The purpose of this practice was to get the great serpent *Mindi* to destroy their enemies.[74]

Mindi, says Smyth, was concomitant with epidemic diseases. When *Mindi* is active people do not stop to bury their dead but leave the district fleeing for their lives.[75] The association of the serpent with what were almost certainly diseases introduced at the time of colonisation was particularly appropriate, for according to both W. Thomas and E.S. Parker *Mindi* was about to take the lives of *all* Whites in the south-eastern Victoria area irrespective of their attitudes toward Aborigines.[76] The incantations and rituals, however, were not addressed to *Mindi* but to *Bunjil*, as the serpent acted only on the All-Father's command. Parker wrote: 'It is believed to be in the power of the large serpent *Mindi*, the supposed incarnation of the destroying spirit, to send this plague forth in answer to the appeals and incantations of those who seek the destruction of their foes'.[77] In a retributively apt logical conclusion to this scenario the anticipated plague that would wipe out Whites, but leave Aborigines unharmed, was identified as smallpox.

Given the track record of ethnographers in nineteenth century Australia for missing new intellectual movements, we might reasonably expect there were many other millennial and nativistic developments that passed unnoticed. Even if their presence was substantially larger than my sample suggests, however, I do not feel they would have achieved the type of major reorientation necessitated by the emergence of the imbalanced cosmos which I documented in the first part of this chapter. The examples I have cited, furthermore, were oriented towards rectifying concrete and relatively transitory injustices; specifically, the arrest and imprisonment of members of their community.[78] To some extent these expectations of the demise of Whites were homologous with earlier practices in frontier contexts designed to remove territorial invaders (*supra*), but in the later cases there could be no genuine hope for the preservation of the pre-colonial locative traditions. Thus although I have labelled these beliefs 'millenarian', and in doing so have merely replicated a common academic tendency to abuse the term, I know of no evidence that Aboriginal people saw the removal of Whites as itself adequate to ensure the salvation of the earth.

While the promise of the millennium may have held some attraction for Aboriginal people, and while they perhaps at times embraced its redemptive offer, I would suggest that, in the final analysis, what preserved the major Aboriginal response as a particularly Aboriginal response was the fact that it resisted the temptation to resolve an imbalanced socio-religious dualism into a monism. To remove Whites and bring the Utopian sky realm to earth would have produced a homogeneity even more divorced from pluralistic traditions than post-colonial life itself. I will argue in the remainder of this chapter that the dominant and persistent Aboriginal orientation was not to overthrow earth with heaven, or Whites with Aborigines, but rather to restructure their relationship to produce a Lawful, balanced and equal dualism which could thus, in the face of time, endure.

In contrast to the momentary upsurge of hope in a future without Whites, the persisting and starkly realistic view of the eschaton was one that comminated the extinction of Aboriginal life. The failure to regenerate the Law, as well, perhaps, as the presence of Lawless beings, threatened the cosmos itself. In one graphically vivid apocalyptic expectation the heavens and earth were about to merge into a formless, flooded mass. The recorded belief, which bears a striking similarity to those associated with the innovative Kimberley *Kuranggara* cult, which I document in chapter 5, was that unless tomahawks were sent to the old man at the end of the earth who tended the pillars which propped up the sky, the heavens would fall, bursting the oceans, and causing a flood in which all people would be drowned.[79] In another documentation it is noted that European materials – axes, saws, ropes and tiers of dray wheels – had been stolen from settlers and passed from community to community in the hope of reaching the guardian of the posts. Fearing their efforts may have been too late, they began to calculate which of the mountains in the district would provide them with the greatest chance of escaping the rising waters.[80]

We are not told who the old man at the earth's end is, but in a Kamilaroi story which also foretells the end of the Aboriginal world, it is *Baiami* who dwells in the distant west instead of his more usual sky home.[81] Since *Baiami*, as I shall presently explain, is often cited as the cause of the eschatological flood, there is a possibility that the two traditions are mythically related. The incompleteness of the records makes a certain evaluation on this matter impossible.

The *Baiami* of the west is described in a rather unusual narrative published by R.H. Mathews. The hero of the story is *Yooneeara*, a Kamilaroi 'chief' who decides to travel to *Baiami*'s home. By Aboriginal standards, the chronicle has a disconcerting historicity to it, and there is nothing to suggest that *Yooneeara*'s journey was anything other than a this-worldly event. On reaching the far west he finds *Baiami* is asleep, shares a meal with the God's daughter, and returns home only to die from the effects of sorcery encountered during his ordeal-ridden trip.[82]

All this seems pointless enough, but Mathews' informant police officer, C.A. Brewster, wrote to Mathews to the effect that the published version was incomplete.[83] After the meal *Yooneeara* asks about *Baiami*'s brother, and *Baiami*, who is now awake, replies that he and his brother had caught a large cod fish which foretold 'the fall of our dynasty'. To avert disaster they caught the fish and, supposedly to prove it was harmless, *Baiami* cooked and ate the cod. His brother, however, thought this an act of greediness and left for the east; he 'had gone away from Australia, and . . . even [*Baiami*] did not know where to'.

This enigmatic end to a prophecy of disaster for Aboriginal people is frustratingly obscure. While the strong Utopian emphasis is in keeping with the ethnographies of this region, we do not know the significance of either the brotherly schism or his departure to an unknown place beyond the vision of even the all-seeing *Baiami*. The hero of the journey nonetheless leaves, telling the God he will relate to his people all he had heard.

If, however, *Baiami* were associated with the possibility of imminent disaster, we would be justified in expecting this to have a major ritual manifestation. This, I suspect, raises what will be the most controversial aspect of my exposition. I believe we have a great deal of documentation for the relevant cult, but have once again mistaken innovation for unchanged tradition. The ceremonies I refer to are most commonly known as *Bora*.

Such a claim will no doubt extract cries of disbelief from scholars committed to the notion that Aboriginal traditions are inherently conservative. I am not, of course, suggesting that initiation ceremonies did not exist in south-east Australia prior to 1788. That would be a patently absurd claim. There is, notwithstanding, evidence that the rituals of initiation took on new forms and meaning following colonisation. Indeed, I cannot conceive how they could have maintained their relevance had this not occurred.

In the following passage, K.L. Parker makes it abundantly clear that the *Bora* was the primary Yualyai vehicle for preventing the eventuation of the envisioned eschaton.

> The oldest wirreenuns could see in their sacred crystals pictures of the past, pictures of what was happening at a distance in the present, and pictures of the future; some of which last filled their minds with dread, for they said as time went on the colours of the blacks, as seen in these magical stones, seemed to grow paler and paler, until at last only the white faces of the Wundah, or spirits of the dead, and white devils were seen, as if it should mean that some day no more blacks should be on this earth.
>
> The reason of this must surely be that the tribes fell away from the Boorah rites, and in his wrath Byamee stirred from his crystal seat in Bullimah. He had said that as long as the blacks kept his sacred

laws, so long should he stay in his crystal seat, and the blacks live on earth; but if they failed to keep up the Boorah rites as he had taught them, then he would move and their end would come, and only the Wundah . . . be in their country.[84]

To understand how the *Bora* could prevent *Baiami* 'stirring' – an act which is in some sources said to cause the final flood – and maintain the Aboriginal place in the world order, it will be necessary to examine the symbolic structure of the rite.

BORA

In his unpublished notes Howitt refers to a myth in which *Bunjil* initially created two men. One of them was light and had straight hair. The other was dark and had curly hair.[85] If the All-Father had made both Aborigines and Whites it would logically follow that he was ultimately responsible for their respective lifestyles, cultures and Laws. The *Bora* grounds, which are in part manifestations of the All-Father's first camp, do in fact reveal this dual creation.

Unfortunately, the documentation we have of *Bora* and cognate ceremonies is very poor. Although we have many truncated descriptions of the physical attributes of the grounds and performances, there is virtually no exegesis at all as to their significance or meaning. R.H. Mathews claimed to possess a 'mass of information' of this kind which he planned to publish, but the work never eventuated and the notes have not survived.[86] While we will therefore never be able to genuinely penetrate the depths of these cults, the incomplete data we have is enough to demand we re-evaluate some of our academic preconceptions about their cosmological message.

To begin with a minor example, the glass plates made by Kerry of a *Bora* ceremony contain photographs of ground sculptures of two introduced species of animal being speared.[87] They are a pig and a bull. Some interpreters might simply dismiss this as 'magical' practices extended to new food sources, but there are several reasons why this would be an overly hasty understanding. Firstly, comparative studies of initiation symbolism, and especially the use of 'increase'-type rituals in such contexts, indicates that their significance does not primarily reside with their ability to procure foodstuffs but rather in their meaningful affiliations with the neophytes.[88] Secondly, pork was apparently unpalatable to Aborigines; a fact that was frequently reported while noting the 'similarity' with Jewish and Muslim customs. Thirdly, although cattle were eaten, they were often killed in numbers exceeding those dictated by survival strategies. It was, for one, a way of hindering settlement without risking the repercussions from killing Whites themselves. And prized sections of the animals were used in ritual. The *Sydney Morning Herald* for 3rd October, 1842, reports that in the Namoi district Aborigines had been driving cattle, killing many of them, and removing for the most part only their tongues and fat. It continues:

> The blacks had a bora, as they call it, which signifies a meeting, and they danced with fat on their heads and beef upon their spears. Unless the stockholders make some effort to prevent them they will lose all their cattle: the blacks tell the men they are afraid to shoot them as the Commissioner will hang them.

Mathews makes related observations. He records the *Bora* representation of a bullock formed by logs covered with earth. A dried skull was placed at the sculpture's head, while sticks were used to represent the tail. He found this icon on more than one occasion.[89] We are never told why cattle are included in the ritual designs, but a passage in an early publication of Howitt's indicates that they do indeed belong in the representation of the All-Father's camp. According to an old informant, *Bunjil* 'possessed great numbers of cattle'.[90]

Cattle, of course, were central to White settlement and were the *raison d'être* for the colonial presence in much of south-east Australia. This, I believe, is the reason they were contextualised in *Bora*-type ritual. The 'figures on the ground and on the marked trees are emblematical' of *Baiami*'s first camp and 'the gifts he presented' to the world.[91] Their inclusion in such a rite brought what was unLawful and indeed destructive of the locative Law within the compass of a new Utopian Law. I will say more of this presently, but I must first proceed to show that cattle, while an apt symbol, were but one of a range of *Baiami*'s gifts.

Mathews, whose training as a surveyor inclined him at times to an almost compulsive measuring and recording of the layout of *Bora* grounds, is our best source for discovering references to components that are at odds with the research paradigms of the time. Even Mathews plays down such phenomena, noting them only in his more exhaustive surveys and even then neglecting to include them in diagrams and speaking of them disparagingly as indications of 'imitative faculties'. That their symbolism was deliberate must have been unthinkable. I will quote at length some of his descriptions:

> At one ground there was a representation of a horse and parts of a vehicle, outlined by carving in the soil . . . ; and near a stump which was naturally in that place, was the effigy of a blackfellow of sticks and old clothes, like a scarecrow, having round his neck a string from which was suspended a crescent shaped piece of tin resembling the brass plate sometimes given by Europeans to aboriginal kings.

At this ground was also a representation of a bullock and a grave containing old clothes. At another ground was

> an effigy made by filling an old pair of trousers and a coat with grass so as to resemble a man and a bundle of something being used for the head. This figure was then propped up against a small tree and represented a white fellow.

A range of more traditional figures is then described although some of these, such as the codfish, quite possibly had a reference to post-colonial life (*supra*). More unexpected are the following items:

> The imitative faculties of the natives were displayed in a few drawings, copied from scenes in the life of the white men, which were intermixed with the others. At one place an attempt had been made to represent a railway train, the carriages with their windows, the numerous wheels, and the two rails on which they were running. At another place a native artist had drawn a chain like those used when working bullocks in a dray. The links of the chain were on a colossal scale, being four feet nine inches long, and one foot three inches wide. The chain was close to the raised figure of the bullock previously described. Another draftsman, apparently a poker player, had succeeded in representing the four aces. Four rectangular spaces, about two feet long and eighteen inches wide, were first made side by side to indicate four cards, and on the middle of each of them one of the aces was delineated.[92]

The dendroglyphs or carved trees of the Bora grounds were also said to represent the All-Father's camp and gifts. These highly geometric designs are mostly undecipherable without the help of Aboriginal interpreters. Some initiated Aboriginal men this century have associated the designs with Christian symbolism,[93] but even as early as 1858 there were references to European cultural items depicted on the trees. Thomas Hall wrote of a Gidabal *Bora* ground just over the Queensland border in which one of the trees revealed a ship in full sail.[94]

Given the range of European items – cattle, horses, pigs, cards, trains, ships and even effigies of Whites themselves – that appear in *Bora* sculptures, and are thus represented as the benefaction of the All-Father, we might be tempted to dub the *Bora* an initiatory version of a 'cargo' cult and interpret it in terms of a general theory of 'cargoism'. But this will not do. 'Cargo,' as Trompf states, 'implies a totality of material, organizational and spiritual welfare, collectively desired as a replacement for current inadequacy, and projected into the imminent future as a coming "salvation".'[95] Cargoism is not defined by the symbolic presence of European goods *per se*, but by the message communicated by those objects and we have already seen in the previous chapter that Aboriginal people have had occasion to use cultic expressions of exotic forms of material culture to underline the reasons why they should *not* incorporate them into their world. Even in Melanesian contexts, as Burridge so perceptively reveals, it is not only a desire for commodities which attracts, but their symbolic moral significance.[96] In Aboriginal Australia, where cultural objects are attributed a very different value to that ascribed to them in Melanesia, we should anticipate that the ritual meaning of White goods will be equally unique.

In this regard the key difference between the *Bora* traditions I have described and 'cargoism' is that we have no indication that the depicted European cultural objects and domesticated animals possess soteriological value. While, as I have shown, there was some quasi-millennial activity in south-east Australia, it was of a transitory, almost pragmatic, nature. *Bora*, on the other hand, was overshadowed by a threatening apocalypse. I have already detailed examples of this mood, but no clearer statement of it is to be found than the central sculpture of the ceremony, the All-Father himself. Our earliest description comes from Henderson, who writes

> The figure . . . represents him in a recumbent position, as he is at present considered to be asleep. There is however a tradition, that once he awoke, and having turned himself on his side, the flood-gates of the salt ocean were immediately thrown open, and the hills and valleys disappeared beneath the rolling waters. It is also reported, that when he next awakes, a similar catastrophe may be expected.[97]

Far from anticipating total salvation or a millennium in which heaven redemptively descends to earth, White cultural items are contextualised in a cult apprehensive of the eschaton and bent on (to use the apt Aboriginal image) propping up the sky whose collapse would only cause disastrous flooding.

How, then, do we interpret the cultic innovations of the south-east of Australia? I confess that the inadequacies of the data mean that any tidy answer must presume as much as it can prove, but I offer the following as the interpretation which I find most convincing.

As I have shown, there were two options explored by Aborigines of the south-east in response to the emergent unbalanced dualism created by the dislocation of the traditional locative cosmology. Both focused on the future. The 'millennial' vision of an end to Whites, while understandably having some attractions, was less prominent than the cults concerned to ward off an imminent and disastrous eschaton. Although the literature will not allow us to specify exactly how these two orientations were historically and sociologically related,[98] we can at least assert that the difference between them was that while the former orientation saw Whites as the central cause of specific worldly problems the latter, while clearly addressing issues of inter-ethnic relations, conceptualised the problem in broader cosmological terms. Burridge expressed this succinctly when he wrote

> The problem is more urgent and more personal than whether they should be ruled by white men. They want to know where they stand in the world as men. And they know that they can only do this with the help of Europeans – moral Europeans.

Burridge proceeded to show that in Papua New Guinea access to European goods was in fact access to moral relationships.[99]

It seems that Aboriginal people in early south-east Australia also used symbols of European power and culture *not* in attempts to eradicate Whites or even merely to overthrow their hegemony, but rather to re-establish moral relationships within an increasingly immoral world. In contrast to Melanesian cases, however, goods were not understood as indications of status or merit in Aboriginal Australia. Nor, in contrast to the pastoral areas discussed later, is there any evidence that Aborigines of the south-east particularly prized the prospect of enhanced access to European commodities. I see no compelling reason to interpret icons of introduced animals and cultural objects as anything other than what they clearly were – symbols of central components of White life and Law.

Bora designs thus brought what I have categorised as the origin of unLawfulness, immorality and 'evil' in Aboriginal thought within the confines of a new, broader Law. *Baiami* had introduced both Aboriginal and White culture and hence both were by definition Lawful. The aim of these ceremonies was not to naïvely return to a pristine pre-colonial life by destroying Whites, but to maintain Aboriginal identity within the cosmos by demarcating its place within post-colonial society. In brief, it aimed to define invasion as a morally controllable act.

This was a precarious worldview; the unleashing of time and its threatening eschaton underscored the dangers. The peril was tolerated because of the promise of the new cosmology. It did not resolve dualism into monism as millennial hopes did. It did not overcome imbalance by having the one subsume the other. Rather, there was an attempt to simultaneously establish ethnic and cosmological balance, to allocate space to both Aboriginal and White Law, and in the face of total destruction, to shore up and demarcate the domain that can most deservedly be considered to have remained authentically Aboriginal.

At the end of the first section of this chapter I listed four summary points which encapsulated the new order of the universe. I argued that the emergence of an unequal dualism from an original single creative principle was an ontology replicating the process of invasion itself. I also suggested that the internal dynamics of such an understanding of the world established a momentum which sought its place of rest and balance in a radically restructured future. I have shown that Aboriginal people of south-east Australia envisioned that future, and on occasions welcomed its coming, but for the most part resisted the cosmos' urge to roll its eschatological waves over their land.

The new Aboriginal ontology shared many features with that of their invaders, bowing, as it did, to the introduced forces of time and Utopia. The central difference lay in their respective dreams for the future. Whereas in colonial Christian thought the world required the scouring intervention of the second coming, Aboriginal people trusted, as some still trust, in the powers of regeneration.

THE RISE AND FATE OF GOD

The sheer bulk of data anomalous to the thesis that the Aboriginal understanding of existence in this area was essentially conservative surely demands that we begin to re-evaluate our presuppositions. I hope to have made a beginning to that process.

We can at the very least be certain the new orientations diffused rapidly through colonial Australia. According to available evidence, the *Mulunga* cult spread from the Diamantina district in central Queensland to Penong on the central-south coast of Australia in just twenty-two years (see chapter 5), thus revealing the effectiveness of cultic exchange between Aboriginal societies. Howitt at times wished to deny that Gippsland initiations (*Jeraeil*), and particularly the representations of the All-Father, could have been influenced by more northerly peoples, yet on other occasions provides evidence that post-colonial innovation reached the area before Whites themselves had arrived. Indeed he actually notes institutionalised gatherings where the 'clever men' came 'to introduce such new beliefs or procedures as may have recommended itself [*sic*] to them'.[100] Others write of new songs and ritual which were communicated from the main regions of first settlement to distant communities of the south-east of Australia.[101]

Was the cult of *Baiami* itself a recent innovation? Our earliest record of it comes from the Wellington Valley mission, and this is a region with the social and intellectual environment to nurture such a doctrine. These people, of course, were heavily missionised, repeatedly requesting baptism even though the missionaries themselves could detect amongst them no true desire to change from their traditions.[102] Aborigines there, however, came to believe the missionaries were deceiving them, providing a context in which they could accept the incorporation of Christian cosmological structure into their own domain. Certainly, Wellington Valley inmates asked questions which appear to relate directly to the symbolism of *Baiami* ceremonies, including whether God made boats, knives and other objects of European extraction, and whether he lay down to sleep[103] (as *Baiami* is ritually depicted as doing). Why such queries presented themselves is something upon which Horatio Hale, the first professional ethnographer in Australia, cast light. He said the cult of God had in fact only reached the area in the late 1820s, writing

> When the missionaries first came to Wellington, the natives used to assemble once a year, in the month of February, to dance and sing a song in honour of Baiami. *This song was brought there from a distance by strange natives, who went about teaching it.* Those who refused to join in the ceremony were supposed to incur the displeasure of the god.[104]

We have no written documentation of *Baiami* that precedes the observations at Wellington Valley, and thus cannot establish where the 'strange natives' came from. My thesis would suggest from a region closer to the Sydney frontier, and there is one, admittedly ambiguous, piece of evidence that points in that direction. According to McCarthy, the iconography of the well known 'Devil's Rock' engravings depicts the mythological motifs found in the ground sculptures of the *Bora*. Other observers, including Mathews himself, did not make this connection, and it is far from a conclusive interpretation. If McCarthy is correct, however, the truly interesting fact is, once again, the ethnographic editing in the published descriptions of designs. For amongst the other mythic representations, and equally weathered, is a representation of a sailing vessel which probably dates the engraving to the late eighteenth century.[105]

Even more telling is an ochre painting which Macintosh claims to represent the same class of figures as the rock engravings of *Baiami*. Like the engravings, it depicts a male anthropomorph with outstretched limbs and having eyes but no nose or mouth. It differs conspicuously from the engravings, however, in one important respect. On the painted figure is a prominent pair of horns, unambiguously announcing it as a post-colonial mythic configuration.[106]

I cannot discern the thread of the *Baiami* cult any further back than this. What is clear is that whenever it is encountered, no matter how early, it is in association with change, innovation, and either the ontological principles or the cultural objects of White Australians. Whilst producing a precise interpretation of its meaning is a task fraught with pitfalls, there seems to be abundant evidence that, whatever it once may have been, by the time reports of it were written the *Bora* had become a cult adapted to colonial existence. The All-Father ceremony, if it was not a *Wanderkult*, then at the very least contained a 'wandering' cultic component which transformed the ceremonial significance of the performances.

Lest the reader feels this an unnecessarily radical stance, I will at this point note some alternative explanations for the anomalous features of Aboriginal traditions in south-east Australia. For, so long as Aboriginal studies have existed, scholars have known that here was a phenomenon demanding explication.

Howitt and his evolutionary colleagues did not hesitate to declare that the fertile climate of the south-east had allowed these Aborigines to advance in their theological development.[107] Both the evolutionism and environmental determinism of this claim were considered

dubious even when the thesis was first pronounced.[108] I also postulate an environmental causality, but one that is easily substantiated.
It was the suitability of the south-east of Australia for European agriculture which established this region as the centre of colonisation.

In his doctoral dissertation, A.P. Elkin offered a diffusionary
explanation for the peculiarity of the south-eastern beliefs, which he
maintained were historically connected with 21st Dynasty Egypt.[109]
This pan-Egyptianism, while given far less prominence, persisted
in his later writings on Aboriginal cultures. Again, I have also
employed 'diffusionary' arguments (although I reject the passive
connotations of the word) but see no reason to search beyond
the period of the most radical event in the history of Aboriginal
Australia – invasion.

The most promising interpretation to date was given in
Durkheim's classic study of Aboriginal religion. When he briefly
focused his attention on the High Gods of south-east Australia, he
intuitively grasped many of the most salient features of this
cosmology. Tantalising, inspired and probably now totally beyond
proof was his suggestion that a single sky-dwelling All-Father was
an emergent transformation of one of the mythically paired birds
that headed moieties.[110] This he correctly identified as a shift from
balanced, reciprocal 'tribal' cults to a tradition stressing a single
creative principle linked to an essentially 'international' socio-
religious base.[111] What induced these people to define themselves as
'one', and against what their collective identity was demarcated, was
something Durkheim should have been pre-eminently in a position
to detect. He baulked at the obvious answer, however, diverted by
one totally inaccurate preconception about the dynamic flexibility
of Aboriginal beliefs and the degree of European mission influence
in the south-east.[112] I welcome Durkheim's informed guess that the
monistic sky-dwelling All-Father had transmuted from the balanced
duality of once earth-bound moiety-linked Ancestral beings. And I
have proposed the social environment which Durkheim required to
explain why these Aborigines would feel compelled to abandon a
view of a homoeostatic and reciprocally ordered cosmos for one
stressing instability and a single yet eccentric notion of power.

Other explanations for the aberrant south-east traditions could no
doubt be fabricated by those with a taste for speculating into
the distant past. If, however, we once admit the possibility that
Aboriginal intellectual constructs can rapidly adjust to a changing
world, then surely we would do well to explore first the decidedly

conspicuous climate for socio-religious innovation created by the processes of conquest.

At present I have read only one statement that encapsulates the mood, if not the detail, of my position. It was made by a Wuradjeri man initiated at around the time Howitt and Mathews were undertaking their field research. His words were these:

> He was always amongst the people long ago . . . [w]hen the white people came out to Australia, Baiami heard that they were coming. He then got 'frightened', and cleared away . . .[113]

Although we each use a language appropriate to our own cultures and to the audiences we respectively address, I like to believe that we are both expressing different facets of a common understanding. If so, then I am content that I am keeping good theoretical company.

As for the fate of the Sky Hero, in those parts of south-east Australia where his story is still told there is clear evidence that his origin in a colonial environment is being explicitly acknowledged, although his *otiose* supra-worldly powers have since been subdued as the brutal brunt of invasion has taken on more subtle and insidious forms. In the closing pages of this chapter, I follow the fate of God into the twentieth century.

There are scattered references throughout New South Wales to Aboriginal people openly equating their narratives with Christian myth. By the 1930s, 'traditional' ceremonial forms had been largely discontinued, although as the recent Murrawon re-creation – for it is hardly a revival – of secret initiation practices reveals, all such obituary notices are perhaps premature.[114] In the main, however, as one mission-based Aborigine in north-west New South Wales said, 'the old Aboriginal beliefs are still there, but the old people that carried them out have gone – there's no one here to do it now'.[115] It is thus that ritual communication was replaced by stories now lacking a ceremonial base, and inevitably this change of medium was equally a transformation of message.

The most notable change in the post-ceremonial period has been the open, non-esoteric identification of the All-Father with the Christian God. This cannot be equated, however, with the thesis that such beliefs are therefore recently emergent, for there are solid links between these notions and those in existence when Victorian ethnography was still being recorded.

Elkin's fieldwork in the north-east of New South Wales in the mid-1930s, and again in 1942, consisted of long discussions with around fifteen initiated men, aged between forty-five and sixty. 'All of them,' he adds, 'had been through and to several rituals – their first Keepara or Burbung at about the age of 14, that is, before 1900.'[116] In other words, these were men initiated at the time Howitt and Mathews were making their pioneering studies of Aboriginal initiatory cults.

In an unpublished paper on 'Kattang Initiation', based on the aforementioned research, Elkin wrote

> The elders told myths of Gulambra, his virgin mother and followers, and showed marks in the rocks where they had been. D.M. [Dick McClement] saw what seemed to him remarkable – a circle with no trees, and where grass only grows for a short time, and then dies. This was a camping place of Gulambra and his men. He saw one near Kupal Kupal, where Gulambra camped performing initiation.
>
> A. Woodlands told of a similar circle at Arakun [*sic*]. In the middle was a stone; there is no grass in the ring. It is the burial ground of the cult hero – 'our saviour' who was killed by a spear which had been thrown very high.
>
> The hero and his men travelled north; he left his girdle and tassel with his mother, telling her that if anything came out of it, this would indicate that he was ill or in trouble. The old fellows told D.M. that Gulambra was killed up north.[117]

How much should we make of small anachronistic details such as references to 'our saviour' and a singling out of a 'virgin mother' in a culture where this was hardly remarkable? After all, these are no more conspicuous – indeed, they are much less so – than the 'aberrations' discussed in earlier accounts. Elkin, for one, seemed to recognise nothing out of the ordinary in what he had recorded, and some readers might wish therefore to allow him final adjudication. Another interpretation, however, is more authoritative, for it seems Aborigines themselves have made pronouncedly explicit those elements many academics have but reluctantly recorded.

Kaatung men have more recently identified *Gulambra* as being the 'Native Christ', and the story, with the decline of initiatory practice, has become increasingly open in terms of secrecy. According to one informant, *Gulambra* was involved with the first agricultural act (planting a sycamore tree seed). Later, when his people were battling, he hung his loincloth in a tree, saying if it bled it meant he was dead. He was eventually speared in the chest, and buried at Cape Hawke.

> And they buried him there, buried him there, and the third day he rose. He rose in the air and he said to his tribe, he says, 'I will put two spots

[stars of the Southern Cross] in the sky, and when they miss, and when they were missing, I am coming. I am coming again.' The grave is there today, at Hawke Head, the Saviour's grave, and the twelve men, his twelve disciples, sat around and where they sat . . . the grass don't grow on it.[118]

This Kaatung interpretation, with a lineage back to the nineteenth century, far from being idiosyncratic, is a story repeated from the mid-north coast of New South Wales up to the Queensland border.

Amongst the Gumbaynggir, the All-Father was known as *Yuludara*. He created all that existed, say our late nineteenth century sources, and had dominion over all spirits. *Yuludara* is also known by the name *Birugan*, literally, 'handsome'.[119] Again, he lives with his mother, is engaged in a battle, hangs a portent (this time a bag of ochre) in a tree and is killed. In the Gambaynggir version, his burial site is that recorded by Elkin, a ringed place at Arakoon.[120]

There are several published, and two unpublished, Gumbaynggir Jesus narratives of which I am aware.[121] John Flanders says *Birugan* was one of two sons of 'God', the other one going to the far side of the world. 'Birroogun is our Jesus,' said Flanders, and an additional intriguing element is that the place of his death was where a racecourse once stood[122] (the ring with no grass Elkin described?). The Arakoon racecourse, I might add, is now long gone, and the grave of 'Jesus' currently lies beneath the fifth green of South West Rocks golfcourse.

Harry Buchanan, initiated in the 1920s, was a well known spokesperson for Gumbaynggir beliefs. Buchanan not only interpreted dendroglyphs as representing the spear thrust in 'Christ's' side,[123] but makes the following comments on *Birugan*.

Birugkan – that's Christ. And the lord himself, they call him Baba. Baba means Father . . . these places – they not let anybody see them see. Even women, see. That's all men's secrets and women got their own secrets . . . there's no women allowed to go there to look at that [diamond tree] . . . they go blind – or do something. You see, that's the blackfellow's bible – he needs that just the same as he's reading the Bible out to you. All those diamonds – that's all lines for him, see. You know the lines where you read – you read all about Christ and all about God – they can read it out to you there – right around the tree.[124]

Buchanan also links the Gumbaynggir tradition with those of the Bandjalang to the north (using a 'Noah's ark' mytheme).[125] Here there had been extensive church influence,[126] and in his famous article on Bandjalang pentecostalism, Malcolm Calley seems to suggest the myth of *Balugan* (Christ) was a relatively recent phenomenon.[127] Since his details, from the virgin mother to the burial beneath the Arakoon racecourse, have, as we have seen, a continuous history going back to the nineteenth century, we are clearly obliged to recognise a more ancient origin.

I have focused on the especially illuminating developments in northern coastal regions of the south-east because their documentation is particularly full, but cognate examples could be drawn from other regions. Caroline Kelly provides some fleeting glimpses from southern Queensland, as does Jeremy Beckett for western New South Wales.[128] At the most recent extreme, we might even consider the words of Burnum Burnum:

> I, like every Aboriginal person, believe in and acknowledge the existence of the Great Spirit. Some of us know it as God, others by other names such as Biami. It is believed that around Wollombi, in a cave there, is a physical manifestation of Biami in the form of a huge cave painting that has exaggerated arms outstretched to embrace all beings.[129]

Generally characterising the post-ritual form of the All-Father is a newly expressed relationship with both Whites and land. The decline of ceremonial traditions in itself marks a weakening of a separate Aboriginal structural autonomy. Thus it is fitting that this was accompanied by a shift from a secret belief in an All-Father who, although having the same attributes, was separate from the Christian God and largely in competition with him, to a model of public identity of a single world Godhead. At the same time, however, this God has also become more localised, with the emphasis shifting to the immanence of his place of death rather than the transcendent 'no-place' or Utopia to which he departed. Faced with ongoing internal-colonialism and the self-destructiveness of clinging overly long to faith in eschatological liberation, Aborigines of south-east Australia have reshaped their All-Father so as to allow some rapprochement between universal and ubietous spatial authority.

Yet to my mind, the Fatherhood of God in Aboriginal Australia always casts an imperial shadow. Short of revoking the deity's transcendence, as Cape York Aborigines had done with their Heroes, the only road open to Aborigines wishing to hold more firmly to their place would be to reform the way God touched the world. In searching for guidance on how this might be achieved, they might discover much – indeed, this has already begun – from those Aboriginal people to the north who fashioned the All-Mother.

NOTES

1. E. Armitage, 'Corroborees of the Aborigines of Great Sandy Island', in 'Vocabularies of Four Representative Tribes of South Eastern Queensland', by F.J. Watson, *Supplement to Journal of the Royal Geographical Society of Australia (Queensland)*, 48 (nd), p. 96.
2. R. Evans & J. Walker, 'These Strangers Where are They Going . . .', *Occasional Papers in Anthropology*, 8 (1977), p. 41. This symbolic interpretation perhaps anticipates the more recent Cook narratives of northern Australia (see Conclusion).
3. D. Collins, *An Account of the English Colony in New South Wales* (London: A.H. & A.W. Reed, 1798), vol. 1, p. 496.
4. ibid., p. 497.
5. N. Butlin, *Our Original Aggression: Aboriginal Populations of Southeastern Australia 1788-1850* (Sydney: George Allen & Unwin, 1983), p. 147. For a more recent resume of the re-evaluations of Aboriginal population figures, and references to some critiques, see T. Dingle, *Aboriginal Economy: Patterns of Experience* (Melbourne/ Sydney: McPhee Gribble/Penguin, 1988), pp. 21-2.
6. A.T. Yarwood and M.J. Knowling, *Race Relations in Australia: A History* (Sydney: Methuen Australia, 1982), p. 102; R.H.W. Reece, *Aborigines and Colonists: Aborigines and Colonial Society in New South Wales in the 1830s and 1840s* (Sydney: University of Sydney Press, 1974), pp. 17-21.
7. Reece, *Aborigines and Colonists*, pp. 21ff.
8. C.D. Rowley, *The Destruction of Aboriginal Society* (Canberra: Australian National University Press, 1970), p. 96.
9. B. Field, *Geographical Memoirs on New South Wales* (London: John Murray,1825), pp. 433-4.
10. E. Kolig, 'Post-Contact Religious Movements in Australian Aboriginal Society', *Anthropos*, 82 (1987), pp. 255-6 & n. 7. Kolig does simply dubs the hinted changes 'syncretisms,' relegated to the position of 'The most facile method of reforming a belief system' (p. 255).
11. For some of the reasons for the failure of scholars to investigate change in Aboriginal religions see D. Rose & T. Swain, 'Introduction', in *Aboriginal Australians and Christian Missions: Ethnographic and Historical Studies*, edited by T. Swain & D. Rose (Adelaide: Australian Association for the Study of Religions, 1988), pp. 2-5.
12. Letter from John Mathew to R.H. Mathews dated 11/12/1907, p. 3, *Elkin Papers*, Fisher Library, p. 130, Box 32, folder 1/9/7.
13. B. Attwood, *The Making of the Aborigines* (Sydney: Allen & Unwin, 1989), p. 78.
14. See especially D.H. Turner, *Life Before Genesis: A Conclusion* (New York: Peter Lang, 1985); also B. Glowczewski, 'Australian Aborigines, Topology and Cross-Cultural Analysis', paper presented at the *Fifth*

International Conference on Hunting and Gathering Societies, Darwin 1988.

15. T. Swain, 'The Ghost of Space: Reflections on Warlpiri Christian Iconography and Ritual', in *Aboriginal Australians and Christian Missions*, edited by Swain & Rose, pp. 452–69.

16. A.W. Howitt, *The Native Tribes of South-East Australia* (London: Macmillan, 1904), p. 440.

17. R.H. Mathews, *Ethnographical Notes on the Aboriginal Tribes of New South Wales and Victoria* (Sydney: Government Printer, 1905), pp. 146 & 99.

18. Howitt, *The Native Tribes . . .*, p. 453.

19. see C. Pardoe, 'The Cemetery as Symbol', *Archaeology in Oceania*, 23 (1988), pp. 11 ff.

20. M.F.A. Montagu, *Coming Into Being Among the Australian Aborigines* (London: Routledge & Kegan Paul, revised edition, 1974), p. 221; Mathews, *Ethnographical Notes . . .*, p. 95.

21. A.R. Radcliffe-Brown, 'Notes on Totemism in Eastern Australia', *Journal of the Royal Anthropological Institute of Great Britain and Ireland*, 59 (1929), pp. 405–6. See also M.J. Calley, 'Aboriginal Pentecostalism: A Study in Change in Religion, North Coast, N.S.W.' (University of Sydney: MA Thesis, 1955), part 2, p. 25.

22. N. Munn, 'The Transformation of Subjects into Objects in Walbiri and Pitjantjatjara Myth', in *Australian Aboriginal Studies: Modern Studies in the Social Anthropology of Australian Aborigines*, edited by R.M. Berndt (Nedlands: University of Western Australia Press, 1970).

23. The sky is not, of course, intrinsically Utopian. In most Aboriginal cosmologies specific regions of the sky also have a locative mythic nature, although sky- and earth-dwelling Ancestors may belong to discrete linguistic categories. The sky does, however, lend itself to becoming the region of unlocatable Ancestors.

24. R.M. Berndt, *Australian Aboriginal Religion*. Iconography of Religions, section V (Leiden: E.J. Brill, 1974), fascicle 1, p. 28.

25. D. Rose, 'Jesus and the Dingo', in *Aboriginal Australians and Christian Missions*, edited by Swain & Rose, p. 361.

26. W.E. Roth, *North Queensland Ethnography: Bulletin No.5: Superstition, Magic and Medicine* (Brisbane: Government Printer, 1903), p. 16.

27. Collins, *An Account of the English Colony . . .*, p. 454.

28. cit. K. Willey, *When the Sky Fell Down: The Destruction of the Tribes of the Sydney Region 1788–1850s* (Sydney: Collins, 1979), pp. 51–2.

29. Howitt, The *Native Tribes . . .*, p. 444.

30. E.J. Eyre, *Journals of Expeditions of Discovery into Central Australia* (London: T. & W. Boone, 1845), vol. 2, pp. 366–7.

31. T.L. Mitchell, *Three Expeditions into the Interior of Eastern Australia* (London: T. & W. Boone, 1839), vol. 1, p. 247.

32. W. Ridley, 'Report on Australian Languages and Traditions', *Journal of the Anthropological Institute of Great Britain and Ireland*, 2 (1873), p. 269.

33. 'Report of the 1845 Parliamentary Committee on the Condition of the Aborigines', reprinted in *Aboriginal Land Rights: A Submission to the Federal Minister for Aboriginal Affairs on the Preferred National Land Rights Model*, CCJP Issues no. 4. (Sydney: Catholic Commission for Justice and Peace, 1985), Appendix 1, p. 19, my emphasis.

34. Rose, 'Jesus and the Dingo', p. 373.

35. My favourite example is the parodying of the well known Catholic missionary Fr. Duncan McNab, as recorded in C.C. Petrie, *Tom Petrie's Reminiscences of Early Queensland* (Brisbane: Queensland Book Depot, 1904), pp. 215–16.

36. Howitt, *The Native Tribes . . .*, p. 504.

37. L. Fison & A.W. Howitt, *Kamilaroi and Kurnai: Group-Marriage and Relationship, and Marriage by Elopement* (Netherlands: Anthropological Publications, 1969), p. 255.

38. This statement was made by J.F. Mann in response to J. Manning's 'Notes on the Aborigines of New Holland', *Journal and Proceedings of the Royal Society of New South Wales*, 16 (1882), p. 170.

39. M. Eliade, *Australian Religions*, p. 7; A. Lang, 'Australian Gods: A Reply', *Folk-Lore*, 10 (1899), pp. 31–2. Eliade is also mistaken in claiming 'The belief [in the All-Father] was witnessed before the installation of Christian missions' (*loc. cit.*). The earliest reference to Baiami in fact comes from the second mission to Aborigines at Wellington. We should not, however, confine Christian influence to missions. Marsden's school at Parramatta began in 1814 and had a substantial proselytising role. Even in the eighteenth century Collins wrote: 'The young people who reside among our houses were very desirous of going to church' (*An Account of the English Colony . . .*, p. 455).

A variation of this argument, used by Howitt and others, depends on finding All-Father beliefs in isolated pockets where missions had not penetrated. My thesis, however, is that we are dealing with a cult spreading in advance of missions. C.G. Seligman's 'An Australian Bible Story', from which I quoted in the previous chapter, provides a nice example of how this occurred in Cape York Peninsula.

40. Some clear examples can be found in Radcliffe-Brown, 'Notes on Totemism . . .', *passim*.

41. Kolig, 'Post-Contact Religious Movements . . .', p. 256.

42. cit., W. Ridley, *Kamilaroi and Other Australian Languages . . .* (Sydney: Government Printer, 1875), p. 135.

43. Howitt, *The Native Tribes . . .*, p. 501.

44. Manning, 'Notes on the Aborigines . . .', p. 160.

45. R.M. Berndt, 'Wuradjeri Magic and "Clever Men" ', *Oceania*, 17 (1947), p. 334, n. 16.

46. J. Macarthur, *New South Wales: Its Present State and Future Prospects* ... (London: D. Walther, 1837), Appendix 55, p. 299.
47. McDonald, 'Two Ways', p. 75.
48. Eyre, *Journals of Expeditions* ..., vol. 2, p. 367. Cf. also p. 357.
49. W. Ridley, 'The Aboriginal "Murri" Race of Australia', *Nature*, 10 (1874), pp. 521–2. Sometimes the 'better country' is equated with England. A Tasmanian example of this can be found in Ling Roth, *The Aborigines of Tasmania*, p. 55.
50. K. Maddock, *The Australian Aborigines*, p. 127.
51. D. Rose, 'The Saga of Captain Cook: Morality in Aboriginal and European Law', *Australian Aboriginal Studies 2* (1988), p. 29.
52. Oldfield, cit. E.B. Tylor, 'On the Limits of Savage Religion', *Journal of the Anthropological Institute of Great Britain and Ireland*, 21 (1891), p. 292; cf. Manning, 'Notes on the Aborigines ...', p. 162, where the reference to a bullock head is more ambiguous.
53. P.E. Strzelecki, *Physical Description of New South Wales and Van Diemens Land* (London: Longman, Brown, Green & Longman, 1845), p. 339.
54. H. Hale, *Ethnography and Philology*, volume 6 of 'United States Exploring Expedition During the Years 1838, 1839, 1840, 1841, 1842', by C. Wilkes (Philadelphia: Lea & Blanchard, 1846), p. 110.
55. J. Woolmington, 'Early Christian Missions to the Australian Aborigines: A Study in Failure', Ph.D. Dissertation (Armidale: University of New England, 1979), p. 164.
56. F.A. Fitzpatrick, *The Early Day Aborigines: Description of the 'Gaboora': As Seen by Phillip Cohen, Esq., in the Hastings River District in the Year 1838* (Wingham, NSW: Wingham Cronicle, nd), p. 12.
57. Manning, 'Notes on the Aborigines ...', p. 165.
58. Yarwood & Knowling, *Race Relations in Australia*, p. 102; cf. Ferry, 'The Failure of the New South Wales Missions ...', p. 34.
59. F.W. Jones, *Tasmania's Vanished Race* (Melbourne: Australian Broadcasting Company, 1935), p. 32.
60. R.M. Berndt in 'Wuradjeri Magic ...', uses Cameron, without critical comment, as his main early source. See p. 329, n. 5.
61. A.L.P. Cameron, 'Notes on Some Tribes of New South Wales', *Journal of the Anthropological Institute of Great Britain and Ireland*, 14 (1885), pp. 364–5.
62. Parker, in T.H. Braim, *A History of New South Wales from its Settlement to the Close of the Year 1844* (London: Bentley, 1846), vol. 2, p. 444.
63. E.S. Hartland, 'The "High Gods" of Australia', *Folk-Lore*, 9 (1898), pp. 290–329, *passim*.
64. Lang, 'Australian Gods', pp. 26ff; E.S. Hartland, 'Australian Gods: Rejoinder', *Folk-Lore*, 10 (1899), p. 53.
65. R.M. Berndt, 'Influence of European Culture on Australian Aborigines', *Oceania*, 21 (1951), p. 235.
66. K.O.L. Burridge, *New Heaven New Earth: A Study of Millenarian Activities* (Oxford: Basil Blackwell, 1969) p. 172, fn. 1.

67. Berndt, 'Wuradjeri Magic . . .', p. 331.
68. Reproduced in A. Massola, *The Aborigines of South-Eastern Australia as they were* (Melbourne: Heinemann, 1971), p. 67.
69. G.S. Lang, cit. S. Bennett, *Australian Discovery and Colonisation* (Sydney: Hanson & Bennett, 1865), vol. 2, pp. 284f.
70. Collins, *An Account of the English Colony . . .*, p. 495.
71. Eyre, *Journals of Expeditions . . .*, p. 358.
72. Howitt, *The Native Tribes . . .*, pp. 331, 415 & 417.
73. O. Siebert, 'Sagen und Sitten der Dieri und Nachbarstämme in Zentral-Australien', *Globus*, 97 (1910), pp. 57–9.
74. A.W. Howitt, papers, State Library of Victoria, Box 9, Folder 3, Paper 8, p. 10.
75. R.B. Smyth, *The Aborigines of Victoria* (Melbourne: John Currey, 1876), vol. 1, p. 445.
76. cit., ibid., p. 446, fn.
77. *loc. cit.*
78. This was emphasised both by Thomas in Smyth, *loc. cit.*; and Eyre, *Journals of Expeditions . . .*, pp. 358–9.
79. Howitt, *The Native Tribes . . .*, p. 427. See also Joseph Shaw, 'Aborigines and Missionary Operations Amongst Them', unpub. ms. H17557, State Library of Victoria, 1868, p. 22.
80. Morgan, *The Life and Adventures of William Buckley . . .*, p. 64.
81. see my fn. 25. In some narratives an unknown distant place on earth replaces the image of an *otiose* sky home. The more significant point is not earth vs. sky but location vs. Utopia.
82. R.H. Mathews, *Folklore of the Australian Aborigines* (Sydney: Hennessey, Harper & Co., 1899), pp. 15–19.
83. C.A. Brewster to R.H. Mathews, undated letter, *Elkin papers*, Fisher Library, p. 130, Box 32, folder 1/9/4.
84. K.L. Parker, *The Euahlayi Tribe* (London: Archibald Constable, 1905), pp. 75–6; Berndt, 'Wuradjeri Magic . . .', p. 331, also notes the power of the clever man to 'thrust his mind forward into the future'.
85. A.W. Howitt, papers, State Library of Victoria, Box 9, Folder 3, Paper 8, p. 3.
86. A.P. Elkin's, 'R.H. Mathews: His Contribution to Aboriginal Studies: Part II', *Oceania*, 46 (1975), p. 143.
87. Reproduced in R.M. Berndt, *Australian Aboriginal Religion*, fascicle 1, plates 49 & 56.
88. Balanced examples can be found in M.J. Meggitt, *Desert People: A Study of the Walbiri Aborigines of Central Australia* (Sydney: Angus & Robertson, 1962), chapter 16.
89. R.H. Mathews, 'Aboriginal Bora Held at Gundabloui in 1894', *Journal and Proceedings of the Royal Society of New South Wales*, 28 (1894), p. 112; 'The Bora of the Kamilaroi Tribes', *Proceedings of the Royal Society of Victoria*, 9 (1897), p. 142.

90. Fison & Howitt, *Kamilaroi and Kurnai*, p. 210, fn.
91. Mathews, 'Aboriginal Bora Held at Gundabloui . . .', p. 114.
92. ibid., p. 110f ('King' was the title given by colonists to Aborigines who wore the brass plates); *idem*, 'The Bora of the Kamilaroi Tribes', p. 142.
93. K.H. Lane, 'Carved Trees and Initiation Ceremonies on the Nambucca River', in *Records of Times Past: Ethnohistorical Essays on the Culture and Ecology of the New England Tribes*, edited by I. McBryde (Canberra: Australian Institute of Aboriginal Studies, 1978), p. 233.
94. cit. J.G. Steele, *Aboriginal Pathways in Southeast Queensland and the Richmond River* (St Lucia: University of Queensland Press, 1984), p. 43.
95. Trompf, 'Introduction', pp. 10–11.
96. K.O.L. Burridge, *Mambu: A Melanesian Millennium* (London: Methuen, 1960), p. 280: 'They do not seek rice; they have it', etc.
97. J. Henderson, *Observations on the Colonies of New South Wales and Van Diemen's Land* (Calcutta: Baptist Mission Press, 1832), p. 147.
98. K.-P. Koepping, 'Nativistic Movements in Aboriginal Australia: Creative Adjustment, Protest or Regeneration of Tradition', in *Aboriginal Australians and Christian Missions*, edited by Swain & Rose, p. 402, distinguishes various social groups coming to the fore at different periods of Kimberley religious history. The texts for the south-east do not allow such detailed discrimination.
99. Burridge, *Mambu*, p. 243; chapter 8, *passim*.
100. Howitt, *The Native Tribes . . .*, pp. 505, 444 & 641.
101. N. Gunson (ed.), *Australian Reminiscences and Papers of L.E. Threlkeld* (Canberra: Australian Institute of Aboriginal Studies, 1974), vol. 1, p. 56. See Gunson's fn. 72 for further examples.
102. Woolmington, 'Early Christian Missions', p. 146.
103. McDonald, ' "Two Ways" ', p. 76.
104. Hale, 'Ethnography and Philology', pp. 110–11.
105. cit. J. Clegg, *Prehistoric Pictures as Evidence About Religion* (Sydney: Author's printed and distributed copies, 1985), pp. 29–34.
106. N.W.G. Macintosh, 'Dingo and Horned Anthropomorph in an Aboriginal Rock Shelter', *Oceania*, 36 (1965), p. 89.
107. Howitt, *The Native Tribes . . .*, pp. 499–500.
108. I have documented this in Swain, *Interpreting Aboriginal Religion*, pp. 93–8.
109. A.P. Elkin, 'Ritual and Mythology in Australia: An Historical Study' (University of London: PhD Thesis, 1927), p. 302.
110. E. Durkheim, *The Elementary Forms of the Religious Life* (New York: The Free Press, 1915), pp. 330f. I suspect Durkheim first came across the idea of the All-Father as a metamorphosed moiety-linked Ancestral being in N.W. Thomas' article 'Baiame and the Bell-Bird', *Man*, 5 (1905), pp .49–52.
111. Durkheim, ibid., pp. 331f. The pan-Aboriginal quality of religious change in post-colonial Australia is emphasised in E. Kolig's *The*

Silent Revolution: The Effects of Modernization on Australian Aboriginal Religion (Philadelphia: Institute for the Study of Human Issues, 1981).

112. Durkheim, ibid., p. 327.

113. Berndt, 'Wuradjeri Magic . . .', p. 334, n. 16.

114. Some twenty Murrawon Aboriginal men have been initiated in the last few years, led by Lenny de Silvia [pers. comm. Lenny de Silvia, August, 1990].

115. cit. Fink, 'The Caste Barrier – An Obstacle to the Assimilation of Part-Aborigines in North-West New South Wales', *Oceania*, 28 (1957), p. 110.

116. Elkin, 'R.H. Mathews', p. 147.

117. A.P. Elkin, 'Kattang Initiation', unpublished ms., *Elkin Papers*, Fisher Library, p. 130, Box 11, Folder 1/3/10, pp. 2-3.

118. N.M. Holmer & V.E. Holmer, *Stories from Two Native Tribes of Eastern Australia* (Uppsala: A.-B. Lundequistska, 1969), pp. 34-6.

119. W.E. Smythe, *Elementary Grammar of the Gumbaingar Language (North Coast of New South Wales)*, Oceania Monograph No. 8 (Sydney: University of Sydney, 1948), p. 296.

120. For a composite version, see W.G. Hoddinott, 'The Languages and Myths of the New England Area', in *Records of Time Past*, edited by McBryde, pp. 52-60; a convenient collated source on this topic is J.S. Ryan (ed.), *The Land of Ulitarra: Early Records of the Aborigines of the Mid-North Coast of New South Wales* (Armidale: University of New England, 1964).

121. One account which I do not discuss here was given by Sharon Smith at the Conference *Aboriginal Spirituality: Past, Present, Future* (Victor Harbor: 2-6 August 1990).

122. R. Robinson, *The Man Who Sold His Dreaming* (Sydney: Currawong, 1965), pp. 37 & 39.

123. cit. Lane, 'Carved Trees . . .', p. 233.

124. H. Buchanan, Transcript of Interview at Nambucca Heads, Source Unknown (nd), p. 1.

125. ibid., p. 4.

126. Calley, 'Aboriginal Pentecostalism'; also R.G. Hausfeld, 'Aspects of Aboriginal Station Management' (MA Dissertation: University of Sydney, 1960), chapter 14.

127. M.J. Calley, 'Pentecostalism Among the Bandjelang', in *Aborigines Now: New Perspectives in the Study of Aboriginal Communities*, edited by M. Reay (Sydney: Angus & Robertson, 1964), pp. 52-3.

128. C. Kelly, 'Some Aspects of Culture Contact in Eastern Australia', *Oceania*, 15 (1944), pp. 151-2; J. Beckett, 'Marginal Men: A Study of Two Half Caste Aborigines', *Oceania*, 29 (1958), pp. 105-7.

129. cit. 'What Australians Believe About God', *Good Weekend* (March 25 1989), p. 31.

CHAPTER 4

Our Mother From Northern Shores

Tidal water flowing, white foam on the waves,
Fresh water from the rain flows into the river,
There are the paperbark trees: the soft bark falls into the water,
Rain falls from the clouds,
Waters of the river are swirling,
She emerges, and walks on dry land.[1]

Aboriginal opinion in the north of Australia is clear: the Mother
of Us All came from across the sea. Her home was often a distant
land. Sometimes that land is Macassar.

The transcendent Father of Us All, said Aborigines in south-
eastern Australia, abandoned the world for a remote heaven. I have
already told the story of that 'New Sky Hero from a Conquered
Land'. This chapter, in contrast, is the history of immanence: the
Earth Mother from Northern Waters.

Between the world and a void; between the womb and the absent
Father: these are the choices strangers bring.

My theme is the art of selecting the Mother.

TRANSCENDENTAL COMPARISONS

Whilst chronicling the emergence of the All-Father I located his
intrusion within the context of a colonial onslaught. My argument
was hardly novel. Reflecting on the conditions under which
Christianity might usurp 'paganism', the young Hegel once wrote:

> despotism . . . chased the human spirit from the earth and spread a misery
> which compelled men to seek and expect happiness in heaven; robbed
> of freedom, their spirit, their eternal and absolute element was forced
> to take flight to the deity.[2]

Yet it is not Hegel's authority that assures me my interpretation
is correct. Nor, in the final instance, is it the ethnographies for that

159

region, which omit nothing save the essential and seem always to fail precisely when they are most needed. It is only possible to fully understand the All-Father by discovering the conditions under which his invading presence might be denied. This is the message of the All-Mother.

I began the tragedy of south-eastern Australia by referring to the presence of Sir Matthew Flinders' ship along that coast in 1802. Aborigines recorded its sighting in a ceremony. In the following year on the northern coast, Flinders in turn recorded his observations in a journal. He discovered the indications of a 'foreign people . . . were almost as numerous, and as widely extended, as those left by the natives',[3] and subsequently learned of the presence of some sixty Macassan praus and the 1,000 men who sailed them. They were, he said, 'Mahometans' of a port-drinking kind who came annually on the monsoons to collect trepang for the Chinese market. Their 'chief', Pobassoo,[4] said the industry had only spread to these waters twenty years earlier, which would make their arrival in Australia virtually simultaneous with the colonial advent in the south-east.

The comparison is irresistible. Even if, as is likely, Pobassoo had underestimated the history of these visits, which current research suggests began towards the beginning of the eighteenth century,[5] we are still presented with two essentially concurrent cases of strangers entering Aboriginal lands.

There is more. In Aboriginal Australia there are only two regions where Ancestral Beings who stand in a single, universal relationship with all people occur. They are the Father of All of the south-east and the All-Mother of the north.

Two cases of intrusion into Aboriginal territories: two cases of atypical Ancestral Beings. Could these incidents be related? And more importantly, if they are, how can the differing types of contact be aligned with the contrasting beliefs? We are here offered a perfect situation for observing the bearing that certain forms of intellectual dynamic have on the genesis of symbolism in cosmologies of disrupted space.

As is the case with the ethnographies from elsewhere in Australia, however, so northern studies too have shied from examining processes of ideological change. Yet the contexts are not always identical. In the south-east it was simply denied any innovation had occurred. In Arnhem Land, although the intercultural associations were far less intense, they were readily acknowledged – and then ignored. Such are the subtleties of anthropological theory.

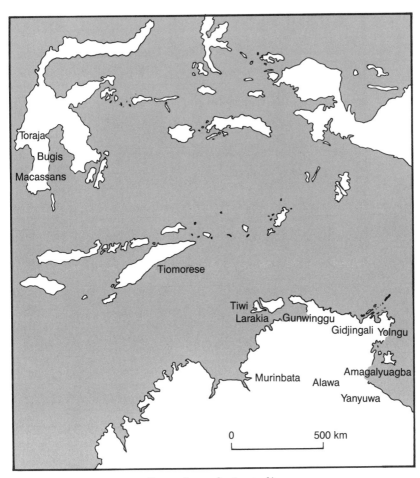

Central-north Australia.

W. Lloyd Warner, who pioneered serious studies of Macassan influences on Aboriginal cultures, begins this record of neglect. While he stresses the influence of distant Aboriginal traditions on Yolngu beliefs, he abruptly concludes, in the face of his own evidence, 'the Malays only slightly influenced Murngin mythology'.[6] Few have accepted his evaluation, although they give every indication they would like to. Finding the sheer bulk of data attesting to reform cannot be denied, they have argued that when Aboriginal cosmologies change nothing changes at all. New motifs are said to have been appended to an immutable order, providing what Macknight dismisses as 'merely an exotic colour to the cultural fabric of Aboriginal societies'.[7]

And finally when all else fails, there is that traditional academic standby, instanced here by the Berndts: 'Aboriginal religion may have been influenced considerably by association with the traders . . . However, to discuss this aspect here . . .'[8]

The dilemma is clear; we cannot deny the evidence but we do not know how to begin to understand it. Capell and Elkin, who believed 'The greatest influence of . . . Macassans was in the field of mythology and religion', advocated intensive comparisons with Indonesian cults.[9] The suggestion has some merit and I make a first exploration of this kind below, but such enquiries only verify the presence of historical connections whose meanings still remain concealed. That compulsive acquisition of data affectionately known as vacuum-cleaner ethnography can never in itself open us to the world of others. At worst it is our attachment to the compendiums of empirical information itself which blinds us. What Urry and Walsh say in regard to the 'Lost "Macassar Language" of Northern Australia' applies equally to the study of northern Australian worldviews:

> mere tabulations of assumed cultural connections based on surviving patterns are an insult to Aboriginal creativity. The important questions to consider in assessing the impact and reaction of 'Macassans' in Aboriginal cultures are not those involving how or where influences occurred on separate aspects of Aboriginal culture but the effects of the contacts on the total pattern of existence.[10]

In this chapter I take this recommendation a step further; for beyond the 'total pattern of existence' is the Abiding Law, the pattern of that totality which is all that might exist. To understand the Macassan impact on Aboriginal ceremonial life is therefore to discover how their ontology could reform in order to accommodate these strangers.

The first section of my account explores the coming of the people from southern Sulawesi and the central issue of their occupation of lands for which Aborigines felt they lacked spiritual entitlement. I examine the myths of shared space which were woven around this problem and the structures which were established to morally confine a people whose eternal abodes must remain elsewhere.

The first section looks outwards to the essence of a distant people. The second is introspective and turns to the All-Mother who came from across the seas to reside within Aboriginal lands. The Mother, I argue, does not address the Macassans *per se* but rather a new concern their arrival introduced into northern Aboriginal Australia – the possibility of unity. I propose that the Mother's genius is her ability to reinforce plurality while acknowledging oneness, and I compare this to the somewhat imperialistic monism of the All-Father in the south-east, offering explanations for the choice of symbolism under various forms of encounter with strangers.

In the final pages of this chapter I unfold the most recent moments of the All-Mother's story, in which she at last emerges simply as the Earth itself. This latest transformation is shown to belong to a post-colonial period in which the All-Father was once again ascending Aboriginal skies. My narrative here comes full circle, ending with the northern Australians grappling with the same cosmological scenario the Aborigines of the south-east had been forced to confront one and a half centuries earlier.

THE MACASSANS

A PLACE FOR STRANGERS

Aborigines today remember with fondness their visitors from the north. This uncomplicated sentiment has, however, led to considerable confusion in scholarship. Those who have mostly relied on Aboriginal oral traditions have tended to romanticise the past while others, who take into account both oral and documentary records of bloody confrontations, paint a bleaker picture. The Berndts have sought a chronological resolution to this apparent contradiction by suggesting tensions only developed during the final decades of the trepang industry[11] – an assessment Pobassoo may have wished to contest as a spear was being removed from his knee. He had, after all, warned Flinders 'to beware of the natives'.[12]

There can be no doubt that violence was a recurrent theme in the Aboriginal association with Macassans. Macknight suspects 'the ahistorical mentality of Aborigines' has edited these episodes from their collective memory,[13] but this too is an unsatisfactory stance. Aborigines remember the conflicts well enough and are not senti-mentalists wallowing nostalgically in their past.[14] When Macassans are presented so favourably against the Whites who succeeded them we are, I believe, being offered a deliberate yet subtle comparison of differing classes of strangers.

I have argued that when Aborigines in the south-east failed to affiliate with and spatially locate the colonists they were forced to conclude these were people who were not governed by Law. Their perceived amorality was manifest particularly in their wholesale appropriation of land and seemingly pointless murder of entire communities. This view of Whites has also been explored in northern Australia,[15] but significantly it was not applied to the Macassans.

With the possible exceptions of disruption caused by intoxication and confusion, disputes with the Indonesians were due either to their sexual relations with Aboriginal women without what some Aborigines deemed to be proper consent, or their alleged failure to fully reciprocate in trade relations.[16] Both cases may be understood as incomplete or inadequately negotiated exchange transactions.[17] I will discuss the significance of the symbolism of trade in a moment, but for now it suffices to say that the existence of this mutually accepted procedure for regulating interrelations bears witness to the presence of an understanding that the Macassans were a people who acknowledged the importance of Law. That they broke the Law would have been no more surprising than the fact that Aboriginal people were constantly compelled to use physical means to punish transgressors within their own society.

Tension and violence are not, in Aboriginal thought, antithetical to the maintenance of the structure of moral order. As Deborah Rose expresses it: 'Boundaries are maintained by being pressed against . . . the process of testing and responding is a process of affirming relationships'.[18] Less abstractly, Lazarus Lamilami prefaced his people's recollection of some particularly grim encounters with the unqualified statement: 'the Aboriginal people were very friendly with the Macassans. They used to address them by the Aboriginal words for brother, uncle and father'.[19]

Yet they were not kin. Here lay the dilemma. While they might be offered classificatory affiliation they could never be accommodated merely by appending them to the pre-existing order which united specific people with the land to which they eternally belonged. Unlike the Melanesians who came to Cape York, the Macassans neither married Aborigines nor brought women on their ships to Australia. Their true homes and families were some ten days distant with a good monsoonal wind. Inaccessible as genuine kin, they were engaged through the most prominent expression of their *raison d'être* – trade. Neither Lawless nor accessible through the locative land-based Law of Aboriginal communities, the moral sanction for their presence was mediated by material goods and other exchange items: iron tools, cloth, alcohol, pipes, tobacco and especially rice, in return for tortoise shell, pearls, pearl shell and, temporarily, women.[20]

While trade networks transverse the entire Australian continent it is widely acknowledged that their rich ceremonial form in Arnhem Land was stimulated by the Macassan presence.[21] Indeed, the word for the northern sector of the Yolngu exchange cycle is derived from a generic term for all goods obtained from Macassans.[22] Although the visitors themselves were confined to the coast, their gifts penetrated into more southerly regions, tying local groups into increasingly widening alliances.

It would be seriously inadequate to suggest that the primary motivation for these ceremonial exchanges was to obtain the items transferred. Thomson actually inverted the truth when he argued that the ceremonies existed merely to encourage Aborigines to work at producing above average artifacts.[23] Rather the value of the goods was 'enhanced and emphasised . . . by the elaboration of the ritual'[24] which at times transformed mundane items into worthy gifts. Just as Burridge reminded us that the 'cargo' of 'cargo' cults in Melanesia must be understood in its symbolic context of the quest for moral Europeans,[25] so too Stanner has warned we must see beyond commodities to interpersonal relationships in northern Australia. Of the *merbok* inter-'tribal' exchanges he wrote:

> It is the *gift* rather than what is given that matters: A gift of *merbok* has always been an affirmation of friendship and attachment: and today one sees withered old men bring some simple little *merbok* gift to a partner who can promise little more in return. One should not miss the symbolism of *merbok*, or the bonds which lie under its show of material gain.[26]

The fact that some Macassan items were particularly prized does not at all alter the fact that the true winning was not wealth but moral relations with a people who were not kin and whose abiding place was an enigma.

The persisting problem with Macassans, however, was precisely the limitation of gifts. They only allied people. Kinships and marriage affiliated space. In a society in which each birth is the manifestation of an eternal potency residing at a known place there can be no demarcation separating a person and their spirit's abode. Marriage was a compact of countries which nonetheless did not threaten the existing spatial boundaries. No matter where a person resided she or he could only ever have one home and the enduringness of these 'promised lands' was affirmed in the gift of affines. As David Turner notes, Aboriginal marriage 'places a part of one Land/People in the form of a "brother/sister" in another Land/People as a spouse, and vice versa without loss of integrity of either'.[27]

The Macassans thus brought the predicament of a Law lacking place. While trade allowed for moral association with strangers it could never be immune from the fickleness of human temporal whims. Even the mere presence of these people threatened locative traditions. The strangers travelled as they willed and the possibility of ubiquity followed them as surely as the wake of their praus. When they had departed, the waves of unity continued to spread through Aboriginal communities like those trade gifts flowing into regions far from coastal waters.

The changes the traders wrought upon the northern Aborigines' understanding of their place within the world might be anticipated from George Windsor Earl's descriptions in the first half of the nineteenth century. He wrote:

> [1] About the month of April, when the prahus congregate at Port Essington, the population of the settlement became a very motley character, from then Australians of perhaps a dozen different tribes might be seen mixed up with natures of Celebes and Sumbawa, Badjus of the coast of Burneo, Timorians and Javanese, with an occasional sprinkling of New Guinea negroes.
> [2] Nearly every prahu on leaving the coast takes two or three natives to Macassar, and brings them back next season. The consequence is that many of the natives all along the coast speak the Macassar dialect of the Malay language. A few have been converted to Mohammedanism.
> [3] The *coast* natives, from frequent intercourse with the Macassan trepang fishers, acquired considerable proficiency in their language . . . They . . . continue to make themselves well understood, not only by the Macassans, but by the people of tribes with whose particular dialect they may not be familiar.[28]

The motifs are clear. The Indonesians, in contrast to the Melanesians, simultaneously widened the world by taking Aboriginal people to previously unknown lands and expanded relationships between communities by providing Aborigines with an otherness against which they might be collectively defined and a pan-Aboriginal *lingua franca* with which to communicate that newfound identity. These transformations are well recognised. Warner suggested long ago that the visitor's presence had dissolved smaller 'tribal' groupings, while Urry and Walsh go so far as to argue that the Yolngu language itself has emerged because of the shared Macassar language and the subsequent cultural exchanges between communities.[29]

All these changes contained within them the threat of the collapse of a social differentiation based on the divisions of space. Much of the thought and practice woven around the Macassan dilemma concerned their inacessibility as kin, their unknown immutable ties to their own lands, and the risk that their seemingly pervasive occupation of Aboriginal coastal territories might be misconstrued as evidence of their spiritual entitlement to these lands. I turn to these themes next, but beyond them was the more deep-rooted disquiet about how Aboriginal people were to maintain their plurality once they had acknowledged their oneness. This unsettling predicament, I later argue, opened the way for the All-Mother.

MYTHS OF SHARED SPACE

The key to the Macassan conundrum rests concealed in Aboriginal myths. Their meaning is veiled by the very richness of their content. When reflecting upon the poetic truths of Aboriginal myth, Stanner once said with characteristic astuteness

> It can scarcely be doubted that propositional and moral truths are being stated, but what are they? The Kerygma of the myth lies obscurely within the paradoxes. One has the sense that antinomes have been stated that would lose their import if the parts could be separated ... It is as though paradox and antinomy were the marrow in the story's bones.

He concluded, wisely, that all methodologies must be 'simply left transcended'; that a science of myth is as impotent as a science of poetry.[30]

I frankly distrust attempts to disclose *the* meaning of myths, and the stories I discuss in this chapter, especially those dealing with the Mother, are anything but exhausted by my readings. I do not pretend to discern the truths of these narratives, but would be rather judged on whether I am true *to* them. To which I might add O'Flaherty's advice that good myths are best cooked lightly.[31]

There is a huge corpus of songs and stories dealing with strangers in northern Australia, most of them as yet unpublished. To date, the most insightful studies of them have been those of neo-structuralists like Maddock and, in particular, Turner, whose findings reinforce many of my arguments thus far.

There is, however, one minor tension in Turner's seminal essay 'Caste Logic in a Clan Society', and as I attempt to resolve it using ideas I have gained from my readings of his more recent works the criticism is equally an acknowledgement. On the one hand he suggests that the myths he examines reveal that the Aborigines felt inferior to the Macassans' technology and thus accorded them a hierarchically superior status. Here he concludes 'the key to our understanding of the phenomena is "domination" '. On one level, the myths analysed here are efforts to explain the Aborigines' subordinate position *vis-à-vis* the Macassans'. Yet on the other hand, he notes the myths are ambiguous about the superiority of the Indonesian culture.[32] Certainly the stories explain why the physical heritage of the two peoples are *different*, just as Cape York narratives stress the otherness of Islander heritage, but as Aborigines did not wish to adopt significant amounts of Macassan material culture as forms of technology[33] we can assume that, even if items were prized, their main value was as symbols of the visitors they related with through trade. I see no envy or hierarchy here.

Turner is nevertheless correct; 'domination' is the key and, as he so forcefully argues here and elsewhere, ascendency results not from superior strength but from the existence of cosmologies which acknowledge that things might be subsumed. This was what Aborigines feared the Macassans brought by their occupation of land to which they had no spiritual entitlement. 'Permitting aliens the ownership of land on a residential basis runs the risk of people moving in and establishing a permanent claim.'[34] Here was a spatial coexistence where one party did not recognise the immutable ties the other had with the land. The *possibility* of domination could not be ignored and, had the Macassans never made a forceful move, their very presence would have still acknowledged 'a Logic that [could] lead to the organized elimination of the other'.[35] This fear was accentuated by the fact that their visits also weakened the plurality of Aboriginal traditions by encouraging Aborigines to define themselves as one.

Turner analyses four myths about Macassans and Aborigines

which I will not re-present here. Three of them stress the dissolving of communication barriers (separateness removed), the subsequent emergence of phenotypical differentiation (separateness reinstated) and the allocation of cultural items to the respective ethnic groups; all within the context of co-residence. The author correctly concludes we are witnessing an Aboriginal attempt to encircle and enfold a vagabond people by erecting an insoluble barrier which nonetheless recognises they are ' "related" to oneself and worthy of life'.[36] But it must be emphasised, the relationships were maintained through goods and not affines. Myths explaining how the two peoples obtained their respective material cultures were, so to speak, warnings against commodity incest.

The following story encapsulates all I have tried to say and needs little commentary. The old Macassan Yoortjing is undeniably friendly and generous. Barwal the dingo-man rejects the gifts and the offer to 'sit down as one company'. No offer of goods or affection can weigh against Barwal's assertion: 'this is my country', and the implicit antagonism between that claim and the possibility of oneness raised by the old Macassan.

Barwal asked: 'Why do you make beds?' 'Why,' said Yoortjing, 'you two are my friends. I would like you to sit down here.' Yoortjing called Barwal 'Grandfather'. He wanted to give Barwal the blankets. He asked Barwal if he wanted a pillow, Barwal answered 'No.' 'Well then,' said Yoortjing, 'what about this meat? Do you want meat?' 'Is it cooked?' said Barwal. 'Yes,' said Yoortjing. 'Then I don't want it,' Barwal said. 'You want raw meat?' Yoortjing asked. 'Yes, raw meat,' Barwal said. Yoortjing gave Barwal and his wife raw meat and Barwal with his wife sat down on the beach and ate the meat raw.

Then Yoortjing asked: 'Do you want to come inside my house?' 'No,' answered Barwal. 'We are going to sleep in the grass.' 'But there is a big rain coming on,' said Yoortjing. 'No matter,' said Barwal. 'You see that rock and that ant-bed? That is where I and my wife will sleep. This is my country. It is better that you go back to your country. You see that fire a long way off in the country Yoormanga? That is your country. It is better that you load up your Miteetjang, your boat, with all your things. Pull down this house and take everything back along your country.'

Yoortjing talked: 'You are angry with me, Barwal. I will give you blankets and tucker. Are you still angry?' 'Yes, I am still angry,' said Barwal. Then Yoortjing said: 'Look, Barwal, you and I can sit down as one company. We can be one company.' 'No,' answered Barwal, 'this is my country. It is better that you go back to your own country. You and I are different colours.'

Yoortjing the Maccassar loaded up his boat. Barwal the dingo-man sat down and watched the Maccassars. 'Pull up everything you have made,' said Barwal. 'Pull up the bamboo you have planted. Pull up your garden. Take everything. Take your iron, your nails with you. You see that smoke? You go there. You stop in that country always. This is my country.'

Barwal and his wife sat down on the beach and watched the Maccassars loading the boat. They saw and heard them pulling on the ropes to haul up the sails. The Maccassars took their wives and children onto the boat. Yoortjing had told all the other Maccassar boats and as the Maccassars pulled up the anchors and the wind filled the sails and the fleet sailed away, Barwal called: 'Go back to your country, and stay there. This is my country. I sit down here.'[37]

This myth, of course, has nothing to do with actual transactions with Macassans but rather establishes the rightful abodes of people and their respective jurisdiction as material cultural repositories. From this primordially demarcated base, moral relationships among living people can proceed through trade. The major difference between mythic and temporal Macassans is that the former were seeking to actualise what was but a perennial possibility for the latter. They sought a permanent place and had brought their wives and families with them. This, the story insists, cannot be.

The problem of perpetual co-residence is probed more extensively in stories dealing with the *Baijini*, another class of trepangers. Said by Aborigines to be a more ancient people, they built substantial stone houses and established their rice-based agricultural subsistence in northern Australia. The word *Baijini* is derived from a Macassarese root meaning 'women',[38] whose presence was a defining difference between them and (other?) Macassans. Whether these people were, as Aborigines believe, actual visitors, or whether they were rather reflections of Aboriginal experiences during their travels to southern Sulawesi transposed onto coastal Australia, is largely irrelevant. Long forgotten as men and women, they endure as poignant fragments in an expansive philosophy of space.

The *Baijini* in some narratives and songs actually precede the All-Mother. This has caused scholars some disquiet[39] but is in fact entirely fitting if we see the Mother as one who resolves the disruption brought by the strangers' occupation of Aboriginal lands. The *Djanggawul* sisters who are called 'Our Mothers' and who gave birth to the first people in a pre-existent world, smelt the *Baijini* long before they reached the Australian mainland.[40] These light-skinned people are later encountered at Port Bradshaw and the following songs, like the preceding myth, announce clearly their preoccupation with the principles underlying rights to land.

> What is that, *waridj* Djanggawul?
> Yes, something is blocking us, *waridj* Bralbral.
>   What can it be?
> Listen, is that the sound of the Baijini talking?
> Are those their words that drift from the roofs of
>   their huts, from the young Baijini playing?
> We hear the noise, *waridj*, of their talking together.
> Yes! That is the shine of their light skin! They are
>   standing about, and working the trepang.
> Yes, because they belong to the Djanala clan.
> What can we do, how can we make them move?
> We, *waridj*, shall quietly chase them away, they
>   can't stop there!
> Why can't they make their place at the other side,
>   by themselves, *waridj* Djanggawul? They
>   can make a big camp there.
> But here, they make the place pale as they stand
>   about together, at Bauwijara, at Janimbilnga
>   (among their huts and their trepang camps).
> We ourselves shall go there, when they have left,
>   walking along with the *mauwulan*.
> We ourselves shall go there, *waridj* Bralbral, go by
>   ourselves, putting our footprints all along
>   the beach.
> We ourselves are making the country, putting a
>   sandhill there, putting our footprints.
> We hear the roar of the sea, and the spray wets us.
> *Waridj* Djanggawul, we are putting our
>   footprints here.
> The roar of the sea! Its foam and spray! We plunge
>   in the point of the *mauwulan*, making
>   wells . . .
> This is for us, *waridj*, this trepang ladle left by the
>   Baijini. We hide it, within the mouth of the
>   ngainmara. Put it with care, *waridj* Bralbral!
> Ourselves we are putting the country, hiding the
>   ladle beneath our arm. It is sacred!
> Yes, *waridj* Djanggawul, and we ourselves are
>   sacred! We shall hide it, putting it in with
>   the sacred *rangga*, *waridj*. [41]

These songs are clearly about the problem of co-residence: 'They can't stay here! Why can't they make a place at the other side?' The

Djanggawul gently force the *Baijini* to move from Port Bradshaw to Daju, not far away, while the land is sanctified. The Mothers say: '*Baijini*, you had better move from here to your own place, for this place must belong to us, and we are going to establish a sacred site.'[42]

Why can't the *Baijini* stay? Not because the *Djanggawul* have the right of superior power or even priority of possession, but because they are giving the land its eternal form. They are putting their footprints along the beach, they are making the land holy. The song could not be more explicit: the spiritual basis of estates eclipses all claims of ownership by occupation and overrides the agriculturalists' ideology of working the self into place.

I will detail the boundaries of the Aboriginal cosmos erected by the Mother in the second part of this chapter, where I will clarify why her presence is rightly understood to be posterior to the *Baijini* problem. Prior to this, however, I deepen my analysis of symbolic exchange between Aborigines and the trepang collectors. I have explored the crucial predicaments the encounters created in both social practice and mythic theory, and now turn to some cultic innovations which permitted a people without land-kin ties to be nonetheless understood in terms of both Aboriginal social organisation and territory.

DIVIDE AND NOT CONQUER

At that place where the Mothers encountered the *Baijini* was another Ancestral Being named *Laindjung*. Although the *Djanggawul* songs suggest all Aboriginal people are descended from the two sisters, other traditions say *Laindjung* was in fact the Father of all those of the *Yirritja* moiety. When they met *Laindjung* offered the *Djanggawul* a piece of cloth given to him by the *Baijini*, but this was refused. Other gifts were then successfully exchanged so that today each moiety is said to have something of themselves within the other half of their society.[43] This process is again most clearly symbolised by the reference in the song just presented to the *Djanggawul* taking the *Baijini* (*Yirritja* moiety) trepang ladle as their own (*Dhuwa*) sacred object.

Our understanding of the 'complementary and co-operative'[44] interchanges between moieties in north-eastern Australia is hampered from the outset because to date most studies have focused on only half of the world. While it is true that *Dhuwa* moiety traditions are today more prominent, those of the *Yirritja* form an integral and essential part of a balanced totality.[45] In a revealing but potentially misleading passage, Warner once wrote: 'Everything in Murngin civilization is divided on this dual basis. There is nothing in the whole universe . . . that has not a place in one of the two categories. The division is as clear cut to the Murngin as heaven and hell to a mediaeval theologian'.[46] I have in the previous chapter tentatively acceded to the view that the sky dwelling All-Father of the south-east was indeed once an earth-bound moiety-linked Ancestor who took flight to the heavens, and in doing so gained supremacy over the earth. This transformation, I argued, replicated the process of conquest. In the north of Australia, however, the moieties were modified in a manner firmly denying ascendency. Both remained rooted in this world and the strangers were given a symbolic place stressing mutuality and reciprocity.

It is well known that it is the *Yirritja* moiety's traditions which are prominently associated with the newcomers to Aboriginal lands, although I am not aware of anyone who has thought this fact worthy of detailed enquiry. What the Berndts call the 'great *Yiritja* moiety trilogy'[47] are songs dealing with *Baijini*, Macassans and the people of 'Badu' (see below), although today Japanese and Europeans are also substantially represented. While I confine my analysis to the Yolngu, it should be noted that cognate developments have occurred throughout other Arnhem Land regions. On Groote Eylandt, for example, numerous localised Dreamings have been reworked within a structure emphasising moiety 'totems' and particularly prominent is that of the 'Macassan ship' mythically associated with the division of humanity into dark- and light-skinned groups.[48]

At the level of individual clans within the *Yirritja* moiety there is also substantial representation of non-Aboriginal themes. The disinterest in appropriating Indonesian material cultural traditions seems to have been inversely related to Aboriginal enthusiasm for replicating those items at a symbolic level – an attitude equally evident in the Cape York 'incorporation' of the bow and arrow. The most oft-cited example is probably that of the form of a square-faced gin bottle carved in ironwood and painted with sacred designs, although available sources are frustratingly silent as to the spiritual significance of this clan 'totem'.[49]

Another example is a particular *narra* ceremony which Thomson cites as 'Proof of Indonesian Influence upon the Aborigines of North

Australia'. *Narra* are arguably the most important ceremonies in eastern Arnhem Land and reaffirm the connection between people and the Ancestor whose activities are being celebrated.[50] In this case the ritual representation of the dog, which Thomson felt to be 'the most remarkable totemic object in the whole of Arnhem Land', was made of Melaleuca bark and string, wool and fabrics which were specifically associated with the Macassans.[51]

Many more instances of this kind could be catalogued. The difficulty is not discerning Indonesian influence but rather in defining its limits. Mountford and Capell believed *all* Arnhem Land sculpture, from a clan's secret *rangga*, used in *narra*, to more public figures, reveal the recent impact of alien artistic techniques.[52] Berndt is more cautious yet concedes 'post-figures' possibly date from the period of the very first visits from the north, while carvings of 'complete figures' are even more modern innovations.[53] The latter class prominently feature representations of *Baijini* and Macassans, and it should be noted that these works may also be used as sacred *rangga* in restricted ceremonies.[54]

This inclusion of symbols of Indonesian culture within Aboriginal spiritual classifications allowed for more intimate exchanges with the traders. While actual marriages with these new people were both undesirable and impossible, the location of things Macassan within the Aboriginal order meant that every marriage between members of the exogamous moieties tied Aborigines to the northern world through affines who were its cultural and, indeed, spiritual custodians. In this way, the somewhat fickle principles of trade began to approach the ideals of land-based alliances.

Yet this ingenious arrangement would in itself have still been left wanting. As Warner clearly revealed, the sacredness of ceremonial objects and designs was dependent upon their associations with the 'totemic wells' which were the core of a 'clan's' land and, equally, the sites from which the spirits of living members of that 'clan' emanated.[55] Ultimately, there could be no resolution until the Macassans were engaged at the level of, to repeat Hegel's words, 'their eternal and absolute element'.

For this the Yolngu were willing to break their soul, pursuing to the full that constant process of dividing and folding in upon themselves, doubling and doubling until at last the displaced strangers were contained. Unlike Aborigines in south-east Australia, those in eastern Arnhem Land did not entrust their spirits to a Utopian ('no place') heaven, but they did create a new Land of the Dead far from their homes. In both regions conflicting and richly paradoxical views of the fate of the soul can be seen to intriguingly entwine.

According to Warner, the soul (*warro* or *birrimbirr*) is inseparably linked to the 'totemic well'. The *birrimbirr*, he writes, 'finally and eternally ties the man whose heart it occupies to his totem, the symbol of all clan unity . . . , since the soul at death is one of the prominent elements in the configuration of associated items found in the clan's totemic water, the water which is the essence of life'.[56] This view belongs to a broader understanding of life which closely approximates that found throughout most of Aboriginal Australia. Ancestral essences, deposited through Abiding Events at specific places, emerge as the life force of people and then return upon death to maintain the potency of its eternal abode. The process is balanced and homeostatic. It establishes the unbreakable bond between 'clan' members and their country; it is, as Warner stresses, *the* classifier of Yolngu social and spiritual structure.[57]

Yet the Yolngu simultaneously insist that the *birrimbirr* travels to the *Dhuwa* or *Yirritja* Land of the Dead,[58] the latter lying within a territory associated with the Macassans. Northern Aborigines, like those in most of Australia, initially classified foreign people as deceased kin; as Earl wrote in 1841, 'The spirits of the dead are also recognised in the strangers . . . who visit their country'.[59] That this was a philosophical construct rather than a perceptual error is established by the fact that as Aborigines travelled to these lands and became intimate with the Indonesians they did not abandon their 'misperception' but rather institutionalised their ideas as the Island of Badu.

Badu is located by Aborigines either in the Torres Strait Islands or, less frequently, in Indonesia itself.[60] Berndt rightly suggests 'the development of the "Badu" song cycle brought in its train the concept of a Land of the Dead' and equally correctly that the people of Badu were engaged through the Macassans who both brought news of them and who also took Aborigines to the Torres Strait, Papua New Guinea and Sulawesi.[61] Carved figures of Badu people are clearly in a style derived from Indonesian sculptures, and Aborigines themselves state, without qualification, that the Badu song cycle is historically posterior to those dealing with Macassans.[62] But perhaps the most telling indicator of all is that the soul is guided to Badu by a rite replicating the departure of a Macassan prau.[63]

The Indonesians had lifted their masts with ceremony at the end of their visits. In turn the Yolngu chant in Macassan pidgin over the corpse as it is taken to the grave and a Macassan prayer is recited for a safe voyage. The ritual masts, complete with cross-bars, rigging and flags, are run up and anchor is ceremoniously weighed.[64] Songs from the *Baijini*-Macassan cycle are sung as the soul departs for the land of the dead.

> [They] looked at it, hanging down from the cross-
> bar, from the mast like falling rain . . .
> On top of the cross-bar, hanging down to the deck,
> the sail at the mast . . .[65]

The *Wuramu* ceremonies associated with mortuary practices also have an explicit Indonesian context.[66] The *Wuramu* sculptures are the probable stylistic precursors of the *Badu* and other carved figures[67] and were originally associated with the officiaries in Macassan mortuary rites, although more recently identified with Dutch customs officials 'stealing' from the Macassans.[68] *Wuramu* sculptures, in their funerary context, are placed on the graves of *Yirritja* moiety men and women.

Whether Badu be in Indonesia or the Torres Strait it is clear that a part of the *Yirritja* soul returns to a territory, largely unknown yet not entirely Utopian, identified with Macassans. Without denying their spirits must forever belong to their 'clan' well, Aborigines were willing to also place their eternal essence within another people's land. This is balanced and fitting, for not only were spirit-Macassans said to have been deposited by Ancestors in Yolngu territories,[69] thus accounting for the actual and indeed rightful arrival of these Indonesians, but further, as I will presently show, the Mother of All had Herself come from an alien northern land. The potential for human life thus came from the abode of strangers to be localised by the Mother in a plurality of 'clan' territories. While this spiritual multiplicity was the very foundation of the Aboriginal world it was nevertheless, and in a deliberately paradoxical manner, juxtaposed with the understanding that, for the *Yirritja* moiety people, their souls must also return to another's place.

This was the most radical of Aboriginal solutions to the Macassan problem. To summarise, I have thus far argued that the strangers introduced the dilemma of a moral and Lawful people whose being in the north of Australia had no spirit/land base. Trade was the immediate medium of reciprocal relationships, but the exchange of (non-affinal) gifts was only as enduring as the partners engaged in the transactions. The 'myths of shared space' probed the short-comings of trade and insisted upon the necessity of a spiritual foundation for relationships with land. The solution established was to give Macassans and Macassan culture a clearly defined yet contained position within the Aboriginal spatial ontology. This was most fully developed in the Yolngu case, where the new cultural items were located within the geo-spiritual order of one half of society so that marriage between the exogamous moieties constantly brought the Macassans, at a symbolic level, into quasi-affinal relationships with Aborigines. This process was further empowered and endorsed by truly acknowledging the eternal basis of their reciprocal relationships and by asserting that, while there could be no possibility of Macassans taking custodianship of Aboriginal lands, both people belonged to a shared cosmos in which one's spirit was something forever at home and yet eternally a part of another people's place.

The changes made by Aborigines to accommodate the Macassans were immense. In 1906 the colonial state government in turn added its contribution. It banned the trepang gatherers from working the coast of Arnhem Land.[70] When it is said, therefore, that the Yolngu *Yirritja* traditions are less prominent than those of the *Dhuwa*, it should be recalled that all our serviceable accounts, from Baldwin Spencer's *Native Tribes of the Northern Territory of Australia* (1914) onwards, were written after the Macassans had departed. It is self-evident that these particular *Yirritja* institutions would have been more vital when the people who brought them into being were a central reality of Aboriginal life and, while such ideologies have to some extent been broadened to include White Australians, Aboriginal people have not considered these new strangers to be of the same order as their predecessors.

Dhuwa beliefs and practices, on the other hand, are commonly said to be the main repository of traditional ideals. I disagree. The difference is not that the *Dhuwa* is 'the more conservative moiety'[71] but rather that it is the more introspective. Whereas the *Yirritja* is concerned explicitly with relations with strangers, the *Dhuwa*, I maintain, is devoted to Aboriginal relations among themselves in the wake of the Indonesian experience.

Having weakened locative ties by placing a part of themselves in a distant land of the dead, how was ubiety to be maintained? Having been required to establish a new Aboriginal unity, how could plurality be perpetrated? And having denied rights to land by occupation how could they themselves ensure they were not swallowed by the very principle of subsumption whose possibility they had so desperately repudiated? These questions remained as shadows more real than the Macassans who had cast them. They persist to this day, reshaped and made more urgent by the succeeding waves of strangers.

And they are answered by the Mother.

THE MOTHER

THE MOTHER FROM THE NORTH

Let me be quite clear from the outset. When I argue that the Mother attended the Macassans this does not mean such beliefs are therefore less 'Aboriginal' or less 'traditional'. The 'traditional Aborigine' is an academic fiction. We are dealing with an inherently dynamic ontological fabric, constantly being made relevant to an ever-changing world. Aboriginal thought can adopt many moods. If in the desert its tenor is contemplative, while in the south-east of Australia it brandished its assertive spirit, then the northern traditions (including, to a lesser extent, those of Cape York) came to be poised dialogically. It is therefore hardly accidental that a growing number of scholars and Aborigines alike derive from this region an understanding of existence which they feel deserves a global audience.

I must equally stress that when I make this first attempt to verify historic associations between Indonesian and Aboriginal Mother cults I do not do so with the conviction that plotting this dif- fusionary path in itself has explanatory value. Like all human beings, Aborigines are concerned with novel concepts only insofar as they enrich their understanding of existence. As Joseph Esherick says in his particularly thorough study of a socio-religious response to intrusion, we must pass 'beyond the idol of origins': 'It is far less important to know where they got their ideas than to understand how their ideas attracted an audience'.[72] The real issue therefore is to establish the conditions of Aboriginal life which permitted the Mother to enter northern Australia. My position is that the All- Mother's appeal was her articulation of the nature of the Macassans' own relationship with the world, which was so problematic for

Aborigines. Just as Aborigines at the tip of the continent appreciated the significance of the vagabond Heroes inspired by Melanesian contacts, and in the south-east people could perceive the bond between invasion and the imperialistic All-Father of their conquerors, so too the Mother's being was conjoined with that of the people from Sulawesi. With Peter Winch I would assert that 'social relations are expressions of ideas about reality'[73] and hence that Aborigines chose to confront intruders at the level of the ontology which sustained them. Or for those who see fertility mothers as an agriculturalist's invention, might I say Aborigines in the north of Australia worked through a neolithic intellectual revolution and rejected its social implications, without ever having set their hands to the plough.

With this caution, I return to the history of the Mother. Many eminent scholars have suspected her origin lay in pre-Islamic Indonesian traditions. Here are the words of Elkin and Capell, who did much pioneering research in this regard. Elkin writes:

> This fertility-mother cult, which has proved very attractive to the Arnhem Land ritualists is not claimed to be indigenous, but to have a northern origin. Moreover, other cults of the north coast . . . are also regarded as diffusions. The detailed study of these cults . . . must be followed by comparison with the fertility-mother cults of the lands to the north.[74]

Capell likewise advocated comparative studies with northern cults, and stated:

> Cults such as that of the Earth Mother appear in this region but not elsewhere, and as they overlay a great basis of normal Australian spiritual beliefs, they are especially intriguing to the student. The interesting and arresting fact would seem that practically all of them have come from the direction of Indonesia, and are assigned by aboriginal belief to either Baijini or Macassan origin.[75]

Both authors appeal to two possible types of testimony – Aboriginal opinion and comparative studies – which I will now examine in turn.

While Elkin and Capell may well have had oral confirmation for their position that Aborigines claimed the Mother *cult* was derived from the visitors, I have not uncovered any published evidence to this effect. The possibility certainly cannot be ruled out, and I myself have attended ceremonies in the very heart of Australia which Aborigines explicitly said had originally been 'given' to coastal Aborigines by Islamic 'Malays'. (See chapter 5.) In the documentary material for Arnhem Land, however, it is not the cult but the Mother herself who is said to have come from across the Timor and Arafura Seas and this is the understanding distributed over the range coterminous with the sphere of Macassan trepang sites.[76]

The Yolngu *Djanggawul* song cycle begins evocatively:

> Although I leave Bralgu, I am close to it. I
>   Djanggawul, am paddling
> Paddling with all the paddles, with their flattened
>   tapering ends
> Close I am coming, with Bildjiwuraroiju
> Coming along from Bralgu.[77]

They are leaving *Bralgu*, their resting place, which was somewhere beyond Groote Eylandt and is today identified as the *Dhuwa* land of the dead. But although the cycle begins here, this was not their home. Beyond *Bralgu* is a now unknown land from whence the Mothers and their brother began their journey.[78] From *Bralgu* they paddled toward Australia's coast, picking up the scent of the *Baijini* long before they reach land.[79] Taken at face value these songs state that the Mothers arrived *after* the first wave of strangers.

The western Arnhem Land equivalent of the *Djanggawul* sisters provides a further clue. Here the Mother or Old Woman can take the guise of *Ngalyod*, an androgynous serpent. In this context it is noteworthy that mythic snakes in this region are sometimes depicted with horns – a striking feature in a country with no indigenous horned animals.[80] About *Ngalyod* the Gunwinngu are specific: 'She came underground from "Macassar", to Madabir, near Cooper's Creek, bringing people inside her – people who later made more people. She made us talk like people, she gave us understanding.' As *Waramurunggundji* she is very like her *Djanggawul* counterparts, arriving with her husband *Wuragag*.[81] Their narrative begins:

> [*Wuragag*] came from the Macassan Islands at the same time as [*Waramurunggundji*], and was her husband. Landing on the north coast, he copulated with her at Melville Island, and left her to produce the children . . .[82]

Most widely diffused of all traditions dealing with the Mother is the *Kunapipi* ('womb') or *Kadjari* ('old woman') cult which changes its aspect radically under local conditions.[83] While its path has been reasonably well plotted since the 1920s, its origins are unclear. Elkin believed it emerged from the Victoria River District, whereas Berndt maintains it spread from the Roper River area throughout Arnhem Land and ultimately into the northern Central Desert and the Kimberley.[84] I favor Berndt's thesis, and it is significant to note that in the Alawa (Roper River people) version of the *Kunapipi*, the Mother is said to have emerged from the waters. I quoted the relevant song as the opening to this chapter and here add Berndt's comment that he felt the suggestion that their content indicates an external origin was an 'attractive' thesis.[85]

As the Mother cult moved westward away from the centre of Macassan influence her northern origin becomes less conspicuous. It is unfortunate that Stanner said nothing of the home of *Mutjingga*, the 'Old Woman' in the Murinbata version of *Kunapipi*. Nor does he dwell on the origin of *Kukpi*, who is also related in an unspecified and historically obscure way to the rite.[86] Yet Robinson's account provides a partial answer. *Kukpi* 'came up out of the salt-water by the Larakia country in the north'.[87]

Aboriginal traditions will take us no further towards affirming historic links with Indonesian beliefs, although the radical increase of female figures in more recent (quite possibly postcontact) rock art perhaps endorses the testimony of oral culture. The Mother, throughout coastal Arnhem Land, came from across northern waters, sometimes specifically from Macassar. But while she herself once resided in the territory of strangers her cult, it is said, was first given to Aborigines.

I am content to accede to Aboriginal opinion here. I see no evidence suggesting a wholesale adoption of the rituals of Sulawesi. The ceremonies are indeed authentically Aboriginal. Nonetheless this does not obviate the possibility that something in the visitors' beliefs and practices ignited a fire of ceremonial creativity in this region. My view is that the Macassans' 'Mother' disclosed much about this agricultural people's relationship to land and it was precisely for this reason that Aborigines sought to incorporate her being into their own order. The process was not one of passive borrowing but rather a vital growth from within the Aboriginal world which strove to reach out and simultaneously embrace and contain an alien understanding of the place of people in the structure of the cosmos.

Surprisingly, no-one has yet actually examined the rites and beliefs of southern Sulawesi in order to see how they articulate with those of Aborigines. Heeren has simply dismissed the suspicions of a generation of Australian anthropologists by boldly stating there is no cognate 'fertility Mother cult' in the pre-Islamic culture of Macassar[88] and Macknight is happy to support this view.[89] Neither scholar offers the slightest evidence for their potentially devastating claims, but happily they are profoundly wrong.

The truth is that when searching for this Indonesian Ancestral Being from the context of the Aboriginal contacts with Macassans, her presence is so conspicuous, so predictably poised, that it is not difficult to guess her positive form from the shape of the experiences which bordered her existence. My research has only confirmed the presence of what I was already assured must be, and I suspect, given some background guidance, most readers of this book will also anticipate the nature of the Macassan Mother.

To begin, 'Macassan', as Aborigines use the word, refers to all trepang collectors of the nineteenth and early twentieth century. They were, as it happens, predominantly people from Macassar, but Bugis and other groups from southern Sulawesi were also well represented. The quotations from Earl (*supra*), furthermore, indicate smatterings of people from a very broad area. It must also be added that maritime sections of 'Macassan' society had their own peculiar beliefs and rituals, and some of these have certainly found their way into Aboriginal tradition.[90]

Unfortunately, very little is published on pre-Islamic Macassan beliefs. According to an eyewitness account written at the time of the beginnings of the trepang industry, the Macassans, who had then belonged to an Islamic 'Kingdom' for 120 years, had 'defaced all the footsteps of the ancient religion, for fear the people should again return to idolatry'. The author could learn little of the old ceremonies and beliefs save vague notions of the complementary duality of heaven and earth giving rise to life.[91] The class of Macassan he describes, however, were certainly not the gin-trading people who sailed to Australia.

Presuming more ancient beliefs persisted in popular Macassan culture we might best discover hints of them by turning to the neighbouring Bugis and Toraja, who have been studied in far more detail. The latter are especially helpful as they held Islam to be 'an abomination' and did not come under Dutch administration until 1906. The southern Toraja, it should be noted, claim more affinity with Macassans and Bugis than other Toraja, so we can expect a reasonable cultural homogeneity among these peoples.[92]

Having demarcated the region in Indonesia where a legitimate search can be made, let me briefly return to Australia to focus our expectations. In Aboriginal song cycles dealing with strangers, two themes are outstanding. One is sea travel, which I have already discussed when dealing with mortuary ritual. The other, also evident in the foregoing discussion, is Macassan items of culture and trade. Now the main cargo and staple food of the sailors, used as a means of payment and brought in quantities allowing a surplus for trade with Aborigines[93] was rice. In the monsoonal seasons when the visitors were present this was a most welcome supplement to the Aboriginal diet. It is therefore not surprising to find that rice is very important in the relevant song cycles. The *Baijini*, in fact, were said to have established their rice-based agriculture in Australia, and Arnhem Land people identify areas where wild rice grows as the sites of *Baijini* homes. The songs dwell on this theme,[94] as they do on the Macassan techniques of cooking rice:

> Cooking rice in the fire; pouring it into a pot from a bag
> Pouring rice from a bag: rice, rice, for food . . .
> Removing its husk and pouring into pots: making it clean.
> Rice from that bag; food from those rice-filled bags . . .
> Rice sticking in lumps, white scum on the boiling water . . .
> Pouring water, washing, cleaning the rice, removing the stems.[95]

And the most prevalent and potent goddess in southern Sulawesi, the deity who maintains all Earthly fecundity is, of course, the Rice Mother. R.E. Downs has gathered some of the relevant Toraja data from Adriani and Kruyt's important but rambling *De Bare'e-Sprekende Toradjas van Midden-Celebes*, emphasising the Earth-bearing *Ndara*, one of a primordial pair, and her guise as *Indo i Tuladidi*, the agricultural goddess with hair of rice ears.[96] Waterson likewise speaks of the 'Mother who Increases', responsible for earthly fertility who is ceremonially acknowledged when the rice is ripening, while Nooy-Palm has detailed the Toraja rice rituals.[97] Indeed in Hatt's survey of Indonesian corn and rice Mothers the Toraja provide the majority of his examples.[98] The evidence for the Bugis Rice Mother is also well documented and despite the fact that since the beginning of the seventeenth century Bugis have been considered among the most devout Muslims in the archipelago, her cult still flourishes to this day.[99]

There is nothing to be gained here, however, by pursuing this line of enquiry beyond the point of merely establishing that the people of southern Sulawesi who sailed to Australia almost certainly brought with them a belief in a fertility Mother intimately associated with the most conspicuous aspect of their subsistence – rice. It seems Aborigines were in turn inspired to generate their All-Mother, who ensured the ongoing fertility of life from their associations with the Indonesians; but more important is the manner in which they reworked her being to sanction and shore up the pre-existing order. The Mother, far more completely than the Heroes of Cape York had done, told of the oneness of earth just as the wandering Macassans were seemingly indifferent to the eternal boundaries of the world, but unlike the invading All-Father's presence in the south-east, she also recognised and fostered the plurality of people and place. Universally the source of human life she nonetheless defends the principles underlying localised traditions.

When the agriculturalists' mother became the Aboriginal Mother she was, so to speak, denied the right to break the ground.

I now turn to examine her essence.

THE MOTHER OF US ALL

The All-Mother is often evoked at the same time as the south-eastern All-Father. They, as Maddock has shown, are the only two instances of 'transcendental powers' in Aboriginal Australia – that is, of Ancestral Beings who transcend the social order and stand in a single ubiquitous relationship with all people.[100] In this regard they are both in contrast to the Heroes of the north-east. Elkin obliquely noted that only the southern 'Sky Hero' could match the Mother's claim to exclusive productive powers,[101] while the Berndts suggest the primacy of the 'Fertility Mother' is commensurate, in a qualified sense, with the notion of an Aboriginal Supreme Being which Eliade felt he had found in the south-east.[102] The affinities are very real indeed, but equally important and often neglected are the divergences. 'The difference between a High God and a multi-centred earth . . . ,' Rose warns, 'is profound.'[103]

As their names imply, the one authentic and important correspondence between the two transcendental beings is their common role as the Ancestral parent of all people. The *Djanggawul*, for instance, brought across the sea their uterine conical mats and phallic sacred poles. In a mythic scenario very similar to at least one from Sulawesi,[104] but quite exceptional in Aboriginal Australia where copulation is almost always absent as a principle of Ancestral fecundity, the Mothers begin to give birth only after an incestuous relationship with their brother. They travel, creating life-containing waterholes with the ritual posts they use as walking sticks and periodically pause to bring children out from their wombs. In this manner the first humans of all of eastern Arnhem Land were born of the one pair of sisters.

In western Arnhem Land, *Waramurunggundji* occupies a similiar position. Again, sexual intercourse precedes procreation. She and her husband mate and then have a rift over etiquette, after which she continues to travel and populate all those regions of Arnhem Land where circumcision is practised. *Waramurunggundji* deposited the spirits of all the 'clans' and, regardless of specific kinship ties, people call her 'mother' or 'mother's mother'.[105]

Kadjari likewise is the All-Mother, although this element has been suppressed where her cult has spread into territories where other Ancestral Beings already perform this task. In the Roper River where she has a primary position, however, there is no ambiguity. People say: 'All the children follow her' or 'she is carrying all those children, and when she stops to camp, she removes and leaves them there'. She, like the *Djanggawul* sisters, populates the land with the spirit essences of her womb.[106] Far to the west, transformed into *Mutjinga*, the Murinbata also recognised her as 'the Mother of Us All'.[107]

While both the All-Father and the All-Mother are beyond a segmentary social order, the Father emerges as doubly transcendent: He is an *otiose* creator remote from the earth. The Mother, in contrast, is the champion of immanence. Even though the *Djanggawul* sisters may have once descended from the sun their narrative is tied to the country. From the northern lands they enter Australia, travelling westward in their procreative journey until at last their story is taken on by neighbouring peoples.[108] *Waramurunggundji* actually becomes eternally localised by transforming herself into a rock on the coast at Blue Mud Bay, and *Kunapipi*, according to Roper River people, has likewise come to abide at a waterhole which is the metamorphosed form of her womb.[109]

It is this immanence of the Mother which underlies ritual in this region. Here there is no appeal to the other-worldly powers of a Sky Hero but rather the release of the life forces from within the earth. The most important of all east Arnhem Land ceremonies are the

Dhuwa narra ('nest', 'womb') which relate the travels and activities of the _Djanggawul_. The rituals' centre is a shelter representing the Mother's womb; the initiates _are_ her children, represented as sacred poles. More generally, the entire ceremonial ground is the uterus, and women and uninitiated boys are symbolically _in utero_ as the men dance the travels of the Mother to the rites where she gave and perennially does give birth.[110]

The western Arnhem Land _Ubar_ rituals have a prepared ground associated with the Rainbow Serpent. In the Oenpelli version, the snake is a guise of _Waramurunggundji_, but on Goulburn Island, where the serpent is male, the ground itself is the Mother's womb. The rites make manifest people's spiritual emergence from the Mother and their sacred identity is proclaimed by the participants entering the enclosure and being reborn as she eternally transverses the country.[111]

The Roper River _Kunapipi_ has largely the same emphasis, with the Mother swallowing the neophytes, who are then ritually contained within her womb, and later releasing them as she 'let out' the first people.[112] Elkin notes that the 'appeal' of _Kunapipi_ resides with 'the concept of the Mother – of birth from the womb . . . We have the Mother symbolised by the ceremonial "Mother Place" and in particular by the earth womb'.[113]

The Mother's immanence within the earth (but not at this stage _as_ the Earth), is complemented by her capacity to maintain plurality. Again the contrast with the monistic Sky Father is stark. Rose suggests the phrase: 'In our mother's body are many wombs'.[114] At the social level, her most distinctive achievement is to simultaneously embrace all the Aboriginal people of an area without undermining their localised individuality and separateness.

An important component of the Mother's being in this regard is the fact that she is neither a creator nor, in the main, even a transformer of the country. Although in recent years she may be sometimes equated with the Earth (see below), contrarily, and in a manner hinting at historical processes, she arrived after the land had taken on its enduring structure. When the _Djanggawul_ began their sojourn, the earth, sky and waters had taken their places, all the species were established and the 'totemic' beings existed.[115] The _Baijini_ too were present and, as Capell suggests, it is difficult not to discern here the more general pattern of locative Aboriginal traditions overlain with a recent glaze of pan-Aboriginality.[116] The

Mother thus inherits and endorses the pre-existent order of the world. To it, the stories say, she adds human life.

Referring to *Kunapipi*, Berndt stresses that while she established the persisting relationships between people and the species with which they are affiliated, the Mother herself is not 'totemic'. 'In this region,' he says, '. . . totemism is a means to an end.' The localised, well-centred traditions in this way manifest themselves as fragments of the Mother's totality.[117] What I suspect we are witnessing, therefore, is a Macassan-inspired conception of socio-religious unity superimposed upon an earlier Aboriginal understanding which was weighted foremost towards maintaining discrete yet interdependent spiritual domains. The resultant synthesis was a manageable, if not always harmonious, balance between cosmological, and hence spatial, plurality and universality.

Perhaps the clearest expression of the Mother's transversing the principles of segmentation and oneness is her role as a namer. As Knight observed in this context, naming is not a passive process of labelling but an act which gives form and structure to the world,[118] and in a society which recognises the esoteric power of names this point is doubly acknowledged. Its significance is patently evident by its highly repetitious prominence in the *Djanggawul* song cycle, where a great deal of the undeniably important activity consists in providing various species with their names.

Whilst naming establishes boundaries and structures within the environment, languages are the vehicle for social inclusiveness and division. Here again the Mother has the fundamental responsibility. When the *Djanggawul* came onto the land they spoke the language later inherited by the people of that area. As they travelled they changed the language or dialect they spoke so that the children from their wombs come to be linguistically separated.[119] The Mothers brought into being all people and all potentiality for speech, but in so doing they took care to check the possibility of an undifferentiated population. They provided the foundation of unification, yet simultaneously undermined its actuality.

The same theme permeates the myths of *Waramurunggundji*. Her story recounts her travels from Cape Don eastwards, crossing to Croker Island, returning inland towards Oenpelli and the East Alligator River, and finally transforming to stone.[120] To the Western ear this narrative of a wayfaring woman, depositing children and changing languages as she roams, is nothing if not dull. To the people who can observe the Mother's enduring presence in their lands it says everything about who they are and, more importantly, who they are not.

Most revealing of all is the famous myth of the *Wawalag* sisters, a story analysed more than any other account of Aboriginal Ancestral Beings. Strictly speaking, they are not All-Mothers, although they clearly absorb some of her responsibilities. They come from the Roper River region, the landing site of *Kunapipi*, and are in some instances equated with her daughters, the *Mangamunga*.[121] They do not give birth to the first humans but are the ones to name animal and plant species. Warner writes

> When they killed the animals, they gave them the names they bear today . . . They gathered all the plants and animals that are in the [Yolngu] country today. They said to each thing they killed or gathered 'you will be *maraïin* [sacred] later on'.[122]

Later, after the sisters have been swallowed by the python *Yulunggur*, he (she?) raises himself in conference with other erect serpents of the Yolngu territory. They comment upon their linguistic diversity saying: 'Ah, what a lot of languages we talk . . . But though our languages are slightly different, we all share the same *mareain* . . . and have the same ceremonies'.[123] This is a realistic reflection of the state of Yolngu dialects[124] and, as I have already noted, Urry and Walsh maintain this linguistic situation arose from the influence of Macassans and the presence of a new *lingua franca* facilitating the bridging of communicative gulfs.

The Mother's essence therefore emerges as an immanence which simultaneously transcends social barriers yet maintains them, unites yet divides and acknowledges oneness while endorsing the necessity of plurality. In this way she accentuated without actually resolving the paradox of post-Macassan Aboriginal life. If the myths, moieties and mortuary practices I discussed in the first part of this chapter were concerned with establishing a place for strangers within the Aboriginal cosmos, then the Mother was devoted to the continuation of places for Aborigines themselves within their now widened understanding of social and spiritual space.

At the heart of the Mother is both hope and foreboding vision intertwining to form a powerfully ambivalent being. Given the commanding appropriateness of her existence for the shifting social climate of Northern Australia, we can no longer avoid those esoteric questions: why a 'Mother'? What precisely is the symbolic value attributed to motherhood? And is there some significance in the distribution of All-Mothers and All-Fathers across differing arenas of intercultural contact?

Before I confront these questions let me briefly review my thesis. Transcendental Beings, unlike the Cape York Heroes, emerged with radical intrusion upon the Aboriginal vision of space, but beyond this there was scope for wide variation in the form of encroachment. I have maintained that the All-Mother replicated the Aboriginal social order after its encounter with Macassans, just as the All-Father reflected the colonial presence in the south-east. The difference between these Ancestral Beings was due to contrasting cases of territorial infringement. The European invasion entailed land appropriation and murder which fractured Aboriginal ties with their spirit abodes. Their new cosmology acknowledged the principles of conquest with the Father of All assuming proportions which replicated the threat of colonisation. The cults were not fatalistic but did have a pessimistic vision of the future, and the earth was abandoned as the location of spiritual promise in favour of the more distant hopes of the heavens.

The Mother, in comparison, was no more a conquistador than the Indonesians with whom she came. She could be threatening, certainly, but never to the detriment of land-based spiritual plurality. Her social transcendence was tempered by geographical immanence; Her All-embracingness with diverse abundancy. She achieved a rapprochement between the one and the many which was beyond the *otiose* All-Father's symbolic powers. The Mother, like the Macassans themselves, did not directly undermine ubiety as an axiom of the Law, but she did acknowledge both the promise and the dangers of the newfound unity which emerged from the encounter with the northerners.

Our enquiry, then, is essentially about a people's confrontation with radical otherness, and it is hardly surprising that they turned to the most primal and powerful of all relationships in search of metaphors which articulated their predicament. The Ancestral parents pronounced, with fundamental authority, the bonds between Aborigines and intruders; between I and thou. To deepen our understanding we therefore need to ask the meaning of motherhood and fatherhood in Aboriginal Australia, all the while keeping watch for broader cultural patterns which might clarify the congruence between the beliefs of the first Australians and those of the various classes of aliens.

For Aborigines parenthood is a metaphysical relationship. I have already reconsidered in chapter 1 the interminable controversy over their knowledge of physiological paternity in order to assert that, whatever else may be a contributing factor, fatherhood is foremost a geographical and spiritual ideology. So too is motherhood,[125] although here self-evident physiological processes are clearly being deliberately downplayed, even 'denied', to enhance philosophic concerns. As Andrew Lang observed long ago, Aborigines here 'ignore that of which they are not ignorant. Not being idiots, they are well aware of the maternal tie of blood'.[126]

The womb is therefore not acclaimed for its biological ingenuity but instead, and in contradistinction, for its sacred significance. Gross has pointed to childbirth as a religious experience for Aboriginal women,[127] but neglects the more fundamental point: in a society in which each person is a manifestation of an Abiding Ancestral essence, the womb, although it threatens to recognise the autonomy of the body, must remain as nothing less than *the* passage linking eternal places and the temporal world. The northern Mother cult makes it abundantly clear that the womb and birth are the core of this sacrality. It is in this respect that the universal experience of motherhood (and Rosaldo would rightly add, the universal experience of women being *designated* as 'mothers')[128] can take us close to the core of one of the most basic symbolic expressions of the human condition.

In the concluding section of the *Djanggawul* myth, the Mothers' sacred objects are stolen by their brother. The older sister consoles the younger:

> I think we can leave that. Men can do it now. They can look after it . . . We know everything. We have really lost nothing, for we remember it all, and we can let them have a small part. For aren't we still sacred, even if we have lost the bags? Haven't we still got our uteri?[129]

At this point of the narrative men will acknowledge that they obtained their secrets from women.[130] They say: 'Women should really be the ritual leaders, for everything belongs to them. Men stole it all. But we still know that they are the real leaders'. The same understanding operates in western Arnhem Land where women are recognised as having the true affinity with the *ubar* grounds which are the Mother's womb.[131]

Perhaps the most concise explanation is that of those Maningrida women dismissing *Kunapipi* as 'men's rubbish': 'Men make secret ceremonies, women make babies'.[132]

And it seems men agree. The appropriation of birth symbols into Aboriginal men's rites is well documented. Wild writes of the *Kadjari* ceremonies in an article appropriately entitled 'Men as Women',[133] while Berndt notes that *Kunapipi*, as well as referring to the Mother and the womb, also means 'whistle cock' or subincised penis; that the men symbolically acquire women's reproductive organs through this operation, and that blood from the subincision is equated with the *Wawalag* sisters' menstrual blood.[134] It is difficult not to at least partially concede Bettleheim's conclusion that many Australian men's rituals are their way of achieving a 'business' in life equal to that of women as mothers;[135] that both birth and men's 'pseudo-procreation'[136] ceremonies are for Aborigines processes of actualising the eternal.

Yet there is a cardinal difference between being born of a woman and being born to men. The difference is this: birth from the Mother's womb spiritually differentiates; (re)birth through the men's ritual womb spiritually incorporates. The Mother's child in Australia, for reasons I have already outlined, rarely shares her land-spirit *identity*[137] – to do so would be to suggest the body's ascendency over land. In contrast the father's (Western secularist sceptics please read 'mother's husband's') child is more often than not cojoined with his or her father by the ideology, if not always the actuality[138] of the patrilineal 'clan'. Anthropological concepts largely fail the reality, but Turner's words are as good as any:

> The territorially-defined patrilineal land-owning group in Aboriginal Australia . . . allows for mythological linkages to be recognised through common totemic affiliations, implying associations with the wanderings of the same Dreaming beings over the geographical landscape.[139]

As territory is defined by the pull of its sacred centre rather than formal boundaries, and as 'ownership' in this context refers to a spiritual accord not to be equated with exclusive occupational rights, it is evident that patrilineal descent entails foremostly an ontologic sameness. These observations provide the equation:

Motherhood : Fatherhood :: Spiritual differentiation : Spiritual incorporation[140]

This formulation highlights some essential features of parental metaphors which come to the forefront when they are raised to the status of Transcendental Beings. The All-Mother can easily overlay a locative tradition with her unifying presence, and the many peoples and traditions she gave birth to can nonetheless maintain that they still differ *in essence* from each other and from her. A single All-creative Father, on the other hand, quickly introduces the threat of monism; one spirit, one earth, one people. While I have argued that the Sky Father arose out of Aboriginal people's enforced estrangement with the land, it is simultaneously true that an All-Father's oppressive spiritual hegemony would be such as to leave no option but to banish him from the earth.

Do not mistake me: I have not ignored the menacing aspect of the Mother. Shapiro's discussion of Aboriginal men's rites of the womb and their quest for the incorporative immortality of the patrilineal lodge in response to their flight from the intimidation of women's carnal qualities has already been examined, and on that occasion I inverted Shapiro's terms to suggest the 'denial' of the body was more accurately understood as an affirmation that Aboriginal people maintained they were born from land.[141] Focusing upon the birth-giving Mother in central-northern Australia, and in particular on the womb as a source, rather than a vehicle, of life, was thus inevitably accompanied by heightened promises of the body's failings and of death and decay, and new hopes in life everlasting (chapter 1). Although the essence of the Mother is her ability to bring forth genuine otherness from her embodied self, the sacredness of life in its abundant forms, she also stands as a ground of existence which ushers in a threat to Abidingness as an ontological premise. While the Mother allows a diversified land-life's initial emergence from a body, she simultaneously introduces the possibility of dissolution into chaos, impermanence and futility.

The minatory side of the Mother is prominent in north Australian myth and rite. Hiatt does not hesitate to call her an 'ogress',[142] for, just as she gave birth to all human life, so too she devours it. In the Daly River area *Mutjinga* consumes the children who have been left in her care, and they are only rescued when the All-Mother is cut open, allowing them to re-emerge, not from her stomach, as we might expect, but from her womb.[143] Likewise, the Roper River *Kunapipi* would kill, cook and eat men who were in theory her offspring, and would incite her daughters to eat their penes. In the north-eastern *Kunapipi* rites the Mother is in this respect replaced by the serpent *Yulunggur*, who Warner reported to be male, but

whom Berndt was told was female. The snake's swallowing of the
Wawalag sisters, the Yolngu say, symbolised the 'return of the
Wauwaluk to the uterus of their Mother'. In western Arnhem Land,
in her guise as the serpent *Ngaljod*, the Mother's appetite for human
flesh is relived in ritual when the neophytes are consumed: 'The
Mother is calling them, they will be swallowed by the snake'.[144]

The Mother's complex and apparently contradictory nature is
compellingly intensified by her androgyny. The phallicism of her
serpentine form, for instance, is quite intentional. Rose, having
briefly referred to a breasted Rainbow snake offers the interpretation
that 'neither exclusively male nor female, the Rainbow is complete'.[145]
This is true, but only within the context of truth's paradoxical form.
A careful analysis of Aboriginal symbols of androgyny does not yet
exist, but Géza Róheim's discussion of the *Alknarintja* women with
their long, penis-like clitorises is relevant as the *Djanggawul* sisters
also have this phallic attribute. In both cases these women are
operated upon (by their 'leader' and brother respectively) so that
eventually they took the form of normal women. 'The long clitoris
is cut,' says the *Djanggawul* song cycle and to make the meaning
unambiguous, the word here used for 'clitoris' is one that can also
be used to refer to a foreskin removed in circumcision.[146] The point
of this comparison is Róheim's observation that, far from exciting
simple feelings of fulfilment and entirety, the mother with a penis
primarily induced anxiety in Aranda and Pitjantjatjara men. We
need not concede his Freudian analysis, but cannot ignore his
informants' advice: 'If you dream of an *alknarintja* woman approach-
ing you, you must speedily awake'. The prospect of being anally
raped by these women, while offering a symbolic means of inverting
and merging sexual roles, was, apparently, not really their idea of
becoming 'complete'.[147]

Berndt, in contrast, has not missed the link between androgyny
and antinomy in the Mother.

Ngalyod, the Rainbow Snake may be referred to as male or female . . .
As the 'good Mother' . . . she is an expression of human and environmental fertility and the sponsor of ritual which concerns the well-being
of the society and its members. In her 'bad Mother' manifestation, she
is fear-inspiring, easily angered and quick to respond to real or supposed
transgression. She is a living symbol of the balance between 'goodness'
and 'badness' . . . This theme is at the root of questions about the destiny
of man.[148]

From here it is but a short step to appreciate the rich insights contained in the closing lines of Wendy O'Flaherty's *tour de force, Women, Androgynes and Other Mythical Beasts*:

> The androgyne . . . serves to express simultaneously love in union and love in separation, merging with god and splitting away from god. It expresses the awe and fear of the deity in whom all oppositions merge. Dangling before us the sweet promise of equality and balance, symbiosis and mutuality, the androgyne, under closer analysis, often furnishes bitter testimony to conflict and aggression, tension and disequilibrium, between female and male and between human and the divine.[149]

I will go no further than this, ending where for many the story just begins. I do not pretend to have penetrated the deeper mysteries of the Mother cult's bitter-sweet philosophy: the paradox of existence Stanner spoke of as 'a joyous thing with maggots at the centre'.[150] My task is merely to document an intellectual revolution, and while thus of necessity dwelling on the socio-political qualities of the emergent tradition, I would not care to be accused of being blind to the rich significances of their beliefs and practices in other domains.

I do suggest, however, that many truths emerge in the polarity of 'being and nothingness'; of autonomous existence against a chaos which drowns or devours human independence and freedom. All I claim to have done is indicate what it means to raise this dichotomy, through the metaphor of the Mother, to a transcendental, all-embracing level and to have chronicled an Aboriginal quest to nurture their interdependent diversity in the face of both the peril and inevitability of a new-found oneness.

When all is said and done, northern Australian Aborigines were simply asking, at both the individual and collective level, that perennial human question: How do I stand in relation to the world?

Sustaining and destroying, constrained by place and world-embracing; I leave the last word on this matter to Gunwinggu women.

> She is like a mother to these boys, looking after them and feeding them – but when they first go there she kills them, and then makes them alive again . . .
>   She is our mother. All of us everywhere, dark skin or light skin, people of every place and of different languages –
>   We all call her mother, our true mother.[151]

THE ALL-FATHER RETURNS: A CONCLUSION?

Our story is not yet over, however, for although the Macassans departed long ago, the Mother still remains. She struggles to survive, contending alike with a new regime of White invaders and more recent symbolic expressions of Aboriginal relationships with other peoples and with their land. In the relatively sheltered social climate of Arnhem Land she to some extent endures as the powerfully ambiguous 'Old Woman', but in the more turbulent environment in which many Aborigines find themselves she is increasingly metamorphosed into the 'Colonised Mother'; the helpless victim of oppression and defilement.

The Colonised Mother is easily recognised by the abstract equation made between her and the Earth – Mother Earth. How she came to assume her new form is a complex and tangled tale.[152] In an argument holding uncanny parallels with my own, Sam Gill has shown how scholars, colonists and Native Americans unwittingly conspired to create the Indian *Mother Earth*.[153] While in Australia the Mother had already emerged with the coming of the Indonesians, there can be no doubt that ethnographers, popular writers, missionaries and others, along with the stark reality of imperialist interests, all contributed to the Aboriginal re-creation of the All-Mother.

Western observers have always been keen to 'discover' Mother Earth among Third and Fourth World peoples. Tylor's claim that the idea of 'Earth as a mother is more simple and obvious . . . than the idea of the Heaven as Father'[154] must be understood not only in terms of 'the sexual politics of Victorian social anthropology'[155] but also the colonial politics of anthropology as a whole. Primitive Mother Earth, today the champion of a new women's spirituality, may more often than not herself be a recent creation of androcentric and imperialist scholarship;[156] which, I hasten to add, does not at all negate her symbolic aptness for either the oppressor or the oppressed.

I cannot fully uncover the way in which ethnographic thought has fed back into Aboriginal opinion, but there is certainly evidence for the predisposition of researchers to proclaim a Mother Earth. Albrecht Dieterich did more than any other scholar to instigate an academic belief in the universality of Mother Earth, and in arguing his case totally misrepresented Central Desert Aboriginal beliefs in order to provide an Australian example for his thesis.[157] Elkin and Capell also both exceeded their data by concluding that the immanent fertility Mother was 'the earth', and Elkin was no doubt inclined to this interpretation because he believed Aboriginal ceremonies were historically connected with the (Eleusinian?) 'mystery cults'.[158] At a more popular level Roland Robinson, who recorded a great deal of useful data in northern Australia, saw with a poet's licence what he thought to be the Aboriginal 'Earth-Mother'.[159] At times the excesses are bizarre, as, for example, when a dubious scholar like Bill Harney makes the absurd claim that Ayers Rock (*Uluru*) was a symbol of 'Earth Mother'.[160] Even the climactic chapter of Deborah Rose's most important study of the Victoria River District, *Dingo Makes us Human*, actually contains but one very brief piece of ethnographic data referring to the Earth as Mother (quoted below) and this is, I believe, quite evidently a recent, post-colonial creation. When Rose turns to Gaia to illuminate her Aboriginal data we witness the circularity of academic traditions, for Dieterich himself had only appealed to Aboriginal and other ethnographical material because of his inability to authenticate the Greek and Roman Mother Earth.[161]

The amorphous association between researcher and Aborigine, however, makes it exceedingly difficult to discern precisely how academic myth-making has in turn nourished Aboriginal myth-making. The mission context is clearer. Both Catholic and Protestant missiologists in Australia have given us pamphlets with titles such as *This Land Our Mother* or *My Mother the Land*. There is an ironic Christian tradition here, dating back perhaps to Saint Augustine, of confronting the 'pagan' belief in an Earth Mother Goddess of which the 'pagans' themselves are innocent. Indeed Dieterich's search for the universal Mother Earth was itself perhaps inspired by Augustine's errors,[162] providing missionaries and academics alike with a most appropriate common ancestor. And today's missionary Mother Earth, now lacking Augustine's vitriolic critique, has readily and with a dangerous astuteness been adopted by Aborigines familiar with mission discourse.

Djiniyini Gondarra, Moderator of the Uniting Church in the Northern Territory, has said:

The land is my mother. Like a human mother, the land gives us protection, enjoyment, and provides for our needs – economic, social and religious. We have a human relationship with the land: Mother-daughter-son. When the land is taken from us or destroyed, we feel hurt because we belong to the land and we are part of it.[163]

This is the colonised Mother, who lacks rich mythological foundations, and is flatly equated with the Earth, defenceless against what Gondarra calls 'oppressors . . . coming into our garden of Eden like a snake'.[164] Patrick Dodson, Chairperson of the Central Lands Council, in an essay which only refers to traditional patrilineal principles within the text, nonetheless opts for a title 'The Land Our Mother, the Church Our Mother'.[165] Elsewhere, he speaks in a little more detail of that Mother with no history save her identity with the Earth:

> The heart was being slowly pierced and living was being substituted with existence, shame and hopelessness. The land herself, our Mother, was being despoiled and defiled – she cried in sorrow and with despair for us, her children, the Aboriginal and Islander people.[166]

Let me be quite clear: I am not belittling the colonised Mother Earth. How, for instance, could one but applaud Riley Young's concerns for the earth as a whole? This is the statement in Rose's work, to which I referred earlier:

> This ground she's my mother. She's mother for everybody. We born top of this ground. This our mother. That's why we worry about this ground.[167]

But the tragedy of these images, though softly spoken, cannot be ignored. The Mother is invariably invoked in juxtaposition with a greater power – the colonialist who defiles her, the Christian God above her. The immensely ambivalent, paradoxical and at times life-threatening All-Mother is retreating. Mother Earth, wounded and bleeding, mutely warns with the very poverty of her being: the tide has turned; the way is open for the All-Father's return.

Here we enter the most recent stratum of North Australia's spiritual history, its opening deposits marbled but its texture increasingly uniform. Old institutions continue to take new forms, moieties once more expand in attempts to contain invaders and their creeds, the soul is again torn, hovering now between heaven and the Land of the Dead.[168]

Since the colonised Mother emerged, the mission Father in Heaven has always been present, either in an ascendent yet complementary way, or in a conflicting role. I will not document here the fundamentalist brand of Christianity now sweeping through Arnhem Land under the banner of that most telling catch-cry: 'Father make us One',[169] nor the constant efforts required to resist the Pentecostal message by those people in the Victoria River area who rally to the side of the threatened Mother Earth.[170] They are long stories in themselves, best reserved for another occasion. My concern in these closing pages is with our earliest glimpses of the All-Father in the north, where he so closely resembles the Father of All who appeared during the turmoil of invasion in south-east Australia. This will bring my investigation full circle.

Rose has noted a vital part of Aboriginal thought that will always remain hidden. She says, 'we have no way of knowing how often people thought of *and rejected* . . . a High God'.[171] There is, however, evidence of northern Australian Aboriginal people conceding his existence only to deny him prominence or ritual expression. Warner, for example, refers in an appendix to a sky dwelling All-Father who heads both moieties. He fathered the *Wawalag*'s children and has power over the Earth's fertility, yet despite all this is given virtually no place in Yolngu cosmology or ceremony.[172]

Paul Foelschue in fact provides an interesting juxtaposition of All-Father and All-Mother beliefs from as early as the 1880s. The view of a Larakia man from the vicinity of Darwin was that

> A very good man called 'Mangarrah' lives in the sky among the Stars, at a place called 'Teelahdlah'; he made all living creatures upon earth, except black fellows. He also made the trees, grass, water, and everything, and makes wind, rain and thunder. He never dies, and likes all black fellows.

But it was 'another good man called "Nanganburrah" ', who made the first Aborigine, *Dawed*, who in turn made the original human beings, instigated their culture and ultimately transformed into a tree. Foelschue's description is intriguing:

> 'Nanganburrah', who lives in the ground, is designated 'All same as Government.' He can read and write, and when black fellows growl writes it down in a book. When black fellows die they go into the ground to 'Nanganburrah,' and if they have been good, which is ascertained by referring to the book, 'Nanganburrah' gives them a letter to give to 'Mangaranrah', with whom they then live among the stars. If they have been bad and growled they are sent to a place deep down in the ground called 'Ohmar', where there is plenty of fire.[173]

Foelschue does not miss the European influences here. But are his data reliable? Apparently so, as he writes, in accord with our other accounts, that only 160 kilometres to the east of Darwin, the cosmology is associated with 'Warahmoorungee' [*Waramurunggundji*], a pregnant woman from the north who arrived at Port Essington and subsequently gave birth to the first people and allocated to each their language.[174] Elsewhere, Foelschue had noted the Malay language in the area,[175] and we readily appreciate we are being given a fascinating still frame from the complex and fluid convergence of several historic traditions: the All-Father from the intense colonial region of Darwin, the Indonesian All-Mother still active in more isolated areas.

Few other accounts are this clear. The Yolngu's *Laindjung*, which I am certain possesses a pre-colonial origin, takes on new proportions in some accounts. Although at one level a localised Ancestor, he is also depicted as a sky dweller who draws spirits to himself in his 'Heaven' connected to earth via a central cosmic tree,[176] itself, as I argued in chapter 1, an atypical symbol of spatial unity.[177]

According to the Berndts, *Laindjung*, the father of all *Yirritja*, competes with and contradicts the *Djanggawul* claim to have mothered *all* people. The full *Laindjung* ceremonial cycle the Berndts promised did not appear,[178] but given their fine ear for detecting synthetic developments, one could be forgiven for suspecting the anachronistic choice of words here is deliberate. Remember we are dealing with a tradition lacking religious specialists, proselytisers or hierarchical authorities in either the human or Ancestral realms. The Berndts write:

> 'I am Laintjung,' said the Ancestral Being, 'I bring all the *yiritja* dreaming and painting: these will belong to you people, no matter what language and what tribe.'
>
> Eventually, he turned himself into a paper-bark tree and his son *Banaidja* took his place. Now *Banaidja* was a great religious leader, who was able to elaborate on the ritual and dogma laid down in the beginning by *Laintjung*, his father. He began to teach men, but his disciples became frightened and talked among themselves. Is this man really connected with *Laintjung*, as a son, as he says? What have we got to do? And they climbed trees with spears, and waiting for an opportunity speared him so that he died. This was in the *Buneraitbi* country at Blue Mud Bay.
>
> But when they had killed him, the murderers realised that *Banaidja* was really a great man, and had a great deal more to tell them; and they were 'sorry'.[179]

Laindjung and *Banaidja* vie with the Mother's cult, emphasising male ritual dominance with little concession to the womb and fertility.[180] But the possibility of the totally incorporative, monistic, All-Father was confined, restricted by moiety constraints and the locative place-bound conclusion to the lives of both *Laindjung* and *Banaidja*.

In the next scenario, the Father broke free. The Port Keats region lacked the buffer of a reserve. Social conditions were appalling and people were being wrenched from their land-based spirits' abodes. It was the context of the Lawless alien. Here Stanner recorded a myth which had not been allowed ritual expression.[181] It was the story of a son, *Djinimin*, incestuously drawn to his sisters, and equally guilty of patricide. He speared his benign Father who, in the agony of death, made a gift of the means of life – fire and water.

While the comparison with Christian myth is far less evident than in the case of *Laindjung* and *Banaidja*, Stanner could not resist the analogy.[182] *Djinimin's* father, *Kunmanggur*, was the Father of All people, the source of all spirit essences. He not only contrasts but symbolically competes with the All-Mother and her 'mysterious female power'.[183] Stanner weighed the Mother cult against the *Kunmanggur-Djinimin* narrative, placed them both in the context of intense social disruption, and saw the truth with a wisdom that was more than profound. It was mantic. In 1958 he wrote that the Aboriginal people at Port Keats had, in the troubled times of the past,

> used a complementary idea which was beautifully appropriate, logically and psychologically – the idea of the All-Mother – . . . the theme was reconstitutive, not revolutionary or millenarian. Still no prophetic elements! Still the guiding conception of continuity with The Dream Time! The bullroarer was swung to summon a new life-principle to a dwindling and needy people. And then the All-Mother in turn began to fail.
>
> 'All this was twenty-five years ago. I was in the same place not long ago. The rites of the All-Mother had not been held for some time . . . It would be only a little fanciful to say the spirit of Tjinimin was abroad.'[184]

Stanner was wrong. It was not 'fanciful' at all.

Five years later, spreading far to the west, the All-Father and his Son had their cult. It was everything Stanner had feared – troubled, millennial and prophetic. The son *Djinimin* had himself become a sky-dwelling deity without equal. He promised as much, and more, as any of the south-eastern High Gods. The world would be purged of the White hegemony if Aborigines only held onto the Old Law. But the pledge was double-edged. *Djinimin* had descended to an 'inter-tribal' meeting. The theme was oneness and equality at the cost of Aborigines themselves becoming White and acquiring the 'cargo' of capitalist wealth.[185] These are the themes of the next chapter. There we will see how, at last, *Djinimin's* secret identity was revealed. For befitting his acquired status as a supreme Sky Hero, he was bequeathed a second name: Jesus.

NOTES

1. Compiled from the 'general translations' in R.M. Berndt, *Kunapipi: A Study of an Australian Aboriginal Religious Cult* (Melbourne: F.W. Cheshire, 1951), pp. 188-9.
2. G.W.F. Hegel, *Early Theological Writings* (Chicago: University of Chicago Press, 1948), pp. 162-3.
3. M. Flinders, *A Voyage to Terra Australis: . . .* (London: G. & W. Nicol, 1814), p. 172.
4. Aboriginal recollections about Pobassoo are recorded in M. Cook, *Makassar and Northeastern Arnhem Land: Missing Links And Living Bridges* (Darwin: Educational Media Unit, Batchelor College, 1987).
5. C.C. Macknight, *The Voyage to Marege: Macassan Trepangers in Northern Australia* (Carlton: Melbourne University Press, 1976), chapter 7.
6. W.L. Warner, *A Black Civilization: A Social Study of an Australian Tribe*, revised edition (New York: Harper & Brothers, 1958), pp. 453 & 465.
7. C.C. Macknight, 'Macassans and Aborigines', *Oceania*, 42 (1972), p. 318.
8. R.M. Berndt & C.H. Berndt, *Arnhem Land: Its History and Its People* (Melbourne: F.W. Cheshire, 1954), p. 45.
9. A. Capell, 'Early Indonesian Contacts with North Australia', *The Journal of the Oriental Society of Australia*, 3 (1965), pp. 74 & 69-70; A.P. Elkin, 'Aboriginal Australia and the Orient', typescript, Fisher Library, *Elkin Papers*, p. 130, Box 109, Folder 8, p. 12.
10. J. Urry & M. Walsh, 'The Lost "Macassar" Language of Northern Australia', *Aboriginal History*, 5 (1981), p. 98.
11. Berndt & Berndt, *Arnhem Land*, pp. 110f.
12. Flinders, *A Voyage to Terra Australis*, p. 232.
13. Macknight, 'Macassans and Aborigines', p. 317.
14. The Berndts give some oral examples in *Arnhem Land*, chapter 12.
15. see D. Rose, 'Jesus and the Dingo', in *Aboriginal Australians and Christian Missions*, edited by Swain & Rose, pp. 361-75.
16. Berndt & Berndt, *Arnhem Land*, p. 111; Macknight, 'Macassans and Aborigines', p. 289.
17. I am not suggesting sexual relations with Macassans were seen only a means of exchange, but certainly this was the aspect of the relationship which Aboriginal *men* sometimes felt had been abused.

18. D. Rose, *Dingo Makes Us Human* (Cambridge: Cambridge University Press, 1992), p. 223.
19. Lamilami, *Lamilami Speaks: An Autobiography* (Sydney: Ure Smith, 1974), p. 72.
20. Macknight, 'Macassans and Aborigines', pp. 285-6 & 304-8.
21. R.M. Berndt, 'Ceremonial Exchange in Western Arnhem Land', *Southwestern Journal of Anthropology*, 7 (1951), pp. 171-3; D.F. Thomson, *Economic Structure and the Ceremonial Exchange in Arnhem Land* (Melbourne: Macmillan, 1949), chapter 6; Worsley, 'Early Asian Contacts with Australia', p. 4; & Macknight, 'Macassans and Aborigines', pp. 308-9.
22. Thomson, ibid., p. 86.
23. ibid., p. 87.
24. Berndt, 'Ceremonial Exchange . . .', p. 174.
25. K.O.L. Burridge, *Mambu: A Melanesian Millennium* (London: Methuen, 1960), pp. 260 ff.
26. W.E.H. Stanner, 'Ceremonial Economics of the Mulluk Mulluk and Madngella Tribes of the Daly River, North Australia: A Preliminary Paper', *Oceania*, 4 (1933), p. 163.
27. D.H. Turner, 'The Incarnation of Nambirrirrma', in *Aboriginal Australians and Christian Missions*, edited by Swain & Rose, p. 476. These principles are developed in the same author's, *Life Before Genesis: A Conclusion: An Understanding of the Significance of Australian Aboriginal Culture* (New York: Peter Lang, 1987).
28. G.W. Earl [1] 'On the Aboriginal Tribes of the Northern Coast of Australia', *Journal of the Royal Geographical Society*, 16 (1846), p. 240; [2] 'An Account of a Visit to Kisser, One of the Serawatti Group on the Indian Archipelago', *Journal of the Royal Geographical Society*, 11 (1841), p. 116; [3] 'On the Aboriginal Tribes . . .', p. 244.
29. Warner, *A Black Civilization*, p. 38; Urry & Walsh, 'The Lost "Macassar" Language . . .', pp. 99-100.
30. W.E.H. Stanner, *On Aboriginal Religion*, Oceania Monograph, no. 11 (Sydney: Australian Medical Publishing Company, 1959-63), pp. 100 & 99.
31. W.D. O'Flaherty, *Women, Androgynes, and Other Mythical Beasts* (Chicago: University of Chicago Press, 1980), p. 10.
32. D.H. Turner, 'Caste Logic in a Clan Society: An Aboriginal Response to Domination', in *Aboriginal Power in Australian Society*, edited by M.C. Howard (St Lucia: University of Queensland Press, 1982), pp. 44-5 & 52.
33. Warner, *A Black Civilization*, p. 459, speaks of 'The conservatism of Aboriginal material culture'. The major non-ceremonial objects adopted were pipes and canoes with mast and sail. Grave posts, hollow log coffins, artistic motifs and other ritual items are likely introductions – see Macknight, 'Macassans and Aborigines', pp. 310-15.

34. D.H. Turner, *Dialectics in Tradition: Myth and Social Structure in Two Hunter-Gatherer Societies* (London: Royal Anthropological Institute of Great Britain and Ireland, 1978), p. 42.
35. Turner, 'Caste Logic . . .', p. 52.
36. *loc. cit.*
37. R. Robinson, *The Feathered Serpent* (Sydney: Edwards & Shaw, 1956), pp. 53–4.
38. Macknight, 'Macassans and Aborigines', p. 313.
39. Capell, 'Early Indonesian Contacts . . .', p. 73, says they are 'almost' a part of the Dreaming. Clearly they are a part of it. R.M. Berndt, *Djanggawul: An Aboriginal Religious Cult of North-Eastern Arnhem Land* (London: Routledge & Kegan Paul, 1952), baulks at the *Baijini* songs, seeing them as 'inconsistent' (p. 55), & argues for a 'possible' superimposition (p. 166), then concludes, with no explanations offered for removing the qualification, that this section '*is* superimposed' (p. 298). I see no reason why this claim should be accepted.
40. Berndt, ibid., p. 65, song 4.
41. ibid., pp. 101–2, song 38.
42. ibid., p. 28.
43. ibid., pp. 28 & 47, n. 1.
44. R.M. & C.H. Berndt, *Man, Land and Myth: The Gunwinggu People* (Sydney: Ure Smith, 1970), p. 117.
45. K. Maddock, 'A Structural Analysis of Paired Ceremonies in a Dual Social Organization', *Bijdragen tot de Taal- Land- en Volkenkunde*, 135 (1979), stresses the polarity and complementarity (p. 85) and unity of opposites (p. 111) of *Yirritja* and *Dhuwa* moiety ritual life.
46. Warner, op. cit., p. 30.
47. Berndt & Berndt, *Arnhem Land*, p. 65.
48. P.M. Worsley, 'Totemism in a Changing Society', *American Anthropologist*, 57 (1955), p. 856. Less obviously, the wind moiety 'totem' of Groote Eylandt may also refer to Macassans. See F. Rose, 'Malay Influence on Aboriginal Totemism in Northern Australia', *Man*, 47 (1947), p. 129, 'Legacy from Makasar', *Hemisphere*, 18 (1974), p. 26; on songs associated with winds bringing Macassans, see A.M. Moyle, 'Bara and Mamariga Songs on Groote Eylandt', *Canon*, 17 (1964), pp. 15–24.
49. Depicted in D.F. Thomson, 'Proof of Indonesian Influence upon the Aborigines of North Australia: The Remarkable Dog Ngarra of the Mildjinji Clan', *The Illustrated London News* (August 12 1939), pp. 277–9.
50. Warner, *A Black Civilization*, pp. 340 ff.
51. Thomson, op. cit., p. 279.
52. C.P. Mountford, *Records of the American-Australian Scientific Expedition to Arnhem Land: 1, Art, Myth and Symbolism* (Carlton:

Melbourne University Press, 1956), pp. 416 ff.; Capell, 'Early Indonesian Contacts . . .', p. 72.

53. R.M. Berndt, 'The Mountford Volume on Arnhem Land Art, Myth and Symbolism: A Critical Review', *Mankind*, 5 (1958), pp. 259-60.

54. R.M. & C.H. Berndt, 'Secular Figures of Northeastern Arnhem Land', *American Anthropologist*, 51 (1949), p. 221.

55. Warner, *A Black Civilization*, pp. 16 ff.

56. ibid., p. 447.

57. ibid., p. 448.

58. H. Morphy, *Journey to the Crocodile's Nest: An Accompanying Monograph to the film Madarrpa Funeral at Gurka'wuy* (Canberra: Australian Institute of Aboriginal Studies, 1984), p. 40; cf. R.M. Berndt, *Australian Aboriginal Religion* (Leiden: E.J. Brill, 1974), fascicle 2, p. 24.

59. Earl, 'On the Aboriginal Tribes . . .', p. 241.

60. Berndt & Berndt, *Arnhem Land*, p. 66. On Badu itself see, for example, J. Beckett, *Torres Strait Islanders: Custom and Colonisation* (Cambridge: Cambridge University Press, 1987). Also see Lamilami, *Lamilami Speaks*, p. 43.

61. Berndt, 'Badu . . .', pp. 94, 99, 101 & 102.

62. ibid., pp. 100-1.

63. Warner, *A Black Civilization*, first reported this, noting it as a 'purely superficial' change to mortuary practice (p. 466). Warner, however, totally neglected the Lands of the Dead in his account and hence would have failed to see the rites' importance.

64. *loc. cit.*

65. R.M. Berndt, 'External Influences on the Aboriginal', *Hemisphere*, 9 (1965), p. 7.

66. Berndt & Berndt, *Arnhem Land*, pp. 60-3, & 'Secular Figures . . .', pp. 214-19.

67. Berndt, 'Badu . . .', p. 101.

68. I suspect this transformation is associated with Aboriginal experiences of Whites in Australia and continuous readjustments of mythemes to accommodate a rapidly changing context. The Yolngu word for a White person is *balanda*, which is derived from the Macassarese for 'Hollander'; see A. Walerk & D. Zurc, 'Austronesian loanwords in Yolngu-Matha of Northeast Arnhem Land', *Aboriginal History*, 5 (1981), p. 124.

69. N. M. Williams, *The Yolngu and Their Land: A System of Land Tenure and the Fight for Its Recognition* (Canberra: Australian Institute of Aboriginal Studies, 1986), p. 28.

70. Macknight, *The Voyage to Marege*, chapter 8. The Northern Territory was then under the jurisdiction of the South Australian State government.

71. R.M. Berndt, 'The Wuradilagu Song Cycle of Northeastern Arnhem Land: Content and Style', *Journal of American Folklore*, 79 (1966), p. 200.
72. J.E. Esherick, *The Origins of the Boxer Uprising* (California: University of California Press, 1987), p. 326; cf. M. Bloch, *The Historian's Craft* (New York: Knopf, 1953).
73. P. Winch, *The Idea of a Social Science and Its Relation to Philosophy* (New York: Routledge and Kegan Paul, 1958), p. 23.
74. Elkin, 'Aboriginal Australia and The Orient', p. 12.
75. Capell, 'Early Indonesian Contacts . . .', pp. 69–70.
76. see Macknight's map in *The Voyage to Marege*, p. 62.
77. Berndt, *Djanggawul*, p. 63.
78. see C.P. Mountford, *Records of the American-Australian Scientific Expedition*, p. 269, n. 16; and R.M. Berndt's critical response, 'The Mountford Volume', p. 257.
79. Berndt, *Djanggawul*, p. 65.
80. R.M. & C.H. Berndt, *The World of the First Australians* (Sydney: Ure Smith, 1977), p. 276; see also L. Taylor, 'The Rainbow Serpent as Visual Metaphor in Western Arnhem Land', *Oceania*, 60 (1990), where, on p. 340, *Ngolyod* is depicted with the head of a buffalo, an animal introduced into Arnhem Land some 150 years ago.
81. Berndt & Berndt, *Man, Land and Myth*, pp. 117–18; cf. W.B. Spencer, *The Native Tribes of the Northern Territory of Australia* (London: Macmillan, 1914), chapter 9.
82. R.M. & C.H. Berndt, *Sexual Behaviour in Western Arnhem Land* (New York: The Viking Fund, 1951), p. 113.
83. In the Warlpiri transformation, for example, the major mythic figures are the male *Mamandabari*, and there is no reference to the Mother, who is quite *otiose* in the rituals. See M.J. Meggitt, *Gadjari Among the Walbiri Aborigines of Central Australia*, Oceania Monographs, no. 14 (Sydney: University of Sydney, 1966).
84. Elkin, 'Introduction', p. xix; Berndt, *Kunapipi*, p. xxviii, and *Australian Aboriginal Religion*, fascicle 3, p. 6.
85. Berndt, *Kunapipi*, p. 188.
86. Stanner, *On Aboriginal Religion*, p. 126. Stanner does note she came from the north (p. 127), and refers to the fact that she spoke of her travels across the sea (p. 128).
87. Robinson, *The Feathered Serpent*, p. 29. In Robinson's version, *Kukpi* is male. Stanner, ibid., p. 126, notes she is identified with both sexes of the black snake, although herself female.
88. H.J. Heeren, 'Indonesische cultuurinvoeden in Australië.' *Indonesië*, 6 (1952), p. 157.
89. Macknight, 'Macassans and Aborigines', p. 315.
90. *idem*, *The Voyage to Marege*, pp. 17 f & 159.

91. D. Gervaise, *An Historical Description of the Kingdom of Macassar In the East-Indies* (London: Tho. Leigh & D. Midwinter, 1701), pp. 119 & 120.

92. ibid., p. 129; R. Waterson, *Ritual and Belief among the Sa'dan Toraja*, Centre for South-East Asian Studies, Occasional Paper no. 2. (Canterbury: University of Kent, 1984), pp. 9 & 10.

93. Macknight, *The Voyage to Marege*, pp. 20, 29, 109–10; 'Macassans and Aborigines', pp. 306–7.

94. Berndt & Berndt, *Arnhem Land*, pp. 36 & 35.

95. R.M. & C.H. Berndt, 'Discovery of Pottery in North-Eastern Arnhem Land', *Journal of the Royal Anthropological Institute of Great Britain and Ireland*, 77 (1947), p. 135.

96. R.E. Downs, *The Religion of The Bare'e-Speaking Toradjan of Central Celebes* ('S-Gravenhage: Uitgeverij Excelsior, 1956), pp. 12–13.

97. Waterson, *Ritual and Belief . . .*, p. 12; H. Nooy-Palm, *The Sa'dan-Toraja: A Study of Their Social Life and Religion: II: Rituals of the East and West* (Pordrecht-Holland: Floris Publications, 1986), chapter 4.

98. G. Hatt, 'The Corn Mother in America and in Indonesia', *Anthropos*, 14 (1951), pp. 882 ff.

99. C. Pelras, ' "Herbe Divine": Le Riz Chez les Bugis (Indonésie)', *Études Rurales*, 53–6 (1974), pp. 357–74; 'Bugis Religion', in *The Encyclopedia of Religion*, editor in chief M. Eliade, vol. 2 (New York: Macmillan, 1987), p. 561.

100. K. Maddock, *The Australian Aborigines: A Portrait of their Society* (Harmondsworth: Penguin, 1974), p. 112; see also K. Maddock, 'Imagery and Social Structure in Two Dalabon Rock Art Sites', *Anthropological Forum*, 2 (1970), pp. 444–63, where the author makes some comparisons of All-Mothers and All-Fathers and their respective locations on and above the earth.

101. Elkin, 'Introduction', pp. xvi f.

102. Berndt & Berndt, *Man, Land and Myth*, p. 227; cf. M. Eliade, *Australian Religions: An Introduction* (Ithaca: Cornell University Press, 1973), chapter 1.

103. Rose, *Dingo Makes Us Human*, p. 230.

104. Downs, *The Religion of the Bare'e-speaking Toradjan . . .*, p. 15. *Ndara* committed incest with her cousin and was banished to the waters, where the foam hardened around her to form land.

105. Berndt & Berndt, *Sexual Behaviour . . .*, p. 110; *Man, Land and Myth*, p. 117.

106. Berndt, *Kunapipi*, p. 159, n. 1 & p. 160.

107. Stanner, *On Aboriginal Religion*, p. 4.

108. Berndt, *Djanggawul*, pp. 2–3 & 48.

109. Berndt & Berndt, *Sexual Behaviour . . .*, pp. 110–20; Berndt, *Kunapipi*, p. 147.

110. Warner, *A Black Civilization*, pp. 340 ff.; Berndt, *Djanggawul*, pp. 14 ff.

111. Berndt & Berndt, *Sexual Behaviour . . .*, pp. 127 ff.

112. Berndt, *Kunapipi*, p. 147.
113. Elkin, 'Introduction', p. xx.
114. Rose, *Dingo Makes us Human*, p. 417.
115. Berndt, *Djanggawul*, pp. 24, 51, 53.
116. Capell, 'Early Indonesian Contacts . . .', p. 69.
117. Berndt, *Kunapipi*, p. xxvii. This is an ideal rather than an actual correspondence as many localised traditions are not woven into the Mother's story. Aborigines nevertheless postulate that the connection must, in principle, exist, even if no one can actually articulate how this occurs.
118. C. Knight, 'Lévi-Strauss and the Dragon: *Mythologiques* reconsidered in the light of an Australian Aboriginal Myth', *Man*, NS, 18 (1983), p. 40.
119. Berndt, *Djanggawul*, *passim*, p. 48.
120. Berndt & Berndt, *Sexual Behaviour . . .*, pp. 110 ff.
121. Berndt, *Kunapipi*, p. 145.
122. Warner, *A Black Civilization*, p. 145.
123. Berndt, *Kunapipi*, p. 24.
124. C. Berndt, 'Monsoon and Honey Wind', pp. 1315-6.
125. M.F.A. Montagu, *Coming Into Being Among the Australian Aborigines: The Procreative Beliefs of the Australian Aborigines* (London: Routledge & Kegan Paul, second edition, 1974). Though simplistic in his interpretation of data, he is correct in insisting that physiological maternity and paternity be differentiated from motherhood and fatherhood as social relationships (p. 342).
126. A. Lang, *The Secret of the Totem* (London: Longmans, Green & Co., 1905), p. 190.
127. R.M. Gross, 'Menstruation and Childbirth and Religious Experiences in the Religion of Australian Aborigines', *Journal of the American Academy of Religion*, 55 (1977), pp. 1147-81.
128. M.Z. Rosaldo, 'The Use and Abuse of Anthropology: Reflections on Feminism and Cross-Cultural Understanding', *Signs: Journal of Women in Culture and Society*, 5 (1980), p. 397.
129. Berndt, *Djanggawul*, pp. 40-1.
130. On the priority of mythic women as ritual authorities, see J. de Leeuwe, 'Male Right and Female Right among the Autochthons of Arnhem Land', *Acta Ethnografica*, 13-14 (1964-5), pp. 313-48; 303-48.
131. Berndt, *Australian Aboriginal Religion*, fascicle 3, p. 2; Berndt & Berndt, *Sexual Behaviour . . .*, p. 122; *Man, Land and Myth*, pp. 120-1.
132. A. Hamilton, cit. L.R. Hiatt, 'Secret Pseudo-Procreation Rites among the Australian Aborigines', in *Anthropology in Oceania: Essays presented to Ian Hogbin*, edited by L.R. Hiatt & C. Jayawardena (Sydney: Angus and Robertson, 1971), p. 88, n. 18.
133. S.A. Wild, 'Men as Women: Female Dance Symbolism in Walbiri Men's Rituals', *Dance Research Journal*, 10 (1977-8), pp. 14-22.
134. R.M. Berndt, 'Subincision in a Non-Subincision Area', *The American Imago: A Psychoanalytic Journal for the Arts and Sciences*, 8 (1951),

p. 166. O'Flaherty, *Women, Androgynes and Other Mythical Beasts*, pp. 288-9, cites Australian data of this kind, but mistakenly says subincision may also simulate a kangaroo's 'pocket'. Rather it has been argued that the split kangaroo penis is being simulated. See J.E. Cawte, N. Djagamara & M.J. Barrett, 'The Meaning of Subincision of the Urethra to Aboriginal Australians', *British Journal of Medical Psychology*, 39 (1966), pp. 245-53; & P. Singer & D. DeSole, 'The Australian Subincision Ceremony Reconsidered: Vaginal Envy or Kangaroo Bifid Penis Envy', *American Anthropologist*, 69 (1967), pp. 355-8. Berndt's Arnhem Land data seem far more explicit in making the vagina/subincised penis equation than Cawte *et al.*, who draw on desert traditions.

135. B. Bettleheim, *Symbolic Wounds: Puberty Rites and the Envious Male* (London: Thames & Hudson, 1955), pp. 165-206.

136. A term coined by Hiatt in 'Secret Pseudo-Procreation Rites . . . .'.

137. I do *not* refer to land or sacred 'rights', which are without doubt transmitted through both men and women. I use the word 'identity' to mean both a metaphysical sameness (the person and the land and the Ancestor share a common essence) and the process of constructing the social and individual self.

138. See N. Peterson on 'patrilineal clan ideology' in 'Rights, Residence and Process in Australian Territorial Organisation', in *Aborigines, Land and Land Rights*, edited by N. Peterson & M. Langton (Canberra: Australian Institute of Aboriginal Studies, 1983), pp. 134-45. See also L.R. Hiatt, 'Local Organisation among the Australian Aborigines', *Oceania*, 32 (1962), pp. 267-86; and Maddock, *The Australian Aborigines*, pp. 29 ff.

139. D.H. Turner, *Australian Aboriginal Social Organisation* (Atlantic Highlands: Humanities Press, 1980), p. 135.

140. This has some similarity with C.P. MacCormack's suggestion that male : female :: colonialist : colonialised, in 'Nature, Culture and Gender: A Critique', in *Nature, Culture and Gender*, edited by C.P. MacCormack & M. Strathern (Cambridge: Cambridge University Press, 1980), pp. 1-21. I would insist, however, that in this context 'motherhood' and 'fatherhood' are more fundamental than 'male' and 'female', and would also reject the stereotypically passive concept of the colonised. The opposite of the monistic coloniser, I maintain, is the very active advocate of pluralism as a social, religious and political principle. The Colonised Mother is nonetheless one of her many possible forms and is considered below.

141. W. Shapiro, 'Ritual Kinship, Ritual Incorporation and the Denial of Death', *Man*, NS 23 (1988), pp. 257-97. Shapiro draws heavily on E. Becker's *The Denial of Death* (New York: The Free Press, 1973), whose discussion of 'The Oedipus Project' and related themes (pp. 34 ff.) is relevant here.

142. L.R. Hiatt, 'Swallowing and Regurgitation in Australian Myth and Rite', in *Australian Aboriginal Mythology*, edited by L.R. Hiatt (Canberra: Australian Institute of Aboriginal Studies, 1975), p. 156.

143. Stanner, *On Aboriginal Religion*, pp. 40-2.

144. Berndt, *Kunapipi*, pp. 184 ff & 31-2; Berndt & Berndt, *Man, Land and Myth*, pp. 139-40.

145. Rose, *Dingo Makes Us Human*, p. 224. F. Merlan dismisses Rose's discussion of androgyny as a 'just so' story: 'Gender in Aboriginal Social Life: A review', in *Social Anthropology and Australian Aboriginal Studies: A Contemporary Overview*, edited by R.M. Berndt & R. Tonkinson (Canberra: Australian Aboriginal Studies, 1988) p. 34. The wholeness of the androgyne, however, is a common view and is certainly not without some foundation. It is, for instance, shared by, C.Jung, 'Psychology of the Transference', in *The Practice of Psychotherapy*, Collected Works Vol. XVI, (London: Routledge & Kegan Paul, 1954); & M. Eliade, *The Two and the One* (New York: Harper & Row, 1962), pp. 78-124.

146. Berndt, *Djanggawul*, pp. 25, 259 & 274.

147. G. Róheim, 'Psycho-Analysis of Primitive Cultural Types', *The International Journal of Psycho-Analysis*, 13 (1932), p. 53.

148. R.M. Berndt, 'A Profile of Good and Bad in Australian Aboriginal Religion', *Colloquium*, 12 (1979), p. 23.

149. O'Flaherty, *Women, Androgynes and Other Mythical Beasts*, p. 334.

150. Stanner, *On Aboriginal Religion*, p. 37.

151. Berndt & Berndt, *Man, Land and Myth*, p. 121.

152. I have recently extended the following analysis of Mother Earth in 'The Mother Earth Conspiracy: An Australian Episode', *Numen*, 58 (1991), pp. 3-26.

153. S.D. Gill, *Mother Earth: The American Story* (Chicago: The University of Chicago Press, 1987).

154. cit. ibid., p. 107.

155. E. Free, 'The Sexual Politics of Victorian Social Anthropology', in *Darwin to Einstein: Historical Studies on Science and Belief*, edited by C. Chant & J. Fauvel (Essex: Longman, 1980), pp. 195-313.

156. U. King, *Women and Spirituality: Voices of Protest and Promise* (London: Macmillan, 1989), pp. 146-53, tries to make the important distinction between the 'Goddess' of women's spirituality and the 'Great Mother' or 'Earth Goddess', but her fanciful understanding of historical processes fails to do justice to the issue.

157. A. Dieterich, *Mutter Erde: Ein Versuch über Volksreligion* (Berlin: E. Ferle, 1905); cf. O. Pettersson, *Mother Earth: An Analysis of the Mother Earth Concept According to Albrecht Dieterich*, Scripta Minora, Regiae Societatis Humanorum Litterum Lundensis, no. 3 (Lund: CWK Gleerup, 1965-6), pp. 23-4.

158. A.P. Elkin, *The Australian Aborigines* (Sydney: Angus & Robertson, 1964), p. 253. M. Eliade, *Australian Religions: An Introduction* (Ithaca:

Cornell University Press, 1973), pp. 27-8, n. 45, asks just what Elkin meant by 'mystery cults', and suggests Eleusis. See also my *Interpreting Aboriginal Religion*, pp. 104-5.

159. R. Robinson, *The Australian Aboriginal* (Sydney: A.H. & A.W. Reed, 1971), chapter 2; cf. *idem. The Shift of Sands: An Autobiography 1952-62* (Melbourne: Macmillan, 1976), pp. 203 ff.
160. A letter by Harney is quoted to this effect in T.G.H. Strehlow, 'Mythology of the Centralian Aborigine', *The Inland Review*, 3 (1969), p. 16; see also W.E. Harney, *The Story of Ayers Rock* (Melbourne: Bread and Cheese Club, 1951). Harney is corrected implictly by Strehlow and explicitly by R. Layton in *Uluru: An Aboriginal History of Ayers Rock* (Canberra: Australian Institute of Aboriginal Studies, 1986).
161. Pettersson, *Mother Earth, passim*.
162. ibid., p. 8.
163. D. Gondarra, in I.R. Yule (ed), *My Mother the Land* (Galiwin'ku: Christian Action Group, 1980), p. 8.
164. ibid., p. 9.
165. P. Dodson, 'The Land Our Mother, The Church Our Mother', *Compass Theology Review*, 22 (1788), pp. 1-3. The only Ancestral reference in the text is: 'When the child is born he calls that part of the country "Father"' (p. 1).
166. *idem*, 'Where are we, after 200 Years of Colonisation?', *Land Rights News*, 2 (1988), p. 5. The inclusion of Torres Strait Islanders here is significant, as their only real cultural link with Aborigines is that of a joint colonial experience.
167. Rose, *Dingo Makes Us Human*, p. 220.
168. Noted in J. Falkenberg, *Kin and Totem: Group Relations of Australian Aborigines in the Port Keats District* (Norway: Oslo University Press, 1962), pp. 187-8; D.H. Turner, *Tradition and Transformation: A Study of the Groote Eylandt Area Aborigines of Northern Australia* (Canberra: Australian Institute of Aboriginal Studies, 1974), pp. 150 ff.
169. see Bos, 'The Dreaming and Social Change . . .'.
170. Rose, 'Jesus and the Dingo'.
171. Rose, *Dingo Makes Us Human*, p. 230. My emphasis.
172. Warner, *A Black Civilization*, p. 542.
173. P. Foelschue, 'On the Manners, Customs, Etc., of Some Tribes of the Aborigines, in the Neighbourhood of Port Darwin and the West Coast of the Gulf of Carpentaria, North Australia', *Journal of the Anthropological Institute of Great Britain and Ireland*, 24 (1895), pp. 191 & 192.
174. ibid., p. 192.
175. P. Foelschue, 'Notes on the Aborigines of North Australia', *Transactions and Proceedings of the Royal Society of South Australia*, 5 (1881), pp. 1-18.

176. A.E. Wells, *This Their Dreaming* (St Lucia: University of Queensland Press, 1971), p. 65. 'The central column of the panel here reveals its true character as the tree connecting the sacred and profane, the heaven and the earth.'

177. In terms of my first chapter, it is also significant that H. Morphy sees the *Laindjung-Banaidja* narrative as being representative of myths of inheritance. See 'Myth, Totemism and the Creation of Clans', *Oceania*, 60 (1990), pp. 316–8.

178. R.M. Berndt and C.H. Berndt, 'Sacred Figures of Ancestral Beings of Arnhem Land', *Oceania*, 18 (1948), p. 314, n. 18.

179. Berndt & Berndt, 'Sacred Figures . . .', p. 314.

180. R. Berndt, *Australian Aboriginal Religion*, fascicle 3, p. 3.

181. Stanner, *On Aboriginal Religion*, chapter 4. Stanner actually believed the rite had been lost, but had no evidence of this and advocated the view only out of his general agreement with the ritual theory of myth. On p. 85, furthermore, Stanner himself acknowledges that the myths were themselves recent and the product of a dynamic, ongoing, mythopeic process. Inversely, I in no way deny that the myth of *Kunmanggur* and *Djinimin* has ancient roots. My concern is only with its newly acquired ontological structure.

182. W.E.H. Stanner, 'Continuity and Change Among the Aborigines', *Australian Journal of Science*, 21 (1958), p. 105.

183. *idem*, *On Aboriginal Religion*, pp. 55, 95 & 97.

184. *idem*, 'Continuity and Change . . .', p. 107.

185. H. Petri & G. Petri-Odermann, 'A Nativistic and Millenarian Movement in North West Australia', *Aboriginal Australians and Christian Missions*; edited by Swain & Rose, pp. 391–6; also *idem*, 'Stability and Change: Present-day Historic Aspects Among Australian Aborigines', in *Australian Aboriginal Studies: Modern Studies in the Social Anthropology of the Australian Aborigines*, edited by R.M. Berndt (Nedlands: University of Western Australia Press, 1970), pp. 248–76.

CHAPTER 5

From the Mother to the Millennium

You steer the plane with both arms,
Sending it straight through the air.
Inside, what a noise!
We are nobody with all our cleverness,
Against the whitefellow.
He can read, and write, and sure enough,
Drive those big things in the sky –
Magic? – He doesn't need it.
Our medicine men, the whole lot
Are utterly useless.[1]

Law flies two ways in the Pilbara. A man like Smiler Narnutjarri might celebrate in song his vision of the 'clever man' soaring 'In full regalia . . ./Beaming, sparkling far ahead . . ./Clearly I see you there aloft,/Your [headdress] burning', but others see different *mapamba*. Pudjipangu's 'magician makes the slim body climb steadily/Up and up it twists the engine's song/Till the double wings are level in the windless sky/Then the clever pilot tunes the engine down,/And aims quietly on high,/It dwindles in the west'.[2]

Here is awe in the presence of power, but the source of that power is not merely 'magic' but a new Law, revealed in the giants of the sky and encoded in a tradition open only to those who 'can read and write'. It was a capricious Law, as changeable as its manifestations, for before the planes there had been trucks and trains, ships, carts, and other bearers of White 'cargo'.

All Aborigines whose places were invaded have been confronted by the White code of being, but in northern Australia, and particularly the north-west, Aborigines responded, or were forced to respond, by playing a reckless and dangerous cosmological game. The prize was moral relationships with Whites within White Law. At stake was the eternal link between Aboriginal spirits and their

212

lands. The game – White invented, White controlled and White imposed – was 'cargoism'. The subject of this chapter is how Aboriginal people were induced to play.

OF LAW AND LABOUR

The north-west of Australia, and especially the Kimberley, stands out in the study of Aboriginal societies as a region with a history. Insofar as I have argued that history in Australia is a European legacy, this means the north-west has been an area where scholars have to some extent admitted, and even reconstructed, time and change. The context of the conceit is, however, revealing.

One domain in which change has been happily acknowledged is at that safe distance where we are dealing with remote eras and non-European contacts (cf. chapter 2). This is, of course, not to say such cultural dynamics did not occur, and were I attempting a prehistory of Aboriginal ontologies, the north-west is almost certainly where my story would begin. Sometime between 50 and 150 thousand years ago, to offer the virtually meaninglessly broad range of dates currently being entertained, humans, but not necessarily *Homo sapiens sapiens*, probably entered the land mass of Greater Australia, which during the intermittent periods of low sea levels stretched from New Guinea in the north to Tasmania in the south, and which extended significantly beyond Australia's present western coastline. Sweeping down through a mainland-locked south-east Asia, these pioneers could have island-hopped as far as Timor from whence, only 80 kilometres to the south-east, lay a vast land, towering one and a half kilometres above sea level. For this route and the data there is no evidence save parsimony: it just seems the simplest path to an empty land.[3]

Whether or not this hypothesised journey has any substance, it remains true that in latter eras, and with the exception of Melanesians, the people of Timor, now some 450 kilometres distant, were Australia's closest neighbours. It is assumed – again, there is no solid evidence – that some of the unique features of Kimberley culture can be attributed to contacts with the Timorese.

No matter how intriguing, to date speculations on this ancient past have succeeded primarily in simply muddying historical waters. If we are honest, we must admit that centuries, perhaps millennia, of creative accommodation of outsiders has left little more than a trace of a record that some adjustment did in fact occur. Both in iconography and in myth there is a layering which bears witness to radical change, but their deeper significance is, and I suspect always will remain, concealed.

If only to help clarify these waters before attempting to see beyond them, I will say a few tentative words about the more distant past of north-western Australian worldviews. One significant observation is that the oldest strata, as revealed in rock art, seem to suggest a vision of life akin to that of traditions which endured within the heart of the continent, thus suggesting a once basic Aboriginal ontologic plan.[4] Arthur Capell believed this past was also accessible through linguistic and mythic analysis, arguing it revealed a tradition associated with the dead who became eternally located and who forever 'stay in a place'.[5] If this were so then it appears the general model I proposed in chapter 1 was also applicable to the Kimberley.

In the initial anthropological reports from the region, however, there were already conflicting doctrines stating that the soul departed for a western Land of the Dead, possibly reflecting contacts with a people (the Timorese?) who brought with them the contextual inspiration for the *Wandjina* motifs. These paintings and their associated myths are certainly more recent, and are focused on the north-western coast (they are absent inland, for instance, amongst the Woljamidi, Guidj and Waladjangari). Often the *Wandjina* stories tell of Ancestral Beings coming from across the sea.[6] Capell concludes:

> It is not beyond the bounds of feasibility that there may be a real kernel of historical truth, and that one has to look north-westward to find the origin of this people. The first land in that direction is Timor, and many have thought to trace the Australians through that path. It is also possible to see the importance of the location of the afterworld, if it is true that immigrant peoples tend to set the afterworld in their old homes. Where the Wandjina cult is found, the afterworld lies on an island westward.[7]

As far as the data take us, it appears we witness here something comparable with the Indonesian impacts on central-northern Australia, which I detailed in the preceding chapter. What is missing is a context. The strangers had long departed before Whites arrived, and the paucity of the records makes it impossible to understand the full significance of these cults. At best, we can establish a chronicle, but a chronicle is not a history.

There are still more unexpected strands in the rich tapestry of Kimberley heritage, with transformations paralleling the Wunambal transformation of *Wandjina* iconography to form the 'children of Kaiara' – allegedly 'traditional' Ancestral beings wearing European clothing and smoking pipes. Thus, it is sometimes said, the soul, besides returning to its place or journeying to the west, might pass on to 'Bundulmiri, said to be the son of Walaro . . . the creator of all things'.[8] An unforeseen belief, indeed, but in the mission-ridden Kimberley we need not be surprised to learn of the corollary: for the Aboriginal people of Forest River, writes Phyllis Kaberry during a pioneering era of research in the area, 'called Christ Bundimiri, and God Wolara'.[9] It appears that here, once again, we witness the High God scenario of chapter 3 re-emerging. *Djamar*, the missionary anthropologist E.A. Worms tells us, was the 'Creator, the great Supreme Being'.[10] I do not want to reiterate my argument for the south-east here, however, for what is important is how the north-west went beyond that scenario. Thus, notes Worms in his discussion of Ancestors who have a particularly uncommon sequentiality to them, *Djamar*, who had usurped *Galalan* and *Mirau*, was himself being overthrown by one of the main heroes of this chapter: *Djanba*.[11]

Djanba is ascribed by Capell to the most recent of his stratum of Kimberley eras. Similarly, archaeologists have associated *Djanba's* cult with the most recent of rock engravings, perhaps belonging to this century.[12] My contention is that *Djanba* not only embodies a post-colonial understanding of the world, but further, that he heralded a new and particularly northern and north-western response to invasion. But before we can begin to understand this great but menacing being, it is necessary to discover his social environment and the context of research into his world.

In specific terms, this chapter deals with four types of cultic moods which emerged in succession in an area focused on a broad band running from north-western Queensland through to the Kimberley, but having impact well beyond that area. Its full demarcation does not correspond to any maps attempting to lay out traditional cultural boundaries in Aboriginal Australia, but is in very close accord with the area plotted to show large-scale pastoral enterprises within Australia. This is the essential key to a specific Aboriginal ontological revolution. The shaded areas on map 5 (page 216) represent an environment which falls midway between the two extremes of the remaining unshaded area. The large south-eastern and smaller south-western corners are fertile enough so that most pastoral enterprises can be managed by an average Australian family group. On the other hand, the remaining unshaded areas represent regions either too dry for cattle, or set aside as, in the first instance, Aboriginal reserves. In the relatively arid areas where grazing is nevertheless still feasible, the leaseholds are of necessity very large, and it is in precisely these regions that White Australians found themselves doing something otherwise more remarkable by its absence: they used Aboriginal labour.

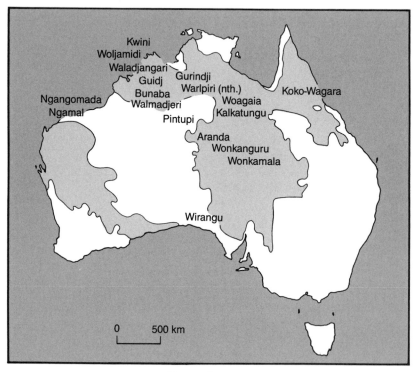

Pastoral areas.

There were other contexts in which Aborigines were employed in early periods – in some mines, and in the pearling and bêche-de-mer industries, for example[13] – but these lacked the continuity which station life provided. Futhermore, as we will see, while Aboriginal people had to be pressurised, even enslaved, before leaving their lands to labour, they eventually at least came to both be expert in and enjoy pastoral work.[14]

On stations Aborigines re-encountered White Australians. It was not the context of the Lawless alien met in chapter 3, and again introduced briefly below. Nor, on the other hand, were Aborigines interacting as equals with traders and their goods, as had been the case with the Macassans. Nonetheless there was a structure of relationship for all that, albeit hierarchical and oppressive. For the first time, White economic necessity forced colonial Australians to offer – even coercing Aborigines to accept – a place within their world. It was an ungenerous offer. Aborigines were presented with the largely unrefusable choice of entering an economic and symbolic world of cash and rations, but never with so much as a nominal promise of control over the representations they were being asked to accept.

Like Elkin before him, Erich Kolig has argued that Aboriginal people did not really understand the material origin of European wealth, believing it sprang somehow from the earth in the homelands of employers,[15] but the point they neglect to stress is that it was the Whites themselves who deliberately decided to safeguard their supremacy by locating the source of their dominance on the cosmological periphery. When discussing a related but somewhat different context, Peter Willis candidly reflected that as a missionary in the Kimberley station area, he too was engaged in an attempt to act as a 'patron', offering unsolicited gifts in order to negotiate a permanent dominance over 'clients' who could never control the goods mediated and hence could never repay the 'debt'.[16] The rules differed in capitalist enterprises, but shared the concern that Aborigines did not have access to the control of the distribution process.

Despite Elkin's infamous assertion that Aborigines radiated towards pastoral stations because they were 'intelligent parasites', the reality is that they were herded into these areas by a cunning predator. It is exceptionally well documented that Aborigines at first physically resisted the spread of pastoralism,[17] and in the Kimberley, as we will soon see, they fought a 'long and savage war' against invasion.[18] When the battles were lost, however, needy station owners were ready to promise Aborigines salvation through work and commodities.

It is in this environment that so-called 'cargoism' emerges in Australia. Some scholars appear almost affronted that it was not more widespread; as though 'primitives' were honour-bound to ritually lust for White goods.[19] Yet as Deborah Rose has observed, in most of Australia the dominant theme was 'conquest, dispossession and eradication' rather than the 'economic manipulation' which provides the fertile medium for 'cargoistic' growth.[20] Where Aborigines have been wooed by the self-declared moral code of European relationships with other cultures – money or commodities – then 'cargoism,' given certain other preconditions, has emerged; which of course means that the responsibility for 'cargo cults' lies not with 'native greed' but deliberate imperialist manipulation.

The word 'cargo' and its derivatives, however, are retained only in order to reshape their significance. It is a term more laden with valuable prejudices than any ceremonial ship or plane was with goods. I will contend that what has been called 'cargoism' is nothing more than *an attempt to (re)establish cosmic balance through the symbolic acquisition of equality within a White Law expressed in terms of commodity wealth*. Having stated as much, this chapter requires little further theory, its history tending to write itself. If the changing relationships with Whites are observed simultaneously with the cultic innovations of pastoral Australia, then, far from an enigma whose explanation requires a 'revolution in anthropology',[21] the slow and reluctant rise of 'cargoism' virtually self-discloses its meaning.

This chapter begins with the expansion of the pastoral frontiers across northern Australia and with militant Aboriginal opposition and its cultic manifestations. I then show how Aboriginal people were brought into the moral world of commodities and the resultant quest for equality which carried with it the 'cargoistic' mood. Finally, I consider what might come after the 'cargo' has arrived with the millennium.

Before turning to the data themselves, it is necessary to comment briefly on the ways in which, in labouring environments, ethnographic texts have refracted and rebuffed Aboriginal beliefs and practices. Initially, we must note that anthropology gets no closer to the 'precontact Aborigines' in the north-west than in the south-east. With a handful of superficial and piecemeal exceptions, field-workers arrived in the north-west a full half century after it had been brutally settled. The next textual adjustment to be made is to realise that Australian-financed anthropology was particularly reluctant to acknowledge that Aboriginal societies were under intense pressure to change. Ralph Piddington, for instance, after a spell of fieldwork in the West Kimberley in 1932, accused the Western Australian government of condoning 'virtual slavery' in the pastoral north. The result was that funding for field-research was threatened and the

Chairman of the Anthropological Committee of the Australian National Research Council, and acting Professor of Anthropology at Sydney University, gave his assurance that anthropologists would in future not criticise the administration publicly.[22] Again, the Berndts, having produced a disturbingly revealing report of pastoral conditions in the Victoria River District in 1944–6, did not publish their findings until 1987.[23] It seems the conservatism of Australian functionalist theory was entirely compatible with institutional inhibitions against researchers speaking out against oppressive and exploitative systems, and I sometimes suspect that living with this situation predisposed local anthropologists to wish Aborigines unchanged precisely because they themselves had done nothing about everything changing for the worse.

The north-west was in this respect blessed by the arrival of the German-financed Frobenius Expedition of 1938, which not only displayed the influence of European historical anthropological thought, but was also free to some extent from restraints imposed by Australian political gatekeepers. True, Helmut Petri and Andreas Lommel do display something of a bias in favour of Catholic missionaries (their gatekeepers) against social-reforming mission critics, but at least their writings are rich in evidence for a dynamic worldview in the Kimberley. Of this, R.M. Berndt would have nothing in the 1950s, and he never repented of his vitriolic critique of those who said there was either a despondent or a revivalistic atmosphere in Aboriginal pastoral domains.[24]

There is nothing to be gained here from pursuing the fact that researchers are constrained by their theory, their political environment and their time, but nor need we apologise for giving scholars trained in the continent more due than has been traditionally their lot amongst audiences in Aboriginal Studies. German and French investigations in fact provide much of the backbone for this chapter.

And so, having dealt with matters of the contexts and constraints of research, I turn back to the last quarter of the nineteenth century, when northern Australia was stained with blood and rich with heroes.

MULUNGA: A COSMIC REBELLION

The northern pastoral frontier pushed up from the south-eastern home of the new Sky Hero, spreading into the north of Queensland, and then arcing across the top of the continent before descending from the Kimberley, where it met a secondary upward thrust from the south-western colonial centre. There was nothing in the least original about the initial north Queensland frenzy of dispossession which began in the 1860s. The unspoken policy was to keep Aborigines out of their lands by any means, and the negotiating strategy was a 'liberal use of the rifle and poison to combat the Aboriginal resistance'. It was enough, at least, to nurture settler wit. When a bullock was speared in the area to the east of the Hodgkinson Goldfield, the carcase was peppered with arsenic and a sign was place upon it saying 'Poison': 'disregarding this caution, a large number of the original monarchs of the soil had injudiciously partaken of the insalubrious "bullocky" and, as a natural consequence most of them had become slightly indisposed'.[25]

The goldrush of the 1870s only intensified the desire to remove Aborigines, and the ruthlessly efficient Native Police were brought in to suppress any resistance. The protracted response was large-scale guerilla warfare.[26] Famed cattle raiders such as 'Hector' and leaders like 'Whistler', who had vowed to kill all Whites and hunt every beast in their lands, gave the settlers very real cause for alarm,[27] but ultimately, their resistance campaigns failed.

It was only toward the very end of the nineteenth century that some Aborigines in north Queensland were 'let in', the pragmatic reason being that, no longer seen as a military threat, 'Aborigines were often very useful for certain kinds of rough, menial or casual labour which no one else would do, or do economically'.[28] By this time, however, the industry had stretched across the continent.

When the first White Australian journeyed through the north-western hinterland in 1879, the most famous of all Aboriginal rebels was then a young boy just six years old. *Djandomarra*, better known as Pigeon, was at the time living in the ranges with his Bunaba people, who had readily adapted to harvesting the new fauna. Suppression inevitably followed, but what is revealing in Pigeon's case is that his rebellion began after he had been 'let in' to the pastoral domain. He became a very skilled station worker but, on returning to the hills to be introduced to his own true spiritual identity, he chose to stay in his country, abandoning the world of labour, and joining those who killed the White pastoralists' stock. His fate is illustrative, and his story worth the telling.

Pigeon was arrested and taken in chains to Derby for imprisonment. As he was a likeable youth, however, the police had him care instead for their horses for a year. Afterwards, he returned home, was bonded to a harsh employer, fled, and was again arrested and made to serve his sentence as a tracker. Having been used to capture some of his own people, he rebelled, shot his sleeping supervising constable, and launched a military offensive against the Whites. He mustered many guerillas to his band, and each victory added to their cache of guns. His ultimate goal was to take Derby itself. Time after time, he evaded seemingly inevitable defeat. Later, sub-inspector Ord reflected, 'it would not matter if the whole British army were sent here, Pigeon would still laugh at them from on top of the range'.[29] He was never subdued by White force. Chained trackers were used to hunt him, and according to White Australian traditions another Aborigine simply killed him. This, however, is not how Banjo Worrumarra tells of his end. In light of more recent cults (which I will discuss later in this chapter), the image of the 'clever man' travelling on the *S.S. Koombana* should not be overlooked.

No matter how many shot he used to take her nothing doin' –
THAT didn't put him back –
anyhow –
one –
maban blackfella witchdoctor –
come from ROEBOURNE –
they used to call 'im ah Minko Mick –
he got onto the boat –
in –
Roebourne –
or Onslow –
boat call – er name ah –
Koombana –
three funnell –
come right up to Derby landed –
anyhow blackfella got onto – mail coaches –
they take-im to Meda and from Meda to Kimberley Downs and
    from Kimberley Downs to Fairfield –
then he ride across with horse –
horseback –
went to Tunnel –
he SLEEP one night there –
he didn't go fast –
but next mornin' –
they stirred-im Pigeon up –
so he got up –
to start shooting – but this bloke seen his life –

soo –
witchdoctor told them boys –
'Alright' –
'I know' he said –
'I take jus one bullet in my rifle,' he said 'I'll kill 'im an' you
  fellas can go an' pick 'im up' –
cut his HEAD off –
so this Pigeon went up aaah –
Minko Mick –
followed the river up –
he got into the boab tree –
he look up –
upwards –
Pigeon was right on top of the cliff –
so he FIRE ONE shot he knock him in his thumb – so he fell
  down an' he sing out –
'I shoot-im you can go in and pick 'im up whenever you want' –
very fright they said, 'NO we can't run to pick-im up' –
'NO – you go in an' see-im' –
'he's finished' –
'alright' –
Oh well they didn't argue with 'im all them fellas around up
  there –
and see –
sure enough Pigeon laying there –
smashed up –
is thumb . . .
so when Minko Mick – went up there he looked 'is – thumb he
  found a little –
little heart –
like a fish –
in his thumb there (shows thumb) –
that where he shot –
an' that was the end of the old Pigeon story – [30]

There is much in Pigeon's saga which makes it memorable and illustrative of broader historical processes. Firstly, it demolishes the image of Aborigines aimlessly drifting towards the 'cargo' of station life. Rather, having realised their need for Aboriginal labour, the pastoralists secured it even when Aborigines, like Pigeon, tried to break free. This was, as Kolig states, slavery not *de jure* but *de facto*.[31] To the south, in the Pilbara, the pearling industry replicated this process, bringing captured labourers in chains to undertake 'employment' which, because of the depths and duration of the dives, would more than likely cost them their lives.[32] Were this 'parasitism', as Elkin contended, it could hardly have been 'intelligent'.

Secondly, Pigeon's biography reveals the speed of the impact of pastoralism. By 1905, the Kimberley was virtually stocked to capacity.[33] The guerilla resistance, whether against invasion *per se* or forced employment, was fated to be a short-lived phenomenon. The choice was unambiguous enough. Aborigines could either accommodate pastoralism in a way acceptable to settler demands (which often meant labouring), or they could die.

And thirdly, Pigeon shows that resistance was costly, not only to human life, but also to the order of the cosmos. He was himself an ambivalent hero, and in other circumstances it might have been his own people seeking to take his life. He flaunted traditional land-order, maintained, amongst other means, through marriage alliance,[34] but his enemies became his followers when it was realised a pan-Aboriginal military front was vital. As territorial boundaries became blurred and as a unified world emerged, so too did the ontologic autonomy of time, not only manifest in Pigeon's own defiance of death, but also in what was to emerge as a millennial ideology. Indeed, this might already have been present within Pigeon's magico-military campaign to free the Kimberley of Whites.

Millennial hopes appear to have emerged with the disruption to place caused by the northern expansion, and to have remained thereafter. In north Queensland, for example, the Koko-Wagara had not only rather realistically redefined the causes of worldly infertility and drought in terms of cosmic watertanks and a bull who drank all the water,[35] but had also engaged the powers of their land to protect it from miners. At Mount Mulligan was a water-dwelling being named *Iku*, to whom sickness was attributed. Only the 'clever men' could enter its lake without fear. *Iku*'s range extended to the mountains, however, and he had been seen sitting in trees near the Mount Mulligan mines. The mine disasters were variously explained by Whites themselves in supernatural terms, but the Koko-Wagara were certain it was the work of *Iku*: 'They say he blew up the mine in anger at the White man's intrusion on his domain. They firmly believe he will again blow up the mine.'[36]

This last, however, is a relatively trifling example, and one belonging to the early twentieth century. The cult which truly captured the atmosphere of early pastoral invasion, and which also spread to the Mount Mulligan area,[37] was the spectacular and widespread *Mulunga* (*Molonga*). It began in north-west Queensland and spread both back to the east and also southwards, following the thin grazeable belt through the heart of the continent before whipping northwards and westwards from the Great Australian Bight. It was not recorded bolting directly for the Kimberley, but we will later see that its descendant did. For the moment, however, it is necessary to trace the story of this often elusive cult.

Much of *Mulunga* remains a mystery, but two things are beyond question. It was a recently emergent ceremonial complex, and it was transmitted with amazing speed. It seems to have been noted everywhere and yet almost never understood, and the best way to begin to unravel its secrets is to follow the sequence of the ethnographic sightings.

Walter Roth was the first to report on *Mulunga*, basing his description on his observation of its ceremonies between 1893 and 1896. He claimed to have witnessed many new dances which had been 'found', usually by 'doctors', and mostly whilst dreaming. These performances had many themes, including the spearing of cattle by Aborigines who are consequently shot by Whites.[38] None, however, could match the appeal of *Mulunga*. Roth's informants could trace it back to the area of the Woagaia on the Georgina Headwaters, although he was not entirely certain this was its place of origin. The Woagaia had passed it on to the people near Camooweal and Lake Nash, and it thus reached Carandotta, where Roth saw it in 1893. From there it was carried in three directions, south, west and east, where he again saw it performed over the next few years.

Roth provides a reasonably painstaking description of the ritual grounds and dress, and the bodily movements. He also informs us women were able to participate in much, but not all, of the celebration. Its meaning, however, eluded him. All he could offer in this regard was the interpretation that *Mulunga* was a 'devil' or evil-doer invisible to all Aborigines except the 'doctors'. *Mulunga* is vengeful, covering his tracks skilfully as he seeks out his enemies, and raping women in districts where his cult is not correctly performed.[39] *Mulunga* himself appears on the fifth and final night, ochred and feathered, and with a long feather-tipped spear. He rushes at the assembled people as though to spear them, retires, and again attacks, as the ceremony reaches its climax.

Several years later, Baldwin Spencer, who deemed all Aboriginal ceremonies 'intensely monotonous', witnessed the most exciting

ritual he had encountered, although 'the only really interesting part
. . . was towards the end'. It was, he soon realised, Roth's *Mulunga*
dance although his Aranda informants called it *Tjitjingalla*. Spencer's
account is enticing and frustrating. He provides all the obvious
details: the ochre, the hair-string, feathers and ritual blood, the
single file dancing and the sticks shaped 'like a gigantic tuning-
fork held in both hands, in such a way that the two prongs pass
on each side of [the dancer's] neck'. Only the finale seems to have
aroused Spencer's interest, when a man, wearing feathered decora-
tions not usually revealed in the presence of women and children,
appears. Some hundred Aborigines wait near an erected ritual
shelter, while a dozen dancers stand before it. Women and children
become frightened.

> After a few minutes pause . . . two figures were seen creeping down the
> low rise close at hand towards the wurley. Both of them crouched down
> low as they crept along peering about . . . the latter was elaborately
> decorated . . . Suddenly, he gazed around as if he had just become aware
> of the group of performers between him and his wurley. Then he sprang
> forward, holding in both hands a spear tipped with a bunch of feathers,
> and charged full-tilt at the dancers as if to force his way through them
> to the wurley, which was supposed to be his own dwelling.

As to what all this meant, Spencer could only offer the suggestion
that the main performer 'represents a man who was renowned for
wisdom and strength'[40] and the other dancers were trying to prevent
him returning to his home so that he would join them.

Between them, Roth and Spencer could do no more than agree
on a core of ritual elements – the forked stick, the hut, the figure
of *Mulunga*, and a combat – but beyond that they were left guessing.
Up to this point in the history of research into the cult, Berndt is
quite correct in arguing that 'the mythic and social significance of
the *Molonga* is missing'.[41]

Before proceeding through the published accounts, it is worth
noting that in May of 1930 Elkin again saw Aranda (and Alwaridja)
people perform this ceremony at Horseshoe Bend. His informants,
in contrast to Spencer's, actually called it *Mulunga* (*Mälongu*),
although in his fieldnote index, Elkin also references it as the 'Red
Ochre Corob[oree]'. If this cursory note has substance, we are in fact
provided with a link between two new cults previously considered
discrete. The remainder of Elkin's description is sketchy and incomplete, and besides confirming once more the various ceremonial

paraphernalia used, his main contribution is in corroborating that
the main actor was called *Kanini* or 'mother's mother'.[42] His interpretation that the climactic dance represented a lost mother and 'the
boys' search for her', is surely either a gross distortion or simply
misinformed opinion, and one can easily understand why he chose
not to publish an account of the cult.

The first and only genuine attempt to offer an interpretation of
Mulunga was made by the missionary Otto Siebert. His account has
divided the very few scholars who have actually read his German
text. Like Eliade before him, Kolig believed 'his testimony is pure
serendipity, as he was the only one among several European observers to recognize the cult's nativistic, xenophobic, and chiliastic
overtones'.[43] In contrast, Luise Hercus denies it was 'anything other
than a new and exciting ceremony',[44] claiming Siebert's descriptions
of anti-European elements of *Mulunga* were 'cautious'. As his interpretation is unique, short and inaccessible to most English-speaking
students of Aboriginal Studies, I provide its full translation in the
following pages. My only prefatory comment is that, far from being
'cautious', Siebert's words are conspicuous as being the only assured
opinion as to *Mulunga's* significance. In comparison with Siebert's
assured, if unexpected, pronouncement, all other accounts appear
superficial, although thankfully not as absurd as Gregory's suggestion, which was based on his witnessing the ceremony at approximately the same time and place as Siebert. Gregory's best guess was
that it was a 'distorted echo' of a Brisbane music-hall's chorus of
'tra-ra-ra-boom-de-ay'.[45]

The Múlunga Dance.[46]

W. Roth has supplied a detailed account of this dance and its migration
from the far north to the Boulia District in Queensland,[47] and Gregory
has told of its appearance in the north-west of Lake Eyre in 1902.[48] This
ceremony was introduced to the Dieri in 1901; thence it migrated still
further south, as far as the Wírangu tribe, north of Port Augusta. I have
seen most of it performed three times, and was able to take a few
photographs, three of which are here reproduced as Plates 6, 7 and 8.[49]
As they show, the ritual dress ornamentation of the performers is
basically identical to that represented by Roth, even though there are
variations; I do not here need to go into details, nor about the manner
in which the dancing and singing was performed: it is unlikely that these
differ greatly from place to place. However, facts about the origin and
the real meaning of the dance were communicated to me, facts of which
the other reporters seem not to have been aware, and which indeed do

not correspond to Roth's version, at least as far as the central figure in the performance as a whole is concerned.

The Múlunga Dance was brought to the Dieri by men from the north. Its leader, Tálatálana, spoke Wónkangúru, although he was not a member of that tribe, but was either a Wónkamála or belonged to a tribe from still further north. This Tálatálana was known to be a very great magician, for which he had enjoyed an enormous reputation. He claimed it as his right that no woman might refuse him sexually. One of the proofs of his magic arts consisted in his remaining under water for a whole day, though he deceived the credulous blacks through the skilful use of hollow reeds.

The ceremony could not be carried out without a long period of tests and rehearsals. As Roth has said, a hut was built on the site of the ritual festival: the one I saw was about 2 metres high and shaped like a beehive. In this hut the spirit of the 'Grandmother' (*Kánini*) was believed to reside, and it was only after I had used all manner of subterfuge that I was able to get this holy of holies of the magical dance onto my photographic plates . . .

According to the information given to me, the Múlunga Dance originated as follows: In the far north, white men had shot down a number of natives, and the magic dance was therefore an act of revenge carried out on all whites. This serves also to explain the otherwise incomprehensible belief, that all those who do not see the dance will be bewitched; otherwise all natives, whether heathen or Christians, are expected, indeed compelled to be present at the performance of the Múlunga Dance. The main theme of the performance is to depict how the blacks were shot down. Roth's Figures 294 and 296 represent riflemen, and the forked objects they are carrying represent rifles.

At the end of the dance the *Kánini*, represented by a man,[50] appears 'out of the water', that is, behind the above-mentioned hut, and mimes the killing of all white men. The *Kánini* is a water-spirit; perhaps the leader's water-test, in which he proves his ability to remain under water for a whole day, is connected with the fact that the 'Grandmother' is a water-spirit.

I have already spoken about the objects called *wólkadará*, carried by some performers under their arms. A special magical power also attached to a neck ornament, *kunimbara*, used in connection with the appearance of *Kánini*. I can still see in my mind's eye the old woman, who had come with the leader from the far north, and after him was the most respected introducer of the Múlunga Dance – how she, when the *kánini* appeared jumped up while she sang the *Múlunga-wíma*, and pointed with her *kunimbara* in all directions, almost in a state of ecstasy, so that all those at whom the magic dance was directed, should be destroyed: the whites and all that belonged to them. Then she pointed with her *kunimbara* at the *Kánini*, partly to give her *kunimbara* in this way more magical power, partly also – I was told – to reinforce the power of the *Kánini* still further. And what the old woman had done, so did all the other initiates, that is, those who had learned the song verbatim, who had passed all the necessary tests and had been present at the whole of the Múlunga Dance at least once.

At the end of the performance, a woman chosen for the purpose had to appear on the festival site, whereupon the men (or only the presenter?) cohabited with her.

If Siebert's report is correct, *Mulunga* was a 'clever-man'-controlled ritual focusing on a water-being who attacks and ceremoniously kills 'rifle'-carrying performers. The climactic appearance of *Kanini*, the water-mother, gives the power to destroy Whites. There is no reason why it is not at least possible that this exegesis would fit all the published accounts. In this regard Kolig is overly hasty in asserting Roth's male '*Molonga*' is missing from Spencer and Gillen's Aranda account, and replaced by '*Kanini*' amongst the Dieri.[51] Roth only assumes *Mulunga* is male because the performer is male, and that performer is present in Spencer and Gillen's, and particularly Elkin's later account, where the mother is again evident. Futhermore, there is no contradiction in the names, as *Kanini* is in fact not a personal name but merely a kinship term.[52]

It is of course possible that, as Kolig writes, the 'chiliastic component recorded by Siebert may have been entirely missing elsewhere',[53] but the simple fact of the matter is no other reports tell us anything of what *Mulunga is about*, so the absence of millennialism is but part of a general absence of *all* interpretation. The most threatening critique of the anti-White theme of the cult, however, comes from the very area of Siebert's observation. Hercus performed the most valuable service by interviewing two Dieri men who danced the *Mulunga* in 1901. Certainly, her informants do not refer to millennial longings, but once again nor do they say anything positive, and we soon realise why this is so. Mick McLean said 'I knew a great lot of it [by rote], but I don't know what it means', while Ben Murray, after only the second night, 'didn't go there any more . . . it was so far away. I just didn't want to'.[54] What makes these men unique is not that they were authorities on Mulunga, but rather that they had seen the cult and were still living, sixty-five years later. Alas, good fortune has its price, for the oldest of Hercus' informants was thirteen years of age in 1901, whilst Murray was only nine. How can we expect the opinion of men who only partially witnessed the rituals as boys over half a century ago to weigh against the contemporary views of cult leaders? While there is little satisfaction in victory by default, we must once again accept the fact that Siebert's is still the *only* explanation of what the *Mulunga* theme entailed.

Hercus does not contest Siebert's ability to understand what was communicated to him, but she suspects he was offered a rather idiosyncratic account.[55] On the other hand, Kolig considers there may have been layers of meaning,[56] in which case Siebert, informed by cult leaders, was offered a rather élite understanding: a concentric core rather than an eccentric deviation. If we take his Dieri informants at their word, then besides *Mulunga's* hunger for vengeance, the main explicit theme of the dances was the White massacre of Aborigines in the far north. I believe if we see the correct context, then it is in fact still possible to locate the origin of *Mulunga*.

Firstly, what Hercus' informants do remind us of is the pastoral setting of *Mulunga*. The ceremony was taught to Dieri who had travelled north along what had become stock routes, and was initially held at a place where water was fetched for the cattle. In reminiscences of their late childhood, both McLean and Murray recall how the ceremonies were dovetailed into ration life: 'It was ration day . . . they managed to get plenty of bullock meat, and so they had a feast of bullock meat and ate damper and sat about drinking tea'; the station owner 'brought them'flour, tea and sugar, he gave them government rations'. These people, it should be recalled, had only six months earlier first entered the station world.[57]

Even more significantly, *Mulunga* impressed the boys with pastoral images: 'The main ritual leader . . . was like a musterer'; 'it was just like mustering'; 'they drove us like cattle'. Is there more to this than similes? Should we recall that Roth also wrote of new cults concerning spearing cattle and White punitive expeditions (*supra*)? How literally should we take McLean's words when he says the performers 'had horns like a bullock'?[58] And, turning now to Siebert's photographs, what was the significance of the dancers on all fours, with those 'horns like a bullock' in a land with no indigenous horned animals?[59]

Let me put these questions to one side for a moment, and turn to the possible place of origin of *Mulunga*. Those witnessing its southern manifestations agreed it came from the north. Daisy Bates, to whose views I will return, said 'from a point east or south-east of Darwin', and with no other substantiating evidence, McCarthy plotted it on a map as seemingly originating in Darwin itself.[60] Micha echoes McCarthy, although also suggesting Arnhem Land as perhaps being the region to which Bates had referred.[61] Elkin, as we have seen, interprets the Aranda theory of its inception as being south-west Arnhem Land (*supra*). All these views, however, suffer from being overly precise translations of very vague descriptions by Aborigines far from the place of origin itself.

Earlier accounts all agree *Mulunga*'s home was south of the Gulf of Carpentaria.[62] Siebert received it from the Wonkamala, while Roth, our earliest source, says he was told it came from the Woagaia.[63] If we accept Roth's general location and Siebert's cultic interpretation, we are left to discover whether there was in fact a skirmish in the region prior to 1893.

There was no skirmish: there was war. The site still bears the name Battle Mountain, in memory of the bloody encounter between Native Police and the Kalkatungu (the immediate neighbours of the Woagaia), in September 1884. Even by the grudging standards of White military codes, it is celebrated as a unique instance of Aborigines who 'stood up to the Whites in open battle'.[64] Holthouse says the protracted campaign which saw the death of the cream of the Kalkatungu was 'the end of the bravest and hardiest fighting men the Australian continent had ever seen', while for Grassby and Hill the Kalkatungu defiance forms the climax of their four detailed studies of spectacular Aboriginal resistances.[65]

On that September day, it was estimated, a staggering 600 Kalkatungu men waited on the crags of Battle Mountain. They had regrouped there after the failure of other prolonged forms of resistance. Their lands had been invaded by pastoralists in the 1870s, and in retaliation whole parties of Whites were murdered and the cattle speared. Alexander Kennedy, foremost amongst the pioneers, withstood intense hostilities for five years 'until the power of the Kalkadoons was finally broken'. A ferocious man, Kennedy had singlehandedly dispersed some forty unarmed Aboriginal men, and soon after, his Aboriginal employee, Sandy, had found the Kalkatungu performing a new 'corroboree'. The dancers moved on all fours as grazing cattle until hunters came and speared them.

> We kill many-legged animal,
> The white man brings the strange beast to our land.

But then the ceremonial focus changed:

> We kill Kennedy in the morning . . .
> Our water is taken by the cattle,
> Kill the White man,
> Kill the White man![66]

An appalling translation, to be sure, but a *Mulunga*-like mood is clearly present here.

Photographs of Kalkatungu and neighbouring ritual designs from this period do not reveal a fixed form of the *Mulunga* complex, although some body markings seem to be of a cognate kind. Nonetheless, the depiction of dancers with leather straps buckled across their torsos, precisely in the manner of the Native Mounted Police Trooper, suggests a frontier employing military ritual motifs.

The rituals continued. Kennedy's partner was found in the blistering sun, with his head bent under his body, his guts spilled and his kidney fat stolen. Kennedy also learned the 'clever men' were calling down lightning 'for the purpose of driving out the white settlers'.[67] And so it was that Urquhart was summoned. After a week of savage police hunts, the pastoral areas were once more temporarily safe. The Kalkatungu retreated to Battle Mountain, and Urquhart led the pursuit. Were it not for a mystifying tactic, the Kalkatungu may have won the day. For, 'without any apparent warning, the Kalkadoon warriors formed ranks like well trained, disciplined soldiers, and . . . advanced in battle formation down the slope of Battle Mountain into the fire of the carbines'.[68]

The Kalkatungu had confronted White pastoral invasion with millennial hopes and a final, unfathomable, perhaps even secret military strategy. The battle was lost more spectacularly and more uncannily than any other Aboriginal war with Europeans, and it surely was an event worthy of the *Mulunga* cult, which erupted in precisely the same area several years later. I am convinced the Kalkatungu final stand was in fact the inspiration for the new cult, although obviously it could have only have been fully developed by their neighbours, such as the Woagaia; the Kalkatungu themselves were now a battered and broken people. Having uncovered its origins, I now want to trace its development and fate.

Our only other recorded sighting of *Mulunga* is provided by Bates, who noted its arrival at Penong on the south coast of Australia in 1915. Three years later it reached Eucla, on the border between South

and Western Australia. Bates did not actually witness the performances and so her testimony is of use only in plotting co-ordinates
and calculating the speed and direction of dispersion. Bates herself
said the transmission from north-west Queensland to Penong took
eleven years[69] but mistakenly uses the date of Roth's publication for
the date of the first recorded performance. Mulvaney says the route
took twenty-five years, but is slightly in error in dating its arrival
at Penong (in 1915, not 1918).[70] It therefore seems to have taken
twenty-two years to cover the distance of some 1,600 kilometres, and
when Bates last saw it it was heading on a north-westerly route which
would, she believed, ultimately take it to the Kimberley via the
western coast. This 'great aboriginal trade route [which] circles the
country'[71] was in fact a route which skirted the perimeter of the
Central and Western Deserts, clinging to the more fertile zones which
encouraged pastoralism. The speed of diffusion almost certainly
owes something to stock routes. Some time later, Petri would note
new cults following train lines, while today they are communicated
by roadways and cars.[72]

Mulunga thus was a ritual complex addressing the situation of
Aboriginal people who had recently had their lands invaded by
pastoral interests. Whilst it persisted amongst the Aranda until the
1930s, and while Elkin's notes hint that it possibly transmuted into
the 'less radically anti-white' (and most poorly researched) Red
Ochre Movement, which gained momentum in the 1940s and which
still endures,[73] the heart of *Mulunga* belonged to a period spanning
from the late 1880s until the early twentieth century. In that time,
people found themselves torn from their places while yet unwilling
to concede the inevitability of a White presence. The solution was
aggressive and pragmatic. With a rich knowledge of their eternal
homes still firmly held in memory, it was possible to envisage a
return to the pre-colonial equilibrium. Time only needed to be set
free for a moment; the future union was not literally a distant
'millennium' but rather a sharp and immediate return to an Abiding
world order still within reach.

With hindsight, the ideological resistance embodied in *Mulunga*
was fated from the outset. The intensity of the old land-spirit connections would of necessity fade with each generation born out of
place. The world would change.

Intriguingly, while it covered all other pastoral frontiers, the one
direction in which *Mulunga* did not travel was immediately to the

adjacent Kimberley. Nonetheless, something other, more subtle and more dangerous, was transmitted to the north-west. It was a small child, who would have been only about three at the time of the massacre at Battle Mountain. He was arguably the most influential individual religious reformer Aboriginal Australia has seen, and today he has been mythologised as a man who singlehandedly revolutionised the Kimberley cosmos, bringing with him the cult of *Djanba*. Always distant from his home, his power nonetheless came from his spiritual estate. He was a displaced Kalkatungu,[74] and his name was Boxer.

DJANBA AND THE PASTORAL MORAL ORDER

In the preceding section, I implied that rebels such as Pigeon were representative of the mood of *Mulunga* – defiant and rebellious and containing radical change within their very quest for an unchanging world.[75] Had these sentiments prevailed, then the cosmic scenario of the invasive south-east may have been replicated on the other side of the continent, and indeed even as it is there are many startling similarities.[76] In the north, and particularly the north-west, however, colonial pressure came to take a new form.

As cattle fanned out from north Queensland toward the Kimberley, frontier stories were repetitive in their reflection of a remorseless hunger for grazing land. Skirting southern Arnhem Land, the pattern was duplicated: intrusion, guerilla warfare, Native Police, 'pacification', 'making people quiet' as it is ironically termed by Roper River people today.[77] Carried along on this early tide of cattle were the occasional adaptable Aboriginal workers. Boxer's mother seems to have been amongst them.

Sweeping into the Kimberley itself, the initial response was once again the same, as we have already seen when discussing Pigeon's resistance. Boxer, in contrast, belonged to a slightly later period when facile millennial dreams had faded. This is not to say that 'pacification' was complete, as cattle were still being speared in the Kimberley as late as 1935.[78] Nevertheless, by 1885, the growing north-west cattle empires had allowed themselves to become dependent upon Aboriginal labour, and whether by enslavery or by more subtle means, it had become apparent that pastoralists required Aborigines.[79] And on the more benign stations, there was room for the creative philosophic thought of people like Boxer.

Boxer's patrons were the members of the famous Durack dynasty,[80] and to read Mary Durack's recollections of Aboriginal workers who gave her the 'gift of laughter and human kindness and true philosophy' is enough to convince all but the most cynical critics that genuine affection existed within the station hierarchies.[81] No Aboriginal worker was more highly regarded, even respected, by Whites than Boxer. The stockman Frank Eipper found him to be strong, efficient, sweet-tempered and nothing short of the best Aboriginal worker in the state; 'I cannot fault him in any way',[82] he wrote. Unlike the taboo-flaunting, charismatic womaniser Pigeon, Boxer was introspective and shunned all women but his one wife. He would retreat to his neat camp, alone, 'and sit smoking his pipe and looking at the moon'. By all accounts, he was enigmatic. Mary Durack recalled 'Boxer's movements are always so mysterious, his comings and goings so sudden, so unannounced'. His healing powers seemed so assured that even some Whites accepted his cures.[83] But most of all, they realised he was 'a "dreamer" of song cycles and corroborees'.[84]

With all these recollections of the Duracks, Aboriginal reminiscences are in accord. His strange excursions and avoidance of women – 'he could not face the girls'[85] – was evidence of his spiritual power. He is remembered as the greatest of all 'clever men': 'No one's like that now, only the old fellers'.[86] His magical skills were many and sprang from his Kalkatungu roots. His kinsmen had uncannily and instantly arrived once to save the lad from another malicious 'clever man',[87] and from that time on his own powers grew. He frequented graveyards, seeking the wisdom of the dead, and amassed amazing skills. He could transform himself into an emu, or open up his own intestines. Bulla remembers, 'I nearly died of fright. This boy old Boxer pulled his guts out and they fell on the ground by Christ. He was very dangerous'.[88] Again, Jack Sullivan says he could bring storms, but unlike his kinsmen of an earlier era, he cheerfully and playfully gave White station owners warning of his powers. Unconvinced, one stationer stayed sitting in the creek bed, 'Oh, you're pulling my fucking leg you old bastard. Fuck you . . . I'll chance it this time',[89] but later he was both wiser and wetter. Boxer, the healer on occasion outshone Western medical services, leaving its practitioners dumbfounded, and his life took on almost messianic proportions. For reasons not altogether clear, he was jailed at Wyndham, but of course he continually left his cell, although he did not try to flee.[90] Eventually, the police simply gave him his freedom. Sometime just before the bombing of Wyndham in 1942, Boxer returned to Queensland, but died and was buried in Darwin.[91] Yet long after, in north Queensland, a White station man saw him in a pub looking younger than ever. He returned to Darwin, sought out Boxer's grave, and found the ground split open. Says Bulla, 'I don't think magic people die . . . He was a terrible big man, not a small man, old Boxer.'[92] And Jack Sullivan – 'Everybody knew what Boxer was, a bloody magic'.[93]

This unparalleled testimony of individual Aboriginal power, however, is insignificant compared to Boxer's ability to dream. His power came from his Kalkatungu home via his visiting kinsfolk, and all his cults were derived from this land. As it is now told, he singlehandedly transformed Kimberley ceremonial life – 'He found all the Corroborees from Queensland', although he quickly passed them on to others. His ceremonies (pre-eminently *Djunba*) drew their authority from *Nangurrurr* waterholes in Kalkatungu territory: 'Boxer sang the Djanba out of that waterhole all round to their country, then right back to the waterhole again and finish it off there'.[94]

The true extent of Boxer's ceremonial innovation is difficult to quantify precisely. He seems to be credited with the greater part of the category of ceremonies known as *Djunba*, while Durack also attributes the *Mulari (Moolari)* song cycle to Boxer.[95] The two traditions are related. Bulla says, '*Djunba* flew in the sky, Mulari went on the ground. *Djunba* started from Wyndham and came past to Argyle right back this way to Darwin. The corroboree belonged in Queensland to those Kaukadunga in mixed English'.[96] While it is of course possible that ceremonies with diverse origins have been added retrogressively to Boxer's fame,[97] it nevertheless appears he was an astoundingly prolific dreamer of ceremonies.

The content of the songs attributed to him have not been adequately studied at all, but they appear to range from tales of his own imprisonment and legendary escapes,[98] to rituals such as *Larrungga, Ngaliwiriwiri, Djimbala* and *Djudu*, which, while not entirely shrouded in secrecy, have names which should at least not be spoken aloud by women.[99] These ceremonies have mostly fallen into disuse without having been recorded, but central to them all was the figure of *Djanba*.

Djanba is that trespassing mythic being whom Worms saw usurping *Djamar* and whom Capell had allocated to a recent stratum of religious innovation (*supra*). Like *Mulunga*, who 'is said to tie up the toes on each foot . . . with a view to obliterating all the tracks',[100] *Djanba* 'walks with his feet bent up . . . Nobody can see his tracks'.[101] According to contemporary Aboriginal opinion, *Djanba* the One could manifest himself as *Djanba* the Many, taking secret dominion over pre-existing cults. Jeff Djanama says

> He's spirit and he's in the sacred Law too. *Djanba* shows how to dance and sing for it. A bloke might sleep and dream if he's good on the brains which way to hold the stick, a long kind of stick they use . . . *Djanba* is a lot of different spirits, a biggest mob like a cloud. There's one *Djanba*, one person, but many different songs.[102]

Jack Sullivan, amplifying the issue, also juxtaposes the One and the Many, saying *Djanba* 'was a wild human' who travelled hunting but then asserting 'the *Djanbas* are not wild animals, they're wild humans'. The multi-faceted *Djanba* has a chameleon-like capacity to conceal himself within ceremonies; he 'puts himself in every corroboree; just fits himself in'.[103] His ability to appropriate perhaps reached its height when, at the request of the Catholic priest who asked that traditional songs accompany mass,[104] *Djanba* entered holy communion: 'He goes through the white fellers now that *Djanba*'.[105]

In all these accounts, there is agreement with the dominant anthropological opinion; 'the *Djanba* corroboree came out lately'.[106] If we return to the reports of the Frobenius expedition of 1938, a time when Boxer was still active in the Kimberley, we are offered further intriguing insights into *Djanba's* being. Like those accredited to Boxer, his cults were in Pidgin-English,[107] but that was just the beginning of European symbolism which *Djanba* had drawn to himself. His home was made of corrugated iron, and behind it he grew poisonous weeds which he used to impart the introduced diseases of syphilis and leprosy.[108] He used iron tools, hunted with a rifle and, to distribute his sacred boards, travelled by motor car, steamer and aeroplane. For his ritual displays, he demanded European foods such as tea, sugar and bread, which were a part of his ceremonial order. Futhermore, his tradition was overseen by a White-style division of labour, complete with a 'clerk' to store sacred objects, a 'mailman' to announce the meals, 'police-boys' to oversee his Law and cultic custodians known as 'the bosses'.[109]

It seems, therefore, that central to cults associated with the hero Boxer are an array of symbolic manifestations as diverse as the two worlds which he himself seems to span. As Rowse has warned, we should not be so literal-minded as to imagine that the Kalkatungu man achieved this unaided, but rather we can assume that subsequent north Kimberley thinkers felt he was the type of person with whom such transformations should be pre-eminently associated.[110] Why this should be so will be explained a little later, but first it is necessary to analyse the content of these new ideologies and practices in more detail.

It is essential to bear in mind we are witnessing developments in a period of pastoral history after the 'wild time' when Aborigines were being lured or herded into labour pools, and Boxer and others like him were perfect social and symbolic mediators. Unlike Pigeon, who was the quintessential resister and instigator of opposition – at times as much of an outsider within his Aboriginal communities as he was in White society – Boxer drew two worlds together. He was one of those that McGrath would say was *Born in the Cattle*, belonging to an era when Aborigines drew links between White Law and their own, believing there were strong connections between the quality of stockmen and community harmony.[111] All things to all men, Boxer bridged rather than separated universes, stepping in to negotiate along with other 'mediators between homeland and bush'. On the one hand, against all the odds, he held determinedly to his place, clinging to the moral order derived from land; on the other, he was equally capable of co-operating within the 'moral order of rationed work'.[112]

If *Mulunga* was a cosmic revolt, those cults which followed, while being related and sharing common themes, seemed to differ in that they accepted the pastoral world as an adjunct in their quest to hold their place. Rations and wages, in this context, proved to be a means by which Aboriginal people could engage in moral relationships with Whites, albeit in a hierarchical, even 'feudal'[113] arrangement. This path was certainly not trodden voluntarily in the first instance, and there was apparently no initial thirst for European goods *per se*, but having been brought into the labour world, sometimes literally at gunpoint, it was necessary that a manageable association be established with the invading peoples. This relationship, *as defined by Whites*, was one encoded in rations, work and wages. At a cosmological level, what better representation of this could there be than the White-goods possessing trickster, *Djanba*, infusing himself into the Aboriginal ceremonial domain?

Yet I see no evidence at this stage that Aboriginal people had in any sense fully conceded the ultimate ontological status of capitalist ideals. The search for a means to morally engage Whites was a necessary step towards maintaining a link with their spirits' abodes, for in pastoral contexts, the connection between a land and its people was stretched to a critical limit.

One clear manifestation of this was observed, but incorrectly interpreted, by Lommel. He was told of the falling birth rate amongst the station Aborigines with whom he worked, attributed to the failure of dreams in which the spirit-child is 'caught'. What Lommel neglects to consider is that the dreamer must return to the place from which the life-forces emanate. It is not just a case of a bad night's sleep, as Lommel intimates, but a withering of the life-giving connection to a people's countries. Theirs were nights not filled with land but 'troubled by visions of the white men, of aeroplanes and ships'.[114]

Despite this seemingly insurmountable obstacle Lommel was overly hasty, as Berndt contended,[115] in prophesying an imminent collapse of the Aboriginal world. For just as *Djanba* fortified cults with White cultural items, so too the now lengthy journeys to promised lands could be made in the invaders' vehicles. Tonkinson had considered a related phenomenon to the south, at Jigalong, and found that while people were far from their homelands they could still dream of their countries and keep them alive. Instead of a conventional spirit image, they had appropriated the very images distracting their dreams to ensure their return. Tonkinson writes:

> Crayon drawings made by Aborigines of *badundjari* [dream-spirits] sometimes resemble aircraft, and vehicles said to be used by *badundjari* to transport others are depicted as aeroplanes, complete with wings, tail, windows and headlights, but with sacred boards, not propellers or jets, supplying the power source.[116]

In other words, these spirit-aircraft were propelled to their lands by icons manifesting the potentiality of place. Beyond dreams filled with invading planes are visions of place-planes offering a ride home.

What we witness here is the attempt to reinforce the now dangerously distended idea of life based on the vitality of sites, with a new understanding of a moral world of White commodities and powers. It is not a case of standing in awe of Western technology as Lommel (and more recently, Kolig)[117] propose, but rather, having of necessity allowed White Law to impose itself upon them, they have sought their salvation partially by employing its representations, but pre-eminently by cojoining it with the Law of their lands and their spirits.

Given this unlikely cosmic marriage, brought into being by those like Boxer who were governed both by their spirits' homes and the Law of labour and rations, it is necessary to delve a little deeper to consider the effects of this alliance upon basic ontological understandings of place, space and time. And it is here that we must briefly introduce the most noted of all *Djanba*'s cults, that of *Kuranggara*.

A variety of *Djanba*'s ceremonies were collected under the secret name of *Kuranggara* – as one Bard man put it simply, '*Djanba* belongs to *gurangara*'.[118] It was, however, Petri and Lommel who provide us with the fullest account of the cult,[119] which they at first suspected came from the south-west,[120] but which almost certainly was derived from southern Arnhem Land.[121] It was, our ethnographers recorded, a cult troubling to those who held to the more ancient locative traditions, as they felt *Kuranggara* would undermine the constant maintenance needed to ensure the fertility of sites and hence the enduring balance of the cosmos. For them, the invading *Djanbas* were place-destructive, sucking the land dry as they went.[122] It was this threat to land-Law that made the elders entertain a pessimistic eschatological vision, uncannily similar to those of south-east Australia, in which the very physical form of the cosmos faces imminent collapse.[123]

For its younger advocates, of course, *Kuranggara* was 'one of the watchwords of . . . revival', and, as well as the aforementioned *Djanba* with his partially White lifestyle, it contained songs, telling amongst other things, of Aborigines flying in aeroplanes and an Ancestral Being named *Mangunba*, who unexpectedly breaks his Dreaming sojourns, 'he walk, he walk . . . till he catch the train at Sandstone'.[124] Its advocates, it seems, at least shared with the older dissenters the view that their new understanding of the cosmos required a radically altered vision of place and time, although in contrast theirs was a partially optimistic hope for the future.

The temporalising of Ancestral Events[125] is one conspicuous aspect of the Kimberley ontologic revolution. Berndt has questioned the pessimistic eschatology of *Kuranggara*, and indeed the very capacity for Aborigines to conceive of a world-end,[126] but there is ample evidence to dispel his doubts. Mandi Munniim, for instance, tells a dreaming story of *Malimburrwana*, who has some of the attributes of a High God and who is significantly paralleled with the Christian God. He states, 'Malimburrwana always found a corroboree about the end of the world all round the place, like'. This was, apparently, the 'same word' the priest delivered in mass, which either is a statement to be interpreted broadly or reveals something intriguing about Kimberley Catholicism, for (presuming the apocalyse takes the same form as the Dreaming Event), it seems the way the world ends is not with a bang but a cosmic fart.[127]

Time is central to the innovations of Boxer, to *Djanba*, and to *Kuranggara*-related cults. This is entirely comprehensible in terms of my discussion of land in the opening chapter, for there I suggested that time can only be satisfactorily denied ontological significance if place endures. Loss of estates, or radical separation from these, requires an intervening temporal element to thus bridge the spatial gulf. Like Boxer, who still retained the promise of his lands, the vast majority of Aborigines in pastoral contexts remembered their place, but the full realisation was beyond their grasp insofar as they must, in order to hold onto the little that remained, also embrace the moral world of station life. Time alone could fully revitalise the association of people and sites.

At the individual level, temporality becomes evident in this period of north-western Aboriginal history as a focus upon the desire for personal immortality. Boxer's resurrection in this regard is as atypical of Aboriginal tradition as it is fitting. More revealing still are his associations with subsections and the moon.

Fortunately we are provided with two rare glimpes of the Aboriginal origins of time in the spread of the pastoral frontier. The first was recorded by Meggitt amongst the northern-most Warlpiri and reveals that not only were subsections recent innovations which were rarely mythologised, but further, when their story was found it was in association with the moon and immortality, as I suggested (in chapter 1) would be the case. Meggitt was told people had originally 'died completely', but Moon, Sun and other Dreamings conspired so that people would return after death. Rain 'then "gave" the subsection system to the Walbiri, saying this too "never finished", for it enabled subsections to cycle continuously through the generations'.[128]

In the Kimberley it was the same scenario, for the person said to have introduced the subsections was none other than Boxer,[129] and it was in association with *Djanba* that time broke free through the body. Whilst equating *Ngabo* ('Father', the Christian God), *Malimburrwana* and *Djanba*, Mandi introduces the personal face of time – remembrance of the body at the expense of a return to place. The culprit is moon.

> Dingo said, 'I'm die. I'm die for good.' And this moon up there on the top said, 'Listen, I'm going die, and come out again'. That was the Father, *Ngabu*. That was the month of the moon who said, 'I'm die on come out again'.[130]

It is clear, therefore, that at both the cosmic and personal levels, time had intervened in the Kimberley to span the vast clefts between places and their human extensions. Paired with this development was the weakening of the absolute integrity of sites and the emergent image of universal space. This is already evident in visions of the entire world confronting the eschaton, and can also be found in myths which speak of a single world origin associated with a flood which stretched to Aboriginal, European and Chinese shores.[131] Spatial unity and cosmic centres are themes we shall see developing as this chapter further unfolds.

For the moment, the only question I will raise is: from where did the *Djanba* cults, and in particular *Kuranggara*, derive their transcendental socio-spatial base? It was not from the south-eastern home of High Gods, although except for the sheer distance this may have added inspiration, but rather from Arnhem Land and the cults of the All-Mother. Once the Mother's ceremonies stepped out of their sheltered original environment, however, they were radically transformed by the current of pastoral invasion running just south of the Top End. Meggitt correctly regards *Kadjari* as the Mother-cult minus the Mother, but still with a spreading and embracive compass, while, more importantly, Berndt has forged a vital link by revealing that *Kuranggara* was once but a segment of the *Kunapipi*, a view that Meggitt endorsed.[132] As *Kuranggara* broke free, it radically altered the significance of spatial transcendence, replacing, as Berndt notes, the Fertility Mother with the great ambivalent male Ancestor named *Djanba*.[133]

In the following pages, I consider various other cults which were cojoined with, or derived from, *Kuranggara* – *Dingari*, *Woagaia* and *Djulurru*; and in each case the Arnhem Land All-Mother tradition, no matter how remote, must be acknowledged as its ultimate ceremonial paradigm. With this in mind, we can draw together some themes from the present and preceding chapters.

The All-Mother, I argued, was conceived out of the *threat* of invasion and dislocation caused by Indonesian visits to northern

Australia, and her cult was one which, with profound delicacy, managed to balance the universal and ubietous worldviews. In the far central-north, millennial hopes and fears remained unnecessary insofar as people stayed in their place. To the south and outside the Arnhem Land buffer, her transcendent foundation was drawn into the vacuum of pastoral expansion exploding across northern Australia. In these contexts, for reasons offered in the last chapter, the Mother herself could not survive, and she was rapidly replaced by more appropriate beings such as *Djanba*. The Mother's transcendent, spatially all-embracive and pan-Aboriginal gift was given over to the cause of those retaining but a fragile hold of place. White moral Law, bred in station life, was incorporated along with time itself, as the transformation was made from the Mother to the millennium.

From here to what is known as 'cargoism' was a small step which, strangely yet wisely, Aboriginal people were reluctant to take. It only required that within a world of lands now in part being sustained by White Law, they ask to be given a 'fair go'.

WOAGAIA: PARITY THROUGH WHITE LAW

In this section, a third and more recent cosmological innovation in the north-western labour world is introduced. To clarify precisely how it relates to its two predecessors, I can think of no better summary than a deceptively simple myth, a Dreaming (*Ngaranggani*) story, told by Mandi. It tells of a pair of spirits who were friends, and who co-operated by working for each other with a balance as equal as reciprocal moiety duties. The two spirits were Blackfeller and Whiteman. In time, discord arose, the balance could not be maintained, and so a hierarchy emerged between the 'bookkeeper' and the worker. Fighting respectively with a rifle and a spear, the order was inevitable: Blackfeller said, 'You whiteman. You after your rifle. I'm blackfeller. I work for you'. A new functional relationship is struck, but Whiteman then makes the bullet and the engine and everything else, and though blackfeller worked for him, he said 'you go to fucking hell. I don't wanta see you. Otherwise I'll shoot you'.[134]

Read the myth backwards and you have our history. In the first period (the last stage of the myth), pastoralists were saying precisely 'you go to fucking hell . . . Otherwise I'll shoot you' and even when they realised their need for Aboriginal labour there was separation, this time instigated by Aborigines like Pigeon and cults like

Mulunga. As we have seen, however, this led eventually and inevitably to the hierarchy of the station world where Aborigines worked for Whites (who had the power, 'you after your rifle'). As oppressive, exploitative or at best paternalistic as this arrangement may have been, it was – in most cases for the first time – a *relationship* with Whites mediated through the White moral code of labour rations and money. Boxer belonged to this world as did *Djanba*, who infused all cults, including the earlier forms of *Kuranggara*, with his dual symbolism. This was at least temporarily a manageable arrangement, but it is clear there was unease, a sense of despair for the future, were this situation to persist. The human suffering was evident, but even more there was the danger to the land of having its custodians held captive by oppressive labour.

The question that demands to be asked is: could the myth be fully reversed by returning to a state in which Whiteman and Blackfeller are equal coworkers? This is the subject of the remainder of this chapter.

The heroes of this final phase are as appropriate as their predecessors. Pigeon was the 'wild black'. Boxer, one man who mastered two worlds, was a 'half caste', some say. In my third stage, however, there was a White man who was indeed working *with* Aborigines, separately yet in co-operation and, despite the critics, probably with reasonable equality. The White man was Donald McLeod, and his most famed Aboriginal partners were Clancy McKenna[135] and, in particular, a Njangomada man named Dooley Bin-Bin. To my knowledge, these three have not been mythologised but they almost instantly became a part of folk-lore. One popular poem began

> Clancy and Dooley and Don McLeod,
> Walked by the wurlies when the wind was loud,
> And their voice was new as the fresh sap running,
> And we kept on fighting and we kept on coming.[136]

McLeod was without doubt more focal than the others in media reports, and for Aboriginal people he was a vital mediator and spokesperson. Nor can we ignore his soteriological promise. The Mob was 'Don McLeod's Mob', their Law 'Don McLeod Law'. If not as a messiah, he at least portrayed himself as 'a martyr'. It has been argued by some that his cause was egalitarian but 'non-millenarian',[137] by others that his promises were 'revivalistic and millenarian . . . as in Melanesian Cargo Cults'. At the very least it would be in keeping with the leader's Marxist roots to say ' "Don

McLeod Law" represents a kind of secularised and social uto-pianism',[138] but the impact of that Law on Aboriginal ritual life went much further than this.

The charismatic McLeod's Law was the beginning of Mandi's myth: parity between Aborigines and Whites.[139] McLeod, who had at various times been a prospector and a well-sinker, developed his contacts with Aboriginal people whilst travelling in the north-west as a buying representative for a mining company. A little research into Western Australian history revealed to him a chronicle of dispos-session and brutality that set him upon his quest. McLeod found himself drawn to Marxist philosophy and the liberation of oppressed classes and, besides founding a branch of the Anti-Fascist League in 1943, was a member of the Communist Party from 1945 to 1948.[140]

On an occasion when McLeod was in the Davis River area of the Pilbara, he was invited to attend an Aboriginal gathering of Law-men, who were consciously attempting to begin a ritual revival in the area. It is difficult to be certain, but I strongly suspect this would have been one of the gatherings for the transmission of the *Kuranggara* to the Pilbara.[141] Certainly John Wilson, one of the main historians of McLeod's activities,[142] was aware of the importance of the new cult at the time. As one old Gnamal man said, 'All this Kurungara business, the north be pushin' the south'. It arrived in the Pilbara as a 'super-corroboree', which 'grew up in times of stress . . . through contact with the competitive western culture',[143] and marked a cultural revival.

During his six-week attendance at this renaissance of Aboriginal Law, McLeod explained that it was possible to bring pressure to bear on changing White Law and offered his services as a spokes-person and a prime organiser of a strike. His proposal was accepted and Dooley was appointed as a representative of local Aboriginal opinion. Dooley himself was bush-born and raised, but his family later emerged from their Desert home and he was drawn into the pastoral world. His station experiences were typical of the time, and his reminiscences were punctuated by events such as meeting Malays, the sinking of the *Koombana*, the early aeroplanes, the later Japanese bombings, and so on,[144] all of which, as we will see, are of great significance to the cultural renewal. As a political speaker, Petri and Petri-Odermann say he was 'without logical sequence', full of 'stereotyped rhetoric' and displayed 'prefabricated concepts', which seems to indicate that Pilbara Aborigines knew precisely who amongst them had all the necessary qualities to make a good politician. On matters of traditional Law, however, the Petris were forced to concede he was keen and flexible, with a concern 'to adapt this to a particular doctrine of Western origin'.[145] He was forceful, could intimidate unco-operative Aborigines and Whites alike, and had a conscripting skill befitting the invasive *Kuranggara* cult itself.

The most pronounced effect on this crusade for equality within White Law was the emergence of so-called 'cargoism'. Although particularly conspicuous in the Pilbara, it was not confined to one area alone, but seems rather to have been a repercussion of the War in parts of northern-pastoral Australia. The War not only altered the working relationship between many Aborigines and Whites, but also brought in its train new classes of high technology endowed outsiders; the allied American forces on the one hand, and the Japanese enemy on the other. The Pilbara strike and the War cannot be separated.

At this point I must once again emphasise that the burgeoning 'cargoism' had little to do with goods *per se,* but rather with a relationship with Whites mediated through commodity wealth. Burridge made the obvious but largely neglected point that Melanesians could acquire their 'cargo' with far less effort had they bought it in from a store,[146] and in the Pilbara, there are developments which appear equally absurd if we reduce the events to economics. One Aboriginal statement encapsulates this perfectly. A protester said 'Me go on strike, me wantum thirty bob a week'. The irony was he was amongst the few Aborigines who in fact already received the award wage of thirty bob. His words seem to be laughable, until, as Biskup adds, we realise this was not a demand for equal money but 'for human dignity'[147] symbolised, in this case, through wages. The search was for the moral European.

The earliest signs of 'cargoism' came with a War effort in which some Aborigines found themselves working side-by-side with Whites, and when they also found abundant proof of the vulnerability of White Law itself. In central Australia, from this time, Fred Rose noted that American soldiers had been cast as the redemptive stranger. Unlike Australians, these new Whites were egalitarian in their exchanges, and after the War they would return to Angus Downs with a large number of trucks laden with gifts of flour, tea and sugar. It was only by trickery that White Australians had stolen the trucks immediately after the war, but the future would bring the

Americans' return. Cans connected to wire to form a wheel (these days a child's toy) were perhaps, said Rose, a quasi-ritual to hasten their second coming. Again, there is Rose's plate depicting a pearl shell pendant engraved with playing card emblems,[148] which seems to indicate the possibility of Aborigines ritually employing a form of White 'cargoism,' gambling.

Rose's data are in themselves rather conjectural, but if we draw comparisons with the west coast, the original home of his pearl shell pendant, his observations are echoed. In this case deliverance would be brought by the Japanese. According to newspaper reports of 1942, Aborigines believed 'Japs were going to come and that all black-fellows would be all right'. They were going to teach them to read and write, enter into marriage alliances with them and 'see we were alright for tucker'. Conversely, Whites would then face retributive justice and would become the servants while Aborigines walked free. Asked how they could be certain of the future, two women replied that they 'knew by studying the stars'.[149]

Unlike Rose's reports of a mild faith in the new (and Allied) American, the longing for the Japanese was widespread and threatening: the enthusiasm for the Japanese was so strong that Aborigines proclaiming their virtues were placed under military arrest and in 1942, a Mobile Force was dispatched to round up unemployed Aborigines in some areas to be interned as 'potential enemies'. Those employed were forbidden to leave their place of normal residence.[150] It was in this already explosive situation that the then-communist McLeod began to be heard.

Admittedly, McLeod himself helped delay the strike until the threat of invasion was past, but when it did begin it brought the Pilbara wool industry to a standstill. Years later, the strike still dragging on, McLeod and his Mob moved into mining ventures, putting some of their considerable initial profits into purchasing their own pastoral stations, the most famed being Yandyerra.[151] By 1954, however, due to a range of unhappy circumstances, the company was forced into voluntary liquidation. The ideal of parity within White Law, on the other hand, was more alive than ever.

During the War period, the Kimberley region had been relatively quiet from the government's point of view, but McLeod Law was spreading northwards just as *Kuranggara* was reciprocally stretching towards the south. Almost a decade after the collapse of the Mob's company, a new face of *Kuranggara* was seen in the area of La

Grange. It was the fully developed messianic, millenarian and 'cargoistic' cult to which I alluded in the closing lines of the previous chapter. Now it is time to examine in detail the rich and complex strands woven to form the Jesus–*Djinimin* tradition.

The random references to *Djinimin* have not previously been brought together, its documenters seemingly unaware they had grasped two ends of the same creature. Only in gathering the scattered data on *Djinimin*'s origins and rise to cultic supremacy do the dynamics of his cosmological innovation become clear.

Djinimin was first noted as a mythic being without a cult amongst the Murinbata. As I remarked in the preceding chapter, Stanner felt that in contrast with that of the All-Mother, the mood of *Djinimin* was profoundly troubled. He himself did not realise there was, or was soon to be, a cult for this Ancestor that was millennial and prophetic, but he seemed to sense it. He conceded that the image of *Djinimin*, profound and inspiring, was the 'kind of stuff on which prophets might have thrived, but no prophets arose, or none of whom we have heard. Yet they did in comparable conditions in Melanesia and Polynesia'. Stanner then adds, almost absently, that he had once read something about an Aboriginal woman who had 'prophesised a time when the whites would be black and the blacks whites', which seemed somehow relevant. 'A search might yield something interesting,' he added, but a search would require a guiding theory to explain the lack of millenarianism and 'cargoism'. Distracted by something shuffling in the undergrowth of ethnography, Stanner then stepped down from the back of that unseen slumbering millennial beast.[152]

The theory Stanner required was simplicity itself, if indeed we need anything so grandiose as 'theory' once we have abandoned the self-congratulatory fetishisation of European wealth which surrounds the discussion of 'cargoism'. Petri and Petri-Odermann, for example, seemed almost relieved to have discovered Aborigines had such beliefs after all.[153] Kolig notes Fred Rose, like other anthropologists, 'was astounded by the almost complete absence of cargoistic and millenarian activity in Aboriginal society' before he goes on to concur that this is indeed a 'baffling question'.[154] If for the moment we concede that Aboriginal people might actually value the Law of place more than a law of commodity wealth, however, our history makes obvious sense.

Millennial or other eschatological beliefs did emerge, as we have seen, with intense disruption to the Aboriginal order of place. This was also true of the *Djinimin* context for, as Stanner notes, people were grasping desperately for a hold on their homes. 'Former territories have been given up long since, but each adult knows his clan territory . . . The corporate clan estate is only a memory, but some of its signs . . . are still jealously guarded rights.'[155] Out of place, people remember and draw their memories into the promises of time and a future world in which they can return to their abodes. There is no balance but only hope that equilibrium might return. Such images are plentiful in the south-east and in pastoral Australia, and 'cargoism' is but one protracted variation in the pre-existent theme.

'Cargoism' arises in Aboriginal societies firstly where people have been enticed or enslaved into the moral world of labour, in order to keep some contact with their lands, and secondly, having done so, when they seek parity *within* that White Law. The second World War and reformers like Don McLeod seem to have been the stimuli which sent north-western Australia into that latter phase. Previous rituals, such as the earlier forms of the *Kuranggara*, had symbolised a White world intruding upon their domain but, so far as I am aware, had not sought to manipulate those symbols in terms of a cosmic balance between two Laws. This was the innovation of *Djinimin*.

Returning now to reconsider Stanner's accounts, his recorded myths take on a new significance. There were, he said, three great Murinbata stories: that of the All-Mother, *Mutinga*; that of a cognate woman, *Kukpi*, who had sung the *Kuranggara* songs, and that of *Kunmanggur* and his son *Djinimin*. Of these, *Kunmanggur* was the most powerful, but had no cult. Stanner believed the myth belonged to a vital ongoing mythopoeic process, and while much of it is surely ancient, careful scrutiny also reveals an unexpected hierarchy in its structure. The retributive and overseeing Rainbow *Kunmanggur*[156] had been killed by his son, *Djinimin*, and 'by his death gives men the fire and water which are the means of perennial life' – symbols we will see recurring below. The structure of the myth, as Stanner observes, is a perfect inversion of the Christian myth in which a benign father sends his son to redeem the world by dying for humanity. Now, the father himself is killed by the son who then enters the world. 'Here,' says Stanner, 'are two remarkably parallel institutions . . . there is of course no historical connection.'[157]

In reality there were two profound historical connections. One was that Stanner collected the myth from men on a Sacred Heart

Catholic mission founded in 1935. The other historic link was only then being forged.

Stanner, I believe, was unsympathetic to a new generation when he said that at the time of *Djinimin*'s spiritual ascent a great materialistic wave had washed across the northern Aboriginal frontier, but he was surely correct in stating that, at some level, there was a new desire for European goods. There was also, without doubt, 'antagonism towards Europeans', and 'a mania for gambling' should perhaps have warned him what was afoot.[158]

When *Djinimin* received his cult is unknown, but by the time he had he was equated with Jesus. Petri and Petri-Odermann were told the movement arose in a mission station and assumed it was Protestant, maybe partially because of their close working relationships with Catholics (who disliked the cult's theology). Yet there were no Protestant missions in these areas where the myth (of which the Petris were unaware) has been recorded, and I am inclined to the Port Keats area, the very region where Stanner made his observations. For this I have no direct evidence, but a solid precedent.

When Father Docherty founded the Port Keats mission in 1935, he showed a man named Mulithin a picture of Mary standing (appropriately) upon a serpent, as well as a picture of Jesus. Mulithin replied he had seen them before. His son later related that Mulithin, a 'kidney-fat man' (i.e. a sorcerer), had been stricken by disease. Mulithin saw a hawk swoop from above (*Kunmanggur*'s closest mythic associate and his mediator, incidentally, was a hawk),[159] and together they ascended. Mulithin saw what he later interpreted as Jesus, God wearing a large headdress, and Mary standing upon the serpent. He also saw the fires of hell and a paradise for the good. Jesus gave Mulithin a *Malgarrin* song cycle and dances, which were introduced and are still known to the Murinbata.[160] It is further noteworthy that the paintings in the Port Keats church said to depict the revelations of Mulithin render Jesus and Mary with black skin. Some Aboriginal interpreters also add that the pictures reveal Jesus' descent to tell people to give up their wayward behaviour and return to their old Law.[161]

Despite pronounced parallels, I repeat that this perhaps proves no more than that Mulithin's revelation shares the same mood as that of Jesus–*Djinimin*. For what the new *Djinimin*, with both black and white skin, did was come to earth precisely in order to give Aborigines a new cult and warn them to hold fast to their old Law.

The *Djinimin*-Jesus cult itself was most prominent to the west, however, at La Grange where, in the early 1960s, it appealed particularly to the advocates of McLeod Law. The ceremonial leaders nevertheless proclaimed its genesis lay somewhere to the east on a mission station. There, *Djinimin*-Jesus had revealed himself to an intertribal gathering of people who claimed they had always been believers in Jesus. They were surprised and afraid by his manifestation, however, and feared to touch him, although they captured his image with a box-camera. The deity with dual skin colour pronounced that 'all the land from the beginning belonged to the Aborigines and that in future there would be no difference between Aborigines and other Australians – all should share equally in that land'.[162] The Petris rightly draw the parallel between this message and that of McLeod Law. *Djinimin*, however, declared the future equality would only arrive if Aboriginal people held true to their own Law and resisted Whites. Then they themselves would be washed White by holy rain.

Djinimin's descent was into a gathering to perform the *Woagaia* ceremonies[163] and, in an act inverting the normal means of ceremonial transmission, took it with him back to Heaven. So, at last, the cultless Ancestor had his ritual, and how fitting it was. For *Woagaia* is itself none other than a manifestation of the earlier All-Mother cults of Arnhem Land, and an extension of that lineage passing from *Kunapipi* through *Kadjari* and *Kuranggara*.[164] When Stanner wrote that the cultless *Djinimin* competed with the All-Mother's ritual places he underestimated the significance of his own words. It seems the Sky God, as he now was, literally stole the Mother's cult, adapting it to his own millennial ends. Thereafter, *Djinimin* and *Woagaia* travelled westwards together. *Woagaia* was now 'God's Law'.[165]

Djinimin also promised 'cargo', for he was in possession of a redemptive stone ship. Noah's Ark had been sent from Heaven with a dual purpose: it was to rescue Aborigines during the second White purging deluge of holy water, and it also contained gold and crystals providing their wealth[166] in a thus equal society. This belief, Kolig maintains, has become well established in the Kimberley. The discolouration of Geikie Gorge is said to be the mark of the first flood, and at that time (and slightly contradicting other accounts) the Ark landed in the Great Sandy Desert. The missionaries who taught that it came to rest in another land were deliberately fraudulent. It was nearby, laden with precious stones and metal, but 'of much more significance than the real or imagined wealth heaped up in the Ark is its redemptive potential'.[167]

The *Djinimin* movement was clearly an attempt at constructing a world in which equality within the White Law of European wealth would provide the means for salvaging Aboriginal associations with their lands. Encouraged by War experiences, and sympathisers like McLeod, the emergent cult played a cosmic game with high stakes. It promised the winner everything, but on the table the world was being wagered, for the solidarity of Aborigines at this time, their pan-Aboriginal front and their unity of cause had themselves changed the shape of those lands longed for but not entirely retained.

This brings me to the persistent element in the *Djinimin* phenomenon which has often been dismissed as an aberration. True, the hero is no longer prominent, and equally undeniably his Ark has now been amalgamated with other millennial causes, but the promise of *Woagaia* and its associated land of *Dingari*,[168] to which I now turn, still lingers in the Aboriginal north, as does the allurement of equality through 'cargo'.

When *Djinimin* spread *Woagaia*, it contained an eschatological structure in which all the Dreaming powers were returning to a cosmic centre called *Dingari* in the far east. In the first chapter, I explained precisely how alien the notion of an *axis mundi* was to precontact Aboriginal thought, and the intrusiveness of its image of spatial unity is matched here by the anachronistic representation of the Ancestors travelling underground from *Dingari* on camels. The Petris also maintained that church symbolism such as bells and the Ark mytheme were initially essential to *Woagaia*, and some said, in words echoing Stanner's, that the dead would be resurrected as Whites. But it is the concept of centralised space that stands out as the most radical and dangerous innovation. Petri and Petri-Odermann summarise the climax of *Woagaia* ideology thus:

> It was God's will that the mythical groups returning as spirits underground from Dingari in the far east . . . continue their immigration as far as . . . the centre of the world . . . where an anticipated future realm of salvation is to exist, and to which the millenarian expectation of various Aborigines were also linked.[169]

Whatever its revivalistic intentions may be, in this compact of a unified world plan and the autonomy of time in its eschatological form we witness the very antithesis of the unqualified authority of the discrete Abiding place explained in chapter 1, and this is a transformation which continues still.

In later times, Kolig found that Aborigines of the Fitzroy Crossing area had melded their affiliation with myriad Ancestors into two macro-_Dingari_ myths and only a few sites. People, he says, can no longer be easily related to their eternal place, and ritual recruitment is now organised by residence rather than birth. 'They have reshaped their religious heritage both to simplify it and to unify themselves organisationally. In the process . . . religious particularism that traditionally divided Aboriginal society into numerous exclusive lodges . . . [has] been discarded.' There is a constant tendency, through the newly imagined underground travels of Ancestors, to thread the Dreaming tracks into a single co-ordinated cosmic fabric.[170]

This surely is a heritage befitting _Djinimin_, but Kolig says these cults no longer seem to be 'syncretistic, nativistic and millennarian'.[171] In many cases I am sure he is correct, but I am also certain the most energised cult currently sweeping through northern Australia is a true descendent of _Djinimin_. It too has _Dingari_ as its focus, has a dual identity godhead, celebrates the symbols of water and fire, and makes promises of 'cargo'. It is called _Djulurru_.

DJULURRU: CLOSER TO UTOPIA

Were it not for _Djulurru_ it might be possible to dismiss _Djinimin_'s _Woagaia_ as something of a sport in this branch of ethnographic literature. As it can be demonstrated, however, that the two cults share a range of cardinal concerns and themes, we have evidence that the innovation of _Djinimin_ has spread and endured through its direct cultic descendant.

Djulurru emerged at the same time and place as _Djinimin_. Those who have seen the ceremonies in the western Kimberley have been told it began on the west coast some time in the late 1950s and 60s.[172] Some see La Grange, the seat of _Djinimin_'s revival, as its home, some Broome, while others say quite explicitly that it began in Nullagine[173] or Port Hedland, which was a flashpoint for much of McLeod's Mob's activities. Rather than adjudicate on a single original source it is perhaps wisest to recognise multiple layers of regional inspiration, although I strongly suspect the Pilbara probably saw the very first spark of this revival.[174]

From its place of origin, _Djulurru_ has spread against the previous tide of ceremonies travelling from the north-east to the north-west. Glowczewski has gathered descriptions of the rituals held at La Grange from Paddy Roe, while Kolig picked it up again at Fitzroy Crossing[175] in the 1970s. In 1975, Moyle observed its transmission from the Walmadjeri of Balgo Hills to the northern and southern Warlpiri in exchange for a Warlpiri ceremony with a shared focal symbolic element, the *Jardiwanpa*, or 'fire ceremony', and at much the same time it also reached the Pintupi. The spread of the 'Balgo Business' or 'Sleeping Business' (as it became known in its later phases) along a path covering almost one quarter of the continent, thus took something in the order of ten to fifteen years. At the time that I witnessed the cult in late 1983, it remained, after a decade, without doubt the most vital and enthusiastically attended of all Warlpiri rituals and was something to which my wife and I were introduced with obvious pride at our anticipated enjoyment. It was a Business 'that made people happy'.[176]

The eastward and thence southern transfer of *Djulurru* has seen it become increasingly esoteric. Kolig did not find it markedly secretive at Fitzroy Crossing,[177] but at Balgo Hills, Moyle said there were major prohibitions surrounding it (so much so that he does not in fact name the cult). Ronald Berndt, however, said he found no such restrictions when he witnessed the ceremony at Balgo,[178] and at Yuendumu the secrecy was relatively mild but structurally significant. It merely separated initiates from non-initiates, but in a radical shift from traditional principles, *anyone*, male or female and literally coming from any place on earth, could be inducted. Place, whilst relevant, was not a recruitment restriction.

As the details of *Djulurru* are available in print, I do not feel any breach of confidence in here clarifying diverse academic opinion concerning the cult, although some as yet unpublished data I too shall omit.[179] The first thing to be noted is that *Djulurru* is a manifestation of *Kuranggara*. Kolig sensed this, saying that 'in some respects [*Djulurru*] bears a close resemblance with *Kurrangarra* suggesting that *Kurrangarra* may have influenced its origin',[180] but it was Hilton Deakin who actually documented the required link. He noted that *Kuranggara* is 'strongly aggressive and anti-white' before going on to describe the transmission of one segment of the cult associated with firesticks. Its Kwini name, he said, is *Tjuluru*, which 'referred to a dramatic moment in the rite, when men and women dancers hit firesticks together in the dark, causing a burst

of sparks to explode around them'.[181] Without doubt, his *Tjuluru*
is the *Djulurru* which thus began as a segment of *Kuranggara*, just
as *Kuranggara* was a segment of *Kunapipi*. As we will see, however,
it is even more explicitly related to the *Dingari-Woagaia* permutations
of *Kuranggara*.

The word *Djulurru* is nonetheless not only used to refer to the
fire-stick cycle. According to Glowczewski, it means 'outside' in a
language her informants could not identify, but this seems rather
conjectural.[182] Akerman, on the other hand, speaks of something
Glowczewski omits. He says *Djulurru* is the personal name of a man
who is the centre of the ceremonies and who is represented by a
carved painted post.[183] This was precisely the meaning suggested by
the southern Warlpiri and hence this can be recognised as an
enduring element of *Djulurru*. His iconic form is an ochred pole
about one metre high, painted with a vertical pipe-clay key motif.
At the base are two small squares with simple, stylistically very
Westernised faces which are said to represent *Djulurru* and his
maliki (dog).

The hero *Djulurru* has other titles. Kolig refers to him as *Wuirangu*,
a spirit who transmitted the cult to a Pilbara song-man. Following
a hypothesised translation by von Brandenstein, Kolig suggests this
name means 'the one of war',[184] which is fitting given the battle
themes of the dance, but is at best an educated guess. What Kolig
says of *Wuirangu* clearly indicates he is *Djulurru* as the Warlpiri
described him – an Ancestral being who lingers dangerously in the
vicinity of his cult.

Kolig also notes *Wuirangu* 'is conceptualised variously as white,
black or as a half-caste',[185] an echo of *Djinimin* which is immensely
amplified when we turn to Warlpiri who refer to *Djulurru* as *Wapirra*,
literally 'Father', and the term used by Christians for both God and
Jesus. When I enquired whether this meant *Djulurru* was the church
Wapirra, there was a slight hesitation amongst some Christians, one
saying 'I can't believe that', although clearly he had been asked to.
Other Christians, also 'bosses' for *Djulurru*, answered 'yes' without
qualification.

Djulurru the 'Father' is not all that the missionaries might have
hoped for, but they can nevertheless perhaps take some credit or
blame. *Djulurru* dresses in white in the style of a cowboy, complete
with hat and pistols. He variously rides his white steed or his
motorbike, and he consumes vast amounts of alcohol. The Berndts,

amongst the few to note the explicitly Christian elements of *Djulurru*, say 'as far as we know, it was not specifically stimulated by missionaries but was designed by Aborigines',[186] and with this I concur. It is possibly worth noting, however, that when I gave this description of the 'Father' to an ex-priest and ex-nun from the Kimberley, they were startled, saying that this (save the alcohol, but this is something Aborigines invariably associate with Catholics) was the revamped image of Jesus (*Yangay*; 'Young Guy') they had used to entice Aboriginal converts.[187]

The figure of *Djulurru* is thus very much akin to that of *Djinimin*, the Black and White Jesus. On the other hand, he also shares similarities with *Djanba*, for his cult is based on symbols of the White moral order of pastoral Australia.

While his ceremonies are being performed, *Djulurru* travels in adjacent areas recruiting those who have avoided his conscripting tradition and playing havoc with European technology. On the one hand he is something of a mechanical saviour, for if an initiate's car runs out of oil or petrol, the Father will come to their rescue. On the other hand, *Djulurru* destroyed the vehicles owned by those who did not share with Aboriginal people. A pearl shell adorned with what appeared to me to be two machine-made circles (this interpretation was denied, however) belonged to the *Djulurru* cult, and could be used to cause cars to crash when drivers failed to offer the person who carried it a lift. This shell was kept in company with another said to depict serpents and aeroplane propellers, and it is significant that similar shells had been collected amongst the Warlpiri, and along the path to the western coast.[188]

Already it is clear that *Djulurru* is surrounded by beliefs striving towards Aboriginal equality within White Law, not only by appropriating the charismatic cowboy Father, but also through his power as an equaliser or at least one who insisted upon the sharing of White commodity wealth. So far, however, I have only skirted the ceremonies themselves, to which I now turn.

Djulurru insists Aborigines join him. I was told he had in the past caught one man unawares in the bush and asked him whether he had been through his Law. When the man answered he had not, he was instantly struck dead, only to be resurrected by this trickster figure. Many Warlpiri people most emphatically did not want to be initiated into the cult and took refuge in a missionary's house to avoid being conscripted, or temporarily fled the area altogether.[189]

Whilst mostly Christians, their reason for resistance was that this New Law was seen as opposing a traditional worldview;[190] that it was coming to replace rather than supplement the 'Old Business'. Over the years, however, nearly all Warlpiri have been conscripted to *Djulurru*.

Hinting at its broad historical sweep, neophytes are referred to as 'prisoners' and those thus captured are kept in a shelter referred to as the 'prison'. In the days before the singing and dancing begins, the inmates are put through a range of onerous trials of deprivation, including spending extensive periods lying immobile (hence 'Sleeping Business') under the watchful eye of the 'policemen'. This, of course, replicates Aboriginal life-experiences within what might be considered a White initiatory institution, the prison.[191] The Aboriginal appropriation of the prison retains its status as a context for a *rite de passage* but inverts the colonial message.

When the prisoners are brought to the main ritual ground, it is soon revealed quite explicitly that this is *not* an Aboriginal cult. Some say it first belonged to the Whites, some the Japanese, Chinese, Afghans or 'half castes', but the most popular understanding is that it was initially a 'Muslim' ceremony which belonged to 'Malays'. For reasons which are not known, the 'Malays' could not handle the tradition, which they found to be 'too strong' and so they 'gave' or 'sold' it on to 'half castes', who in turn transferred it inland. The Islamic/'Malay' element is apparent in the brightly coloured head-gear made of looped and twisted red, blue, yellow, white, pink and green wool (purchased in the Warlpiri case by women from Alice Springs) and icons such as a shell showing a man wearing a turban but with the tail of a fish.[192]

The ceremonies begin with the women distant from the main camp. The men huddle to consult a piece of paper, *mili* (mail), which when opened reveals a drawing of a dancer and the words '8 o'clock'.[193] The women receive a similar 'letter,' and thus the Business starts with a White message form announcing an onset symbolically co-ordinated by clock-time.

The grounds are a typically simple affair with a shelter (called *Jirripa*), an adjacent tree, and, running east-west at the southern end, a long clearing, said to be *wantarpa* (for the aeroplane).[194] Officiating are four classes of men. As with Lommel's account of *Kuranggara*, the owners of this cult are not people linked with it through land affiliation, but are aspirants, often relatively young and ritually ambitious, who have taken upon themselves the position of 'boss'. These *Nyinurru*, as they are called, are the main singers and overseers of the ritual procedure. The *Katurunja* are the guards who care for the prisoners, although they are also present in a central dance. Like the *Kankarra*, who are workers controlling the two key symbols of *Djulurru*, they consistently wear European hats. The *Kankarra* are obliged, when appropriate, to light and extinguish fires, and also to provide water in drums which some say are for watering the unseen *Djulurru's* horses. According to Glowczewski's informants, *Kankarra* are 'Whites' or 'men of the sun' and control water and fire, central elements which parallel the focal themes of the *Djinimin* myth in which the wounded father descends into the water with all fire, and hence the means of life itself. Here 'Whites' control these elements. Finally, there are the 'Table-men' who are something of a mediating group, building and embodying the New Law. Rather felicitously, I think, the concept of 'Table'[195] is to be conceived generally as a Law standing above and separated from the land, and also obviously reflecting the Aboriginal image of White Law, both clerical and judicial, which is always associated with books resting upon tables.

Glowczewski has admirably charted the proceedings of the various days' performances, and I will here but note the main songs and dances of the opening days. In the first performance, called *Jukura-kakarra* (tomorrow eastwards), the bodily designs of the dancers seem related to Meggitt's illustration of *Djanba* spirits. They have a white 'Y' painted on their torso, and wear in their feathered headdress two antenna-like sticks, as well as having a wooden slab pushed through the back of their 'turban.' The club in the 'belt' possibly represents a sword. No-one I consulted was certain as to the meaning of the words they sang, and no other account has as yet provided this detail, but Glowczewski's La Grange informant pointed to a general Uto-pian theme: 'In the future ("tomorrow") Ancestors will take men to the dream country of the East'.[196]

A second dance, *Wanjarri Wanjarri*, consists of a line of people emerging from the screen *Jirripa*, and while at one level it is said to represent people being released from a serpent (a traditional *Kuranggara/Kunapipi* motif), it is said more explicitly to reveal the 'spirits of the drowned' people from a shipwreck off the coast of Broome. This is a persistent element of *Djulurru*. Kolig refers to it but, in a rather indirect manner, reconstructs the vessel as being the schooner *S.S. Colac*, sunk by a tidal wave in 1910. This seems at best but a secondary view, for the sinking which Mary Durack says permeated history for so many Aborigines, and to which men like Dooley Bin-Bin referred, was that of the *Koombana*.[197] This is precisely the ship Glowczewski's informant, Paddy Roe, specifies; the same ship said to have carried the *maban* who finally killed Pigeon (*supra*).

This theme is also present in the next dance, known as *Wanpukardakarda*, which evokes people jumping from the wrecked ship. Its texts were tentatively translated to mean 'jumping with shivering lips' and was said to recall 'Malay' people dying but two men surviving to pass on the Law to Aborigines. Another performance to be noted is the spectacular fire dance which like the ritual shelter is known as *Jirripa*.[198] The *Kardrurunja* dance has been translated as the 'battle of the cross'.[199] Paddy Roe says this 'represents the distress rockets which had been sent by the sinking boat',[200] but possibly another interpretation holds simultaneously. Glowczewski, or her informant, may have confused 'battle of the cross' (cross = Warlpiri *wanta wanta*) with 'battle of the planes' (plane = *wanta*). Kolig, at least, was told that the two 'blokes' involved in the fighting symbolised in the rituals were called Hitler and German. The motifs of bombing and gunfire which also featured in them may actually have been inspired by the Japanese raid on Broome during the war on the third of March, 1942.[201] This event, at the very least, has been celebrated in Pilbara song:

> They're coming in from the east
>   – terrifying!
> Seven they are – coming in from the east.
> Coming in from the east
>   – terrifying!
> Those chaps with the protruding eyes.[202]

It should be noted, however, that the firefighting protagonists in *Djulurru* are men and women of ideal intermarrying subsection pairs, and thus there is clearly also an interpersonal and social facet to this segment.[203]

The two themes thus far in evidence, the sinking of a ship and the manifestation of planes, provide the key to *Djulurru* and its explicitly 'cargoistic' climax. The historic episode of the sinking of the *Koombana* was initially dreamt by a Port Hedland man named Coffin.[204] He must have been one of two famous Coffin brothers.

Jack Coppin (Coffin) went on strike in 1943 because he felt victimised by legislation which, as we have seen, restricted Aboriginal movement because of their pro-Japanese attitudes. Coffin and his sympathisers were firmly suppressed by the police, but his protest was not really a failure, as it paved the way for McLeod. His brother Peter Coppin was later director of 'McLeod's' mining ventures and eventually came to challenge McLeod's leadership itself: 'Don's right all the time. Pig's arse he is!' he said.[205] *Djulurru* thus began with either McLeod's predecessor or his successor. It is said he was visited by the dead souls of the *Koombana*, who charged him with transmitting their message to Aborigines in the form of *Djulurru*.[206] The second theme was an event contemporaneous with the Coffins' protests – the Japanese bombing of Broome.

At the climax of *Djulurru*, these elements are juxtaposed. On the final day, three canvases are erected, which some accounts suggest depicted ship sails (although the *Koombana* was a steamer, a 'three funnell' as Worrumarra notes in Pigeon's story), but which Paddy Roe says were the 'tents' of its 'three captains'.[207] These dancers are also known as the 'Three Kings' and their dance is the *Table-karra*. Roe also notes that two of the 'captains' are traditional doctors, whilst the third is the spirit of Coffin himself. Glowczewski's interpretation in terms of the roles of Aborigines, Whites and a shared Law is on the right track, I feel, but her symbolic gymnastics are regrettably more tidy than convincing.[208]

The ship and the three captains or kings are followed, however, by a greater mystery. After the *Table-karra*, attention turns to the *wantarpa* – 'for the aeroplane'. Along it comes – first a huge string cross, some two metres in diameter, which screws backwards and forwards. This is followed by a second string cross, fully four metres high, but rectangular with rounded ends, which proceeds, pauses, dips and passes. This is finally followed by the third cross, which is identical to the first. They come to rest before the three tents and then depart. The first and final crosses are called *pitia* or 'cool wind'. The middle one is a *wanta*. They are a plane's wing and its propellers, and they are powered by traditional doctors. I was told that a picture of a public Mowanjum dance of an aeroplane associated with the Flying Doctor Service displayed the same string cross arrangement in miniature.[209] The massive *Djulurru* plane, however, was said to embody the promise of tea, flour and tobacco.

Djulurru is a 'cargo' cult, but like all such cults it is far more than that term implies. In forming a general interpretation of *Djulurru* we must always recall that its aesthetics are paramount. It is 'a good show' with more appeal in the pure pleasure of performance than any other celebration in living memory. It follows that much of its contents are cherished for their intuitive fit, and given the disparate sources and number of years of its emergence, we are bound to be frustrated if we attempt too tidy a meaning. Yet, tantalising us with impressionistic images comparable to the dreams which conjured them, a theme and a mood emerge.

This much can be said: *Djulurru* lingers upon the memories of non-White outsiders – Japanese and 'Malays' – who invert White hegemony over their own Law. Ships are destroyed and towns bombed, but then the order is reversed and those very boats and planes are brought within the Aboriginal world, empowered, however, by the traditional Aboriginal 'doctor'. The neophytes, or prisoners, are finally set free not, as had been history's lesson, when they are deemed ready to bow to an imposed Law, but when they learn parity can be obtained within their own Law, expanded to embrace the Law of commodities and wealth. Thus, ultimately, *Djulurru* repeats and prolongs the message of its twin *Djinimin*, ritualising the pledge of equality within the White symbolic domains which become apparent with the War and in ideals such as McLeod Law.

As is often equally true for the display of wealth amongst White Australians, there is for Aboriginal people little interest in the 'cargo' stripped of its symbolic value. An incident illustrates my point nicely. On one occasion, I joined a long discussion between a small party of elderly men at an 'outstation'. There were a handful of tin sheds there, and one man, a 'boss' for *Djulurru*, was bringing heavy pressure to bear upon the man whose homeland we were on to demand that the Department of Aboriginal Affairs pour concrete floors for his sheds. I could not (and still cannot) think of any pragmatic value in such floors, and so remarked that this was an expensive option when people hated sleeping indoors and, even were they to be forced to escape from rain, a soft earth floor was infinitely more comfortable than cold concrete. The owner conceded this, but we were told, quite firmly, we had in effect missed the point. The floor was not something Aborigines should want, but rather something that Whites should want to give them. It was an equitable exchange, a sign of parity, not a commodity or a piece of 'cargo'.

This is the promise of *Djulurru*, what Burridge calls the quest for the moral European.[210] It is a noble quest, but what is often ignored is its cost.

In a fine segment of analysis of the 'Cargo cult' *Djulurru* as a 'Symbolic Manifestation of Economic Transition', Glowczewski notes foremostly that it has broken the basic Aboriginal ritual transaction between place and people:

> What Aborigines depend upon is not a transcendent being, it is, as it were, their own identity, defined as an incarnation of the vital force of terrestrial species . . . The transmission or transaction [is] between men and the sacred earth . . . In contrast, with *Juluru*, the value of transformed object . . . becomes those of men who thus attribute to themselves the mastery of that which this object represents.

Put more simply, there is a shift from a Law in which people's being is defined by place to one where they are defined by objects.

> The Aboriginal Law resides in sacred objects (or sites) as long as they are the metamorphoses of the same 'essence' . . . which makes humans, while the Law of the Whites resides in these 'riches,' without a common essence with men.[211]

From this she develops the corollary that because there is no essential identity between the person and the object mediated by place, the new power reduces boundaries and opens up a new unity: 'The power of collective appropriation. The discourse on a pan-Aboriginal identity is thus in progress, and the notion of "God", like place "empty" of power, can be dissolved in that of the State.'[212] Here Glowczewski points towards, without apparently having fully seen it, the deeper and darker side of *Djulurru*. The sacrifice of the search for moral relations with Whites is a ubiquitous transcendence and a world emptied into homogeneous space. Another Aboriginal man of the Kimberley once expressed the logic of this transformation in a rather different context: 'You can see that [the Dreamings] are dying . . . Do you think they will go to heaven?'[213]

It is not only that the Fatherhood of *Djulurru*, like *Djinimin*, has many of the High God qualities, but further, that they both have the same ultimate destiny. For just as *Djinimin* drew all Dreaming powers from the earth towards *Dingari*, so too *Djulurru* is responsible for uniting once disparate Dreaming tracks at a place.[214] *Dingari* is now said to be off the coast of Broome, beneath the sea, in the place from whence all the Dreaming lines emanated. The site is said to be marked by a fire beneath the ocean, and the glowing beneath the waves is variously linked with the sinking ship and planes.

Djulurru's task is to track down the Dreamings and bring them back to *Dingari*. His success marks the millennial hope of *Djulurru*, but in the process he will literally strip the earth of its sacred powers, taking them to a new Utopian realm.

Amongst the various communities where *Djulurru* is celebrated, songlines which once ended within their lands are now provided with a subterrestrial postscript which sees the Ancestors disappearing toward the west coast. This is not a cult which passively unifies all people and all places. Its pan-Aboriginal platform is conscriptive, and the locative powers of the world are being absorbed into a new domain.

According to the Warlpiri, one of the songs of *Djulurru* refers to the mythic figures, the two brothers we met at the end of chapter 1's discussion of 'Worlds to Endure'. In the earlier version of the myth, the brothers enter the earth and head towards their eternal home. In the *Djulurru* song, however, the reference is to flux and all the country 'walking away'. Paired with the song is a new conclusion to the myth, although its focus is in this case actually to the south of *Dingari* itself. The brothers plunge below the earth's surface, heading westward, along the path of *Djulurru's* transmission, towards Broome. In the country of the Lungu people, they made a *kayut, kayut*[215] call before they moved on to *Wanjari Wanjari*, a land of one of the *Djulurru* songs. They continued, at one place becoming itchy with 'witchdoctor stones' in their heads. Along the coast they again meet strange Aboriginal people and continue to call, *kayut, kayut*. Finally, they reach a place in the Pilbara known as *Kukarn-kukarba*. The brothers smell sacred objects there (*juju*) and then a wind blows up pushing rocks to cover the brothers in the ground with their medicine stones and sacred objects. There they remained until the land was opened by mining groups. I was told that as a White person I could go to see these powers emerging from the mineshafts, but Aborigines would be killed if they approached the area. The location of this site was in the vicinity of Abydos Station, the very place Don McLeod had tried to purchase just prior to the famed Pilbara strike, and Yandyerra, a station McLeod had acquired for the Mob as a focus for their own mining ventures. Its manager was none other than Peter Coffin (Coppin).[216]

The rise of Aboriginal 'cargoism' appears at every turn to be linked with those movements, associated with men such as McLeod and the Coppin brothers, who sought equality within the world of labour and wages. This quest continues, but increasingly Aboriginal people are turning toward another option. For the danger of the 'cargo' solution is that it concedes much to the symbolic authority of commodity wealth and hence, ultimately, threatens to fulfil assimilationist ideals of inducing Aborigines to define themselves in terms of White Law.

The movement away from 'cargoistic' principles was also tied to the striking action. The Gurindji from Newcastle Waters went out, again on the first of May (1966), over delays in introducing award wages, but there was far more to their protests than this. Nonetheless, the Pastoral Award came into operation in 1969, and resulted in endemic unemployment. As Rose writes, 'Aboriginal peoples' productive capacity, in relation to the national economy, had changed from the status of being appropriated under conditions of virtual slavery, to the status of being virtually irrelevant'.[217]

Perhaps the Gurindji anticipated as much, for at the same time as they demanded recognition within White Law, they also began retreating from it. Specifically, they petitioned the Governor-General, Lord Casey, to return to them 500 square miles of their land, an action which has been seen ever since to mark the birth of the modern Land Rights movement.

I cannot here pursue the massive rush of events following that initial action – it has literally reshaped a nation and the entire Aboriginal world – but I will in closing simply note what the Gurindji claim signified. It stated a renewed desire, one never truly vanquished, of a people to hold on to their place. It meant that instead of seeking to change White Law in order to give Aboriginal people equality within its terms, there was a concern to reshape that Law so as to recognise the Aboriginal understanding of land-being. 'Unlike cargo cults which flatter our sense of mastery and, on the surface, suggest that it is others who want to change,' Rose argues, this more recent orientation reverses the terms so that 'the dispossessed claim to have indeed understood . . . And . . . *they* are offering *us* redemption'.[218]

I began the discussion of invasion in south-east Australia (chapter 3) with a Badjala song recording the *Endeavour* sailing past their country. Precisely 200 years later, Hobbles Danayari, having himself participated in the Gurindji actions, told of a different experience of Captain Cook and his Law. He said it was a lie; he said he wanted a reinstatement of land-power; but more importantly, he said this was also the concealed truth within White Law. His words, which bring to a conclusion the 'cargoist' vision by refusing to acknowledge its terms, need no explanation save to note the aptness of his choice of representative for the moral White person. For the same Queensland Native Police used to murder the Kalkatungu (discussed in the first part of this chapter) had only a few years earlier been sent to track down the White outlaw Ned Kelly, and the fact that Kelly was hunted by 'police boys', just as their own rebellious heroes had been, was something well remembered by Aborigines in the western Kimberley.[219] Danayari's words were these:

> First there was water here and then it went back so that there was the Northern Territory. Then a thousand million Aborigines were here and lived on the land for a long time. The first cudeba (white-man) who came was Ned Kelly and he brought with him the first horses, a stallion and a mare, which bred here and the first bullock, a very hairy one whose picture you can see on some rocks in Victoria River Downs country. Ned Kelly was a friend of and helped the Aborigines. The second cudeba who came was Captain Cook. He looked at the land and saw that it was very good and wanted it for himself. He decided to clear the Aborigines off the land. So he shot many of them and he shot Ned Kelly too and he stole the land.
>
> But now we want the land back.[220]

NOTES

1. C.G. von Brandenstein and A.P. Thomas, *Taruru: Aboriginal Song Poetry from the Pilbara* (Adelaide: Rigby, 1974), p. 12.
2. ibid., pp. 33 & 30.
3. S.J. Hallman, 'The First Western Australians', in *A New History of Western Australia*, edited by C.T. Stannage (Nedlands: University of Western Australia Press, 1981), pp. 38–40.
4. Hallman, 'The First Western Australians', p. 61.
5. A. Capell, 'Mythology in the Northern Kimberley, North-West Australia', *Oceania*, 9 (1939), p. 385.
6. A. Capell, *Cave Painting Myths: Northern Kimberley*, Oceania Linguistic Monographs, no. 18 (Sydney: University of Sydney, 1972), chapter 5 & p. 12.
7. Capell, 'Mythology . . .', p. 392.
8. This rock art gallery is shown in C. Hill, 'Did Aboriginal Spirits Smoke?' *Australian Geographic*, 21 (1991), p. 23, Capell, 'Mythology . . .', p. 385.
9. P. Kaberry, 'The Forest River and Lyme River Tribes of North-west Australia', *Oceania*, 5 (1935), p. 434.

10. E.A. Worms, 'Djamar, The Creator: A Myth of the Bad (West Kimberley, Australia)', *Anthropos*, 45 (1950), p. 642.
11. E.A. Worms, 'Djamar and His Relation to Other Culture Heroes', *Anthropos*, 47 (1952), pp. 543-4.
12. Capell, 'Mythology . . .', p. 403; B.J. Wright, *Rock Art of the Pilbara Region, North-West Australia*, Occasional Papers in Aboriginal Studies, no. 11 (Canberra: Australian Institute of Aboriginal Studies, 1968).
13. See H. Reynolds, *With the White People* (Melbourne: Penguin, 1990); C. Anderson, 'Aborigines and Tin Mining in North Queensland: A Case Study in the Anthropology of Contact History', *Mankind*, 13 (1983), pp. 473-98; A. Chase, '"All Kind of Nation": Aborigines and Asians in Cape York Peninsula', *Aboriginal History*, 5 (1981), pp. 7-19.
14. see F. Stevens, *Aborigines in the Northern Territory Cattle Industry* (Canberra: Australian National University Press, 1974).
15. E. Kolig, 'An Obituary for Ritual Power', in *Aboriginal Power in Australian Society*, edited by M.C. Howard (St Lucia: University of Queensland Press, 1982), p. 284.
16. P. Willis, 'Riders in the Chariot: Aboriginal Conversion to Christianity at Kununurra', in *Aboriginal Australians and Christian Missions*, edited by Swain & Rose, pp. 308-20.
17. H. Reynolds, *The Other Side of the Frontier: An Interpretation of the Aboriginal Response to the Invasion and Settlement of Australia* (Townsville: James Cook University, 1981); R. Broome, *Aboriginal Australians: Black Response to White Dominance 1788-1980* (Sydney: George Allen & Unwin, 1982).
18. N. Green, 'Aborigines and White Settlement in the Nineteenth Century', in *A New History of Western Australia*, edited by Stannage, p. 115.
19. H. Petri & G. Petri-Odermann, 'A Nativistic and Millennarian Movement in North-West Australia', in *Aboriginal Australians and Christian Missions*, edited by Swain & Rose, p. 391.
20. D. Rose, *Ned Kelly Died for Our Sins*, the 1988 Charles Strong Memorial Lecture (Adelaide: Charles Strong, 1988), p. 4.
21. The search for an adequate interpretation of cargo cults forms the core of I.C. Jarvie's *The Revolution in Anthropology* (Chicago: Henry Regnery, 1964).
22. P. Biskup, *Not Slaves Not Citizens: The Aboriginal Problem in Western Australia 1898-1954* (St Lucia: University of Queensland Press, 1973), p. 94.
23. R.M. & C.H. Berndt, *End of an Era: Aboriginal Labour in the Northern Territory* (Canberra: Australian Institute of Aboriginal Studies, 1987). See D. Rose's extensive review in *Australian Aboriginal Studies*, 1 (1988), pp. 93-9, and her comment that the Berndts' silence was a 'matter at that time . . . of life and death with action or inaction making the difference', p. 98.

24. R.M. Berndt, 'Influence of European Culture on Australian Aborigines', *Oceania*, 21 (1951), pp. 229-35; Berndt & Berndt, *End of an Era*, p. 276.

25. N. Loos, *Invasion and Resistance: Aboriginal-European Relations on the North Queensland Frontier, 1861-1897* (Canberra: Australian National University Press, 1982), p. 61 & cit. p. 58.

26. C.D. Rowley, *The Destruction of Aboriginal Society: Aboriginal Policy and Practice* (Canberra: Australian National University Press, 1970), pp. 169 ff & 137-8.

27. Loos, *Invasion . . .*, pp. 56-7.

28. ibid., chapter 6; p. 162.

29. H. Pedersen, '"Pigeon": An Australian Aboriginal Rebel', in *European Aboriginal Relations in Western Australian History*, Studies in Western Australian History VIII, edited by B. Reece & T. Stannage (Nedlands: University of Western Australia Press, 1984), p. 13; see also S. Muecke; A. Rumsey; & B. Wirrunmarra, 'Pigeon the Outlaw: History as Texts', *Aboriginal History*, 9 (1985), pp. 81-100.

30. B. Worrumarra (S. Muecke transcriber), 'Pigeon Story', in *Paperbark: A Collection of Black Australian Writings*, edited by J. Davis *et al.*, pp. 158-63 (St Lucia: University of Queensland Press, 1990), pp. 161-3; cf. E. Kolig, *The Noonkanbah Story* (Dunedin: University of Otago Press, 1987), p. 27.

31. ibid., chapter 3.

32. Broome, *Aboriginal Australians*, p. 121.

33. G.C. Bolton, 'Black and White after 1897', in *A New History of Western Australia*, edited by T. Stannage, p. 126.

34. Pedersen, 'Pigeon', p. 10.

35. F. Richards, 'Customs and Language of the Western Hodgkinson Aboriginals', *Memoirs of the Queensland Museum*, 8 (1926), p. 258.

36. Richards, 'Customs . . .', p. 256.

37. W.E. Roth, *Ethnological Studies Among the North-West-Central Queensland Aborigines* (Brisbane: Government Printer, 1897), p. 118.

38. ibid., p. 117.

39. ibid., p. 121.

40. W.B. Spencer, *Wanderings in Wild Australia* (London: Macmillan, 1928), pp. 231, 234, 235 & 238.

41. R.M. Berndt, *Australian Aboriginal Religion* (Leiden: E.J. Brill, 1974), fascicle 2, p. 2.

42. See Siebert's account below. Elkin's fieldnotes are housed in the Fisher Library, University of Sydney, Box 9, 1/2/5.

43. E. Kolig, 'Post-Contact Religious Movements in Australian Aboriginal Society', *Anthropos*, 82 (1987), p. 255.

44. L.A. Hercus, ' "How We Danced the Mudlungga": Memories of 1901 and 1902', *Aboriginal History*, 4 (1980), p. 7, n. 4.

45. J.W. Gregory, *The Dead Heart of Australia: A Journey Around Lake Eyre in the Summer of 1901-1902 . . .* (London: John Murray, 1906), p. 216.

46. The following translation is from O. Siebert, 'Sagen und Sitten der Dieri und Nachbarstämme in Zentral-Australien', *Globus*, 97 (1910), pp. 57-9. The careful translation has been made by E.J. Sharpe, to whom I am particularly grateful.
Siebert's note: I have always heard it referred to as Múlunga and not Molonga, although this of course does not rule out the possibility that farther north the word is pronounced, as Roth has it, Molonga.

47. *Siebert's note:* [W. Roth, *Ethnological Studies*], pp. 120 ff.

48. *Siebert's note:* Gregory, *The Dead Heart of Australia*, pp. 209-10; see also A.W. Howitt [*The Native Tribes of South-East Australia* (London: Macmillan, 1904)], pp. 416 & 787; & W.B. Spencer & F.J. Gillen, *Northern Tribes* [*of Central Australia* (London, Macmillan, 1904)], pp. 718-9.

49. *Siebert's note:* One of my photographs has been used by Gregory (*The Dead Heart*, p. 211) and two by Howitt (*The Native Tribes*, pp. 415 & 417).

50. *Siebert's note:* See Roth, Figure 304.

51. Kolig, *Dreamtime Politics*, p. 79.

52. A.R. [Radcliffe-] Brown, 'The Relationship System of the Dieri Tribe', *Man*, 14 (1914), pp. 53-6.

53. Kolig, *Dreamtime Politics*, p. 79.

54. In Hercus, ' "How We Danced the Mudlungga" ', pp. 17 & 27.

55. ibid., p. 7, n. 4.

56. Kolig, *Dreamtime Politics*, p. 80.

57. Hercus, ' "How We Danced the Mudlungga" ', pp. 18, 20, 27 & 27, n. 16.

58. ibid., pp. 18, 19 & 21.

59. Siebert, 'Sagen und Sitten', p. 58, plate 7.

60. D. Bates, *The Passing of the Aborigines: A Lifetime Spent Among the Natives of Australia*, second edition (London: John Murray, 1947), p. 125; F.D. McCarthy, ' "Trade" in Aboriginal Australia and "Trade" Relationships with Torres Strait, New Guinea and Malaya', *Oceania*, 10 (1939), p. 84, map 11.

61. F.J. Micha, 'Der Handel der Zentralaustralischen Eingeborenen', *Annali Lateranensi*, 22 (1958), p. 80; also 'Trade and Change in Australian Aboriginal Cultures: Australian Aboriginal Trade as an Expression of Close Cultural Contact and as a Mediator of Cultural Change', in *Diprotodon to Detribalization: Studies of Change Among Australian Aborigines*, edited by A.R. Pilling & R.A. Waterman (East Lansing: Michigan State University Press, 1970), p. 298.

62. E. Kolig, 'Religious Movements', in *The Australian People: An Encyclopedia of the Nation, Its People and Their Origins*, edited by J. Jupp (Sydney: Angus & Robertson, 1988), p. 165.

63. Roth, *Ethnological Studies . . .*, p. 118.

64. cit. R.E.M. Armstrong, *The Kalkadoons: A Study of an Aboriginal Tribe on the Queensland Frontier* (Brisbane: William Brooks, nd [c.1980]), p. 145; H. Holthouse, *Up Rode the Squatter* (Adelaide: Rigby, 1970), p. 120.

65. A. Grassby & M. Hill, *Six Australian Battlefields: The Black Resistance to Invasion and the White Struggle Against Colonial Oppression* (Sydney: Angus & Robertson, 1988), chapter 9.
66. H. Fysh, *Taming the North* (Sydney: Angus & Robertson, 1933), pp. 122 & 123-4.
67. ibid., opp. pp. 143, 95, 144 & 139.
68. Armstrong, *The Kalkadoons*, p. 144.
69. D. Bates, 'Aborigines of the West Coast of South Australia . . .', *Transactions and Proceedings of the Royal Society of South Australia*, 42 (1918), p. 165.
70. D.J. Mulvaney, ' "The Chain of Connections": The Material Evidence', in *Tribes and Boundaries*, edited by Peterson, p. 92.
71. Bates, *The Passing . . .*, p. 123.
72. H. Petri, 'Dynamik in Stammesleben Nordwest-Australiens', *Paideuma: Mitteilungen zur Kulturkunde*, 6 (1956), pp. 167-8; E. Kolig, *The Silent Revolution: The Effects of Modernization on Australian Aboriginal Religion* (Philadelphia: Institute for the Study of Human Issues, 1981), pp. 27-8.
73. Kolig, *Dreamtime Politics*, p. 80. In 1984, Warlpiri people I was driving from Yuendumu to Alice Springs were very nervous about the possibility of encountering the Aranda 'Red Ochre Mob' preparing for ceremonies.
74. B. Shaw, *Banggaiyerri: The Story of Jack Sullivan* (Canberra: Australian Institute of Aboriginal Studies, 1983), p. 158.
75. Compare with the biographical details of Major in B. Shaw, *Countrymen: The Life Histories of Four Aboriginal Men as Told to Bruce Shaw* (Canberra: Australian Institute of Aboriginal Studies, 1986), pp. 98-101.
76. The data for the two regions are compared in H. Petri, 'Das Weltende im Glauben Australischer Eingeborener', *Paideuma*, 4 (1950), pp. 349-62.
77. F. Merlan, ' "Making People Quiet" in the Pastoral North: Reminiscences of Elsey Station', *Aboriginal History*, 2 (1978), pp. 70-106.
78. T. Rowse, 'Were you Ever Savages?: Aboriginal Insiders and Pastoralist Patronage', *Oceania*, 58 (1987), p. 81.
79. N. Green, 'The Cry for Justice and Equality: Some Exceptional Protestant Missionaries in Western Australia', in *Aboriginal Australians and Christian Missions*, edited by Swain & Rose, p. 161.
80. M. Durack, *Kings in Grass Castles* (London: Corgi, 1967).
81. M. & E. Durack, *All-About: The Story of a Black Community on Argyle Station, Kimberley* (Sydney: The Bulletin, 1935), dedication.
82. M. Durack, *Sons in the Saddle* (London: Constable, 1983), p. 155.
83. Durack & Durack, *All-About*, pp. 68, 53 & 45.
84. Durack, *Sons . . .*, p. 379, n. 3.
85. Shaw, *Banggaiyerri*, p. 164.

86. Shaw, *Countrymen*, p. 180.
87. Shaw, *Banggaiyerri*, p. 161.
88. Shaw, *Countrymen*, p. 180 & 181.
89. Shaw, *Banggaiyerri*, p. 165.
90. Shaw, *Countrymen*, pp. 181-2; cf. B. Shaw, *My Country of the Pelican Dreaming: The Life of an Australian Aborigine of the Gadjerong, Grant Ngabidj, 1904-1977* (Canberra: Australian Institute of Aboriginal Studies, 1981), pp. 133-4.
91. Shaw, *Banggaiyerri*, pp. 165-6.
92. Shaw, *Countrymen*, p. 183.
93. Shaw, *Banggaiyerri*, p. 167.
94. ibid., pp. 58 & 59.
95. Durack, *Sons* . . ., p. 379, n. 3.
96. Shaw, *Countrymen*, p. 180.
97. Rowse, 'Were You Ever Savages? . . .', p. 94.
98. Shaw, *My Country* . . ., pp. 133-4.
99. Shaw, *Banggaiyerri*, pp. 58-9.
100. Roth, *Ethnological Studies* . . ., p. 121.
101. Worms, 'Djamar and His Relations', pp. 551-2.
102. Shaw, *Countrymen*, pp. 195-6.
103. Shaw, *Banggaiyerri*, pp. 60 & 157.
104. cf. Willis, 'Riders in the Chariot', pp. 312-13.
105. Shaw, *Countrymen*, p. 154; cf. *My Country* . . ., p. 119.
106. Shaw, *Banggaiyerri*, p. 157.
107. A. Lommel, 'Modern Cultural Influences on the Aborigines', *Oceania*, 21 (1950), p. 23.
108. Considering Boxer's place of birth it is worth noting the Kalkatungu suffered heavily from sexually transmitted diseases. R. Evans; K. Saunders; & K. Cronin, *Exclusion, Exploitation and Extermination: Race Relations in Colonial Queensland* (Sydney: Australia and New Zealand Book Company, 1975), p. 386.
109. Lommel, 'Modern Cultural Influences . . .', p. 23.
110. Rowse, 'Were You Ever Savages? . . .', p. 96.
111. A. McGrath, *'Born in the Cattle': Aborigines in Cattle Country* (Sydney: Allen & Unwin, 1987), p. 37.
112. Rowse, 'Were You Ever Savages? . . .', pp. 87 & 83.
113. Bolton, 'Black and White . . .', p. 126.
114. Lommel, 'Modern Cultural Influences . . .', pp. 15-17 & 12.
115. Berndt, 'Influence of European Culture . . .'. Berndt and Lommel both seem to radiate to unrealistic extremes. Lommel can only predict cosmic collapse, Berndt can only see continuity. Neither, it seems, entertained the possibility of an enduring reformulation of the Aboriginal worldview.
116. R. Tonkinson, 'Aboriginal Dream-Spirit Beliefs in a Contact Situation: Jigalong, Western Australia', in *Australian Aboriginal Anthropology:*

Modern Studies in the Social Anthropology of the Australian Aborigines,
edited by R.M. Berndt (Nedlands: University of Western Australia
Press, 1970), p. 289.

117. Lommel, 'Modern Cultural Influences . . .', p. 20; Kolig, *Dreamtime Politics*, chapter 4, *passim*.
118. Worms, 'Djamar and His Relations', pp. 550 & 554.
119. A. Lommel, *Die Unambal: Ein Stamm in Nordwest-Australien* (Hamburg: Druck, 1952); H. Petri, *Sterbende Welt in Nordwest-Australien* (Braunschweig: Albert Limbach, 1954).
120. E.A. Worms [and H. Petri], *Australian Aboriginal Religions* (Richmond: Nelen Yubu, 1986), pp. 30–3. Whilst probably not simply a rather ruthless means of elevating the Catholic publisher's missionary anthropologist, I am still at a loss as to why Petri (the co-author and editor of this book) has had his name omitted from the title page of the English translation. Petri's data, added in indented paragraphs, frankly save this book from being totally unreliable. On the pages in question, he adds some essential scepticism to Worms' highly dubious claim that *Kuranggara* came from central Australia.
121. Worms, 'Djamar and His Relations', pp. 557–8, contains a postscript written when the author belatedly discovered *Kuranggara* as a part of the *Kunapipi* rituals, and in a last *post hoc* attempt to save his thesis he makes the messy claim that the *Kunapipi* must have recently added the allegedly desert-derived *Kuranggara* segment.
122. K.-P. Koepping, 'Nativistic Movements in Aboriginal Australia: Creative Adjustment, Protest or Regeneration of Tradition', in *Aboriginal Australians and Christian Missions*, edited by Swain & Rose, p. 402.
123. cf. chapter 3; & Petri, 'Das Weltende . . .'.
124. J. Wilson, 'Kurungura: Aboriginal Cultural Revival', *Walkabout* (May 1st 1954), pp. 15 & 19.
125. Koepping, 'Nativistic Movements . . .', p. 403, refers to 'a diachronization of different layers of Dreaming stories'.
126. Berndt, 'Influence of European Culture . . .', p. 235.
127. Shaw, *Countrymen*, pp. 131 & 178.
128. M.J. Meggitt, *Desert People: A Study of the Walbiri Aborigines of Central Australia* (London: Angus & Robertson, 1962), p. 167.
129. Shaw, *Banggaiyerri*, p. 164.
130. Shaw, *Countrymen*, p. 132.
131. ibid., p. 139
132. R.M. Berndt, *Kunapipi: A Study of an Australian Aboriginal Religious Cult* (Melbourne: Cheshire, 1951), p. 48; M.J. Meggitt, *Gadjari Among the Walbiri Aborigines of Central Australia*, The Oceania Monographs, no. 14 (Sydney: The University of Sydney, 1966), p. 89.
133. Berndt, 'Influence of European Culture . . .', p. 233.
134. Shaw, *Countrymen*, pp. 138 & 139.

135. K. Palmer & C. McKenna, *Somewhere Between Black and White* (Melbourne: Macmillan, 1978).
136. cit. H. Middleton, *But Now We Want The Land Back* (Sydney: New Age Publishers, 1977), p. 98.
137. cit. Biskup, *Not Slaves . . .*, pp. 212 & 221.
138. H. Petri & G. Petri-Odermann, 'Stability and Change: Present-Day Historic Aspects Among Australian Aborigines', in *Australian Aboriginal Anthropology*, edited by Berndt, pp. 256 & 266.
139. M. Brown, *The Black Eureka* (Sydney: Australasian Book Society, 1976), pp. 91 ff.
140. Biskup, *Not Slaves . . .*, pp. 212–13.
141. Brown, *The Black Eureka*, pp. 96 & 208.
142. J. Wilson, 'Authority and Leadership in a "New Style" Australian Aboriginal Community: Pindan, Western Australia', MA dissertation (University of Western Australia, 1961); cf. K. Wilson, 'Pindan: A Preliminary Comment', in *Diprotodon to Detribalization*, edited by Pilling & Waterman, pp. 333–46.
143. Wilson, 'Kurungura', pp. 16 & 19.
144. Brown, *The Black Eureka*, pp. 99 ff & 100; also D. Stuart, *Yandy* (Melbourne: Australasian Book Society, 1959), *passim*.
145. Petri & Petri-Odermann, 'Stability . . .', p. 257.
146. K.O.L. Burridge, *Mambu: A Melanesian Millennium* (London: Methuen, 1960), p. 280.
147. Biskup, *Not Slaves . . .*, p. 221.
148. F. Rose, *The Wind of Change in Central Australia: The Aborigines at Angus Downs*, 1962 (Berlin: Akademie, 1965), pp. 90–1 & plate 62.
149. Biskup, *Not Slaves . . .*, pp. 209–10.
150. ibid., p. 210.
151. Brown, *The Black Eureka, passim*; Stuart, *Yandy, passim*. Both of these novelists were present whilst many of the events they describe were unfolding.
152. W.E.H. Stanner, 'Continuity and Change Among the Aborigines', *The Australian Journal of Science*, 21 (1958), p. 109.
153. Petri & Petri-Odermann, 'A Nativistic . . .', p. 397.
154. Kolig, *Dreamtime Politics*, p. 49.
155. Stanner, 'Continuity and Change . . .', p. 108.
156. W.E.H. Stanner, *On Aboriginal Religion*, The Oceania Monographs, no. 11 (Sydney: University of Sydney, 1959–61), pp. 83, 85, 97, 100 & 130.
157. Stanner, 'Continuity and Change . . .', p. 105.
158. See W.E.H. Stanner, 'The Founding of the Port Keats Mission' (unpublished ms., nd), p. 108.
159. ibid., p. 94.
160. E.D. Stockton, 'Mulithin's Dream', *Nelen Yubu*, 22 (1985), pp. 3–11.
161. I thank Fr Barry Tunks for drawing my attention to the possible congruence between the revelation of *Djinimin* and Mulithin's dream,

and also for providing me with photographs of the Port Keats Church paintings and Aboriginal interpretations of them.

162. Petri & Petri-Odermann, 'Stability and Change', p. 258.

163. For a discussion of *Woagaia*'s innovations and a comparison with other cults such as *Mulunga*, see E. Kolig, 'Woagaia: Weltanschaulicher Wandel und neue Formen der Religiosität in Nordwest-Australien', *Baessler-Archiv*, 29 (1981), pp. 387–422.

164. Petri & Petri-Odermann, 'Stability and Change', pp. 266–7; 'A Nativistic Movement . . .', p. 393. Woagaia is also the name of a 'tribe' adjacent to the Kalkatungu, but like Petri & Petri-Odermann ('A Nativistic Movement . . .', p. 395, n. 4), I cannot establish any direct link. Were there one it would be intriguing, as these are the people to whom Roth attributes the *Mulunga*'s origin, and thus a shared historic thread would weave through all the cults discussed in this chapter.

165. Petri & Petri-Odermann, 'Stability and Change', p. 259.

166. idem, 'A Nativistic Movement . . .', p. 393.

167. E. Kolig, 'Mission Not Accomplished: Christianity in the Kimberleys', in *Aboriginal Australians and Christian Missions*, edited by Swain & Rose, p. 379; cf. E. Kolig, 'Noah's Ark Revisited: On the Myth-Land Connection in Traditional Aboriginal Thought', *Oceania*, 51 (1980), pp. 118–32.

168. *Dingari* certainly did not come into being *ex nihilo* and it was previously associated with *Kuranggara* in an (ethnographically) obscure manner. These are discussed by R.M. Berndt in, among other published works, 'The Walmajderi and Gudadja', in *Hunters and Gatherers Today: A Socioeconomic Study of Eleven Such Cultures in the Twentieth Century*, edited by M.G. Bicchieri (New York: Holt, Rinehart & Winston, 1972), pp. 206 ff. In Berndt's accounts there is ambiguity even as to whether *Dingari* is a place, a myth, or a ritual, and if the latter, how it relates to (or equates with) *Kuranggara*. F. Myers, *Pintupi Country, Pintupi Self: Sentiment, Place, and Politics Among Western Desert Aborigines* (Canberra: Australian Institute of Aboriginal Studies, 1986), p. 300, n. 8, notes this 'polysemy'. In the early 1960s, however, when Petri studied it, *Dingari* traditions were associated with an Ancestral movement (some say led by none other than *Djanba* himself) toward the Pilbara. This was nothing short of a transference of diffused plural earthly sacred powers to a single site. For a sound summary, see Koepping, 'Nativistic Movements . . .', pp. 403–4.

169. Petri & Petri-Odermann, 'Stability and Change', pp. 263, 264–5 & 272. The *Dingari* traditions, focusing on Badur Hill, are discussed extensively in H. Petri, ' "Badur" (Parda-Hills) ein Felsbilder-und Kultzentrum im Norden der Weslichen Wüste Australiens', *Baessler-Archiv*, 14 (1966), pp. 331–70. His account is further extended in

' "Wandji-Kurang-gara", ein Mythischer Traditionskomplex aus der Wüste Australiens', *Baessler-Archiv*, 15 (1967), pp. 1–34.
170. Kolig, *The Silent Revolution*, pp. 27–8, 37, 39, 40 & 43.
171. ibid., p. 160.
172. Kolig, *Dreamtime Politics*, p. 120; see also E. Kolig, 'Djuluru: Ein Synkretistischer Kult Nordwest-Australiens', *Baessler-Archiv*, 27 (1979), pp. 419–48.
173. K. Akerman, 'The Renascence of the Law in the Kimberleys', in *Aborigines of the West: Their Past and Their Present*, edited by R.M. & C.H. Berndt (Nedlands: University of Western Australia Press, 1979), p. 235.
174. B. Glowczewski, 'Manifestations Symboliques D'une Transition Economique: Le "Juluru", Culte Intertribal du "Cargo" ', *L'Homme*, 23 (1984), p. 8.
175. Glowczewski, 'Manifestations . . .', p. 7. Her informant, spelled 'Paddy Row', is in fact Paddy Roe, author of *Gularabulu: Stories from the West Kimberley*, edited by S. Muecke (Fremantle: Fremantle Arts Centre Press, 1983); Kolig, 'Djuluru', *passim*.
176. R. Moyle, *Songs of the Pintupi: Musical Life in A Central Australian Society* (Canberra: Australian Institute of Aboriginal Studies, 1979), pp. 6 & 60 ff.
177. Kolig, *Dreamtime Politics*, p. 120.
178. R.M. Berndt, pers. comm., 1988.
179. Secrecy is a relative matter. At certain sections of initiation ceremonies, Warlpiri neophytes are still told they will be killed if they inform others of some of the revelations, and recording or photographing these segments would be totally unthinkable (although it did occur before the implications of this were fully understood). Using such matters as a yardstick, *Djulurru* is clearly a more open affair than other rituals.

The restrictions on access to *Djulurru* are instated as much to protect against power as they are to prohibit knowledge. Our small son, who like other children was permitted to be present, was later diagnosed as having become mildly ill from being a little too close to the sacred objects. Again, to my surprise, I was pragmatically told the easiest way to learn the songs was to bring a tape recorder with me, and I was even reminded that a White cattle worker had photographed the climactic ritual emblems. His pictures did not come out, however, because of the forces emanated. There was power and danger here, but the point is the secrecy was not to structurally divide predetermined insiders from all others so much as to protect people.
180. Kolig, *Dreamtime Politics*, p. 85.
181. H. Deakin, 'Some Thoughts on Transcendence in Tribal Societies', in *Ways of Transcendence: Insights from Major Religions and Modern Thought*, edited by E. Dowdy (Adelaide: Australian Association for the Study of Religions, 1982), p. 106.

182. Glowczewski, op. cit., p. 9.
183. Akerman, 'The Renascence . . .', p. 241.
184. Kolig, *Dreamtime Politics*, p. 121.
185. loc. cit.
186. R.M. & C.H. Berndt, 'Body and Soul: More than an Episode!' in *Aboriginal Australians and Christian Missions*, edited by Swain & Rose, p. 52.
187. P. & E. Willis, pers. comm., 1987.
188. R.E. Barwick, 'The Anatomy of an Aircraft: A Warlpiri Engraving', *Aboriginal History*, 6 (1982), pp. 75-80.
189. M. Laughren, 'Religious Movements Observed at Yuendumu, 1975-81', in *Symposium on Contemporary Aboriginal Religious Movements*, unpublished, p. 2; Glowczewski, 'Manifestations . . .', pp. 14-15.
190. Laughren, 'Religious Movements . . .', p. 2.
191. M. Foucault, *Discipline and Punish: The Birth of the Prison* (Penguin: Harmondsworth, 1979); I have applied Foucault's analysis of prisons to missions, which are equally and relatedly evident in *Djulurru* symbolism, in T. Swain, 'Love and Other Bullets', *Religious Traditions* (1990).
192. Photograph of pendant in author's collection.
193. cf. Kolig, *The Silent Revolution*, p. 135.
194. Glowczewski, 'Manifestations . . .', p. 19.
195. Akerman, 'The Renascence . . .', p. 241; Glowczewski, 'Manifestations . . .', p. 25; Stanner, 'Continuity and Change', p. 105 (Stanner sees these as key symbols of 'the means of perennial life'); Glowczewski, 'Manifestations . . .', pp. 28-9.
196. M.J. Meggitt, 'Djanba Among the Walbiri, Central Australia', *Anthropos*, 50 (1955), p. 395; Glowczewski, 'Manifestations . . .', p. 8; Kolig, *Dreamtime Politics*, p. 122.
197. Glowczewski, 'Manifestations . . .', p. 27; Kolig, *Dreamtime Politics*, p. 122; Durack, *Sons . . .*, p. 301. As well as some historical background, J. Hardie, *Nor'Westers of the Pilbara Breed* (Port Hedland: Shire of Port Hedland, 1981), discusses the sinking of the *Koombana* on pp. 120-2. It is depicted in Plate 5.
198. Glowczewski calls this *juju*, which, however, is only a generic Warlpiri word for sacred power.
199. This is Glowczewski's translation (p. 25), but it is possible that the word for cross (*wanta wanta*) has been confused with that for aeroplane (*wanta*) and hence this could be the 'battle of the planes', which makes more contextual sense.
200. Glowczewski, 'Manifestations . . .', p. 8.
201. Kolig, *Dreamtime Politics*, p. 121.
202. von Brandenstein & Thomas, *Taruru*, p. 29.
203. Glowczewski, 'Manifestations . . .', p. 33.
204. ibid., p. 9.

205. Biskup, *Not Slaves . . .*, p. 213; Wilson, 'Pindan', p. 335; Brown, *The Black Eureka*, p. 226. For further details on the Coppin brothers see Stuart, *Yandy, passim*.
206. Glowczewski, 'Manifestations . . .', p. 9.
207. loc. cit.
208. Glowczewski, 'Manifestations . . .', pp. 9 & 34.
209. The picture is in E. Allen, 'Australian Aboriginal Dance', in *The Australian Aboriginal Heritage: An Introduction Through the Arts*, edited by R.M. Berndt & E.S. Phillips (Sydney: Australian Association for Education Through the Arts/Ure Smith, 1978), p. 277, plate 242.
210. Burridge, *Mambu*, pp. 266 ff.
211. Glowczewski, 'Manifestations . . .', pp. 11 & 12.
212. loc. cit.
213. cit. D.B. Rose, 'Passive Violence', *Australian Aboriginal Studies*, 1 (1986), p. 24.
214. Akerman, 'The Renascence', p. 241.
215. Glowczewski, 'Manifestations . . .', pp. 8 & 19.
216. Brown, *The Black Eureka*, p. 41.
217. D.B. Rose, 'Jesus and the Dingo', in *Aboriginal Australians and Christian Missions*, edited by Swain & Rose, p. 363.
218. Rose, *Ned Kelly . . .*, p. 24.
219. A. Whittington, 'The Queensland Native Mounted Police', *Journal of the Royal Historical Society of Queensland*, 7 (1920), pp. 516–17 on Ned Kelly, and pp. 518–19 on the Kalkatungu. Bulla in Shaw, *Countrymen*, pp. 100–1, says the same police and 'police boys' who killed the rebel Major had also sought Ned Kelly. I might add that the widespread Aboriginal awareness of Kelly's activities seems to undermine D.B. Rose's attempted reconstruction in 'Ned Lives!', *Australian Aboriginal Studies*, 2 (1989), pp. 51–19, which, however fortuitously, only provides for an extremely localised explanation of how Aborigines learned of Kelly.
220. cit. Middleton, *But Now We Want the Land Back*, p. 7.

Conclusion

> That's how we did it all the time. That was the way, the Law, you see. We don't do that now. We do it like the white man because we all belong in the community. When the man is lost he's taken out to the graveyard, and you become free. You're taken in to Heaven, whether he's a good man or not a good man. That's all I know. The white man idea is the same Law as the blackfeller, my fucking oath.[1]

With these words of Mandi Munniim we return, with all of the vigour and something less of the elegance, to the paradox of the song-text with which this book began. Again – but this time following an historical excursion which I trust has opened readers to the antinomy's fuller meaning – we are confronted by two modes of being which are equated, and which for all this are evidently, indeed literally, worlds apart.

As I said at the outset, this book is about the juxtaposition of Heaven and 'the waterhole' and all that that juxtaposition might entail. It embraces, as we have seen, the gulf separating each place from Utopia, the Abiding from the temporal, and the ubietous self from the free spirit.

In these closing pages, I will draw together my preceding arguments, highlighting both the pattern of this story and its broader value in expanding our understanding of human constructions of existence, before finally retreating a little from the constraints of the past to fleetingly note an old dilemma the future will bring with renewed vigour to the first Australians.

While almost totally ignored – indeed I have argued it has been at times most enthusiastically suppressed – everything I have considered in detail in this book has been at least suspected of being true by many of my predecessors. I do not claim to have uncovered anything

276

new, only to have taken past speculations seriously and to have provided them with a context. Having postulated a trans-Aboriginal 'architectonic idea' I have in turn shown how variations on this plan in Cape York Peninsula, south-east Australia, Arnhem Land and adjacent regions, and pastoral areas (particularly the Kimberley) can be best understood by considering those divergences against a background of various types of alien intrusion upon Aboriginal existence. If this is so then the cultic variations can be understood as very recent transformations in Aboriginal ontology.

Meggitt has in fact previously brought key elements of each of my chapters together in the form of a brief yet most insightful statement on the structure of supra-'totemic' traditions in Aboriginal societies. He wrote that the Fertility Mothers of Arnhem Land

> post-date the ordinary totems and rarely are they totems in themselves, tied to specific localities or descent groups; indeed, some are explicitly not totems at all. Rather they are all extra-totemic or even super-totemic and inter-tribal or international in character, and their cults involve all initiated men.
>
> This state of affairs is analogous to that concerning Iwai, the crocodile hero whose cult extends through the Cape York peninsula, and it resembles also certain cult situations in and near the Kimberleys, where exotic culture heroes . . . such as Djamar, Djanba, the Kurangara-Dingari, [etc.] . . . enter the area and disseminate new social rules, religious dogma and ritual objects as they travel about. These supernatural beings are also super-totemic in that they provide an embracing explanatory context into which local forms of totemic tenet and ritual may be integrated. In short, all of these northern beings are cosmoplastic and elevated in somewhat the same way as are Daramulun and Baiame of the eastern Australian tribes, who are probably the closest approximation to high gods to be found in Australian religion.[2]

A full understanding of Meggitt's fleeting observation, and further, an understanding of the equally significant *differences* between the Fertility Mothers, Heroes, *Djanba, et al.*, and the High Gods, together with the divergent contexts which produced those differences, have been the goal toward which my journey through Australian ethnography has been directed.

All that has been required to make this reconstruction possible is the acknowledgement of history. It is certainly true, as I have shown in each of the preceding four chapters, that scholars have strongly suspected the effects of external influences in each of these cases of revised worldview, but they have done so in a manner which effectively nullified the possibility of genuine historiography.

Academic ingenuity and consistency in denying history as an element in the persistence of Aboriginal ontology is so marked that I cannot but suspect that the 'timeless Aborigine' is itself a deeply cherished component of White mythology; a domain into which we have projected our own 'terror of history', as Eliade would say,[3] and our own retreat from the overwhelming sovereignty the West has given to time in recent centuries. Faced with unprecedented change and 'progress' anthropology arose – and despite all protests to the contrary to some extent still persists[4] – because European worldviews needed to retain faith in the enduring, the primordial and the primitive within humanity.[5]

It is thus that ancient or comparably 'primitive' influences on Aborigines are acceptable, for these do not tarnish our myth, but the devastating and obvious impacts of colonisation on the very core of Aboriginal being have for the most part become ethnographically invisible. We can accept that Melanesian beliefs softly drifted toward their southern neighbour's land, but cannot see that an invasion which totally changed a way of life, and which in the south-east took ninety six per cent of the people's lives, might have influenced Aboriginal notions of existence. As long as Indonesian impacts are relegated to the distant past, and deemed superficial, they too are acceptably safe; yet remove people from their lands, conscript them to a life of labour and wages or rations, and the naked truth, it seems, is something from which colonial-bred scholarship must shade its eyes. Aboriginalists, like the culture which shaped such scholars, need their primitives to be timeless. Today, all too belatedly, we can recognise that Aboriginal subsistence and social life have been transformed to a remarkable degree, but what we still cannot accept is that the very essence of Aboriginality has been touched by our presence. Acknowledging this would indeed open us to the 'terror of history', for it would mean not only that the primitive (that is the original or primary) was not eternal but also, insofar as changes were irreversible, that there could not even be an 'eternal return'.

Indeed, it was this predicament and our need for the primitive which led to the White invention of Aborigines themselves, for, as Attwood and Reece[6] have reminded us, that collective label of identity of course had no indigenous precedent. The 'Aborigine' (Latin 'from the beginning'), which, like *primitivus* ('first of its kind'), conjures the image of an timeless essence, was defined *vis-à-vis* the colonists as unchanging and when they did, undeniably, change, this was ignored as the focus shifted to the 'traditional' Aborigines or the 'traditionally oriented' Aborigines. As Gillian Cowlishaw writes perceptively

> The only integrity recognised in an Aboriginal society, until recently at least, was the integrity of tradition. A whole body of literature in anthropology, valuable as it is in recording past traditions, did not see itself *simply* recording past traditions. Rather it saw itself defining what Aborigines were, and are. This literature is dominated by the false notion that there *are* traditional Aboriginal societies.[7]

My working assumption has been that 'traditional Aboriginal society' never existed. Rather I have considered tradition*s* as entities which are forever becoming. This is not to say there was no structure at one time shared, perhaps for centuries, by all Aboriginal societies. What I am saying is that everything we know of the first Australians has been recorded since 1788, and most of our knowledge was collected much more recently than that.

If we open our understanding of Aboriginal existence to history, we are not denied a trans-Australian model of being. How ancient that ontology was will, I suspect, always remain unknown, but it is recorded as being distributed across the continent in our earliest ethnographies, and that is where our history must begin. I outlined that conception of the world in chapter 1 and took care to reveal its presence beneath more recent ideals in the ensuing chapters. Having identified that paradigm as something upon which Aboriginal communities were in agreement some two centuries ago, it then becomes a matter of merely reading the variations on, departures from, and even inversions of that theme within their ethno-graphically contemporary historical contexts. When we do so, static traditional Aboriginal societies take on a new life as the ongoing vital traditions they truly are and have surely always been.

The bald fact is that, with the exception of the Central and Western Desert regions (which thus provide much of my data for chapter 1), written records of any value on Aboriginal beliefs and practices were compiled at least a half a century after the arrival of outsiders. We do not know how long Melanesian people had been in contact with Cape York Aborigines, but it was at least one and a half centuries, and possibly a millennium more, before ethnographers reached the area. As I have argued, in Arnhem Land the Indonesians had perhaps arrived as late as the early eighteenth century, but again we are waiting a full two centuries for the first White researchers to arrive. As for the contexts for chapters 3 and 5, we are left with Maddock's sobering words: 'one has only to add L.R. Hiatt's observation that anthropologists in Australia have moved behind the advancing frontier to A.W. Howitt's observation that the frontier in Australia has been marked with a line of blood'.[8]

Once we acknowledge that in Cape York, Arnhem Land, the south-east and pastoral Australia, effective field-work was undertaken generations after the intrusion of outsiders, Meggitt's remarks concerning the Hero cults, Fertility Mothers, *Djanba* and the High Gods immediately find their frame of reference. The rest, as they say, is history.

The focus of this history has been ontology. This, as I said in my 'Introduction', is because I believe this is a difficult yet essential area to reassess, but it is also because Aboriginal traditions demand this approach to penetrate their patterns of change. Anyone tied to the more superficial categories of 'religion' or 'mythology' would find the tracks of innovation carefully concealed. While there are enough exceptions to warn the researcher that some radical reforms have in fact occurred, by and large there is a relative absence of conspicuous 'syncretisms' or 'synthesisms' within Aboriginal thought. The majority of scholars have seen this as sufficient reason to abandon enquiries into this domain, but thankfully Klaus-Peter Koepping has alerted us to the rewards of deeper investigations. He suggests Australian ethnography has been blinkered by narrow definitions of intellectual remodelling and that were we to return to the data with a researcher's 'fine tooth-comb' guided by adequate focus to our investigations, we would discover that 'not only is [the] Aboriginal world-view not stagnant, but it adapts with great, and almost feverish speed to new challenges'.[9]

In undertaking the re-examination of data Koepping advocated, I have found that nothing short of the very nature of existence will serve adequately as a point of reference. My exposition has concentrated upon ontology both as cosmology and as individual and collective processes of becoming and hence being-in-the-world. Once we allow such matters to guide us, and once we turn our gaze beyond culturally-bound notions of 'religion', 'myth' and so on, the shape of history begins to emerge from the timeless world of anthropological literature.

My task, however, has not primarily been to uncover laws of intellectual and social dynamics. I have pursued not *Deutung* but *Verstehen*;[10] I hope to have been faithful to the ideals of a meaningful story – 'a story which can change the conventions for understanding things'[11] – rather than those of social science. As such, I have attempted not to harness data to some grand theoretical cause, but instead, and as far as possible, to allow a narrative to unfold from texts by arranging its components and peeling back the occasional concealing foliage.

At the broader level of the arrangement of chapters, this has meant the avoidance of a hierarchical typological order in favour of a somewhat collage-like, yet chronologically justifiable, organisation. No doubt I have broken some unwritten rule by placing a discussion of invasion between chapters on Melanesian and Indonesian impacts, only to pursue the colonial presence once again at a later point. Besides the fact that the sequence is historically defensible, however, this order refuses to acknowledge the subtle narcissism in the assumption that the contemporary Western influences are the biggest, if not the best. As I understand this history, the truth is that Aboriginal traditions made more radical accommodations in the early years of invasion than of late (an inversion of accepted academic wisdom), and the arrival of Whites was then but one of several adjustments to outsiders. This, furthermore, represents only the minute slice of the past open to history. Revolutions in Aboriginal understanding of the world had no doubt a past millennia-old and, of course, a future yet untold.

The above notwithstanding, in this summary I will reflect upon the preceding chapters in a manner highlighting degrees within a continuum of territorial intrusion upon Aboriginal domains and underlying principles of historical reponse. From the proposed model of precontact ontology during the nineteenth and twentieth centuries discussed in chapter 1, I suggest the degree of cosmological adjustment intensifies as we pass from the relatively mild, equitable trade and marriage-based contacts with Melanesians; through to the more land-threatening, affineless, associations with Indonesians from a distant land; followed by the ration/wage-labour morality of the pastoral world; and finally, to the amoral associations with Whites on the frontiers of invasion.

In the chapters on each of these contexts (chapters 2, 4, 5 and 3 respectively), I have pursued several strands of a single phenomenon introduced in chapter 1. Woven into ensuing chapters is a consideration of the effect of strangers upon an ontology of place in its individual, social and cosmological levels. Cosmologically, the continuum runs from the uncompromisingly locative Abiding place to the temporalised Utopian vision. The social form of the same reality is the polarity of the site-lodge and the pan-Aboriginal organisation. Individually, the extremes are the land-spirit and the immortal body. I will consider each of these separately, although they are no more separable than, as the Samkhya philosophers would say, the three *Gunas* of an indivisible *Prakriti*.[12]

1. I began the first chapter of this book by redefining the so-called Aboriginal 'Dreamtime' to show that in fact Desert traditions, from which the word was derived, are rather governed by Abiding Events: events for which temporality is irrelevant and which are rather defined by their embeddedness in places. I argued that the radical plurality of autonomous yet related place-Events could not without compromise coexist with conceptions of an original creative act, cosmic centre or any other principle of spatial unification. Time, too, was denied determinative status insofar as it threatened spatial immutability. Because of the interdependence of people and places, however (to which I shall return in a moment), this world-plan could endure without qualification only insofar as all people acknowledge this principle of being.

Melanesian traditions posed a significant philosophical threat to the Aboriginal horizon of existence in northern Cape York, insofar as they operated from an assumption (one I suggested is shared by all agriculturalist and post-agriculturalist societies) that another people's land-being might be subsumed. Yet I also revealed how this ideological danger was prevented from becoming intimidating in practice. A mutually recognised ontological barrier was erected in the form of the Hero Cults, and in the main the Aboriginal order was free to continue. The only shift was a stretching of space to include places of another world, places that were celebrated in the songs of the Heroes.

The Indonesian presence off the coast of Arnhem Land was far more troubling, however, as those peoples, themselves from an unknown land, travelled at will without recognition of the Aboriginal conception of place. The *possibility* of territorial invasion could not be overlooked, but the genius of the All-Mother tradition was its ability to accommodate a new notion of space without directly undermining locative ideals. Her cult certainly embraced a broad earthly domain – even though she was not a Mother Earth *per se* – yet ubiety endured and time was not permitted to alter the shape of the land.

Colonial conditions, however, radically transform Aboriginal visions of their place. In pastoral environments with long-term White occupation, the authority of sites inevitably waned over the generations of lost contact with homelands. It is only in these situations that spatial unity began to take on proportions which threatened rather than complemented discrete estates. We saw, on occasion, locative powers being marshalled towards world-centres such as *Dingari*, and the promise of time breaking free of the constraints of eternal lands. It is here that pessimistic eschatologies and redemptive millenniums emerged.

The true antithesis to Aboriginal cosmology, however, is the notion that sacred power is neither earthly nor plural. It is only in south-east Australia, where Aborigines faced the ruthless thrust of invasion, that this ideal took on widespread proportions, and indeed, such beliefs have even there softened in this century. In nineteenth century accounts, however, the Supreme Deity had not only amassed all life's essences to himself, but had also removed them to an unknown, and for the living, unknowable, realm above the clouds – a refracted ideology of invasion chilling in its familiarity.

2. As I stressed in the first chapter, the demarcation between the geographical and the social was not a meaningful one in (nineteenth and twentieth century) precontact Aboriginal traditions, as people expressed their relationships as the relationship of places from which they emanated. 'Cosmology is "Kinship" ' to repeat Turner's words, and again, as Glowczewski wrote, 'Aboriginal kinship neither determines nor is determined by cosmology but . . . the two are applied forms of a specific logic . . .'[13] which, I believe, is the logic of their territorial ontology.

In the opening chapter I also indicated, however, that especially in northern Australian the identity of kinship and cosmology was weakened, perhaps through contacts with outsiders, by the emergent autonomy of the kinline, and in particular, the patrilineage. This parental link became a vital factor when it was shifted to the metaphysical level as an expression of transcendence.

In Cape York Peninsula, full transcendence did not emerge. Here there was not only a tussle between principles of patri- and matri-estates, but even more significantly the Heroes had begun to take on a pan-Aboriginal significance. They were poised to break loose of land itself, but, just as the shape of the world ultimately survived in this region so too the Heroes, despite their 'inter-tribal' appeal, in the final analysis were firmly chthonic beings.

It is in Arnhem Land with the powerful and ambivalent figure of the All-Mother that a fully transcendental Ancestor first stepped into Australian worldviews. To repeat the Gunwinggu words, she was the mother of 'All of us everywhere . . . people of every place and of different languages – We all call her mother, our true mother'. While arguably drawing an unwanted degree of attention toward the body, the Mother, as a mother, had, as I proposed in chapter 4, the advantage of standing outside what had become the mode of land-lodge recruitment – the patri-identity. It was thus that, despite her universal significance, she left largely unimpaired the now complementary ideals of site-based spiritual determination.

Outside the sheltered corner of the north-eastern Northern Territory, however, the Mother's cult's transcendental base was taken over by a more disruptive cause. *Djanba, Djinimin* and *Djulurru* stand as male usurpers of the Mother's ceremonial base (the *Kuranggara, Woagaia* and *Djulurru* transformations respectively), and their conscriptive spiritual powers at times directly threaten the moral law of ubiety. Socially, while not explicitly 'All-Fathers', they transcend kin-lands, with *Djanba* infusing every ritual, and *Djinimin* and *Djulurru* having an ubiquitous significance with all the aptly borrowed trappings from the god of their Christian proselytisers.

In the south-east in the nineteenth century this scenario took on its most extreme form, with the not only transcendent but also *otiose* All-Father, who dwelt somewhat imperiously it seems, above his newly subjugated devotees. For a people who had lost much of their lands and most of their kinfolk, the High God's elevation from the land was simultaneously a rise beyond localised affiliations and a politico-religious premise which theoretically could, and in other hands has, embraced or conquered worlds.

3. As was true for 'social' relations and cosmology, so too the individual was land-construed. In chapter 1 I diverted the tedious debate on ignorance of the physiology of procreation to show it must be understood not as nescience but as a positive affirmation of the

priority of land-being over the carnal body. Inversely, death could be seen as a return of a site's essence to itself, leaving no room for the discrete survival of the individual spirit as a separate existent.

Alien intrusions upon Aboriginal domains have invariably, although not equally, compromised the once unqualified recognition that individual lives were but an extension of estates. There is in both Cape York Peninsula and Arnhem Land greater recognition of physiological maternity and paternity, that is, of the human contribution to the embodied self, and with this appears a nostalgia, associated conspicuously with moon-myths, that death must intervene. These notions, I argued, perhaps mark the first germ of the autonomy of time from within an ontology of place. This connection was again repeated in chapter 5, where we saw that moon, as well as being linked to the material body, was also tied to the social immortality of the newly introduced subsection system.

This wistfulness notwithstanding, it was yet acknowledged in Cape York and Arnhem Land that death was indeed final. The fate of the deceased's spirit, however, opened up further innovative possibilities reflecting spatial disruption. In the tip of the Cape there was a seemingly minor shift of emphasis with the spirit returning to a person's mother's estate – perhaps, as I suggested in chapter 2, to separate land-powers from the ascendency of the Heroes' potentiality. In Arnhem Land, on the other hand, a radical accommodation of strangers entailed a literal split of the spirit so that while it returned to its 'well' it was also set free of its site to journey to a Land of the Dead which was either in the Gulf of Carpentaria (*Dhuwa* moiety) or the Torres Strait Islands (*Yirritja*).

In pastoral regions I then showed how the spirit-land tie was stretched to breaking point, and at times it was said to have become impossible for the requisite dreams to occur in order to bring life from land. Inversely, upon death, there was something of an indecisive moment, and in the case of great personalities – themselves indicative of excessive accord being given to the individual as an individual – it was suggested they may in fact not die but become immortals.

In nineteenth century south-east Australia, however, the dominant notion was even more weighted toward the carnal at the expense of the land. To recall the widely reported opinion from this area, Aborigines anticipated death fondly, not so that their lands may be replenished, but so they might leave the earth, making their way, apparently as individual spirits, to a better sky-home.

The ontological movement informing cosmology, social formations and individual ontogeny might be distilled to the polarity of the locative event and the Utopian universe – the 'waterhole' and 'Heaven' of my opening quotation in this book. Time is tied to this continuum as, when universal space opens as a possibility, time begins to receive power of determination and, like homogeneous space, becomes an arena in which events occur, thus taking ontological priority over events themselves. The ever-intensifying intrusion of outsiders upon Aboriginal Abiding places thus introduced intellectual revolutions driving people from Abiding Events toward temporalised hopes for an other-worldly Utopia; a non-territorial pan-Aboriginality and an immortal individual self, freed from land. (See table 1, opposite, for a schematisation of this summary.)

Having, somewhat reluctantly, systematised history into its underlying principles, or perhaps, better, having specified what appears to have been the rules of a 'game' of existence,[14] I will go further and draw some tentative conclusions as to what our story might contribute to a broader understanding of intellectual processes.

Once we admit history into the Aboriginal mode of being-in-the-world, we are richly rewarded. Even in this immensely incomplete study – for I have only sought to begin the movement *'Towards* a History of Aboriginal Being' – we have seen the Aboriginal invention of so many doctrines which have fascinated Western scholars for a century and more. I have, for instance, followed the first rise of transcendent Beings, not only the Supreme Deity or High God, but also the Fertility and Earth Mothers. The origin of the body's autonomy and the quest for immortality have been seen, as have notions of an individual's enduring life beyond death, and lands for the dead, either in the form of distant islands or as a Heaven. There have also been insights into the emergence of kinship determination and the ascent of lineages, and the recognition of, but resistance to, agriculturalist ideology and the wars of conquest. These themes are not buried but scattered conspicuously across the surface of the preceding pages, and I leave readers to gather for themselves those pieces which take their fancy.

In these closing pages, I elect to reintroduce and focus on just three ideas which were observed to emerge in the preceding pages: the origins of time, the origins of Utopia, and the origins of 'cargoism'.

strangers	intrusion	cosmology	social form	the individual
Precontact	nil	ubietous	locative with focus on site-lodge	personhood defined as extension of place
Melanesians	spatially confined, morally mediated through trade and marriage	some stretching of place but entirely ubietous	locative with one estate taking on broader pan-Aboriginal significance	land defined but with a matrilineal reform
Indonesians	potentially invasive, lacking marriage alliances	some Utopian elements but not place-disruptive	transcendent and pan-Aboriginal but acknowledging estate identity	nostalgia for life after death and spirit shift to Utopian realm
Pastoralism	invasive with moral regulations of labour and wages	Utopian and temporalised but largely earth based	transcendent and heavily pan-Aboriginal	emergence of notion of immortals and spirit freed of place
Invasion	invasive in context of amoral alien	Utopian and non-earthly (i.e. sky based)	transcendent and heavily pan-Aboriginal; no land restraints.	focus of individual shifts to sky-life after death

Table 1 *Summary*

First let me offer what I hope will be an unnecessary word of caution. By 'origin' I do not mean any more than their first Aboriginal occasion. Aboriginal people, of course, have inevitably been evoked as representing the point from which either evolution began or from which we must mark the fall.[15] I will not enter into such debates. What I do say, and what the data surely substantiate, is that Aboriginal cultures are profoundly different to those that entered Australia at later dates, particularly those of European extraction.

Each culture's portrait of existence frames and contours 'reality' in terms of its own intellectual aesthetic. All are selective; all make choices as to what should be lovingly represented, what omitted. And all, I believe, to some extent fail. It is only in the past few years that Western scholars have realised there might be a profound price to pay were the Aboriginal way of existence to be lost. Whether that price will ultimately bankrupt us or whether it can by any means be justified cannot be answered by scientific Law. Appeals to 'evolution', 'devolution' or whatever mask our true responsibility. We are faced not with a theoretical but with a moral choice.

More than any other cultures for which we have historical evidence, those of Aboriginal Australia pursued a philosophy of the enduring immanence of autonomous yet related places. The emergence of time, the quest for Utopia and the moral order of 'cargo' each contradicted that worldview, but have each been to some extent acknowledged. Whether this was a birth or a death (to anticipate the words of my closing quotation from T.S. Eliot), is not for me to say.

1. I have argued that prior to contacts with outsiders, Aboriginal traditions of the nineteenth and twentieth centuries did not allow time ontological status. It was neither measured nor numbered, and hence their world was governed instead by the qualitative values of the enduring place. This indeed is precisely what was embedded in the concepts which were alas mistranslated as 'Dreaming' or even worse, 'Dream*time*'. There were stories revealing Abiding Events which permeated lands.

Time escaped from the bounds of place in several ways. It is first glimpsed, only fleetingly, at the individual level in the longing for life everlasting, and soon after is seen in its social guise in the form of subsections. I will not here reiterate how these were both associated with lunar narratives. Rather I turn to the more significant construction of time in its cosmological form.

For Aborigines, as indeed it may have been true for the ancient Hebrews,[16] cosmic time emerged with the breaking of the connection between a land and its people. When a people are displaced, yet remember and long for their homes, time steps in to forge a future-oriented link to a land with which they are yet spiritually bound. Whether coincidentally or not, it is thus intriguing to note Aboriginal people today increasingly speaking of their 'promised Lands'.[17]

Melanesian and Indonesian contacts did not force Aborigines from their homes, and cosmological time is absent in the relevant ethnographies for these cases. It is only in colonial contexts that – and despite the academic disclaimers – we witness millennial hopes and, when hope fades, pessimistic eschatologies. The 'Millenniums', however, are not a 'new earth' but a return to a still-remembered order, while the eschatologies are a vision that the lands themselves might finally fail. I can find nothing not wholly realistic in these new temporal worldviews; they encapsulate precisely the options open to Aborigines and the fickleness of the promises made to those who trust, or who are forced to trust, in time.

2. When Erich Kolig speaks of Aboriginal Utopias as the unleashing of revolutionary potential by breaking with 'the existing order, the "topia" ',[18] he both mistranslates a word and a world. For *topos* is 'a place' and Aboriginal Utopias are born not merely by bucking the colonial system but more importantly when people lose hold of their countries. For Aborigines, Utopianism is at best a dangerous option.

It begins, cautiously enough, with the Arnhem Land distant Lands of the Dead, but as befits the fact that Indonesians only threatened possible land appropriation, the departing spirit remains simultaneously in its eternal home. The power of 'no-place', like time, only becomes apparent when people are, or are likely to be, dispossessed of their lands.

Utopias apparently take two forms within Aboriginal Australia. They may be distant places on earth, such as *Dingari*, which makes them still potentially accessible to the living and hence a fitting focus of ongoing political action. Such notions, for example, accompanied the industrial actions and subsequent fights for equality in north-west Western Australia. On the other hand, in the most oppressive land-denying conditions, as witnessed in nineteenth century south-east Australia, the Utopian realm may actually become entirely divorced from the world. In these contexts, short of the heavens descending, the only salvation is for each individual to make his or her way to the sky-kingdom upon death.

Like time, Utopia has been assumed by those who approach others from a land-transcendent tradition to be a universal human construct, but from another vantage, Utopia is a belated longing for enduringness in timeworn worlds which have lost their sense of place. As Marcuse said 'the end of utopia . . . can also be understood as the "end of history" ' for 'utopia is a historical concept'. Whether Aborigines can succeed in putting an end to their Utopian images through its *denial*, and through a return to *topos* is, ironically, itself something still embedded in time – for 'even "ahistoricity" has a historical limit'.[19]

3. Lastly, Aboriginal 'cargoism' too can be understood in terms of the dissolving of ties of place. It belongs to a wider class of Aboriginal symbolic representations of the material culture of outsiders, but is defined by its particular message.

It must again be stated that subsistence and technology cannot be separated from ontology. This is true for Australia, Melanesia and the West. It has indeed been unfair that 'cargoists' have been seen as those who ritualise the acquisition of commodities, for surely ritualisation, let alone 'fetishisation', has always been a part of capitalist productive life. Rather, what has occurred has been but a changing of ceremonial forms.

Aborigines symbolically expressed the material face of alien being for each class of outsider to reach their shores. Melanesian agriculture and the bow and arrow were a part of the Hero's cult, although they were never appropriated as a way of life. Indonesian agricultural ideals were also found in central-northern myths, as were a vast array of Macassan (and later European and Japanese) cultural items. And in the areas of extensive White contacts, we again find the fruit of strangers' being represented in Aboriginal ritual thought.

In the above instances, however, the items symbolised were not presented in contexts of incorporation. In fact, the inverse was often the case, the manifestations serving to reinforce that which did not and should not belong to Aboriginal domains. 'Cargoism' can therefore be seen as but a reversal of the more usual valuation placed upon representations of another's mode of existence.

For Aborigines, this was a major step, for it marks a shift from an identity exclusively determined by place to one which at least partially recognises humanly constructed cultural objects as having power of definition. As I explained in chapter 5, the transition required several phases: the (conspicuously rare) use of Aboriginal bodies within the White moral order of wage/ration-labour; the enforced or coercive removal of people from their lands; and finally, the emergent desire within Aboriginal communities to be treated with equality *within* White Law. When such volatile ingredients are brought together, 'cargoism' follows. That it has been infrequently observed in Australia indicates a racist history in which colonists did not even feel their indigenous predecessors worthy of the compliment of exploitation and a tenacious Aboriginal reluctance to be determined by existants other than land.

No people, however, can resist forever an ontological invasion. Is it, as Victor Hugo once wrote, that 'a stand can be made against invasion by an army; no stand can be made against invasion by an idea?';[20] or is it that the wars of bodies and minds are inseparable? Can Aboriginal people go beyond Utopian futures? Can they transcend the enticements of its 'cargo'?

It was at this point, on the brink of adjoining worlds, that my narrative ended. I have summarised the foregoing history, and drawn out what I believe to be its core elements, but in closing I must once again emphasise that this story remains embedded in lives, refusing to allow any conclusion to even pretend to be complete.

This book only begins the task of infusing our understanding of Aboriginal being with history. I have, for instance, left largely to one side the enormous but scattered impact of Christian missions, even though this is an area in which I can claim some scholarly contribution.[21] My preference, however, has been to paint this first canvas with a broad brush, considering larger cultural revisions rather than changes confined to isolated proselytisers' regimes. I have also chosen to focus upon this area because it is the most ethnographically clouded and historically obscure. This has required a reinterpretation of virtually everything previously written on Aboriginal intellectual and ceremonial life, but with this framework in place it becomes possible to construct future historical research with a new assuredness.

I have also left to one side the matter of Aboriginal spirituality in settled rural and urban areas – although again this is an area in which I have shared in recent pioneering investigations;[22] and finally, I have omitted, deliberately, the huge episode – itself another book – which leads on from the end of chapter 5. The gist of that matter, however, is as follows.

As I briefly indicated at the end of the previous chapter, Aborigines attempting to gain parity through White Law finally succeeded in being granted entitlement to award wages before they saw the sting in the tail of colonialism. When they could not be exploited, they simply got the sack. Yet even whilst the Gurindji were striking for monetary recognition of their labours, they seem to have been thinking beyond the White symbolic word, for they also demanded some of their land be returned. This seemingly simple act was of monumental significance.[23]

From this time onward, there were several fronts to a revival of hope in the power of land to restore the Aboriginal world. Instead of Aborigines seeking equality through White Law it was insisted that White Law should, and in fact primordially *did*, acknowledge Aboriginal Law. In the religious domain, God was said to endorse Abiding land-Events.[24] In political spheres, Captain Cook Law was deemed to be false, deceiving Blacks and Whites alike, for a true law, the real White Law, lay beneath that colonial lie.[25] All this, of course, accompanied the massive, continent-wide co-ordinated Aboriginal awareness of *the* issue – Land Rights.

Beyond legislation, however, a return of land poses a dilemma of existence for Aborigines. How do urban Aborigines truly reclaim their place? Can generations of separation from one's eternal home be no more than a momentary and reversible breach? And faced with the mammoth revision of their Law I have documented, to what extent can even the most isolated of Aboriginal communities return in full spirit and body to their 'settle down country'?[26] What, in short, can it mean in its most absolute sense, to say: 'But now we want the land back'?

These are not rhetorical questions. They do, however, represent the greatest challenge Aboriginal Australian societies have had to face in historic times.

It is perhaps cold comfort for me to close by recalling that this is not the first time a people have faced such a bittersweet homecoming.

> All this was a long time ago, I remember
> And I would do it again, but set down
> This set down

This: were we led all this way for
Birth or death? There was a birth, certainly,
We had evidence and no doubt. I had seen birth and death,
But had thought they were different; this birth was
Hard and bitter agony for us, like Death, our death.
We returned to our places . . .,
But no longer at ease here, in the old dispensation,
With an alien people clutching their gods.[27]

NOTES

1. B. Shaw, *Countrymen: The Life Histories of Four Aboriginal Men* (Canberra: Australian Institute of Aboriginal Studies, 1986), pp. 125–6.
2. M.J. Meggitt, *Gadjari among the Walbiri Aborigines of Central Australia.* The Oceania Monographs, no. 14 (Sydney: The University of Sydney, 1966), pp. 82–3.
3. M. Eliade, *Cosmos and History: The Myth of the Eternal Return* (New York: Harper, 1959), chapter 4.
4. A lovely and most perceptive anecdote is candidly provided by Diane Bell. She was asked by a taxi driver:
   'What do you do?'
   'I'm an anthropologist.'
   'Oh, they study monkeys don't they?'
   'Well, mostly they study people.'
   'Oh, that's right: they study people as if they were monkeys.'
   D. Bell, 'Academia's Lost Tribe: Anthropologists Have Come Wandering out of the Universities Into the Public Domain', *Australian Society*, 4 (1985), p. 37.
5. S. Diamond, *In Search of the Primitive: A Critique of Civilization* (New Brunswick: Transaction Books, 1981).
6. B. Attwood, *The Making of the Aborigines* (Sydney: Allen & Unwin, 1989); R.H.W. Reece, 'Inventing Aborigines', *Aboriginal History*, 11 (1987), pp. 14–33.
7. G.K. Cowlishaw, 'Aborigines and Anthropologists', *Australian Aboriginal Studies*, 1 (1986), p. 9.
8. K. Maddock, *The Australian Aborigines: A Portrait of their Society* (Harmondsworth: Penguin, 1974), p. ix.
9. K.-P. Koepping, 'Nativistic Movements in Aboriginal Australia: Creative Adjustment, Protest or Regeneration of Tradition', in *Aboriginal Australians and Christian Missions: Ethnographic and Historical Studies*, edited by T. Swain & D. Rose (Adelaide: Australian Association for the Study of Religions, 1988), p. 401.
10. A sound overview of this distinction can be found in W. Outhwaite, *Understanding Social Science: The Method Called Verstehen* (London: Allen & Unwin, 1975).

11. K. Benterrak, S. Muecke, & P. Roe, *Reading the Country: Introduction to Nomadology* (Fremantle: Fremantle Arts Centre, 1984), p. 173.

12. The classic exposition of the doctrine to which I refer is the *Samkhyakarika*, contained in translation in G.L. Larson, *Classical Samkhya: An Interpretation of its History and Meaning* (Santa Barbara: Ross/Erickson, 1979).

13. D. H. Turner, 'Cosmology is "Kinship": The Aboriginal Transcendence of Material Determination', *Mankind*, 19 (1989), pp. 215–26; B. Glowczewski, 'A Topological Approach to Australian Cosmology and Social Organisation', *Mankind*, 19 (1989), p. 227. I should add that although I frequently find Glowczewski's analysis insightful, to my mind her appeal to topological models is entirely unnecessary and unenlightening.

14. Some time ago I proposed that an adequate approach to 'meaning' within Aboriginal traditions could be realised by focusing upon ontology in terms of Wittgensteinian 'rules'; see T. Swain, *On 'Understanding' Australian Aboriginal Religion*, Charles Strong Young Australian Lecture (Adelaide: Charles Strong Memorial Trust, 1985). As alluded to in the 'Introduction' of this book, I now hold to a qualified version of that position, but would align myself rather with a more dynamic view of both being and understanding as contained in Gadamer's 'ontological hermeneutics'. This is not a particularly radical shift. For a coherent comparison of Wittgenstein/Winch and Gadamer, see T. McCarthy, *The Critical Theory of Jügen Habermas* (Cambridge: Polity Press, 1978), pp. 162–93.

15. For a concise overview see T. Swain, 'A Bicentenary of the Study of Australian Aboriginal Religion', *Religion*, 21 (1991): 165–195.

16. see M. Weippert, 'Frage des israelitischen Geschichtsbewusstseins', *Vetus Testamentum*, 23 (1973), pp. 415–42. Weippert strongly emphasises that Israel's historical consciousness was linked to their not being autochthonous to the land with which they came to identify.

17. I noted this at both of the first two Aboriginal conferences on their Spirituality, held respectively at Victor Harbor in South Australia and Brisbane, in 1990. The difference between Aboriginal and Hebrew traditions, of course, is that the Israelites' Promised Land was not their own, which they had abandoned in search of 'a prosperous land . . . where you will want nothing' (Deuteronomy, 8: 7–10, *Jerusalem Bible*).

18. E. Kolig, *Dreamtime Politics: Religion, World View and Utopian Thought in Australian Aboriginal Society* (Berlin: Dietrich Reimer, 1989), p. 8.

19. H. Marcuse, 'The End of Utopia', in *Five Lectures: Psychoanalysis, Politics, and Utopia* (London: Allen Lane, 1970), pp. 62–3.

20. Victor Hugo, *Histoire d'un Crime* (Paris: L'Imprimerie Nationale, 1907), 'La Chute', chapter x, p. 187.

21. See the major collection, *Aboriginal Australians and Christian Missions*, which I instigated and co-edited with D.B. Rose.

22. I refer here to the conference and forthcoming published report, *Aboriginal Spirituality: Past, Present, Future*, organised by the University of Sydney's Department of Religious Studies. This pioneering occasion was jointly instigated by G.W. Trompf and me, and brought to fruition with the seemingly tireless assistance of Jani Klotz.

23. see F. Hardy, *The Unlucky Australians* (Melbourne: Nelson, 1968); and H. Middleton, *But Now We Want the Land Back: A History of the Australian Aboriginal People* (Sydney: New Age Publishers, 1977).

24. See my 'The Ghost of Space: Reflections on Warlpiri Christian Iconography and Ritual', in *Aboriginal Australians and Christian Missions*, edited by Swain & Rose, pp. 452-69. This is a development comparable to that documented by R.M. Berndt in *An Adjustment Movement In Arnhem Land: Northern Territory of Australia* (Paris: Mouton, 1962), and more adequately interpreted in H. Morphy, ' "Now You Understand": An Analysis of the Way Yolngu Have Used Sacred Knowledge to Retain Their Autonomy', in *Aborigines, Land and Land Rights*, edited by N. Peterson & M. Langton, pp. 110-13 (Canberra: Australian Institute of Aboriginal Studies, 1983). Another cognate episode is recorded in A.E. Wells, *This Their Dreaming* (St Lucia: University of Queensland Press, 1971). The historic connection between the presentation of land-based icons in a Christian setting and legal struggles for land is provided by Morphy, and this link is also evident if one reads Wells' account in conjunction with E. Wells' *Reward and Punishment in Arnhem Land 1962-1963* (Canberra: Australian Institute of Aboriginal Studies, 1982), or my study in light of T. Fleming, 'A History of the [Baptist] Aboriginal Missions' (unpublished ms.).

25. Captain Cook stories are widespread in Aboriginal traditions. See K. Maddock, 'Gli Aborigeni Australiani e il Capitano Cook: Quando il Mito Incontra la Storia', *Materiali Filosofici*, 14 (1985), pp. 57-70; K. Maddock, 'Myth, History and a Sense of Oneself', in *Past and Present: the Construction of Aboriginality*, edited by J.R. Beckett, pp. 11-30 (Canberra: Aboriginal Studies Press, 1988); B. Congoo, *Stories from Palm Island* (Townsville: Townsville Cultural Association, 1981); E. Kolig, 'Captain Cook in the Western Kimberley', in *Aborigines of the West: Their Past and Their Present*, edited by R.M. & C.H. Berndt, pp. 274-82 (Nedlands, W.A.: University of Western Australia Press, 1979); D. Rose, 'The Saga of Captain Cook: Morality in Aboriginal and European Law', *Australian Aboriginal Studies*, 2 (1984), pp. 24-39; C. Mackinolty, & P. Wainburranga, 'Too Many Captain Cooks', in *Aboriginal Australians and Christian Missions*, edited by Swain & Rose, pp. 355-60. In some cases the true Captain Cook is portrayed as a moral White person who preceded the 'historic' Captain Cook. In other cases his predecessor was a different European, such as the outlaw Ned Kelly. On the latter see; D.B. Rose, *Ned Kelly*

Died for Our Sins. The 1988 Charles Strong Memorial Lecture (Adelaide: Charles Strong, 1988); & D.B. Rose, 'Ned Lives!', *Australian Aboriginal Studies*, 2 (1989), pp. 51–9. In this regard, Ned Kelly was akin to Aboriginal outlaws hunted by Whites, a point made explicitly by Bulla in B. Shaw, *Countrymen: The Life Histories of Four Aboriginal Men as Told to Bruce Shaw* (Canberra: Australian Institute of Aboriginal Studies, 1986), p. 101.

26. On the homelands movement, see the aptly named books, D.L. Japananka and P. Nathan, *Settle Down Country* (Malmsbury: Kibble Books, 1983); and House of Representatives Standing Committee on Aboriginal Affairs, *Return to Country: The Aboriginal Homelands Movement in Australia* (Canberra: Australian Government Publishing Service, 1987).

27. T.S. Eliot, 'Journey of the Magi', in *Collected Poems 1909–1935* (London: Faber & Faber, 1936), p. 108.

Index

297

DATE DUE

MAR 1 9 2003		
		/

Brodart Co.   Cat. # 55 137 001   Pr